KITCHEN & BATH
RESIDENTIAL CONSTRUCTION AND SYSTEMS

KITCHEN & BATH
RESIDENTIAL CONSTRUCTION AND SYSTEMS

Second Edition

JERRY GERMER

National Kitchen & Bath Association

Cover image: (left) © iStockphoto.com/tonda (right) Design by Peter Ross Salerno, CMKBD/co-designer Shannon Gallaher Hall; photograph by Peter Rymwid
Cover design: Anne Michele Abbott

This book is printed on acid-free paper.

National Kitchen & Bath Association
687 Willow Grove Street
Hackettstown, NJ 07840
Phone: 800-THE-NKBA (800-843-6522)
Fax: 908-852-1695
Website: NKBA.org

Published by John Wiley & Sons, Inc., Hoboken, New Jersey.

Published simultaneously in Canada.

For general information about our other products and services, please contact our Customer Care Department within the United States at (800) 762–2974, outside the United States at (317) 572–3993 or fax (317) 572–4002.

Wiley publishes in a variety of print and electronic formats and by print-on-demand. Some material included with standard print versions of this book may not be included in e-books or in print-on-demand. If this book refers to media such as a CD or DVD that is not included in the version you purchased, you may download this material at http://booksupport.wiley.com.

For more information about Wiley products, visit www.wiley.com.

Library of Congress Cataloging-in-Publication Data

Germer, Jerry, 1938-
 [Works. Selections]
 Kitchen & bath residential construction and systems / Jerry Germer. – Second Edition.
      pages cm
   "Residential Construction and Systems is a compilation of the material originally published by the NKBA in two prior books, Residential Construction : Systems, Materials, Codes, 2006 and Kitchen & Bath Systems : Mechanical, Electrical, Plumbing, 2006."
 Includes index.
  ISBN 978-1-118-43910-4 (cloth); 978-1-118-69302-5 (ebk.); 978-1-118-71104-0 (ebk.)
  1. House construction–Handbooks, manuals, etc   2. Building–Details–Handbooks, manuals, etc.
3. Kitchens–Remodeling.   4. Bathrooms–Remodeling.   5. Buildings–Mechanical equipment.
I. Germer, Jerry, 1938- Residential construction.   II. Germer, Jerry, 1938- Kitchen & bath systems.
III. National Kitchen and Bath Association (U.S.)   IV. Title. V. Title: Kitchen and bath residential construction and systems.
  TH4813.G47 2013
  690'.42–dc23

                                                                    2013009462

Printed in the United States of America

SKY10027927_070221

Sponsors

The National Kitchen and Bath Association recognizes, with gratitude, the following companies whose generous contributions supported the development of this second edition volume which combines the newly revised Residential Construction and Kitchen & Bath Systems volumes of the NKBA Professional Resource Library.

PLATINUM SPONSORS

WWW.FISHERPAYKEL.COM

WWW.DCSAPPLIANCES.COM

WWW.LYNXGRILLS.COM

About the National Kitchen & Bath Association

The National Kitchen & Bath Association (NKBA) is the only non-profit trade association dedicated exclusively to the kitchen and bath industry and is the leading source of information and education for professionals in the field. Fifty years after its inception, the NKBA has a membership of more than 55,000 and is the proud owner of the Kitchen & Bath Industry Show (KBIS).

The NKBA's mission is to enhance member success and excellence, promote professionalism and ethical business practices, and provide leadership and direction for the kitchen and bath industry worldwide.

The NKBA has pioneered innovative industry research, developed effective business management tools, and set groundbreaking design standards for safe, functional, and comfortable kitchens and baths.

Recognized as the kitchen and bath industry's leader in learning and professional development, the NKBA offers professionals of all levels of experience essential reference materials, conferences, virtual learning opportunities, marketing assistance, design competitions, consumer referrals, internships, and opportunities to serve in leadership positions.

The NKBA's internationally recognized certification program provides professionals the opportunity to demonstrate knowledge and excellence as Associate Kitchen & Bath Designer (AKBD), Certified Kitchen Designer (CKD), Certified Bath Designer (CBD), Certified Master Kitchen & Bath Designer (CMKBD), and Certified Kitchen & Bath Professional (CKBP).

For students entering the industry, the NKBA offers Accredited and Supported Programs, which provide NKBA-approved curriculum at more than 60 learning institutions throughout the United States and Canada.

For consumers, the NKBA showcases award winning designs and provides information on remodeling, green design, safety, and more at NKBA.org. The NKBA Pro Search tool helps consumers locate kitchen and bath professionals in their area.

The NKBA offers membership in 11 different industry segments: dealers, designers, manufacturers and suppliers, multi-branch retailers and home centers, decorative plumbing and hardware, manufacturer's representatives, builders and remodelers, installers, fabricators, cabinet shops, and distributors. For more information, visit NKBA.org.

Table of Contents

Preface

Residential design and construction continues to change and affects two of the most important rooms—the kitchen and bath. Even in lean economic times, such as the one we are just now emerging from, new building materials and products come on the market in a steady stream, and changes continue to be made to tried and true products. Some of these changes are in response to concerns consumers have for the environment and represent positive change. Others are merely updated versions of their predecessors. To be successful, kitchen and bath designers need to keep abreast the changes that affect their areas of expertise. But these rooms don't exist as disparate entities; they are part of a larger entity, the home. That's why K&B designers need a general knowledge of residential design and construction—the focus of this book.

Residential Construction and Systems is a compilation of the material originally published by the NKBA in two prior books, *Residential Construction—Systems, Materials, Codes* (2006), and *Kitchen & Bath Systems—Mechanical, Electrical, Plumbing* (2006).

The present volume is an overview of all the elements that go into building a new or modifying an existing home, beginning with a description of who does what in the process and how they interrelate, followed by a description of the codes and permitting process that confront all designers.

Chapters 3, 4, and 5 cover healthy houses, maximizing energy efficiency and using natural energies—topics that have become ever more important to homeowners in an era of dwindling natural resources, increasing energy costs, and concern for the environment. Chapters 6 through 12 describe how homes go together, from the foundation to the finishes. The remaining chapters of the book deal with the mechanical and electrical systems that are necessary to create the desired interior environment and enable the home's appliances and equipment to operate.

While combining the two predecessor books into a single volume the author has updated the content to reflect changes in residential design and construction. One of the improvements in home construction cited is the use of a drainage plain "rain screen" between siding and the substrate which extends the life of the siding and coatings. Throughout the book there is mention of developments in the industry that have come about in response to growing consciousness to create environments that are sustainable and use energy wisely. For example, building codes, ever changing, now include the International Green Construction Code. Concern over indoor air quality has resulted in the availability of paints and panels that contain low or no harmful VOC emissions. Daylighting and new lighting products such as

LED lamps are discussed as ways to conserve household energy, along with trends in insulation that include growing use of spray foam. There is expanded coverage of solar heating, both active and passive. New products mentioned include fiberglass windows, polyethylene gas piping, and dual-flush toilets.

Many contributors made this book possible. Special thanks go to Johanna Baars, publication specialist at the NKBA, Paul Drougas, editor at John Wiley & Sons, and Mike New, editorial assistant. The following peer reviewers provided many useful comments and suggestions: David Alderman, CMKBD, Spencer Hinkle, CKD, Corey Klassen, CKD, and David Newton, CMKBD.

Acknowledgements

The NKBA gratefully acknowledges the following peer reviewers of this book:

David Alderman, CMKBD
Spencer Hinkle, CKD
Corey Klassen, CKD
David Newton, CMKBD

The Building Team

As a kitchen and bath designer, you won't be working alone. To begin with, you'll obviously need clients. Beyond that you'll depend on a number of other professionals and installers to realize your design concepts. You should know your own strengths and weaknesses and what specialists to call on for project tasks outside your own expertise. Working smoothly with this team of building specialists will require courtesy, respect, and patience. This chapter gives you an overview of some of the major players on the building team and where they fit in the game.

The teams that design and build commercial or industrial projects have narrower, more clearly defined roles than those involved with residences. Architects and engineers basically design and look in, from time to time, to ensure that the work is being constructed as specified. A general contractor manages the construction, with subcontractors installing various parts.

With residences, many variations are possible. The overall design may not come from an architect or building designer at all but from a magazine or other source, sometimes adapted by a designer for the specific project. The heating system might be designed by the same firm who installs it. The same holds for electrical work. A general contractor, or homebuilder, may coordinate the various subparts, or it may be left to the owner. And the owner often installs some of the work.

How do you fit in? There's no general answer. As a kitchen and bath designer, you play an important part in realizing a residential project. To do this effectively, you need first to know your craft, understand the project, and be able to work smoothly with the other players on the team.

Before you do anything else with a project, you should pin down the organizational model, who does what, and who answers to whom.

Learning Objective 1: Describe the areas of expertise of those who may interact in the design of a residence.

Learning Objective 2: Describe the areas of expertise of those who may install or construct all or portions of a residence.

Learning Objective 3: Differentiate the roles of each member of a building team.

GENERALIST DESIGNERS

The design process starts with a program statement that lists the client's needs and goals. Your task is to translate the program into a concept that ultimately can be built. Building design is a huge field that contains both generalists and specialists. The overall design may be entrusted to an architect or building designer who coordinates the work of the other specialized design professionals. The list of specialists required to fill out the team varies according to the size and type of project and may include engineers, landscape architects, interior designers, and—here's where you fit in—kitchen and bath designers.

Architects

The role of architects has changed dramatically from the days when they were "master builders" who orchestrated the entire production of a building, from design through the driving of the last nail. Today architects mostly design, with limited oversight responsibilities during the construction phase. To be called an architect, one must be licensed by the state, which requires a professional degree, a supervised internship, and successfully passing a professional examination. Even though trained as generalists, architects today are increasingly specializing in a niche, such as hospitals, prisons, schools, or residences. Architects who do residential design may include the detailed design of kitchens and baths in the scope of their services or leave it to specialist designers, once the general concept has been established. In this case, the specialist designer may work through the architect or, more likely, answer directly to the client.

Building Designers

Unlike architects, building designers do not need professional licenses to practice, but they are limited to buildings of a certain type and/or size. Most specialize in residential design. This doesn't mean building designers are untrained, though. Some may have little training in their craft, but others may have substantial formal education and/or practical experience. To qualify as a certified professional building designer by the American Institute of Building Designers (AIBD), one must meet specific educational and professional design experience requirements; submit work samples for extensive peer review; and pass an examination covering such topics as architecture, engineering, building systems and materials, project administration, problem solving, and professional ethics. AIBD also encourages its members to seek qualification from the National Council of Building Designer Certification (NCBDC) and its certification program for professional building. If you are called in to consult on a project for which a building designer has prepared the plans, you may work for either the designer or the client.

Engineers

Like architects, engineers are licensed by the state and obtain their qualifications via a professional degree and professional exam. Most engineers specialize in a particular area, such as mechanical, electrical, structural, and civil engineering. Multistory housing may require the services of any or all of these specialties. The majority of single-family housing gets built without the services of any engineer, except perhaps for a civil engineer to survey the site. In high-end housing, mechanical engineers may be entrusted with the design of the heating, ventilation, and air-conditioning (HVAC) systems. An electrical engineer might design the power and lighting, communications, and other electrical systems. To work effectively with an engineer, you will need a final layout of your portions of the house in hand, along with the particular equipment that will be installed. If a mechanical engineer is charged with designing the HVAC or plumbing system, be prepared to provide the engineer with any plumbing, ducting, and power requirements for the fixtures and equipment you specify. Get these requirements from catalogs and pass them along as soon as possible in the design process. If an architect is in charge of the overall design, you probably will communicate this information through him or her.

Interior Designers

The design team of high-end residential projects may include an interior designer, who specializes in organizing the interior and specifying furnishings and color schemes. If an interior designer is involved with the project, you will need to clarify the various design responsibilities early on. Confusion and bruised egos will surely result if all the players don't know how they fit into the team and how project communication will work.

Other Designers

Various other designers may design particular systems in a residence, including the heating, cooling, lighting, security, automation, solar systems, fire suppression, landscaping, water purification, flooring, and other systems. The professionals who design these systems gain their expertise in various ways, which may include a college major or experience in their field. They may or may not hold professional licenses or certification by a professional association. For example, a lighting designer may be a licensed electrical engineer, an electrician, or a person who has developed skills in that area from working for a company that manufactures or sells lighting.

BUILDERS AND INSTALLERS

Once the planning work is complete, another team enters the project: builders and installers. A residential project may require the services of a very few or several specialists, according to the complexity of the project.

General Contractors

All building projects need someone to coordinate the various actors involved in the construction. Whoever takes on this important charge must schedule the construction, recruit the subcontractors (subs), usually pay them, and oversee the construction. The task is daunting, rather like herding cats. Owners who act as their own general contractors often encounter rough waters—work that doesn't happen when it is supposed to, unforeseen costs, and numerous other frustrations. Hiring a general contractor helps avoid these kinds of headaches. Even with a pro managing the show, owners still can reserve portions of the work to do themselves, such as installing drywall or painting.

Plumbers

If you think of plumbers as the experts on systems that move water in and out of kitchens and baths, it's obvious how crucial these installers are to the project team. Plumbers need to know their way around the myriad of pipes, fittings, and fixtures while keeping up to date with the latest code provisions. It's in your interest to get to know a few competent plumbers in your area so you can pick their brains when you confront plumbing-related questions in your design work. And, naturally, the plumber on your project will need to know the layout and plumbing requirements of the kitchen and bath fixtures.

Electricians

Electricians are also indispensable to kitchen and bath projects. Their work begins where yours leaves off. If your design shows the proposed locations of power outlets and lighting fixtures, the electrician has to make sure all of these devices work as intended. Like plumbers, electricians must follow the latest provisions of a reference code, most likely the National Electrical Code (NEC). Electricians usually determine the circuiting arrangements in residential work. For this, they'll need to know the voltage requirements of large appliances and which lighting fixtures are low voltage, along with any other electrical requirements.

Home Technology Specialists

Home electrical systems used to consist of a high-voltage power system and a low-voltage telephone system. The power system brought power to the house via a service panel with circuits for power and lighting. A wiring network distributed the electricity to the various points of use. Telephone wiring amounted to a box on the outside wall, connected to one or more phones inside by low-voltage wiring. No more. The "smart house" came on the scene in the 1980s with low-voltage systems to control appliances and lighting automatically. The technology was slow to catch on but has progressed steadily. Many of today's new homes contain some provisions for home automation, ranging from data wiring in the walls to complete home automation systems with programmable options capable of controlling a multitude of electronic devices. Not surprisingly, these systems are complicated enough to require specialist designers and installers—either electrical engineers specialized in home automation or the vendors themselves. Because these systems affect the whole house, it is in your interest to be aware of them and know how and where they fit into your kitchen and bath design.

SUMMARY

As a kitchen and bath designer, you play an important part in realizing a residential project. To do this effectively, you need to know your craft, understand the client's objectives, and know who will make up the project team. The team may range in size and include any of these specialists:

- Architects or building designers, for overall project design
- Engineers, for design of specific portions of the project
- Builders or general contractors, for management of the overall project
- Plumbers, electricians, and other subcontractors for installation of the various systems that will go into the project

To work smoothly within the planning and building process, you should understand how the project has been organized, who will be on the building team, and what each member's role will be. Understanding and executing your role on the building team in a competent manner with due consideration of the ideas and contribution of other members can result in a successful project and solid referral base for years to come.

CHAPTER REVIEW

1. What is a program statement? (See "Generalist Designers" page 2)
2. What type of engineer would most likely be involved with a single-family house? (See "Engineers" page 2)
3. Are building designers required to be licensed in order to practice their trade? (See "Building Designers" page 2)
4. What is a general contractor responsible for? (See "General Contractors" page 3)

Codes and Permits

Most buildings require a building permit for construction and renovation. Obtaining a permit usually requires that the proposed construction satisfy the conditions of one or more codes. The codes that apply depend on the location of the project, its size, and its type. If you limit your work to installing cabinets on walls, you may avoid worrying about codes altogether. But you'll probably need to comply with a building code for any rough carpentry required to support the cabinetry. Any plumbing or electrical work proposed falls under the purview of mechanical and electrical codes. Other codes that may apply set standards for fire safety, energy conservation, and handicap accessibility.

Before undertaking any design work on a project, you'll save time and hassles by finding out which codes apply. Cities and towns often have some kind of building and inspection department to enforce the codes in their area. Rural areas may or may not have a building official to enforce their codes and may not even have codes in force for residential structures. However, even if there are no local codes, state codes may apply. Before you begin, check to see if there are state codes in force in the locality.

Learning Objective 1: Recognize the history and objectives of building codes.

Learning Objective 2: Differentiate between codes that address specific systems in the building.

Learning Objective 3: Identify codes that have developed to address emergent concerns for the environment, energy efficiency, sustainability, and persons with special needs.

BUILDING CODES

Designers and installers often complain about codes, but, in doing so, they lose sight of the reason for them: to protect the public's safety and welfare by establishing uniform minimum standards.

Prior to 1994, three so-called model codes were in force in the United States that set standards for buildings of all types:

1. The BOCA National Building Code, published by the Building Officials and Code Administrators International (BOCA). Used primarily in the Northeast and Midwest

2. The Uniform Building Code, published by the International Conference of Building Officials (ICBO) and in use in the western states
3. The Southern Building Code, published by the Southern Building Code Conference International (SBCCI) and in use in the majority of southern states

A fourth code, One- and Two-Family Dwelling Code, often called the CABO code after its publisher, the Council of American Building Officials (CABO), addressed issues of particular concern to detached houses. As such, it complemented the other three model codes for residential construction.

These codes were called "model" codes because they were developed to serve as models for further refinement or alteration by local municipalities. Some large cities, such as New York City, have their own building code. More commonly, though, municipalities adopted the applicable model code as is or amended it to suit local needs. For example, areas where there is inordinately high danger from hurricanes, fire, or earthquakes amended the model codes with stricter requirements.

Some municipalities still retain their own codes, which address conditions specific to their region, and several states, provinces, and territories either have building codes or leave it up to local jurisdictions as to which code to adopt. Fourteen states, as of this writing, are included in this group. All others have adopted the International Building Code (IBC) and its companion, the International Residential Code (IRC), which replaces the One- and Two-Family Dwelling Code.

In addition to these codes, which address general building requirements, there are a number of codes specific to specific building systems, such as mechanical or electrical, and others that address particular concerns, such as fire safety. Keeping up with codes and their areas of applicability can be confusing. Your best first step, as a kitchen and bath designer, is to consult with the local building official, who can steer you to the applicable code or codes and alert you to any specific concerns that might apply to your work.

International Building Code

One of the reasons the designers and installers didn't like codes in the past was the confusion resulting from their multiplicity. The time was clearly ripe for the building industry to press for a single unified building code that applied to all parts of the United States. The first concrete steps toward that goal were taken in 1994, with the establishment of an umbrella organization, the International Code Council (ICC). The goal was to create a code that would not only eventually supersede the regional codes in force in the United States but would allow other countries to be part of the system in the future. The first draft of the new international code was published three years later for review. Since that time, the IBC has gained acceptance by an increasing number of jurisdictions and is updated periodically.

International Residential Code

Whereas the IBC addresses buildings in general, its companion the IRC covers topics more specific to home construction. For that reason, it is the code you will most likely deal with in your sphere of activity. This code applies to one- and two-family detached dwellings and apartment buildings up to three stories. It contains a stand-alone set of standards, with chapters on foundations, framing, plumbing, electrical, mechanical, fuel, gas, and energy. The code is more complete than its only other predecessor code, the CABO. The IRC also contains detailed requirements for emerging techniques, such as steel-stud construction, frost-protected shallow foundations and insulated concrete forms.

Like the CABO, the IRC addresses regional variations of such factors as frost depths, snow loads, and termite threat potential, but it also includes criteria for building in areas prone to floods, high winds, and seismic activity.

Canadian Codes

As in the United States, Canadian model national building, fire, and plumbing codes are prepared under a central agency, the Canadian Commission on Building and Fire Codes. Canada's centralized system for model code development and maintenance began in the 1930s and the Canadian Codes Center published the first National Building Code of Canada (NBC) in 1941 and has issued an updated version approximately every five years since. Other Canadian codes include the National Energy Code of Canada for Buildings, National Fire Code of Canada, National Plumbing Code of Canada, Model National Energy Code of Canada for Houses, and National Farm Building Code of Canada. Codes from the provinces and territories that supersede the national or provincial/territorial codes give the ten provinces and three territories jurisdiction over construction. Before undertaking any work in a Canadian location, you should find out which codes are in effect by contacting the local municipal building inspection office.

Energy Codes

The energy shortages of the 1970s sparked widespread concern for conserving energy in buildings and spawned new technologies for utilizing renewable energy from solar, wind, and geothermal sources in homes. Concurrently, new and better ways were found to make buildings less dependent on *any* outside energy source. To encourage conservation in building construction, federal, state, and local governments developed standards, which found their way into various energy codes. The first uniform energy codes were developed under the name Model Energy Code (MEC).

The MEC accomplishes conservation goals by allowing designers to comply in one of two approaches. The first is to supply design calculations that ensure that the building as a whole meets the performance standards of the code. The second—and more often used—is simply to comply with the minimum prescriptive standards of the code. Choosing the performance standard method allows the designer greater flexibility but requires an ability and desire to deal with engineering calculations. For example, you might increase the glazing in one part of the building if you compensate by using a higher level of insulation in another. The second, prescriptive-standards, approach simply spells out just how much glazing can be used and what R-value the walls must have. This approach is usually the simplest way to satisfy the code.

The MEC has been succeeded by the International Energy Conservation Code (IECC). Introduced in 1998, the IECC addresses energy efficiency on several fronts, including cost savings, reduced energy usage, conservation of natural resources, and impact of energy usage on the environment. Important changes in the sixth edition that affect residential design include measures to improve the thermal envelope, heating, ventilation, and air-conditioning (HVAC), and electrical systems.

Still, only 28 states have adopted the IECC code as of this writing. Some others base their mandatory energy requirements on the ASHRAE 90.1 code, published by the American Society of Heating, Refrigeration, and Air Conditioning Engineers (ASHRAE). Still others have state or local energy codes or no codes at all. As with building codes, the situation is constantly changing, so find out the status of energy code acceptance in your state by contacting your local building department or state energy office.

Canadian energy conservation requirements are published in the 2011 edition of the National Energy Code for Buildings, replacing the 1997 Model Energy Code for Buildings, which allows designers to follow multiple paths to ensure the proposed building designs are compliant. The NBC applies to residential buildings of three stories or fewer and additions of more than 10 square meters in area. In response to the cold climates of Canadian provinces and territories, the emphasis is on high insulation and air tightness.

Accessibility Codes

The push to make buildings more accessible to people with physical limitations was codified into law by the Americans with Disabilities Act (ADA), which became effective in 1992.

Because the law applies to buildings of "public accommodation" rather than private dwellings, its requirements are not mandatory for private residential work. Even so, the legislation is evidence of a growing concern for "universal design," a trend whose aim is to accommodate the needs of people who do not conform to the "average" able adult.

In Canada, requirements regarding access for persons with disabilities were included for the first time in the NBC in 1975 under "Building Standards for the Handicapped." The 1985 NBC edition integrated all requirements and intended to facilitate the use of buildings by persons with physical disabilities, particular those in wheelchairs. This was the first time the newly defined term *barrier-free access* was integrated into a Canadian building code.

People in wheelchairs and those with impaired sight, mobility, or hearing all use kitchens and baths. And the world's population is aging. Thus, it wouldn't be unusual for you to have clients with some kind of special needs at some point in your career. Because the ADA is a civil rights law, it does not specifically address design standards. Guidelines have, however, been issued in various federal publications. These include the Fair Housing Accessibility Guidelines and the Design Guidelines for Accessible/Adaptable Dwellings, published by the U.S. Department of Housing and Urban Development, Office of Fair Housing and Urban Development. Contact the housing agencies in your state to see what standards apply. For design information on accessibility issues, you may wish to obtain the *Bath Planning and Kitchen Planning volumes,* published by Wiley.

PERMITS AND INSPECTIONS

The type and number of permits required for a particular project depend on the extent of the work planned. Most municipalities require a building permit for any new residential construction and for remodeling if it exceeds a specific value. The general contractor normally obtains this permit upon approval of an application and payment of a fee. The fee is normally a percentage of the construction value of the project. A straightforward interior remodeling project may require no other documentation. A permit for a new residence probably will require a site plan, drawn to scale and showing the house on the property, property lines, site setbacks, utility lines, walks and driveway, and possibly a floor plan and exterior elevations.

Plumbing and electrical work often require separate permits. The municipality may require the work to be installed by a licensed plumber and electrician. Expect at least one inspection for each permit granted. The building permit will trigger an inspection at the time the rough framing is completed and one after the project is complete. Plumbing and electrical work usually are inspected after rough-in is completed but before any finish work is completed. For example, the inspector will check out the electrical rough-in after the wiring is installed but before it is covered by drywall. If your responsibilities for a project extend beyond design to include oversight during the construction phase, you will need to be aware of the required inspections and make sure they occur at a time that will prevent construction delays.

Working with Building Officials

Working with local building departments can go smoothly or become a nightmare. In general, the bigger the municipality, the larger the bureaucracy you will face in getting permits and inspections. Another difference is the level of expertise. The inspectors of a city building department may be more knowledgeable about codes and construction than those in small rural districts, who may be part-timers with another primary occupation. In any case, some general rules of thumb can help minimize hassles with the local building authority.

- Visit the local building department to familiarize yourself with the process and obtain information about permits, fees, and inspection procedures.
- Get a copy of the local zoning ordinance and check its provisions for each project you propose.
- Find out which codes are in force and get a copy of them. Familiarize yourself with the provisions of the codes that affect your sphere of operation.

- While the project is still in the planning/design stage, take preliminary drawings in to get input and advice. You won't get written approval at that stage, but officials appreciate being consulted while there is still time for changes, and you can use their input to make sure your design doesn't fly in the face of local laws or regulations.
- Make sure any plans you submit have the professional stamp required (architect, engineer, surveyor).
- Notify the appropriate inspectors in a timely manner when inspections are due.
- Don't be confrontational with building officials. Listen to their concerns, express your own, and seek compromise. Sometimes it pays to let some time pass and tempers cool before you respond. If you feel you are in over your head, seek outside advice from the appropriate professional—an architect, engineer, or attorney—before taking on the building department.
- Budget time in your project for the inspection process.

SUMMARY

The historic general and specific building codes came into being to promote uniform construction standards that would ensure public safety. Other codes, such as energy and accessibility codes, have been devised to foster goals deemed worthwhile for society. Building permits and inspections are ways of ensuring conformance with the codes. As you become more familiar with codes and permits, you will see them less as obstacles to the progress of a project and simply as another task to be accomplished in a logical and planned sequence.

CHAPTER REVIEW

1. Where can you find out which codes apply in your region? (See "Building Codes" pages 5–7)
2. What is a "model" code? (See "Building Codes" page 6)
3. How do the IBC and IRC codes differ? (See "International Residential Code" page 6)
4. What energy sources does the Model Energy Code promote? (See "Energy Codes" page 7)
5. What is the difference between the prescriptive and performance standard approach? (See "Energy Codes" page 7)
6. Why is it important to be familiar with ADA requirements? (See "Accessibility Codes" pages 7–8)
7. Do you request a plumbing inspection before or after the drywall is installed? (See "Permits and Inspections" page 8)

Designing Healthy Houses

Children with brain damage from ingesting lead paint chips. People getting respiratory diseases from moldy basements. Cancer cases suspected from drinking water contaminated with the fuel additive methyl tertiary-butyl ether (MBTE) or breathing radon gas. Every day seems to bring a new health scare from some peril lurking in the home. Why? Two reasons. First, we know more today about environmental health hazards than ever before. Second, today's homes contain numerous synthetic materials—everything from manufactured lumber to carpets and furniture—whose gases can't escape to the outside as they did in the past, when houses were draftier and contained fewer manufactured materials. In today's more tightly sealed homes, indoor air quality has become a primary concern to ensure the health and well-being of the occupants.

This chapter describes some of the hazards to health encountered in residences and suggests what you as a kitchen and bath designer can do to minimize them in your projects. Doing so will not only create safer, healthier environments for your clients but will also result in better job site safety for the installers on the job.

Learning Objective 1: Identify the substances produced by certain building materials that that can permeate the interior and pose health risks to occupants.

Learning Objective 2: Recognize substances that pose health risks through absorption through the skin or eyes or by ingestion.

Learning Objective 3: List measures a designer can utilize to minimize the health risks of building materials to the occupants.

AIRBORNE HAZARDS

Human lungs and nasal passages are pretty well equipped to deal with most kinds of natural dust. Saw-cut or router dust is about 33 microns or larger (a micron is 1 millionth of a meter). Particles of this size don't pose much risk to the lungs, since they are easily expelled, but they can definitely irritate the eyes and nose. Other irritants of this type are fibers of mineral wool or fiberglass insulation.

Particles larger than 10 microns are usually trapped by mucus in the larger respiratory passages and eventually expelled. Extremely small particles, such as dust from sanding or grinding materials such as wood, drywall, or concrete, may be as small as 1.3 microns, small enough to be trapped in the lungs and pose a health hazard. If your project responsibilities encompass job site supervision, make sure the areas of operation are sealed off from the house with effective temporary dust barriers and that the workers wear goggles, respirators, and protective covering for their skin.

In the following sections, we'll learn more about the dangers of particular hazards and how to best deal with them.

Asbestos

Asbestos is a mineral that is as soft and flexible as cotton or flax, yet it is fireproof. Because of this property, it has been used since the dawn of civilization. The ancient Greeks used asbestos for the wicks of the eternal flames of the Vestal Virgins, as the funeral dress during the cremation of kings, and as napkins. In modern times, asbestos was used in many industrial applications, such as insulation for boilers, steam pipes, turbines, ovens, kilns, and other high-temperature equipment.

A 1906 study determined that there was an uncommonly high mortality rate among asbestos workers and suspected that this probably was due to the amount of dust that accumulated in the poor working conditions. In 1917 and 1918, several studies in the United States concluded that asbestos workers were dying unnaturally young, and in 1924, the first diagnosis of asbestosis was made. England passed laws in 1931 to improve ventilation and to recognize asbestosis as a work-related disease. It took until 1930 for the first autopsy to establish the existence of asbestos lung disease in North America. The following years saw laws passed to allow asbestosis in workers' compensation cases. But these laws often allowed employees only a very short time period after leaving work to file a claim.

Asbestos particles smaller than 10 microns have been linked to lung cancer and other respiratory maladies. Thus, asbestos-containing products have not been used in construction since approximately 1975. Even so, the products already in place present a clear danger to individuals involved in repair and demolition of structures containing asbestos products.

Asbestos may turn up during remodeling of older houses in any of several locations: pipe and duct insulation, ceiling tiles, sprayed ("popcorn") ceiling material, or—less likely—floor tiles. Left undisturbed, asbestos poses little risk to occupants. The danger comes when the particles become airborne or friable, as they often do in remodeling.

Visit the project before you complete the plans. Federal regulations enforced as part of the Clean Air Act now require that facilities be inspected for asbestos prior to demolition or renovation. Contact the appropriate agency in your state to clarify the enforcement and procedures before engaging in any renovation work. Notify the appropriate contractor(s) to have material (flooring, ceiling tiles, insulation, etc.) tested. If, after testing, asbestos is found on the site, remediation can take four forms:

1. Encapsulation, whereby the asbestos-containing material (ACM) is covered with a sealant to prevent fiber release
2. Encasement, whereby the ACM is covered with a hard-setting sealing material
3. Enclosure, whereby the ACM is placed in an airtight barrier
4. Removal from the site

The appropriate remedy will be determined according to specific federal guidelines. In residential work, removal is the most likely option, but it must be done by a contractor certified to do this kind of work. Remodeling work should not begin before the site has been tested and any remedial work has been certified as completed.

Formaldehyde

Formaldehyde is a colorless, pungent-smelling gas that can cause watery eyes, burning sensations in the eyes and throat, nausea, and difficulty in breathing, at levels above 0.1 parts per million (ppm), according to the Environmental Protection Agency (EPA). Plywood, particleboard, and other pressed wood products—common components of residential construction—achieve their high strength through a process whereby the wood fibers or chips are forced together under high heat and pressure, using formaldehyde-containing bonding agents. Over time, the formaldehyde escapes in gaseous form (outgases) into the environment. In older, leakier homes, this wasn't much of a concern. However, the current trend to tighten up houses to conserve energy has meant a lower exchange of inside with outside air. The potential for airborne hazards has mounted, posing a potential health hazard to the occupants. New homes usually contain significant amounts of pressed wood products that can release formaldehyde levels greater than 0.3 ppm, such as medium-density overlay (MDF) panels, particleboard, and hardboard, all of which are commonly used in the cabinets and underlayments of kitchen and baths. However, many manufacturers have recently developed ultra-low-emitting and no-added-urea-formaldehyde products, resulting in a wide variety of products available with reduced formaldehyde levels as well as a growing number of non-formaldehyde alternatives. Also, panel products that are faced with melamine, laminate, or other nonporous materials prevent the release of formaldehyde.

If possible, specify formaldehyde-free panel products. If this is not possible, two job site measures can minimize the amount of gases released by panel products during and immediately after installation:

1. Use air conditioning and dehumidifiers to maintain moderate temperature and reduce humidity levels.
2. Increase ventilation after bringing new sources of formaldehyde into the home.

Volatile Organic Compounds

The fumes from solvents in oil- and lacquer-based paints and adhesives have long been linked to respiratory illnesses, memory impairment, and cancer, as well as hazards to the environment. Many of the coatings, solvents, and adhesives typically used in kitchen and bath work contain these volatile organic compounds (VOCs), which are emitted during drying and/or curing. The oil- and lacquer-based paints that contain the highest levels of VOCs have been largely replaced by water-based latex paints in residential applications, but even these release some levels of VOCs as they dry. Several paints have recently emerged on the market claiming low or zero levels of VOCs. However, the "zero" claim is probably a misnomer.

There are other products commonly used in kitchen and bath installations that contain VOCs, such as adhesives, cleaners, and solvents. As a designer, you should be familiar with every coating and adhesive you specify, along with the potential risks they may pose to workers on the job or building occupants. If and when you must specify chemicals containing VOCs, take whatever measures are necessary to protect the installers and occupants. This may include specifying low-VOC products and ensuring that there is adequate ventilation during installation.

Radon

Radon, a colorless, odorless gas, is a radioactive product of the radium that naturally occurs in the earth's crust. Radon in levels exceeding 4 picocuries per liter poses a risk to people in regions with high concentrations of certain types of rock strata. Radon is believed responsible for 5% to 15% of all lung cancer. Radon seeps into houses through minuscule cracks in foundations and basement floors and also can occur in well water. Scientists consider the amount of radon emitted by granite used in countertops too small to pose a health risk.

The International Residential Code (IRC) lists counties that have strong probabilities of high radon concentrations. The soil at the site of a new home or air inside an existing one should be tested, so that the results can guide design strategies to mitigate unsafe levels of radon. Preventing radon from getting into a house is easier at the construction stage than after it is built. Local codes in radon-prone regions may require radon control measures. The IBC suggests several methods for radon-resistant construction in new dwellings, such as installing a gravel bed below the basement slab. This gravel bed acts as a continuous evacuation path to the outside when equipped with a fan that pulls air through the gravel and exhausts it to the outside. Measures that may or may not be feasible in remodeling include sealing up cracks in the floors and walls, waterproofing foundations on the outside, and ventilating the interior, as discussed in Chapter 15, to evacuate any remaining radon.

OTHER HAZARDS

Arsenic

Moisture is a fact of life in most of the United States. Except for naturally decay-resistant wood species, such as redwood, cedar, and cypress, most woods deteriorate under long-term exposure to moisture. Wood in direct contact with concrete, masonry, or soil comes in constant contact with moisture, which facilitates attack by insects and fungus. To withstand this onslaught, the wood must be naturally rot resistant or treated with a chemical. The most common chemical treatment used to be chromated copper arsenic (CCA), which was forced into the wood under pressure. Pressure-treated wood typically was southern yellow pine, which had a label attached to the end of each piece and usually had a slightly greenish tinge.

The arsenic used in the compound has come under increasing attack in recent years as a hazard to health, particularly in playground equipment children regularly come in contact with. The wood decks in homes may also be made of CCA-treated lumber. The arsenic in these applications poses a hazard when it is ingested or absorbed through the skin by handling the material. Arsenic may also enter the lungs, by inhaling either the sawdust released when it is cut, or the smoke when it is burned.

Alternatives to CCA-treated wood include the naturally rot-resistant species mentioned above or woods treated with newer and safer chemicals. Two of these in current use include ammoniacal copper quaternary (ACQ) and copper azole. A number of materials for decks have emerged that are made of wood fibers or plastics, all of which are rot resistant and arsenic free.

To protect installers working with CCA-treated wood, the EPA recommends:

- Always wear gloves and a dust mask when cutting CCA-treated wood.
- Protect eyes by wearing goggles.
- If possible, do any cutting outdoors.
- Wash hands before eating, drinking, or smoking.
- Wash work clothes exposed to CCA separately from other clothing.

Guidelines for protecting householders are less precise. In general:

- Don't leave CCA-treated scraps on the job site.
- Make sure any CCA-treated wood is enclosed or inaccessible to the inhabitants.

Site-Applied Wood Preservatives

Before installing wood in a location prone to moisture, cut ends of treated wood (whatever treatment) and any non–rot-resistant species should be spot treated by brushing or dipping in a preservative solution. A typical example in a kitchen/bath job is the inside edge of a plywood countertop cutout that will support a sink. Another is any pipe cutout in a plywood subfloor. Preservatives that contain lindane, pentachlorophenol (PCB), or tributyl tin oxide (TBTO) are toxic. Safer treatments are based on borax, soda, potash, linseed oil, or beeswax. The label should state whether the substance is toxic or safe.

Lead

Lead, ingested or inhaled, is a toxic substance that can damage the heart, bones, intestines, kidneys, and reproductive and nervous systems. In the latter category, it is particularly toxic to children, where it can cause permanent learning and behavior disorders.

In homes, the sources of lead are paint, water supply, and plumbing. Lead provided a stable, effective pigment for paints up until the 1970s, when its toxic effects were finally recognized and it was banned. By then it had already done untold damage to the health of hapless homeowners and professional builders alike, in the form of hypertension, anemia, kidney failure, and memory loss. A report in Massachusetts identified 380 cases of severe lead poisoning in construction workers from 1991 to 1995. Of these, 101 were painters. The main concern today is protecting inhabitants and remodelers in existing housing, and the potential of children who may eat lead-paint chips and acquire brain damage as a consequence.

Lead poisoning from paint is, fortunately, avoidable. Like undisturbed asbestos, undisturbed lead-based paint poses no hazard. But sanding, scraping, or burning off the paint creates clouds of lead dust that can be inhaled or swallowed. This makes for difficult decisions when it comes to renovating. A U.S. federal law in effect since April 2010 requires that all contractors performing renovation, painting, and repairs that disturb lead-based paint in homes built before 1978 to be EPA certified and follow specific work practices to prevent lead contamination. Any paint applied before the 1970s likely contains lead and should be analyzed and removed by a specialized lead abatement contractor before other finishes are applied. If you are charged with job site supervision, you can minimize your legal vulnerability by having homeowners get the paint tested and have any required abatement work done before you begin your operations.

Lead can pollute drinking water from a well or from lead pipes found in homes built before 1950 and from lead-based solder. Traditional solder used to join copper water pipes was made of lead and tin. When the acid in soft water runs through the pipes, some of the lead is released into the water. Lead-free solder containing silver is now required for pipes containing drinking water. If a kitchen/bath remodel entails extensive replacement of the water pipes, it may be a good idea to test the solder in the remaining pipes. If lead is found, the pipes should be resoldered. Simple test kits are available from building supply stores. Lead in the water supply can be treated by point-of-use devices discussed in Chapter 16.

Toxic Paint Additives

The list of construction materials once thought to be benign but subsequently found to be toxic continues to expand. In the past, mercury was added to latex paints to control bacteria and mildew. It was banned by the EPA in the early 1970s. Although the ban was subsequently replaced by a requirement to post a warning on the label of interior paints containing more than 200 parts per million mercury. Cadmium, once a reliable common paint pigment, is also no longer used.

A POSITIVE APPROACH TO DESIGN

So far we've talked about what to avoid in your design. Some hazards are dire enough that they may even scare you away from design entirely. But they shouldn't. Understanding these hazards will enable you to deal with them competently in your design work. One of the first things you might do when beginning a project is to ask your clients what specific allergies any household members might have. Take this information into account when specifying materials. Design adequate ventilation to remove not only any airborne pathogens resulting from the construction but also those resulting from the use of the space after the construction is complete.

But don't stop there. Good design goes beyond minimizing hazards to provide positive benefits to the occupants. The goal of the project should be to make their lives better than they were before. As you acquire knowledge and design skills, you'll find ways to make sure your designs transcend the merely safe or adequate to reach the level of wonderful.

Adequately designed lighting, for example, will ensure that users can see what they are doing. Wonderful lighting incorporates creative light sources, locations, and controls that enable the occupants to direct the light where they want it and create different moods. It extends to finding ways to use sunlight in the space, through creative use of windows and skylights. Colors, forms, and textures can all be used to design spaces that will be delightful as well as healthy areas of the home.

SUMMARY

We know a great deal today about the materials used in home construction and their effects on the inhabitants. Once-common toxic materials, such as lead and asbestos, have been replaced with safer alternatives. But today's homes, built tighter in order to conserve energy, also risk accumulating harmful gases from the many synthetic materials used in their construction. Designers can do much to ensure a healthy indoor environment by understanding which materials pose hazards and how to deal with them.

CHAPTER REVIEW

1. Why are particles smaller than 33 microns dangerous to health? (See "Airborne Hazards" page 11)
2. What are the four methods of dealing with asbestos found on a construction site? (See "Asbestos" page 12)
3. What products commonly used in a kitchen or bath may contain formaldehyde? (See "Formaldehyde" pages 12–13)
4. Which products, other than paints, are likely sources of VOCs? (See "Volitile Organic Compounds" page 13)
5. What is ammoniacal copper quaternary (ACQ) used for? (See "Arsenic" page 14)
6. What are the sources of lead hazards in homes? (See "Lead" pages 14–15)

Maximizing Energy Efficiency

The cost of energy to homeowners has increased in recent years and will continue to do so, eating up an ever greater percentage of the household budget. Because so many of the components that go into the construction of a home affect its use of energy, maximizing energy efficiency affects the entire design and construction, from the building envelope down to the choice of equipment.

Kitchens and baths use more energy than any other rooms in the house. Both require lots of hot water, and kitchens require energy to both heat foods and keep them cool. Rural houses with wells must also pump the water to the point of use. Electrical power is required for ventilation to remove odors, moisture, and cooking gases. A variety of appliances depend on gas or electricity to operate. Finally, lighting is likely more extensive, especially in kitchens.

Designers have become aware in recent years of the environmental consequences their design choices. The concept of "green" building has come into recent use and covers a wide range of decisions made during the the design and construction process that promote a more efficient use of resources in order to have a smaller impact on the environment. Organizations such as the National Association of Home Builders (NAHB) and Leadership in Energy and Environmental Design (LEED) have developed standards to promote green building.

The NAHB along with the International Code Council established the ICC National Green Building Standard in 2007, which defines green building for single- and multifamily homes, residential remodeling projects, and site development while still allowing for the flexibility required for regionally appropriate best green practices. Certification for the standard is provided by the NAHB Research Center. Copies can be obtained from the organization's Web site, www.nahbgreen.org/ngbs.

LEED was conceived by U.S. Green Building Council to develop standards that promote the efficient use of resources in construction. LEED certification provides independent, third-party verification that a building, home, or community was designed and built using strategies aimed at achieving high performance in key areas of human and environmental health, sustainable site development, water savings, energy efficiency, materials selection, and indoor environmental quality. Information on how to become an LEED-certified designer can be obtained from the organization's Web site, usgbc.org.

These organizations, along with energy codes, can provide useful sources for making the best use of household energy. As a kitchen and bath designer, you can do your part by understanding how energy is used in these rooms and selecting appliances and equipment that makes the best use of it. Doing so will not only save your clients money on operating expenses; it also will provide them with a pleasant, comfortable interior environment. In this chapter, we see how each of these conservation strategies comes into play.

> *Learning Objective 1: Explain how to maximize energy conservation in the design of the building envelope.*

> *Learning Objective 2: Identify natural energies that can contribute to the heating, cooling, ventilation, and lighting of the building.*

> *Learning Objective 3: Recognize how specifying efficient equipment can augment the use of natural energies.*

AN ENERGY-CONSERVING BUILDING ENVELOPE

An energy-conserving envelope is a building enclosure in which walls and roof exclude heat in the hot seasons and retain it in the cold seasons. Because North America contains several climate zones, each with its own particular characteristics, there is no one-size-fits-all rule for a building envelope that optimizes energy efficiency. An efficient design begins with an understanding of the region's climate and ends with a design that makes the best use of the region's assets while countering its liabilities. Regardless of the region, the process begins with managing the flow of heat in and out of the building shell.

Thermal Insulation

Heat passes through the building envelope primarily by conduction, though radiation and convection also play a part. The best way to minimize conduction is by insulating the parts of the envelope that have direct contact with the outside weather—the exterior walls and the roof/ceiling. Include the floor in the equation if it sits above a ventilated crawl space.

Homes in all locations need some amount of thermal insulation in the envelope to control heat gain and loss. The standard for rating insulation is its R-value, an index of the ability of the material to resist heat flow by conduction. The higher the number, the more conductive heat it blocks. Although the state energy department or local building inspection department is the final source for determining the recommend levels of insulation for a particular region, Table 4.1 and the map in Figure 4.1 give a general idea of the recommended R-values in North America.

TABLE 4.1 Recommended Minimum Total R-values

Insulation Zone	Ceilings[1]		Floors[2]	Walls	Foundations[3]
	Oil, Gas, Heat Pump	Electric Resistance	All Fuels	All Fuels	All Fuels
1	19	30	0	19	11
2	30	30	0	19	19
3	30	38	0	19	19
4	30	38	19	19	19
5	38	38	19	19	19
6	38	38	19	19	19
7	38	49	19	19	19
8	49	49	19	19	19
9	49	49	19	19	19
10	55	55	19	19	19

[1] Cathedral ceilings and ceilings below ventilated attics.
[2] Recommended levels for floors above crawl spaces or basements with uninsulated foundations.
[3] Recommended levels for foundation walls if floors are not insulated.

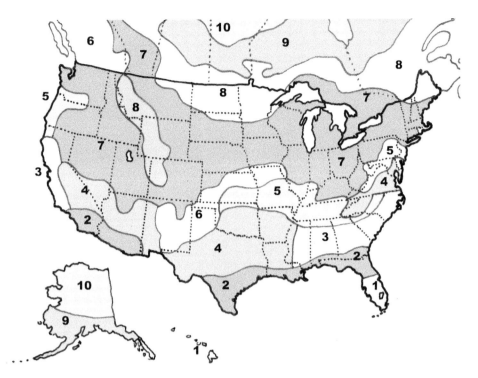

FIGURE 4.1 Zones for Recommended R-Values

Choosing the right type of insulation from the many available options requires matching the insulation to the application, balancing R-values with cost, and weighing the ease or difficulty of installation. Table 4.2 rates and describes some of the most common types of insulation used in homes.

Blankets and Batts

Fiberglass and mineral wool blanket and batt insulation has been the most widely used insulation in homes in the past and continues to be popular because of its economy and ease of installation. Thicknesses range between 3½" to 12" (89 to 254 mm), with R-values ranging between R-11 and R-38. Widths are sized to fit between framing members spaced 16" (406 mm) or 24" (610 mm) centers. Insulation is packed into bundles containing 4'-long batts or rolled blankets (see Figure 4.2).

Fiberglass blanket/batt insulation consists of glass fibers pressed together with a binding substance, unfaced or sandwiched between facings of kraft paper or aluminum. The standard type is messy to work with. As fibers come loose, they cause the skin to itch and eyes and nose to run. The binder has been improved in some brands to lessen the scratching and keep the fibers from breaking off and becoming airborne. A still-newer innovation is a plastic wrap that completely encloses the batt. Fiberglass batts and blankets also come unfaced, for friction fitting between framing, or faced with kraft paper or foil that you staple to the face of the framing. The foil facing can also serve as a vapor barrier, but only if the edges are thoroughly sealed with tape or caulk. Kraft paper facing is only a marginal vapor barrier.

Mineral wool, sometimes called rock wool, costs slightly more than fiberglass. It is similar to fiberglass in facings and installation but is an even greater irritant to the skin, eyes, and nasal passages.

Cotton insulation, also available in batts, has come on the market in recent years. Although more expensive than fiberglass, it is less harmful to health, since it contains no toxic substances. This attribute and the fact that cotton insulation is a sustainable product made largely from recycled sources qualifies it as a green product.

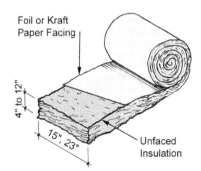

FIGURE 4.2 Fiberglass or mineral wool batt and blanket insulation is available in various thicknesses and widths, sized to fit between framing spaced 16 or 24" (406 or 610 mm) on center.

ENGLISH

TABLE 4.2 Comparing Types of Insulation

Key: • Usually □ Sometimes L Low M Medium H High	R per inch	Relative cost	Suitable Applications				
			Vapor barrier integral	Wall/ceiling cavities	Wall, ceiling or roof surfaces	Foundations	Under concrete slabs
Blanket and Batt Insulation							
Fiberglass, 15" (381 mm), 23" (584 mm) wide, various lengths	3.3	L	□[1]	•			
Mineral Wool, 15" (381 mm), 23" (584 mm) wide, various lengths	3.6	L	□[1]	•			
Rigid Sheet Insulation							
Phenolic Foam, 4' × 8' (1,219 mm × 2,438 mm)	8.5	H	•[2]		•	•	•
Polyurethane, Isocyanurate, 4' × 8' (1,219 mm × 2,438 mm) sheets:	7.2	M	•[2]		•	•	•
Extruded Polystyrene, 4' × 8' (1,219 mm × 2,438 mm), 2' × 8' (610 mm × 2,438 mm)	5.0	M			•	•	•
Expanded Polystyrene (beadboard) 4' × 8' (1,219 mm × 2,438 mm), 2' × 8' (610 mm × 2,438 mm)	4.0	M			•	•	•
Foamed-in-Place Insulation							
Open-cell polyisocyanurate	3.5	H		•	•	•	
Closed-cell polyisocyanurate	6	H	•[4]	•	•	•	
Loose Fill Insulation							
Cellulose, blown in	3.7	M		•			
Cellulose, bagged	3.7	L		•			
Perlite pellets, bagged	2.7	L		•			
Fiberglass, blown in	2.2	M		•			
Mineral Wool, blown in	2.9	M		•			
Sprayed Cellulose							
Cellulose	3.5	M	•	•[3]			

[1] The foil facing on some batt and blanket insulation can serve as a vapor barrier only if the joints are taped adequately.
[2] Applies if the boards are faced with aluminum foil and all joints are taped or caulked.
[3] Spray cellulose limited to wall cavities.
[4] The claim that no separate vapor barrier is needed has not yet been universally accepted.

Rigid Foam Insulation

In rigid foam insulation, various polymers are converted into a foam state with blowing agents, then used in spray form or made into rigid sheets to insulate buildings. Rigid foam sheets come in thicknesses of ½" to 4" (13 to 102 mm) and in various widths and lengths. The material costs more than batts, in terms of R-value, but makes up for it in compressing more R-value into a thinner volume and other advantages.

Rigid foam insulation has many applications in homes, applied to the inner or outer structures of walls and roofs and the undersides of concrete slabs (see Figure 4.3). In remodeling work, rigid foam sheets also provide a way to increase the R-value of an existing stud wall or cathedral ceiling without tearing the wall or ceiling apart. When faced with foil and taped together, the sheets can serve as a vapor barrier if the joints are taped. The material cuts easily with a sharp knife and can be secured by nails, screws, or adhesives. Tin washers must be used with nails and screws to keep the heads from punching through the surface.

Spray Foam Insulation

Spray foam insulation offers not only very high R-values but also fills voids that are difficult to fill with other types of insulation. And because of spray seal cracks and openings in the building skin, it provides excellent resistance to the passage of air and moisture. With these advantages over other types, spray foam is gaining in residential applications, despite its higher cost.

The material comes in two parts, which are mixed together as it is sprayed through a nozzle against a building surface, where it expands, hardens, and cures. At that time, any foam that expands outside the cavities is trimmed off with special tools.

Two types of spray foam are currently used: open cell and closed cell. The best type for a given application depends on the circumstances. Open-cell foam is more economical but has a lower R-value. It also requires a dry location to cure. Closed-cell foam cures in locations prone to moisture, so is a better choice for foundations. And with a greater R-value per inch thickness than open-cell foam, closed-cell foam might be the only choice where space is limited. Applying either type successfully is a tricky task best done by experienced franchised applicators.

Loose Fill and Blown-in Insulation

Making remodeling work weather tight often requires insulating nooks and crannies that are hard to fill with standard insulation. Cellulose, perlite, fiberglass, and mineral wool are available as loose fibers or pellets and bagged for pouring by hand into hard-to-reach areas or for blowing into walls or ceilings by pneumatic equipment. Cellulose insulation is made from recycled newspapers treated with a fire-retarding chemical. Its R-value is slightly lower than fiberglass or mineral wool, but its slightly greater density makes it less susceptible to being blown about by sudden gusts whipping through the attic. Because it is made from recycled newsprint, it qualifies as a green material. Its main drawback is its tendency to attract and hold moisture, making a good vapor barrier mandatory. Over time, all loose-fill and blown-in insulation settles, resulting in some decrease in R-value.

Sprayed Cellulose

The same cellulose available as loose fill can be sprayed into building cavities with pneumatic equipment. It is sprayed dry into horizontal areas, such as floors and attics, and mixed with water and adhesives and sprayed wet into vertical wall cavities. Damp-sprayed cellulose then clings to the cavities without falling down. After drying, the excess material is scraped (scrubbed) flush with the stud faces. Its ability to completely fill the voids, lack of need for a separate vapor barrier (some claim), and a cost just slightly above fiberglass batts make this type of insulation a popular option for houses.

Radiant Barriers

Thermal insulation is not quite as effective for keeping the sun's heat out of roofs and attics as is another class of materials called radiant barriers. Where thermal insulation blocks conduction only, radiant barriers have a shiny metallic surface that reflects the sun's radiant heat. Radiant barrier materials are available as rigid sheets of foil-faced foam or plywood and rolls of flexible sheet. They are of greatest benefit to homes south of the Mason-Dixon Line. To be most effective, radiant barriers must be installed with an airspace between the reflective layer and an adjacent material to prevent conductive heat flow. The preferred installation in a roof is to place the radiant barrier just below the rafters. It doesn't matter which way the shiny surface faces.

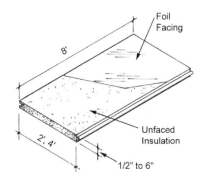

FIGURE 4.3 Rigid foam insulation comes faced with foil or unfaced in thicknesses up to 6″ (152 mm). The total R-value depends on the type of foam and thickness.

Air and Vapor Barriers

Thermal insulation reduces heat transfer by blocking conduction through the construction materials that make up wall and roof assemblies. Because the materials do not fit together perfectly, the inevitable gaps allow air to infiltrate, bypassing the insulation and leaking heat to the outdoors in cold climates and cool air out in hot climates and also leaking hot air indoors in hot climates and cool air indoors in cold climates. Several other items present possible paths for leaks, including wall receptacles, pipe penetrations, and tub cutouts. Caulking and weather-stripping windows and doors go a long way to tighten the envelope against convective heat flow, and spray foam can seal the envelope from the inside. With other types of insulation, an air barrier material that wraps the house just under the exterior cladding provides a needed second line of defense.

So-called housewrap materials let moisture vapor pass through while blocking air infiltration. Housewrap comes in rolls and is stapled to the sheathing. Joints are then taped with a plastic sealing tape (contractor's tape). Some experts think covering the entire wall surface is redundant, because only the joints leak air. These experts maintain that taping only the joints and leaving the solid portions of the sheathing unwrapped makes an effective air barrier. Special types of sheathing plus joint tape are now available to enable this type of approach.

Conserving energy in the building envelope also requires keeping moisture out of the structure. In heating-dominated climates, warm, moist air migrates through walls and roofs to the colder outdoors in winter; it condenses at some point along the path. Depending on where this occurs in the wall or roof, this moisture can cause insulation to lose efficiency, wood framing and sheathing to decay, and outside paint to peel. In cooling-dominated climates, the reverse can happen when the house is being cooled.

The accepted way to avoid these woes is to seal the envelope on the inside in regions where heating is the dominant need and on the outside in warm climates where air conditioning is the primary need.

A good, continuous vapor barrier material has a low permeance rating (the index of a material's ability to block the passage of moisture). Polyethylene sheet and aluminum foil both have very low permeability to moisture and can be used on both new and existing construction. Vapor barriers are always recommended in cold climates to keep moisture out of the structure in winter. The barrier always goes between the insulation and heated space, usually just under the wall finish material. The reverse is true in warm, humid climates, such as Alabama, Florida, Georgia, Louisiana, Mississippi, South Carolina, and the southern half of Texas, where the barrier goes near the outer surface, to keep the more humid outside air from entering the air-conditioned interior.

Sealing up a house against air infiltration (or exfiltration) yields a "tight" house that can lack sufficient fresh air for the occupants and combustion air for fuel-burning appliances. Various ways to ensure an adequate supply of fresh air are discussed in Chapter 15.

Energy-Efficient Equipment

All homes depend on equipment and appliances, which use energy. The next chapter shows some ways to reduce this dependence by using natural energies to heat and cool houses. Regardless of the source of the energy, minimizing its use benefits both the homeowner and environment.

Many factors influence homeowners' buying patterns, and energy efficiency is not always at the top of the list. This is borne out by the recent trends toward outdoor kitchens, full-body showers, and professional-size ranges and refrigerators. Even so, heating/cooling equipment and appliances have gotten much better at conserving energy, and designers can do much to educate and encourage their clients to obtain the most efficient equipment.

Refrigerators and other appliances whose efficiency is independent of the climate come with an Energy Guide Label affixed to the appliance, which states their energy efficiency rating

(EER). Appliances whose operation varies with the season, such as air conditioners, contain a seasonal energy efficiency rating (SEER). In either case, the higher the number, the more efficient the appliance.

Incorporating energy efficiency into every aspect of your design work is the right thing to do. Not only is it environmentally responsible, but it results in comfortable, functional, pleasant interior environments that will save your clients money over time.

SUMMARY

Homes use energy to provide heat and cooling and to power appliances and equipment. Minimizing the dependence on energy imported into the home benefits the homeowner as well as the environment. Reaching this goal begins with a building envelope designed to control the flow of heat in and out, through adequate insulation, housewraps, and sealing, and ends with the selection of energy-conserving equipment and appliances. We have described in this chapter the various types of insulation and air- and moisture-sealing strategies.

CHAPTER REVIEW

1. What are some of the ways kitchens use energy? (See "Chapter introduction" page 17)
2. What are the three ways heat passes through the building envelope? (See "Thermal Insulation" page 18)
3. What does R-value measure? (See "Thermal Insulation" page 18)
4. What newer type of batt insulation is less harmful to health? (See "Blankets and Batts" page 19)
5. What advantage does open-cell spray foam insulation have over closed-cell insulation? (See "Spray Foam Insulation" page 21)
6. What is the best way to block radiant heat flow? (See "Thermal Insulation" page 18)
7. What material is used to block moisture migration through exterior walls? (See "Air and Vapor Barriers" page 22)
8. What type of efficiency rating is appropriate to an air conditioner? (See "Energy-Efficient Equipment", page 23)

Using Natural Energies

The cost of energy derived from fossil fuels has gone up and down over the past forty years. Despite a continued attraction to gas-guzzling cars, overall fuel efficiency has increased, and we now have a number of efficient models to choose from.

We see similar patterns in home construction. Although many social and economic factors affect the design and size of homes, the cost of heating, cooling, and operating them with gas, fuel oil, and electricity is expected to continually rise. At the same time, we have become increasingly aware of how extracting and utilizing these fuels negatively affects the environment. Home design can respond to these trends in two ways: by conserving energy, as described in chapter 4, and by using natural forces whenever possible to provide light, heat, and cooling. This chapter gives an overview of how these energies can be exploited to the benefit of the occupants as well as the environment.

Learning Objective 1: Recognize the potential of natural energies for minimizing a home's dependence on imported energy.

Learning Objective 2: Describe alternate methods of using solar energy for space heat.

Learning Objective 3: Use light from the sun to augment electric lighting.

Learning Objective 4: Apply the potential of a specific climate region in the design process.

HOME HEATING WITH THE SUN

The sun is a constant source of heat and light. Far more solar energy falls on the surface of the earth than we need. It would be foolish not to use it. Unfortunately, although the energy is free for the taking, capturing it has costs, as does storing the energy for when we need it. The energy crises of the 1970s spawned many technologies for using the sun's energy for heating, cooling, lighting, and electricity. Some of these technologies fell by the wayside in the intervening years, because they were either too costly or too complicated. Drops in energy prices and the abandonment of government incentives also contributed to the decline in interest in these technologies. Spikes in energy costs in recent years have combined with greater environmental awareness to bring these technologies once again into the building mainstream.

Using solar energy to provide all or part of a home's heat started with the Greeks and Romans but didn't see much activity in industrial countries until the 1970s. At that time, oil from the Middle East suddenly became expensive and spurred interest in conservation and renewable energies. Out of this ferment grew two techniques for using the sun to heat houses: active and passive. Active solar heating systems use rooftop collectors to trap solar heat into a liquid medium or air that circulates the heated liquid into the house via heat exchangers and fans. Because of the unattractive appearance of solar collectors on roofs, and the cost, complexity, and high maintenance requirements of active systems, their appeal has been limited, mainly confined to southern locations, where they can provide most of the heat needed and heat water for swimming pools in the warm season. In other areas, the passive solar heating approach has proven more popular.

Of the numerous devices invented to turn sunshine into useful home heat, the most cost-effective approaches to date have also been the simplest. They use the house itself to collect, distribute, and store solar heat rather than depending on complicated systems of panels, pumps, distribution lines, and controls (see Figure 5.1).

The ideal passive solar house has a well-insulated envelope and compact footprint, with the longest side facing as close to due south as possible. Most passive solar houses in North America collect the sun's heat directly or indirectly, through a sunspace.

Direct Gain

Because windows are necessary in any case, they can also help heat the house if located on the south side, where they receive the greatest solar exposure on an annual basis. By far the simplest way to get heat from the sun into a house is through the windows. But the windows have to face the sun, which means southward for houses in the Northern Hemisphere. Solar rays penetrate the glass and strike an opaque surface, which radiates the energy as heat to

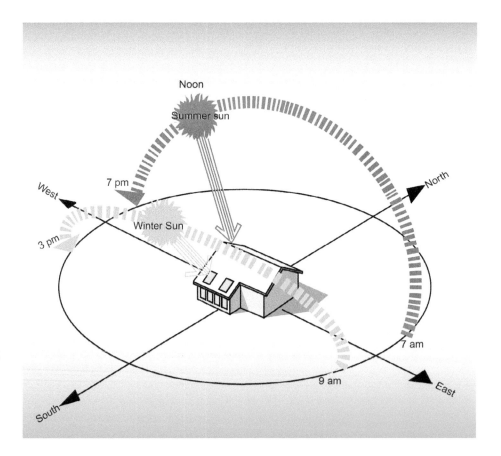

FIGURE 5.1 The path of the sun in summer is higher than in winter. To get the most benefit from solar heat and light, a house should be sited with its long façade facing southward and sufficient glazing in this façade to capture the sun's rays.

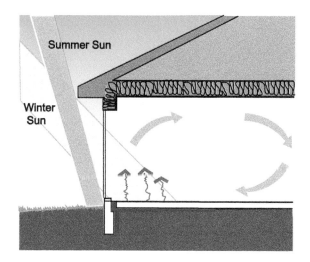

FIGURE 5.2 Direct gain is the simplest way to trap solar heat. A house designed for this approach has ample south-facing glazing to collect solar light and heat and a means of shading to block unwanted heat in warm seasons. In this illustration, the roof overhangs just enough to block summer sunshine while admitting lower-angle winter rays. A massive floor, such as a concrete slab, can absorb solar heat to even out day-to-night temperature fluctuations.

the space. If the surface is a dark-colored dense material, such as brick, stone, tile, or colored concrete, some of the heat is trapped—or stored—in the material and slowly released, an ideal situation for the times when the sun isn't shining. Windows for passive solar heating should be energy efficient, preferably coated with low-e coating, as described under "Glazing Choices" in chapter 9. Roof overhangs or other shading devices should be part of the design to protect against overheating in times of the year when the solar heat isn't wanted (see Figure 5.2).

Windows used for direct gain need some means of protection against heat during times of the year when warmth is not needed. Inside controls, such as blinds and drapes, work to control light but don't keep out much heat, because it has already penetrated the glass. Awnings or roof overhangs, mounted outside, work better. A simple rule of thumb for sizing an overhanging awning or roof eave is:

Horizontal overhang projection = Vertical distance × Overhang factor

The overhang projection and vertical distance to be used are shown in Figure 5.3. You can find the appropriate overhang factor by looking up your latitude on a map and matching it with Table 5.1.

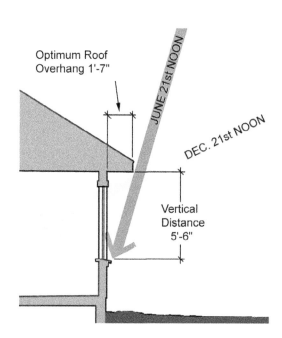

FIGURE 5.3 The optimum overhang for summer shading and winter solar heat gain can be obtained by multiplying the vertical distance shown here by the overhang factor in Table 5.1.

TABLE 5.1 Roof Overhang Factors

Latitude	Representative Location	Overhang Factor
28°	Tampa, FL., San Antonio, TX	0.09
32°	San Diego, CA, Dallas, TX	0.16
36°	Las Vegas, NV, Nashville, TN	0.22
40°	Denver, CO, Philadelphia, PA	0.29
44°	Boise, ID, Minneapolis, MN	0.37
48°	U.S./Canadian border, western	0.45
52°	Calgary, Regina	0.54

For example, if you want to find the necessary overhang length to arrive at the correct overhang factor for a south-facing kitchen window in Salt Lake City, you first determine that Salt Lake City is at north latitude 40°. The sill height above the floor is 42" (1,067 mm). If the eave height is 9 feet (108", 2,743 mm) above the floor, you will have a vertical distance of 108 – 42" (2,743 mm – 1,067 mm), or 66" (1,676 mm) to enter in the formula. The required overhang length will thus be 66 × 0.29 = 19" (1,676 mm × 0.29 = 486 mm). This rule of thumb is generally good for areas that can benefit from some solar heat. For climate zones that always need cooling, such as south Florida, the overhangs should block as much of the sun as possible, year-round.

Sunspaces

The sun's heat can also be collected indirectly, through an adjoining room, also known as a sunspace or solarium, as shown in Figures 5.4 and 5.5. This approach has the advantage of greater control of heat flow than direct gain. Because the space can be isolated from the main living area at night, it won't draw heat from the house on cold winter nights (although it may be desirable to either allow some heat from the house in or to provide an auxiliary

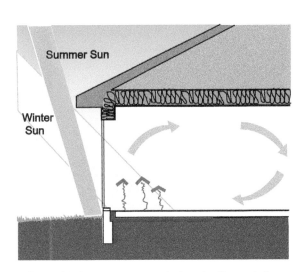

FIGURE 5.4 A sunspace traps solar heat by direct gain but supplies it to the house indirectly through doors or windows that control the heat transfer in or out of the living spaces.

FIGURE 5.5 The sunspace serves as a bright, cheerful entrance to a two-story colonial house. Tall vertical glazing faces south to capture the rays of the low winter sun.

heater on the coldest nights to keep plants from freezing). Sunspaces can serve functional needs as well as providing solar heat. Properly designed, they can make a welcoming entry–mudroom and place to grow plants (see Figure 5.6). As with direct gain systems, sunspace design must provide means for shading during warm seasons.

Daylighting

Light from the sun, called daylighting by architects and engineers, is most always welcome in kitchens and baths, for the free light it provides and even more for the cheerful way it enlivens a room. Any plants used to enhance the space thrive better in natural light as well. Sunlight can enter a space from a skylight or window in any wall, but the direction the window faces affects the amount of heat and light it will admit. "High-performance" windows contain improvements that make the control of heat and light that streams through much easier than the single- and double-glazed windows of the past, as we explain in chapter 9. But even efficient windows will contribute more to the home's lighting if the following four guidelines are observed.

South-facing Windows
Windows on southern walls receive the most total light year-round. The light is direct when the sky is clear, and glare is thus a problem. Overhangs, awnings, or other shading devices designed for the latitude, as described previously, can protect against unwanted heat during warm seasons.

North-facing Windows
Windows situated in the north walls receive direct sunlight only during early mornings and late afternoons in North America. At all other times the light is diffuse, with no glare. Although these windows are not cursed with glare and unwanted heat, north-facing windows are always a heat loss liability in the winter, so their total areas should be minimized in energy-conserving homes and the windows themselves should be be energy efficient.

East-facing Windows
The early-morning sunlight from windows facing east is especially welcome in kitchens, dining areas, and baths. Except in very warm climates, east-facing windows probably do not need shade protection, unless possibly to minimize glare and ensure privacy.

West-facing Windows
The afternoon light that streams in through west-facing windows also admits heat. However, this light doesn't help much in winter, when it is needed, because of the shorter days and angle of the sun. In summer, it can add a great amount of unwanted heat. Shade trees of proper size and location provide the best control. In their absence, vertical blinds or shutters, preferably mounted outside for warm-season control of heat and glare, are recommended.

Energy Design by Climate

We have seen so far how the design and construction of an energy-efficient home begins with an envelope that conserves imported energy, then exploits the sun's energy as much as feasible for free heat and daylight. North America contains several climate zones, as indicated in Figure 5.7. A successful home design makes the best use of the features of its location. The next sections describe the characteristics of each region and some energy-conserving design strategies for each one. These guidelines are not intended to replace but to supplement any requirements of state or local energy codes that may be in force in an area.

Northern United States/Southern Canada
Summers are short and mostly pleasant in the band that stretches across the northern portion of the United States and Canada. Autumns can be spectacular. The downside is the cold, long winters that dominate the climate and are the major focus of energy-efficient design. Homes

FIGURE 5.6 Plants thrive inside this sunspace without heat from the house. The brick floor and rear wall absorb solar heat during the day and slowly release it at night to keep the interior warm.

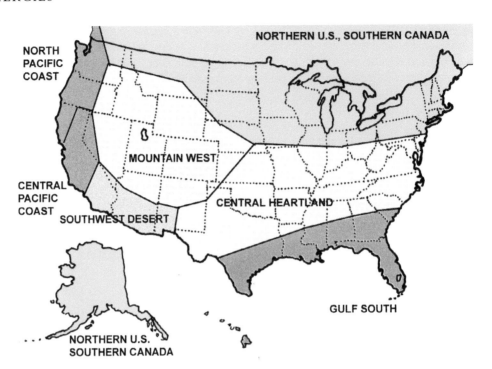

FIGURE 5.7 The United States and Canada span several climate zones. Designing an energy-efficient house requires understanding how to deal with the assets and liabilities of the zone in which it is located.

in this zone need a well-insulated envelope to keep heat loss to a minimum, with roofs insulated to a minimum of R-38, walls and foundations to R-19, and floors above crawl spaces to R-19. Trees and other natural features should be used to protect against winter winds. The envelope should be well sealed against infiltration. Choose the most efficient windows (R-3 or better) and make generous use of south-facing windows to collect winter sun.

Mountain West

Dryness and abundant sunshine mark the climate of the western states that lie between the Sierra Nevadas and Great Plains. Numerous mountains, valleys, and canyons create a variety of microclimates. Winters can be cold and stormy, with cold winds barreling down out of the northwest. In spring, winds often blast down out of canyons. The good news, outside of the dryness, is that the winters in this region are tempered by plentiful sunshine. Summers in the mountains are cool enough to require some heating throughout the year. Low-lying areas can be hot, but low humidity and cool nights make them bearable.

Start with a tight, well-insulated envelope. Insulate roofs/ceilings to a minimum R-38; and walls, foundations, and floors above crawl spaces to R-19. Locations in the higher mountains or those prone to winter winds coming down out of the mountains should receive higher insulation levels. Orient the main windows southward to capitalize on solar heating. Massive interior materials, such as tile-on-concrete floors and masonry walls, can help with both comfort and energy savings by absorbing solar heat during the day and releasing it during the night. Protect windows with overhangs or plants against the strong summer sun and minimize glass on the west-facing side, if possible. Divert or screen winter winds by landscaping, but allow breezes to cool the interior in summer. Ponds near exterior walls can help cool the building by cooling air before it enters.

North Pacific Coast

The rain, fog, and steady Pacific breezes of the coastal zone west of the Cascades make for cool and gray conditions much of the year. Even so, this climate is one of the easiest to design for. Despite the lack of sunshine, solar heating is worth the effort because so little heat is needed. South-facing windows can transmit solar heat to massive floors, which will absorb and store the energy. Window placement should defend against the cold, wet winds that plague this region. Insulate roofs/ceilings to R-38; and walls, foundations, and floors above crawl spaces to R-19.

Central Pacific Coast

Hot dry summers and abundant sunshine mark the Mediterranean climate of California's Central Valley, which stretches from Oregon to Los Angeles. Winters are moderately rainy, colder in the north than in the south. Variations in elevation and proximity to mountains and sea create numerous microclimates.

We can learn much from the ranch houses, missions, and adobes indigenous to this region. Long and low, with the long sides oriented toward the winter sun, their overhangs block summertime solar heat. Floors and interior walls are often masonry, which absorbs heat during the day and releases it during the cooler night. Patios and courtyards offer outdoor living during the abundant periods of mild weather. Operable windows on upper and lower levels allow cooling breezes inside at night. If fences contain outdoor living spaces, they are held away from these windows so as not to block the ventilation. Insulate roofs/ceilings to R-30, and walls and foundations to R-19.

Southwest Desert

Vacationers and retirees flock to the desert climate of the Southwest for the warm, dry climate that prevails there for most of the year. But many leave in summer when things get really hot. The searing temperatures of a summer day are often followed by a chilly night. Wide temperature swings combine with more sunshine than anywhere else in the United States to make this region the best location for solar heating. Massive construction materials should be used for floors and walls to store solar heat and balance the diurnal temperature extremes. Trees and man-made shading devices can help cool buildings by blocking the sun, while water near the building can cool nearby air through evaporation. Recommended levels of insulation are of R-30 in roofs/ceilings, R-19 in walls, and R-11 in foundations.

Central Heartland

The region stretching westward from the mid-Atlantic coast to the plains of Texas and northward from the Gulf states to Great Lakes has a relatively temperate climate with four distinct seasons. Summers are hot and humid. Winters are mild along the Atlantic coast, colder farther inland. Rainfall, also heaviest along the Atlantic slope, prevails throughout the region. The ever-present winds sometimes become tornadoes or hurricanes in summer and fall. Climate-responsive design in this region starts with walls insulated to R-19, roofs/ceilings to R-38, and foundations and floors above crawl spaces to R-19. Windows should be placed to catch winter sun and cooling breezes in warm periods but to shield them from the summer sun and hurricane winds.

Gulf South

For most of the year, heat and humidity dominate the coastal areas that lie on the Gulf of Mexico. Heavy rains and hurricane-force winds also plague the region. On the upside, very mild winters make the heating season short—even nonexistent in southern Florida. Sunlight is a liability in this region for most of the year, so windows should be placed for light, view, and ventilation rather than to capture solar heat. Provide windows with roof overhangs or awnings to block unwanted heat and protect them from high winds and heavy rains. Exterior shutters that completely close over windows are a good option here. Climate control is easier with an array of many smaller windows than with a few large ones. Heavy wind damage incurred by homes in this region in recent years has resulted in stricter construction requirements. Insulate roofs/ceilings to R-30, walls to R-19, and foundations to R-19 except in southern Florida, where R-19 suffices. Floors need no insulation.

SUMMARY

Today's well-designed homes not only guard against the natural forces that create unlivable conditions but also make use of natural energies to heat, cool, and light the interiors. Solar energy can be put to good use—actively with mechanical equipment to convert it to usable heat, or passively, relying on the design of the building itself to heat it directly.

The sun can also lessen the building's dependence on electricity through openings in the envelope designed to admit sunlight but block unwanted solar heat with the use of natural features and artificial shading devices.

North America contains several climate zones, each with particular features. Understanding these features and how to best counter the region's liabilities while exploiting its assets is the key to successful energy design.

CHAPTER REVIEW

1. What two ways can design lessen the dependence of homes on outside energy? (See "Home Heating With the Sun" pages 25–26)
2. What is the difference between active and passive systems? (See "Home Heating With the Sun" pages 25–26)
3. What role do dark-colored, passive materials play in solar heating? (See "Direct Gain" page 27)
4. What factor determines the size of a shading device in a particular region? (See "Direct Gain" page 27)
5. What uses can sunspaces serve, other than solar heating? (See "Sunspaces" pages 28–29)
6. Which building wall-facing is the least likely to cause glare from windows? (See "Daylighting" page 29)
7. In what ways do the indigenous houses of the central Pacific Coast respond positively to the region's environmental factors? (See "Central Pacific Coast" page 31)

Foundations

Every house sits on some kind of foundation, which carries its weight and anchors it to the ground with a footing, which underlies the foundation. The foundation may extend no deeper than necessary to prevent it from frost damage or deep enough to contain a basement. Although most foundations are made of concrete or masonry, they can also be made of wood. In this chapter, we scan the types of foundations you will most likely encounter in residential construction.

Learning Objective 1: Differentiate the four categories of foundations.

Learning Objective 2: List the parameters that influence the proper choice of foundation type.

Learning Objective 3: Describe the suitability of common materials used in residential foundations.

HOW DEEP A FOUNDATION?

The foundation of a structure must be deep enough to:

- Extend below the frost line.
- Extend down to a solid bearing layer.
- Accommodate a full basement or crawl space, if present.

The requirement to extend below the frost line is to ensure that the foundation will not freeze. When concrete and masonry freeze, they can crack, which reduces their structural capacity and creates pathways for water to seep through. Section R403.1.4 of the International Residential Code (2012) requires that all footings be at least 12" (305 mm) below the undisturbed ground surface and have adequate frost protection, which usually entails extending the footing to a depth below the frost line of the locality. Because the frost line varies from place to place, the required minimum depth of footings also varies. For example, homes in Florida can get by with very shallow foundations. In New England, footings must extend down to 4' below grade. The National Building Code (NBC) of Canada defines minimum foundation depth according to a table that includes factors such as soil type, drainage, and whether the house sits over a heated or unheated basement/crawl space. Where the NBC requires foundations to extend below the frost line, it leaves determining the exact depth of the frost line up to "local experience."

Making sure the foundation extends into solid bearing material is even more complicated. Soils vary greatly in their ability to support imposed loads. Topsoils are poor risks as bearing material, because they are rich in organic material. Clays are iffy. Loams and mixed soil are better, gravel is better still, and rock is best. Typically, during building design, the soil is tested by boring into the ground and obtaining samples at different depths. Then the foundation and footings are designed accordingly.

TYPES OF FOUNDATIONS

There are several types of foundations for residential applications. The homeowner's requirements will determine how much space, if any, is needed below the first floor. Local climatic conditions and type of soil also play a part in the decision.

Full-Basement Foundations

Homeowners use basements primarily to store seldom-used items and sometimes finish off certain areas for living space. As with mechanical/electrical equipment, these functions most often could be accommodated on an aboveground floor, if there were no basement. All homes need some storage space. Because basements are usually as large as the floor above, they can store a lot. Living space below grade is sometimes advantageous, particularly if the house sits on a slope that allows the basement rooms to open onto the outdoors for access, light, and view. But moisture must be dealt with in all below-grade construction, as we discuss later.

Houses with basements require continuous wall foundations between the main structure and the ground. The foundations must carry the vertical load of the building to the footings while withstanding the horizontal forces of the earth and resisting penetration of water and moisture. Foundations in cold climates should be insulated on either the outside or the inside. Foundations are erected on continuous footings that run below the foundation walls and are wide enough to distribute the building loads into the soil. The floor inside usually consists of a concrete slab, isolated from the ground with an impermeable poly vapor barrier. Well-designed foundation-footing systems contain gravel or a permeable mat next to the outer wall to relieve water pressure and conduct it downward. Perforated pipes are placed next to the footing to collect the water and conduct it away from the foundation (see Figure 6.1).

Crawl Space Foundations

If the homeowner doesn't need a full basement for storage or mechanical equipment, the extra expense and potential problems that may arise from extending the structure deep into the ground can be eliminated by a shallow, or crawl space, foundation. In cold regions, footings are required to go down just below the frost line, which is always less than required for a full basement. Although the space between the ground and the first floor isn't sufficient for storage, it provides a useful area in which to run pipes, wires, and ducts. There is one downside compared to a full basement: no space for traditional furnaces or water heaters.

Crawl space foundations typically consist of concrete or masonry walls set on continuous concrete footings, although wood can also be used, as we see later under "Wood Foundations." Because the floor below a crawl space is often the earth itself, two problems occur. First, moisture wicking up through the soil can damage any wood above and can carry pathogens, such as radon and mold. Second, rodents and other pests can easily burrow into the house through an earth floor. One way to address these problems is to pour a concrete rat slab over a poly vapor barrier (see Figure 6.2). The slab doesn't have to be troweled smooth, as in a basement, since it is not intended for an occupied space. Another approach is to simply lay a 6-millimeter poly vapor barrier directly over the soil, with seams overlapped and taped and edges taped to the foundation wall or run up the wall and sealed to the sill plate, the horizontal board that anchors the wall framing to the foundation. This approach keeps moisture out of the crawl space but does not prevent rodents from entering.

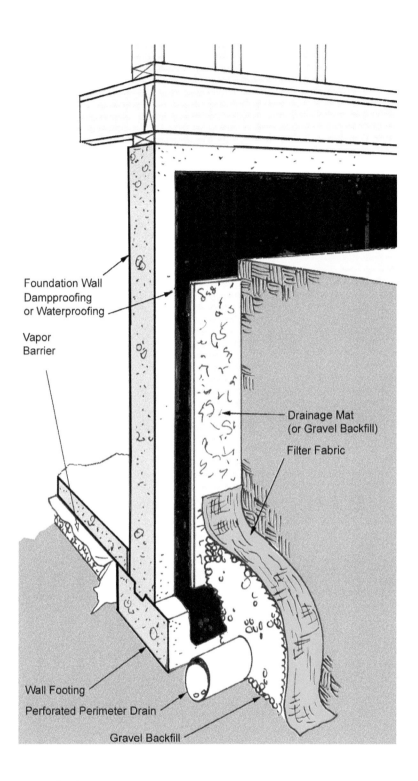

Foundation Wall
Dampproofing
or Waterproofing

Vapor
Barrier

Drainage Mat
(or Gravel Backfill)

Filter Fabric

Wall Footing

Perforated Perimeter Drain

Gravel Backfill

FIGURE 6.1 A well-designed full-basement foundation includes thermal insulation on the inner or outer face and provisions to allow surface water to drain down the outside of the wall and into a foundation drain, which empties onto grade or into a sump pit.

Pier Foundations

Sometimes the house or a portion of the house is disconnected from the grade completely, which reduces the foundation cost while eliminating the problems of soil-borne moisture getting into the superstructure. Instead of resting on a full foundation, the structure bears on an array of piers or posts (see Figure 6.3). This method is the most common way to support porches and decks and also suits certain room additions. One trade-off for the cost savings is the appearance. A house on stilts may look fine near the seashore but out of place in an urban or suburban setting. Another downside is the loss of a contained space below the floor to house equipment, pipes, and ducts. However, if they are well insulated, pipes and ducts

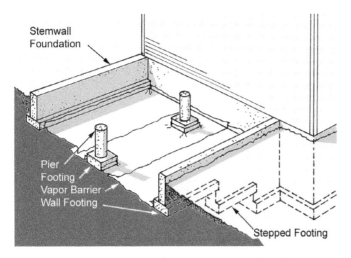

FIGURE 6.2 A crawl space foundation typically extends just below the frost line. A continuous vapor barrier is needed to prevent ground moisture from wicking up into the space and damaging the wood floor framing above.

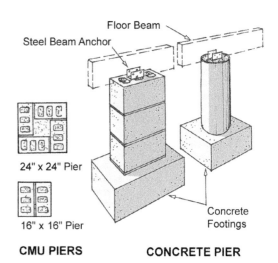

FIGURE 6.3 Piers made of concrete or concrete block may be used as the entire foundation or as supports within an exterior foundation wall.

can be located within the floor structure. Post and pier supports must bear on concrete footings that are properly engineered to distribute their weight onto the soil without sinking.

Grade-Beam Foundations

Not all homes need space below the first floor to house equipment or for storage. Furnaces, air conditioners, water heaters, and pumps can all be housed above grade if provisions are made for their distribution systems and certain other details are accommodated. For example, fresh air intake and exhaust provisions must be made for heating/ventilating equipment. Ducts and water pipes in attics must be insulated. Noise must be isolated from living spaces.

Getting to and from below-grade space requires stairs. With an aging population, we can expect more homes in the future to be built directly on grade. Houses without basements often rest on a concrete slab floor thickened at the outer perimeter to form a grade beam (see Figure 6.4). The slab portion consists of cast-in-place concrete, usually 4″ thick and

FIGURE 6.4 A grade-beam foundation consists of a concrete beam at the periphery, which encloses a concrete slab floor, insulated to stem heat loss to the earth.

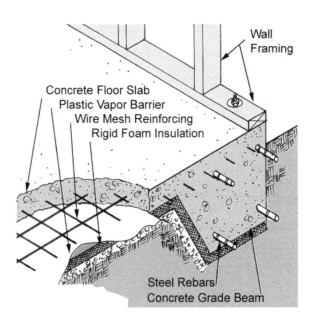

reinforced with wire mesh, while the grade-beam portion contains horizontal reinforcing bars engineered to make it strong enough to distribute the weight of the walls of the structure onto the soil without breaking apart. Grade-beam foundations go up quickly and economically but do have some drawbacks. Rather than installing below the slab, mechanical, electrical, and plumbing distribution systems that would otherwise have space in a crawl space or basement will have to be installed in ceilings or walls, where they are more easily accessible for repairs or future alterations.

FOUNDATION MATERIALS

Any material used for exterior walls below grade must withstand the vertical forces of the building and the horizontal forces of the earth and resist water, a tall order. Fortunately, several materials can meet the challenge, each with its own assets and liabilities.

Poured Concrete

Long life, structural stability, strength, and resistance to water have made poured-in-place concrete the most used material for below-grade construction. To perform up to its potential, however, concrete must be:

- Mixed with the proper ratio of water, gravel, sand, and cement.
- Poured without delay.
- Kept from freezing in cold weather and drying out too rapidly in hot weather while it cures.

Reinforcement of some sort is always required in concrete. The loads imposed by the structure above and conditions of the soil usually determine the type and extent of reinforcement needed.

Concrete foundations traditionally have been poured into wood forms that must first be erected and braced, then taken down after the concrete has cured. The recent trend toward more energy-efficient construction has generated a new technique that incorporates foam plastic insulation into the forms. The forms then remain in place to insulate the wall. These insulated concrete foundations (ICFs) rely on expanded polystyrene (EPS, or beadboard) foam as the base material and contain vertical and horizontal cavities in which to run reinforcing steel (see Figure 6.5).

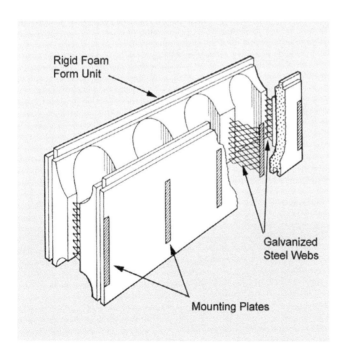

FIGURE 6.5 ICFs consist of rigid foam insulations and galvanized steel webs that hold the foam in place when concrete is poured inside, resulting in a system that provides both insulation and formwork.

Concrete Block

Many houses in North America sit on foundations made of concrete block consisting of modular blocks (concrete masonry units, or CMUs) laid one by one in a bed of mortar (see Figure 6.6). Vertical and horizontal steel reinforcing is required to resist both the vertical forces of the superstructure and the lateral force of the earth. Ladder-shape wire mesh is often used in horizontal joints, while steel rebars that extend from the footing up through the cores of the blocks form the vertical reinforcement.

Surface bonding (also called dry setting) provides a faster and easier method of joining concrete blocks. Rather than laying blocks one by one in mortar joints, they are simply stacked on each other. Both faces are then coated with a prepackaged surface-bonding mix composed of Portland cement, sand, and chopped fiberglass, which locks the blocks tightly together. Because both faces are coated, a separate application of mortar to the wall is not required for waterproofing, as it is with mortar-set blocks. However, as with blocks set in mortar joints, cores to receive vertical reinforcing bars still have to be filled with mortar.

Both mortar-set and surface-bonded block foundations can be insulated on either face, as with poured concrete, or by loose-fill insulation poured into the block cores. Special blocks containing built-in foam insulation are also available.

Wood Foundations

Wood, a most unlikely foundation material, has nonetheless been used successfully for the foundations of thousands of homes. While not accepted by all local codes, wood foundations are included in chapter 4 of the 2012 International Residential Code. Wood foundations have certain advantages over concrete. They provide an alternative to concrete on sites where it would be difficult or impossible to place concrete. They go up faster and can be erected by carpenters. And because wood is an organic, renewable material, as opposed to concrete, which requires very high amounts of energy to manufacture, wood foundations are less stressful to the environment. A final advantage of wood over concrete is the cavities between the studs can be insulated easily, just as wood stud walls above grade can be.

To perform well, a wood foundation must be constructed to tight specifications, available from the National Forest Products Association. Lumber must be treated to resist moisture or of a naturally rot-resistant species, such as clear heart cedar, redwood, or cypress. Nails must be stainless steel. Wood foundations must rest on footings of granular fill (coarse gravel) rather than concrete (see Figure 6.7). Framed with 2 × 6 or 2 × 8 studs and plates, wood foundations are clad on the outside with pressure-treated plywood sheathing. Walls are built

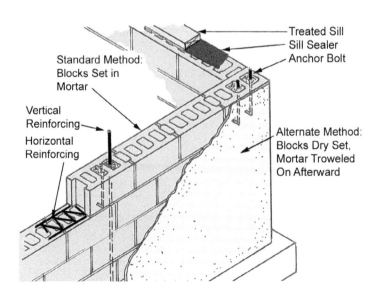

FIGURE 6.6 CMU foundations traditionally contain mortar joints but also can be constructed by setting the blocks on each other without mortar, then applying mortar to the interior and exterior faces (surface bonding).

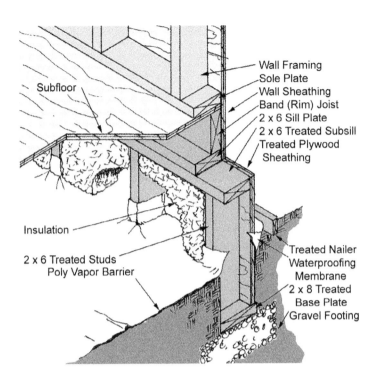

Subfloor

Wall Framing
Sole Plate
Wall Sheathing
Band (Rim) Joist
2 x 6 Sill Plate
2 x 6 Treated Subsill
Treated Plywood
Sheathing

Insulation

2 x 6 Treated Studs
Poly Vapor Barrier

Treated Nailer
Waterproofing
Membrane
2 x 8 Treated
Base Plate
Gravel Footing

FIGURE 6.7 Foundations may be constructed with pressure-treated wood set on a compacted gravel footing. If there is no concrete slab floor, a continuous moisture barrier is necessary to keep soil moisture from entering the crawl space or basement.

on the ground in 8' wide sections and then tilted up into place over the gravel footing. Once in place, the outside of the wall can be covered, damp-proofed or waterproofed, and back-filled. The cavities can be insulated and enclosed. If there is a full basement, the finish can be applied directly to the studs of the foundation.

SUMMARY

A foundation of some sort is required to support any type of residential structure. The type of foundation most suited to a specific structure depends on several factors. The amount and configuration of space below the first floor are determined by the requirements of the living space and storage space and by type and location of mechanical and electrical equipment to be accommodated. The structural loads of the superstructure, soil type, and climate conditions all play a part in the materials and structural design of the foundation.

A foundation may extend deep enough to provide a full basement, be a shallow crawl space, or not extend beyond the first-floor level. It may be constructed of concrete, concrete block, or wood.

CHAPTER REVIEW

1. Name two dangers that can result when a foundation freezes (See "How Deep a Foundation?" pages 33–34).
2. Why is it unwise to build a foundation over topsoil? (See "How Deep a Foundation?" pages 33–34)
3. How far into the ground must a crawl space foundation extend? (See "Crawl Space Foundations" page 34)
4. What two forces must a full-basement foundation resist? (See "Full-Basement Foundations" page 34)
5. What are the downsides of using grade-beam foundations? (See "Grade-Beam Foundations" pages 36–37)
6. What applications would benefit from a pier foundation? (See "Pier Foundations" page 35)
7. What alternative is there to a poured-in-place concrete foundation? (See "Concrete Block" page 38)

Floors

Floors must be designed as strong, durable platforms to reliably support the loads imposed on them without movement. Kitchen floors need to be dead level to enable the cabinetry to be installed true and flush. This chapter describes the various types of floors used in residential construction and where each type is most suitable.

We begin with the structural materials that support the floor surface, followed by an overview of the various types of underlayment. Floor finishes are discussed in Chapter 12. We explain where insulation is necessary in floors and the ways it is done. Because remodeling work often entails the need to level a floor, we lay out some of the ways in which this can be done.

The supporting structures of floors in houses are either a monolithic concrete slab or a framing system, consisting of beams and joists. Joists span between foundation walls or—more often—between an outside foundation wall and one or more beams that run parallel to the foundation. Beams, in turn, bear on internal bearing walls or columns.

Learning Objective 1: Discuss the pros and cons of framing systems used in residential construction.

Learning Objective 2: List the criteria for selecting a framed floor over a slab-on-grade floor.

Learning Objective 3: Describe the trade-offs of using engineered lumber over sawn lumber for floor framing.

Learning Objective 4: Discuss some common problems encountered in remodeling floors and their solutions.

Learning Objective 5: Differentiate the ways to insulate floors.

WOOD-FRAMED FLOORS

In the past, all framed floors were made of wood, but the quality of sawn lumber has declined in recent years. Fortunately, a variety of alternate materials have come along to replace it, often with superior performance. Examples include lightweight steel framing and composition wood of various types, used in a variety of joists and beams. Nevertheless, sawn lumber is still in wide use in residential floors as well as in the studs, joists, posts, and beams that comprise the house's superstructure, so it is important to understand the basics of the material (see Figure 7.1).

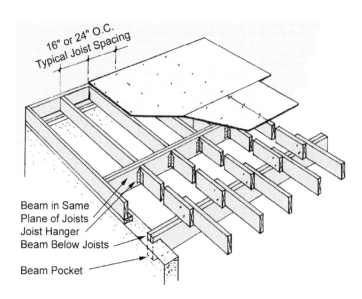

FIGURE 7.1 A typical wood-framed floor consists of joists that span between the foundation walls and over any interior beams. Joists can either run over the tops of the beams or frame into them flush, attached by metal joist hangers. Plywood or oriented strandboard (OSB) subflooring should be applied with the face grain running perpendicular to the joists and glued and screwed into position.

Sawn Lumber

The term *sawn lumber* includes a wide class of softwood milled to standard sizes and shapes. Structural lumber bears a grade stamp that indicates its species and stress rating. It includes shapes 2 or more inches in nominal thickness and width, suitable for joists, planks, beams, stringers, posts, and timbers. With the exception of joists and planks, structural lumber is at least 5" in one dimension.

Lumber used to make structural components comes primarily from conifer (evergreen) trees, such as pine, fir, hemlock, and spruce, which are considered softwoods, as opposed to the hardwoods, which come from deciduous trees that seasonally shed their leaves, such as maple, elm, and walnut. The terms are somewhat arbitrary, however, since some softwoods are harder than some hardwoods and vice versa. Still, the labels are useful to differentiate lumber according to its end use. Softwoods are used mostly for structural purposes, while hardwoods end up in finish materials, cabinets, and furniture.

Lumber Cuts

The cells that carry water and nutrients up and down in the trunk of the tree while it is growing comprise the fibers that give wood its structural strength. Just under the bark are active fiber cells—sapwood—that carry nutrients to the leaves. Sapwood cells are added more quickly during warm seasons than during cool seasons, creating annular growth rings that show up as grain on the lumber. Inactive cells at the core comprise the heartwood, the darker portion of the cross section of the log. How pieces are cut from this cross section affect qualities such as grain, texture, color, workability, stability, and resistance to decay.

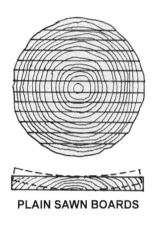

PLAIN SAWN BOARDS

Logs sliced with parallel cuts yield *flat-sawn* or *slash-grained* lumber in softwoods and *plain-sawn* lumber in hardwoods. The grain pattern varies from wide and wavy at the outer slices to narrow and vertical at the slices near the center. Logs cut perpendicular to the rings are termed *vertical grain* or *edge grained* in softwoods and *quarter sawn* in hardwoods (see Figure 7.2). This type of cut yields a thin, vertical grain pattern with boards more dimensionally stable and warp resistant than flat-sawn boards.

QUARTER SAWN BOARDS

Moisture Content

All wood cut from living trees contains moisture, which can comprise as much as 20 percent of the total weight, when cut. Exposing wood to air (seasoning it) or heating it in a kiln removes some of the moisture, leaving the wood stiffer, stronger, and less prone to shrinkage than green wood. Wood used for exterior framing and finish work should have a maximum

FIGURE 7.2 Plain-sawn boards are sliced from the log in parallel planes, whereas quarter-sawn boards are cut perpendicular to the growth rings.

TABLE **7.1** Lumber Grading Standards

Grade	Category	Dimension (nominal)	Use
CONST (construction) **STAND** (standard) **UTIL** (utility)	Light framing	2–4" thick, 2–4" wide	Where high strength not required
SEL STR (select structural), **#1 & BTR** (#1 and better), **#1, #2, #3**	Structural light framing	2–4" thick, 2–4" wide	Trusses, tall concrete forms, and where higher strength needed
SEL STR (select structural), **#1, #2, #3**	Structural joists and planks	2–4" thick, 5" and wider	Floor and ceiling joists, rafters
STUD	Stud	2–4" thick, 2" and wider	Studs of 10' or less. Suitable for load-bearing walls
Data from American Softwood Lumber Standard, U.S. D.O.C. PS 20–70.			

19 percent moisture content. Interior wood moisture content should not exceed 10 percent to 12 percent. Higher moisture content causes internal stresses in the wood that deform it over time, producing checking, cupping, and warping. Also, as the wood dries out, it shrinks, with softwoods generally shrinking more than hardwoods. Shrinkage is greatest parallel to the grain. Thus, quarter-sawn lumber incurs less shrinkage than plain sawn.

Lumber Grading
Imperfections, such as cupping, warping, and knots, make wood harder to cut, shape, and build in straight and true assemblies. Trade associations develop and maintain grading standards that rate lumber according to the extent of its imperfections (see Table 7.1). Building codes typically require that all lumber and wood-based panels used for structural purposes bear the grade stamp of an approved grading agency, and building inspectors look for grading stamps as a way of knowing whether the lumber is up to the task. Grade stamps look confusing at first, but once you crack the code, they tell you important qualities of lumber, such as its grade, species, moisture content, (see Table 7.2) source mill, and grading agency (see Figure 7.3).

The standard for grading Canadian lumber is the Standard Grading Rules for Canadian Lumber, published by the National Lumber Grades Authority (NLGA). These standards meet those of the United States, and grades and sizes of lumber in Canada are identical to those in use in the United States.

Lumber Sizes
Softwood lumber is sold either by the lineal foot or board foot. One board foot represents a piece whose nominal size is 1' square by 1" thick. For example, a lineal foot of 1 × 12 contains

TABLE **7.2** Moisture Content of Graded Lumber

Moisture Content Indication	Elaboration
S-GRN	Surfaced while green. The moisture content when the lumber was planed exceeded 19%.
S-DRY	Surfaced while dry. The moisture content when the lumber was planed was 19% or less.
KD-19 or KD	The lumber has been dried in a kiln to a moisture content of 19% or less.
MC-15 or KD-15	The lumber has been dried to a moisture content of 15% or less.

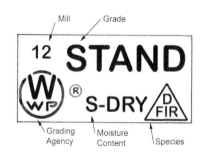

FIGURE **7.3** The lumber grading stamp tells the source, grade, moisture content, and species of the wood.

TABLE 7.3 Sizes of Milled Lumber Based on Western Wood Products Association Rules

Thicknesses (in.)		Face Widths (in.)	
Nominal	Actual (seasoned)	Nominal	Actual (seasoned)
1	¾	2	1½
1¼*	1	**3**	**2½**
1½†	1¼	**4**	3½
2	**1½**	5	4½
2½	2	**6**	**5½**
3	2½	7	6½
3½	3	**8**	**7¼**
4	3½	9 **10** 11 **12**	8¼ **9¼** 10¼ **11¼**

* Sometimes called "five quarters" and written 5/4.
† Sometimes called "six quarters" and written 6/4.
Sizes indicated in boldface type are those most readily available.

Data from American Softwood Lumber Standard, U.S. D.O.C. PS 20–70.

one board foot, while a lineal foot of 2 × 12 contains two board feet. Sawmills cut boards to their true-size dimensions. After the boards are seasoned, they are milled to their final dimensions, which trim off ¾ or ½". A 2 × 4, for example, emerges with final dimensions of 1½" × 3½" (see Table 7.3).

Engineered Lumber

Trees are a renewable resource, yet the rate of replacement has not kept up with the demand, at least when the term *replacement* is understood to mean trees of the same size. The result is that younger trees are cut and the lumber has more imperfections than that of older-growth trees. Among the alternative products available to take up the slack is "engineered" or "manufactured" lumber, made by bonding wood fibers or flakes together with resins under heat and high pressure (see Figure 7.4). The resulting structural shapes cost a bit more but have many advantages over sawn lumber, as described next.

- **Longer lengths**. Because joists and beams are made in a continuous process, lengths are limited only by shipping constraints. If a floor is 30' wide, you can get 30' long joists to span the distance without intermediate supports.
- **Less moisture**. With about half the moisture content of sawn lumber, engineered lumber shrinks less after installation. Floor joists will not shrink and cause squeaky floors when the heat is turned on.
- **Uniform sizes and shapes**. Joists and beams do not deform by checking, cupping, or warping.
- **Randomized defects**. Instead of large knots that go completely through the member, reducing its strength, knots in engineered lumber are as thin as the layer in which they occur and are more random in location.
- **Lighter weight**. Engineered lumber is made in the most efficient structural shapes for the intended uses, with the result that it supports the same loads with less material than sawn lumber.
- **Holes for ducts and pipes**. Larger-diameter holes can be cut through manufactured joists than through standard lumber. Prepunched cutouts are even provided in some members.

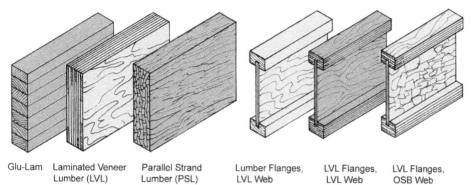

Glu-Lam   Laminated Veneer   Parallel Strand
           Lumber (LVL)   Lumber (PSL)

ENGINEERED LUMBER BEAMS

Lumber Flanges,   LVL Flanges,   LVL Flanges,
LVL Web   LVL Web   OSB Web

ENGINEERED LUMBER JOISTS

FIGURE 7.4 Some of the types of engineered lumber beams and joists currently available as alternatives to sawn lumber.

Engineered lumber is made by various processes. One consists of veneers glued together similar to plywood, except that the grain of each ply runs along the long length of the member. This lumber is called laminated veneer lumber (LVL). LVL is made into rectangular beams and I-shaped joists. Another process arranges wood fibers to run in the same directions, as they do in sawn lumber. The resulting parallel strand lumber (PSL) yields long, straight beams, posts, and studs. The third main type of engineered lumber consists of solid 2 × 4s or 2 × 6s glued together to form beams, called glue-laminated beams, or glue-lams.

Engineered lumber components install with standard carpentry tools and methods and are secured with nails, screws, and bolts. They should be installed in accordance with the manufacturer's recommendations.

Sizing Floor Joists

Floor joist sizes can be determined from tables, once the loads and span lengths are determined. Two types of loads must be considered: dead loads and live loads. Dead loads include the weights of the floor materials and any permanent items they support, such as spas and partitions. Live loads are the weights of nonpermanent items, such as furniture and people. Most codes require a minimum live load of 40 pounds per square foot (psf) (1.92 kN/m^2) for occupied rooms. Kitchens and baths often contain items that impose concentrated live loads over a specific area, such as islands topped with stone countertops and whirlpools. The weights of these items should be calculated, and the results should be used to determine the proper size and spacing of joists below the concentrated loads.

As for dead loads, most residential floors weigh in at around 5 to 7 psf (0.24–0.34 kN/m^2) for the framing and subfloor. Tile set in mortar adds around 20 psf (0.96 kN/m^2), assuming an average 2" thickness, and spas can add 60 psf (2.87 kN/m^2) or more when full of water. Get exact weights from the supplier.

Next, you must decide how much deflection, or give, is acceptable in the floor. Deflection is the distance the joists will sag at the midpoint when the floor is fully loaded. It is limited to 1/360 of the joist span if the floor covering or ceiling below is a rigid material that will crack when flexed, such as plaster or drywall. Deflection for all other floors is limited to 1/240 . Still, many designers limit deflection to 1/360 because occupants do not like springy or bouncy floors.

Now you can go to a joist span table to see what the options are. Lumber trade associations, such as the Western Wood Products Association and Southern Pine Marketing Council, publish span tables for sawn lumber joists. Span tables for engineered lumber are available from the manufactures. The next example shows how to select floor joists for a kitchen addition.

Let us assume the proposed addition extends 14' beyond the main house and is 24' long. A full basement is to be added under the addition, and the client does not want the space encumbered with supporting posts. The most obvious solution is to select joists that span out over the 14' to bear on the new foundation.

TABLE 7.4 Solid Lumber Floor Joists

Southern Pine, 40-psf live load, 10-psf dead load, L/360									
Size	Spacing	Grade and Spacing (ft–in.)							
	(inches on center)	Select Structure	Non-Dense Select Structure	No. 1 Dense	No. 1	No. 1 Non-Dense	No. 2 Dense	No. 2	No. 2 Non-Dense
2 × 6	12	11–2	10–11	11–2	10–11	10–9	10–11	10–9	10–3
	16	10–2	9–11	10–2	9–11	9–9	9–11	9–9	9–4
	24	8–10	8–8	8–10	8–8	8–6	8–8	8–6	8–2
2 × 8	12	14–8	14–5	14–8	14–5	14–2	14–5	14–2	13–6
	16	13–4	13–1	13–4	13–1	12–10	13–1	12–10	12–3
	24	11–8	11–5	11–8	11–5	11–3	11–5	11–0	10–6
2 × 10	12	18–9	18–5	18–9	18–5	18–0	18–5	18–0	17–3
	16	17–0	16–9	17–0	16–9	16–5	16–9	16–1	15–3
	24	14–11	14–7	14–11	14–7	14–0	14–0	13–2	12–6
2 × 12	12	22–10	22–5	22–10	22–5	21–11	22–5	21–9	20–11
	16	20–9	20–4	20–9	20–4	19–11	20–4	18–10	18–2
	24	18–1	17–9	18–1	17–5	16–8	16–8	15–4	14–10
Source: Southern Pine Marketing Council, *Maximum Spans: Southern Pine Joists & Rafters, 1993.*									

Use a book of span tables to find possible joists and spacing. Find the table that applies to a floor with a 40-psf live load (the load for occupied rooms). Table 7.4 is one such table, excerpted from *Maximum Spans: Southern Pine Joists & Rafters,* published by the Southern Pine Marketing Council.

The table yields several possibilities, depending on the grade, size of the joist and spacing:

2 × 8 No. 2, spaced at 12″ on center
2 × 10 No. 2 Dense, spaced at 24″ on center
2 × 10 No. 2 Non-Dense, spaced at 16″ on center
2 × 12 No. 2 Non-Dense, spaced at 24″ on center

Now let's check Table 7.5 to see how these possibilities compare with I-joists, for the same loading and deflection.

Possible joists from Table 7.5 are 9½″ deep I-joists spaced at 24″ or 11⅞″ deep joists spaced at 32″.

You might next use the desired joist depth to narrow the field. For example, if you want to match the depth of the 2 × 0 floor joists of the main house, your choices of solid lumber

TABLE 7.5 Engineered Lumber Floor Joists (I-Joists)

40-psf live load, 10-psf dead load, 1/360					
Depth (in.)	Spacing (in.)	Span (ft-in.)	Depth (in.)	Spacing (in.)	Span (ft-in.)
9½	12	18–8	11⅞	12	22–3
	16	17–1		16	20–4
	19.2	16–2		19.2	18–10
	24	14–11		24	15
Source: Truss Joist MacMillan, *TJI/Pro,* 150, 250, 350 & 550 Joists					

decrease to two and your options for I-joists to one (the 9½"-deep one). The final choice might be made on economics. Fewer joists will be required if spaced 24" on center than if set 12 or 16" apart. But costs saved must be compared to the higher cost of the thicker subfloor required to span a greater distance. Subfloor materials are rated for spans of 16 and 24" on center, depending on the thickness.

Supporting the Joists

Joists bear onto walls or beams (girders), which must be designed to accept the accumulated loading of all joists that bear onto them. In the previous example, the joists span between a ledger board attached to the band (rim, or edge) joist and a new foundation wall, so no intermediate beams are necessary. If one were, such as is usually required down the center of a full-width basement, it could consist of multiple members of solid lumber or engineered lumber or a steel beam. Sizing beams requires knowledge of structural theory beyond the scope of this book. If and when you need to select beams, get help from an architect or structural engineer.

Joists can connect to beams by running over their tops or by flush framing into their face. In flush framing, the tops of the joists are at the same level as the tops of the supporting members. This framing method is used when it is necessary to achieve maximum headroom below. Metal joist hangers connect the joists to their supporting member in a flush-framed application. These joist hangers vary in size and type to suit a wide variety of joist sizes and loads.

Framing Bump-out Floors

Bumping out the walls of a kitchen or bath without expanding the foundation can yield a few more feet of space (see Figure 7.5). Although this would not mean much to a living room, the few extra feet in a small kitchen or bath might expand the planning options substantially. A tub might be placed in a bump-out, for example. Bumping out the floor parallel to the existing floor joists can be done by first removing the band joist in the bump-out area and adding "sister" joists next to and parallel to the existing joists, with the outside ends cantilevering out over the foundation. Limit the overhang to one-quarter of the total length

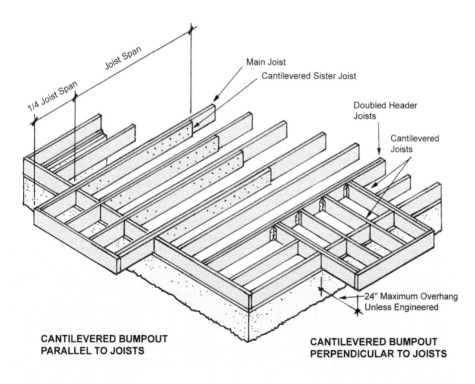

FIGURE 7.5 Bump-outs can cantilever out from the floor framing either parallel or perpendicular to the floor joists. The overhanging projection should not exceed one quarter of the bump-out joist overhang unless the system is engineered.

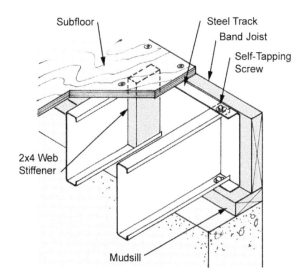

Subfloor   Steel Track
Band Joist
Self-Tapping
Screw

2x4 Web
Stiffener

Mudsill

FIGURE 7.6 Lightweight steel joists are an alternative to wood. A wood band (rim) joist provides a way to attach wall sheathing and siding.

of the sister joists. (For new floors, simply run the joists out one quarter of the total span of the joist between supports.) To bump out part of the floor perpendicular to the floor joists, extend the cantilever joists into the normal floor framing at least two joist bays into a doubled joist header and limit the amount of overhang to 24″ (610 mm), unless the system has been designed by an architect or engineer.

LIGHTWEIGHT STEEL-FRAMED FLOORS

Lightweight steel studs and joists, long used in commercial buildings, are becoming another increasingly popular alternative to sawn lumber in home construction (see Figure 7.6). Steel floor joists are cold formed from galvanized sheet steel in various thicknesses, or gauges, then formed into structural shapes. They are made in lengths up to 40′ and have several advantages over sawn lumber:

- Pound for pound, steel is much stronger than wood.
- Steel floor joists are perfectly true and straight, free of checks, warps, and knots.
- Moisture does not cause steel to swell or move.
- Steel joists offer a choice of stiffness for a given depth.

There are two downsides. Steel joists cost more than wood, and house framers may not be familiar with the special techniques and tools required for steel, which include cutting with tin snips or a metal-cutting power saw and joining members with sheet metal screws.

Steel joists are C shape, in gauges of 18, 16, 14, and 12. Flanges vary from 2 to 3½″ (51 to 89 mm) in width. Standard depths are 6, 8, 10, 12, and 14″ (152, 203, 254, 305, and 356 mm). Some come with prepunched cutouts in their webs to allow wiring and piping to pass through (plastic grommets must be snapped into wiring holes to prevent the sheet metal from cutting into the wiring insulation).

TRUSSED JOISTS

The maximum spans are limited for all joists, regardless of the material. For example, the longest span of a southern pine 2 × 12 spaced 16″ (406 mm) on center is 21′ 1″ (6.42 m), for a standard 40-psf (1.92 kN/m^2) live load. But this is for the best grade—dense select structural. The maximum span for the worst grade, #3, drops to 14′ 5″ (4.39 m). Reducing the spacing to 12″ on center (o.c.) increases the span but also the cost. Wood I-joists get spans up to 26′ (7.92 m) and have other advantages over lumber, as described previously.

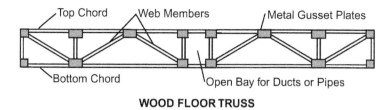

WOOD FLOOR TRUSS

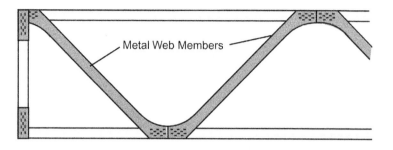

METAL WEB WOOD FLOOR TRUSS

FIGURE 7.7 Several types of floor trusses make large spans possible in applications where intermediate supports below are not desired. Wiring and ductwork can run through the spaces between the web (triangular) members.

Some floors need to span lengths even greater than feasible with engineered lumber. Steel or wood floor trusses make this possible, as they are capable of spans up to about 35′ (10.66 m) (see Figure 7.7). Trusses consist of continuous horizontal members, or chords, held apart by a series of short struts (web members) arranged in triangles. The assembly makes the best use of a given amount of material to distribute the vertical loads to the supports. Ducts and pipes can be run through the spaces in the web, whereas holes must be cut in solid joists and the size and location of the holes are restricted. Residential floor trusses typically use 2 × 4s for the top and bottom chords and wood or steel web members. Depths vary from 12 to 24″ (305 to 610 mm). Trusses are expensive and have one other drawback—they must be ordered to exact length and cannot be altered on the job. Because of that fact, the ductwork layout must be checked against the proposed trusses to ensure that any ducts that run through the web members will fit.

REMODELING EXISTING WOOD FLOORS

When designing upgrades to existing kitchen and bath floors, you may encounter floors too uneven or out of level to accept a new floor covering. Or the supporting structure may be rotted from years of exposure to moisture. Even if the floor is sound, it might need modification in order to reroute piping for plumbing fixtures or support a spa. If the floor sits above a cold crawl space, it will need insulation to conserve heat and keep pipes from freezing. Depending on what is there and what is required for the proposed changes, the work can be as minor as modifying the finish surface or as major as ripping out the floor completely and installing new joists, subfloor, underlayment, and floor covering.

Upgrading Floor Framing

During a remodeling project, the framing that supports a floor may require any of these improvements:

- Replacement of joists damaged by dry rot or insects
- Additional strength to support higher loads or to yield a stiffer floor
- Openings in joists to accommodate piping or ducts

Any joists damaged by moisture or dry rot should be replaced, after correcting the cause of the damage to ensure that it will not recur. The next step is to make sure the remodeled floor will support the intended loads. A special item to watch out for in baths is the extra load imposed by a proposed whirlpool. Always inform the builder, architect, or whoever is in charge of the structural integrity of the home that a whirlpool is proposed and supply the weight of the unit when full. This information should be available from the supplier. For example, a unit containing 50 gallons (192 L) of water and two people will weigh about 800 pounds (362 kg). This weight must be distributed over a small area, amounting to about 60 psf (2.87 kN/m^2), which is considered a dead load in any structural calculations. The joists below the spa will have to be increased accordingly (see Figure 7.8).

Framing floors to accommodate new plumbing inevitably requires cutting or notching the joists. Doing this without compromising the structural integrity of the joists requires planning. Some of the adjustments to the floor framing that may be required for various fixtures are listed next.

- **Tub traps**. Allow at least 4" (102 mm) clear from each side of the drain centerline and 12" (305 mm) from the wall to the drain.
- **Shower drains**. Allow an 8 × 8" (203 × 203-mm) space for the trap, centered below the drain and at least 3" (76 mm) additional clear space for access.
- **Shower pans**. Tiled shower floors typically require a recess in the framing to allow for mortar.
- **Spas**. Determine total weight of unit when full of water and provide framing adequate for the load. If the unit is to be set in mortar, add the weight of the mortar to the total.
- **Drains and vents**. Pipes from fixtures and appliances that require water supply and drainage sometimes must run through the floor framing.

With regard to the last item, piping that runs below joists, as in a floor above an unfinished basement, can be rerouted without affecting the floor structure. But some situations can jeopardize the structure. Joists have to be left largely intact in order to maintain their capacity to support the loads of the floor. Any cutting or notching of a joist must be done in a manner that leaves the joist with a safe carrying capacity (see Figure 7.9). For example, you may propose moving a toilet out into the room a few feet from its original location. Although this looks fine in plan, it has serious implications for the joists below. The drain line can run clear of any obstructions if the joists run parallel to it, but it will be too large to pass through a joist running perpendicular, regardless of the joist's depth and wood species. Holes and

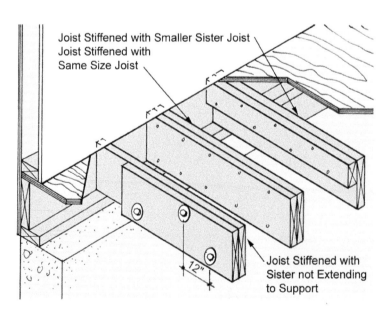

FIGURE 7.8 Existing wood floor framing can be strengthened by attaching sister joists, which ideally should run full length to the bearing points.

Joist Stiffened with Smaller Sister Joist
Joist Stiffened with Same Size Joist
Joist Stiffened with Sister not Extending to Support
12"

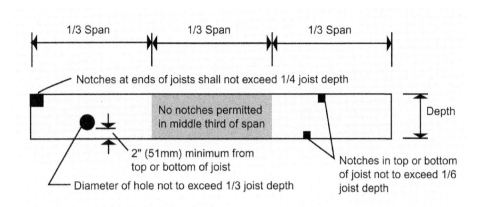

FIGURE 7.9 When holes or notches must be made in joists for wiring or piping, care must be taken not to weaken the structural capacity of the joists.

notches in joists are limited by both their size and their location in the joist. Section 2308.8.2 of the International Building Code 2000 limits notching as follows:

Notches on the ends of joists shall not exceed one-fourth the joist depth. Holes bored in joists shall not be within 2" (51 mm) of the top or bottom of the joist and the diameter of any such hole shall not exceed one-third the depth of the joist. Notches in the top or bottom of joists shall not exceed one-sixth the depth and shall not be located in the middle third of the span.

Insulating a Floor above a Crawl Space

Kitchen and bath floors above crawl spaces should contain insulation to stem heat loss and a vapor barrier to keep moisture out. Insulation can go either between the floor joists or at the foundation wall. Insulating the floor itself allows the crawl space to be ventilated continuously (required by some local codes) but is harder to do. Also, any water pipes and heating ducts that run under or within the floor must be wrapped (see Figure 7.10).

Insulating the foundation itself offers another way to stem heat transfer from the floor to the outside and creates a frost-protected crawl space for pipes and equipment. Insulating a foundation can be done with any type of insulation on the inside face or rigid foam on the outside of the crawl space (see Figure 7.11). However, any vents in the wall must be able to be closed during the cold season. The location of the insulation also affects where the vapor-control barrier goes. If the floor joist cavities are insulated, the barrier should go between the insulation and the room above, usually between the floor joists and subfloor. The best vapor barrier is a sheet of polyethylene at least 4 millimeters thick. The foil or kraft paper facing on

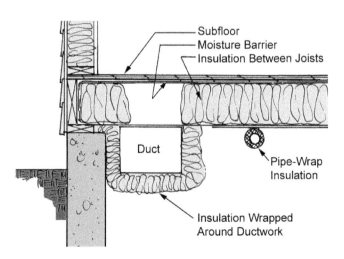

FIGURE 7.10 When insulating between floor joists, the insulation also must enclose any water supply piping and heating ducts.

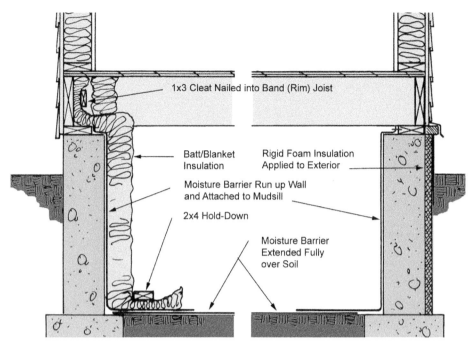

1x3 Cleat Nailed into Band (Rim) Joist

Batt/Blanket Insulation

Rigid Foam Insulation Applied to Exterior

Moisture Barrier Run up Wall and Attached to Mudsill

2x4 Hold-Down

Moisture Barrier Extended Fully over Soil

CRAWL SPACE, INSULATED INSIDE

CRAWL SPACE, INSULATED OUTSIDE

FIGURE 7.11 Crawl space foundation walls can be insulated on either the inside or the outside face. If there is no concrete floor, a continuous moisture barrier is necessary over the earth and should extend up the walls to the sill plate.

batt and blanket insulation is not a reliable vapor barrier. If you choose to insulate the foundation walls rather than the floor, the vapor barrier should go next to the inside face of the wall and extend completely over the soil below the crawl space.

Rigid foam is applied to the outer face of the crawl space more easily on new construction, since before the rigid foam is applied, an existing foundation will have to be excavated down to the footing.

Leveling Wood Floors

Wood-framed floors in old houses often slope from years of unequal settling. There are two main ways to level them:

1. Remove the flooring and subfloor and add sister joists to the sides of the existing joists.
2. Apply a self-leveling compound over the surface.

Leveling compounds consist of gypsum- or Portland cement–based mixes that are poured over almost any solid substrate, including wood and ceramic or vinyl tiles. These compounds are available in bags for job site mixing or can be installed by franchisers. You must first assess the condition of the framing to ensure that it is strong enough to bear the additional load of the leveling compound. For example, adding ¾″ (19 mm) of a gypsum-based leveling compound can add about 7 psf (0.34 kN/m^2) to the floor. Any rotted subfloor must be replaced first, preferably with ¾″ plywood or oriented strandboard (OSB). Loose subfloor must be screwed down firmly to the joists. Small holes must be filled and large holes covered with sheet metal or plywood. Cracks and edges must be sealed with drywall joint compound. Then the leveling compound can be applied.

CONCRETE FLOORS

If concrete is the universal material for basement floors, why can't it be used for above-grade floors in homes with no basement? It can in many homes, especially in locations having mild climates where there is less danger of concrete cracking due to freezing. Concrete floors often are used in multistory apartment buildings. They form the basement floors of houses with basements and the main floors of homes built with slab-on-grade construction. The typical slab-on-grade floor consists of a poured concrete slab over a layer of granular material, such as sand or gravel, a vapor barrier, and, in colder climates, rigid foam insulation. The granular layer distributes the load of the concrete evenly over the ground and allows any water below to drain without being trapped. The vapor barrier, usually a 4- or 6-mil-thick sheet of polyethylene plastic, prevents soil moisture from wicking up through the concrete. The insulation stems heat loss to the ground and varies in thickness with the severity of the climate.

Slab-on-grade floors make an excellent substrate for several finish materials and are well suited to radiant floor heating systems, where the tubing carrying hot water is embedded in the slab, as we discuss in Chapter 14. The slab distributes heat from the tubes evenly over the entire surface, without hot or cold spots. And because concrete is dense, it holds heat well, so it evens out the temperature swings over the course of a 24-hour period. Concrete floors are often seen in passive solar homes, where they are placed near south-facing windows to soak up solar heat during the day and release it at night, yielding comfort and lowering heating bills in the process.

Downsides

All of the pipes, wires, and ducts that snake through a typical basement ceiling or below a crawl space still need to be accommodated in a concrete floor. Water supply and drainage piping can run below the slab, as can wiring. Locating heating ducts below slabs, although possible, is expensive and inflexible, should any future changes have to be made. Locating the ducts in a ceiling or attic is a better choice, even if they must be insulated. Any electrical wiring below a slab will have to be encased in conduit. As with heating ducts, placing wiring below the slab makes it inaccessible to change, so it usually makes better sense to run wiring in partitions or attics.

Cracking and differential settling are the main problems with concrete slabs themselves. Concrete shrinks when cooled, and the shrinking can cause cracking. Reinforcing slabs with steel can help but does not prevent shrinkage cracking. A more reliable approach is to make sure the concrete itself is strong. The thickness (slump) and composition of the concrete mix influence its compressive strength. An interior slab should have a maximum slump of 4" (101.6 mm) and minimum compressive strength of 4,000 pounds per square inch (psi) (27.6 MPa). Fiberglass strands added to the mix boost its resistance to shrinkage and cracking. Specifications should also require the slab to be poured when the weather is not too hot or too cold. Slabs poured in hot weather should be kept moist and covered with a plastic membrane for a few days until curing is adequate. Cold-weather concrete can contain accelerator chemicals to hasten curing and—in very cold weather—be enclosed within a heated tent. After pouring and finishing, the slab should be covered and kept wet to allow it to develop full strength before drying out. In cold climates, a layer of rigid foam insulation under the slab not only helps avoid the temperature swings that can crack the slab but provides better comfort above it.

Remodeling Concerns

Settling occurs in some slabs over time. It happens most often when the base material is not solid or adequately compacted. Soils containing organic material (topsoils), clay, and silt are not stable, and thus not suitable substrates. Well-compacted gravel and sand make good substrates (see Figure 7.12).

Slab-on-grade floors are constructed in two common configurations: "floating" within the concrete perimeter foundation or as an integral part of a shallow-grade beam foundation. Floating slabs, if not tied to the foundation with reinforcing steel, can settle over time at the joint. When remodeling a bathroom in a house with such a slab, you might notice a gap

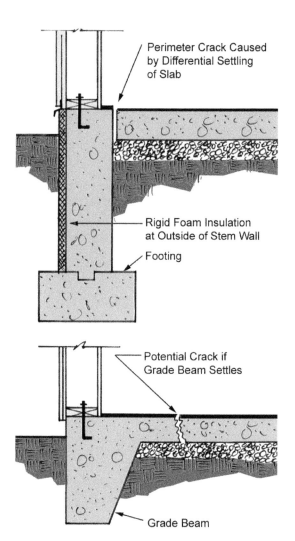

FIGURE 7.12 Slab-on-grade floors are vulnerable to cracking and settling at the perimeter. The settling in the slab in the upper example can be prevented with steel rebars doweled into the slab and foundation. The best preventive for cracks near the grade beam in the lower example is an adequate base material, well compacted.

between the wall and the floor baseboard. If the gap is significant, you might address the problem by stripping the finish from the slab and applying a floor-leveling compound before applying a new finish material.

Integral slab-on-grade/grade-beam floors tend to crack out away from the edge. If the crack produces a change in level of the floor, it, too, might be leveled with leveling compound. Extreme settling can be halted with a hydraulic pour under the slab to prevent future settling.

Because moisture passes through concrete easily, it can wreak havoc on any floor finish material applied to the slab. When inspecting the floor for a kitchen/bath project, look for curled seams or bubbles under sheet flooring. Specify that all existing flooring be completely removed, along with the adhesive, before new flooring is applied. If moisture is detected, the new floor covering should not be applied to the slab. One way to install the new floor covering is over a new subfloor attached to wood strips ("sleepers") over the slab. Another—if there is sufficient space between floor and ceiling—is to install a poly barrier over the existing slab, over which a new slab or leveling compound can be poured.

Another concern is the piping and heating ducts that may underlie a slab in a slab-on-grade home. If it is necessary to reroute these lines, it may entail removing a portion of the slab, which can be costly.

Old slabs may have settled unevenly, putting them out of level. If it can be determined that the slab has been in place long enough that it is not likely to settle any more, it can be put right with self-leveling compound, as described earlier for out-of-level wood floor.

SUBFLOORS AND UNDERLAYMENTS

A quality floor finish starts with what lies beneath. Concrete slabs, if dry and smooth, can serve well as the substrate for ceramic tile, sheet flooring, or carpeting. Selecting the right substrate for framed floors is more complicated than for a concrete slab because the substrate of a framed floor consists of two components: the subfloor and the underlayment. The subfloor is the platform that carries the loads imposed on the floor. The underlayment is a material that makes a suitable transition to the floor covering. If the subfloor does double duty as a platform plus underlayment, its surface must suit the intended floor covering.

Subfloor Materials

When specifying a substrate for a wood- or steel-framed floor, consider first the strength requirements of the subfloor. It must be stiff enough to span between the joists, so make sure the material is rated for the actual joist spacing to be used. Sheets of plywood and OSB, the two most common subfloor materials in use today, usually bear a stamped span rating number. Some of the most common subfloor materials are discussed next.

Plywood
Plywood, the most universal underlayment, is available in a species and grade suited to every floor covering. The American Plywood Association classifies plywood as "exposure 1" or "exterior." Exposure 1 plywood resists limited exposure to weather during construction but is not as dependable against long-term moisture as exterior plywood, which is a better choice for bathroom floors. B or C face veneers are suitable for ceramic tile. Resilient flooring requires a smooth, fully sanded face for direct application or an underlayment. PTS plywood is sanded only in spots, hence is not as desirable as plywood stamped "sanded face."

Oriented Strandboard
OSB consists of long, narrow wood chips produced by slicing the wood across the grain. The strands are oriented in cross directions, with the outer layers running essentially parallel to the length of the panel, similar to plywood and about as stiff. Heat and phenolic resin bonds the strands together. OSB subflooring comes in 4 × 8' (1,209 × 2,438 mm) sheets with tongue-and-groove joints. The most common thickness is ¾" (19 mm). Like plywood, OSB bears grade stamps that indicate its quality and uses.

Underlayments

The type of floor covering material determines what type of underlayment, if any, is required, as described in Chapter 12. Some of the underlayment materials in use today are described next.

Plywood Subfloors
Fir and pine plywood used for the subfloor may also serve as an underlayment if the surface grade meets the requirements of the floor covering and if all joints and imperfections are filled and sanded smooth.

Luan Plywood
Luan, a species of mahogany available in ¼" (6 mm) thickness, has met with increasing acceptance for resilient flooring. It carries two ratings from the International Hardwood Products Association: Type 1 has exterior glue, and Type 2 has water-resistant glue. Only Type 1 should be used for underlayment under resilient floor covering. (Look for the grade on the edge rather than on the face of the panel.)

Particleboard
The perfectly smooth, knot-free, and impact-resistant surface of particleboard make it highly desirable for an underlayment for carpet. But its tendency to absorb moisture, particularly at

the edges, makes it an unsuitable underlayment for resilient floor covering, ceramic tile, and stone. Particleboard made with urea formaldehyde can outgas vapors that may cause reactions in people who have sensitivities or allergies. The greatest amount of particleboard outgassing occurs during the first year after the piece is manufactured. After the first or second year, the rate at which formaldehyde seeps out of the piece drops off considerably. Even so, the material can continue emitting small amounts of gas for up to 10 years.

Hardboard

Like particleboard, hardboard's surface is smooth and consistent. It remains a popular underlayment material despite newer materials, but resilient flooring manufacturers differ in their acceptance of it for resilient tiles or sheet goods. The Resilient Floor Covering Institute recommends it as one of two acceptable underlayments for resilient flooring. (The other material is plywood of the appropriate grade.) However, the recommendation applies only to Class 4 service-grade hardboard, 0.215" (5 mm) thick, which is scarce. Some resilient flooring manufacturers do not allow hardboard for fully adhered floor coverings because of its alleged poor uniformity, dimensional stability and variable surface porosity. The tightly packed fibers also make it unsuited to moist environments. Although hardboard may work for a kitchen floor, it is a poor choice in a bathroom.

Cement Board

An excellent underlayment for ceramic tile floors, other than inside showers, is made of Portland cement reinforced with thin wire mesh, called cement board or cement backerboard. Cement board panels, 24" by 48" by ½" thick (610 mm by 1,219 mm by 13 mm), are screwed or nailed to the subfloor. After the joints are taped with fiberglass-mesh joint tape using drywall compound, the substrate is ready for ceramic tile.

Membrane Underlayments

Ceramic tile can be set in mortar (mudset) or thinset with an adhesive. Thinsetting tile directly over a plywood or OSB substrate poses two risks. The tile may crack when the substrate expands and contracts at a different rate form the tile, and moisture can migrate into the substrate. Both of these problems can be minimized with the use of a flexible membrane underlayment made of a polyethylene, embossed in order to hold the thinset adhesive (see Figure 7.13).

Self-Leveling Compounds

If a self-leveling compound is used to even out a sloping floor (as described earlier under "Leveling Wood Floors"), the compound also provides a suitable substrate for resilient floor coverings and carpets. (See Figure 7.14.) However, ceramic tile is applied more successfully over a membrane underlayment.

FIGURE 7.13 A membrane underlayment installed between a plywood substrate and tile finish material uncouples the two materials, which prevents possible cracking of the tile.

Courtesy of Schlutter, Inc.

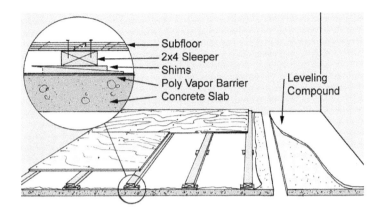

FIGURE 7.14 Concrete floors can be leveled by applying wood sleepers, shimmed (left side of drawing), or by a leveling compound poured over the surface (right). Sleepers offer other benefits, such as cavities that can contain wiring or insulation as well as a substrate for various floor coverings.

SUMMARY

The floor in a kitchen or bath is the most important surface. It must bear the weight of fixtures, equipment, and the occupants and do this without movement. The surface must be true and level to enable cabinetry and other items to be installed properly. Both framed and concrete slab floors can achieve these goals with proper design and construction.

Framed floors consist of a structural system of beams and joists made of steel or wood, topped with a subfloor, underlayment, and floor-covering material. Wood, either as sawn lumber or manufactured into a panel product, figures prominently in the materials used for the structural elements as well as the subfloor choices, and the proper selection of species and grade is critical to a successful project.

Engineered lumber provides a useful alternative to sawn lumber in applications with longer spans and offers other advantages. Lightweight steel framing offers yet another alternative.

Concrete floors are constructed above grade or on grade, designed to suit the application. Although they require no subfloor, they may need an underlayment, depending on the type of floor covering to be applied.

There are many choices of underlayment materials, each suited to the type of subfloor and floor covering.

CHAPTER REVIEW

1. Why must a kitchen floor be level? (See "Chapter introduction" page 41)
2. What type of trees produce lumber used for structural purposes? (See "Sawn Lumber" page 42)
3. What is meant by the term *vertical grain*? (See "Lumber Cuts" page 42)
4. What happens when wood has a high moisture content? (See "Moisture Content" pages 42–43)
5. What are randomized defects? (See "Engineered Lumber" page 44)
6. What is deflection? (See "Sizing Floor Joists" page 45)
7. How are joists connected to supporting members in a flush-framed floor? (See "Supporting the Joists" page 47)
8. When would you most likely use a truss-framed floor? (See "Trussed Joists" pages 48–49)
9. Why does ceramic tile need to be isolated from its substrate? (See "Membrane Underlayments" page 56)

Exterior Walls

This book began by presenting a house as a collection of systems. In the previous chapter, we saw how floor systems are constructed to meet specific criteria. Exterior walls comprise another important system that keeps the weather out, provides privacy, and supports fixtures and cabinetry. Some outside walls also support other parts of the structure, such as other walls or a roof. In this chapter, we discuss how various wall systems are designed to meet these challenges.

Learning Objective 1: Differentiate between the various wall framing systems used in residential construction.

Learning Objective 2: Describe the nonframed wall systems and where they are most suitable.

Learning Objective 3: Discuss some of the issues encountered in insulating new and remodeled walls.

Learning Objective 4: List some of the common exterior wall finishes and their pros and cons.

WALL FRAMING SYSTEMS

Framed walls take several forms. Most of your kitchen and bath work probably will focus on homes built of lightweight structural systems, but other systems are also in use, so you should be prepared to deal with them.

Log Homes

When the first European settlers set foot on North America, trees covered the eastern coast. Not surprisingly, they used this most readily available material to build their homes. Even unskilled people could put up a shelter quickly by stacking logs on each other horizontally. The only part that required any carpentry skills were the corners, which had to be notched to interlock. The gaps between logs were chinked (packed) with mud or, if available, mortar to seal out drafts. Nostalgia among some homeowners to return this rustic simplicity has spurred a resurgence of log homes in recent decades. Today specialty

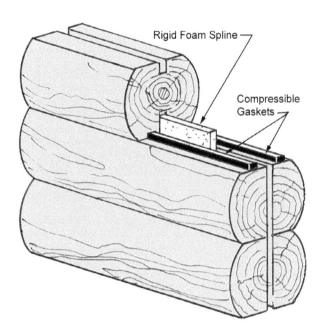

FIGURE 8.1 One log home system sandwiches rigid foam strips into grooves in the logs and uses compressible gaskets to make an air seal between the logs.

manufacturers supply log homes as kits of preshaped logs, cut to length and erected by franchised contractors.

Cedar makes up most of today's log homes. The logs are left exposed on the outside and may or may not be exposed on the inside, depending on the interior finish and insulation requirements. And insulation is the Achilles' heel of log home construction. Wood is inherently a poor insulator. To bring a log wall up to an R-19 level as required by most energy codes, the logs must be about 19" (432 mm) thick. Since the standard thickness of logs used to build log homes is 6" (152 mm), additional insulation must be added. Some systems do this by fitting pieces of rigid foam in slots cut into the logs. Others simply rely on insulation added inside, which conceals the logs. Manufacturers have been more successful at controlling infiltration by creatively using gaskets and other types of seals between logs (see Figure 8.1).

Because plumbing cannot be run through log walls, any pipes for kitchen and bath walls must be located inside the exterior walls and concealed behind a finish material.

Timber Framing

Another wall framing system that has gained ground in recent years also has its roots in colonial times. In timber framing (also called post-and-beam framing), beams support floors and roofs and transfer their loads to vertical posts, which take them down to the foundation. Structural joints shaped with mortise and tenon joints fit precisely, with nothing more than wood pegs to connect the parts. All the infill wall portions between the posts have to do is keep the weather outside.

Today specialty manufacturers (timber framers) scattered around the United States design timber framing systems, sometimes collaborating with architects or home designers. After cutting and shaping the parts, the manufacturers ship them to the site and either erect them or engage a knowledgeable local contractor for this task. Infill wall panels are either standard stud wall construction or structural-insulated panels (SIPs), which are sandwiches of rigid foam insulation cores faced with oriented strandboard (OSB) or plywood (see Figure 8.2). SIPs go up quickly and make very tight, well-insulated envelopes for post-and-beam houses (see Figure 8.3).

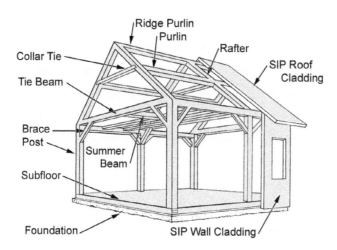

FIGURE 8.2 A typical timber-framed home structure clad with SIP panels, which provide closure and insulation while allowing the framing members to be exposed on the interior.

Stud Wall Framing

The advent of wire nails combined with improved sawmill technology in the first half of the nineteenth century revolutionized housing construction. Instead of a few heavy wood posts and beams that could be joined only by skilled craftsmen, houses could be constructed entirely with much lighter members, studs, braced by the outer skin, or wall sheathing.

The roofs of single-story houses built this way rested directly on a plate supported by the studs. For two-story houses, two systems emerged to carry the upper floor. In the first, balloon framing, studs extended from the mudsill to the roof, with the upper floor joists resting on a ledger notched into the studs (see Figure 8.4). But the system had one major downside: The joist spacing had to match the stud spacing exactly. Because of this, balloon framing gave way to a simpler system, platform framing. Studs in platform-framed walls terminate below the upper floor framing, which simply rests on the studs, like a platform (see Figure 8.5). Any successive floors simply extend upward in the same manner. Because of its simpler and faster construction, platform framing is the method of choice today.

If the stud wall is a bearing wall, the studs carry any vertical loads from the roof and floors down to the foundation. Stud walls also must be braced to resist horizontal wind

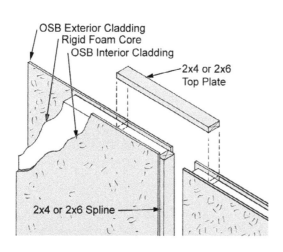

FIGURE 8.3 SIP panels sandwich rigid foam insulation between sheets of OSB or plywood with sawn lumber around the perimeters.

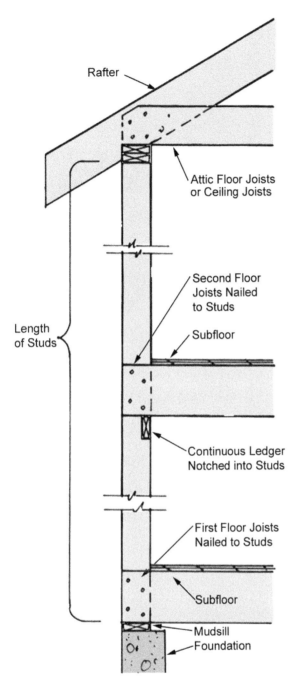

FIGURE 8.4 In balloon framing, the studs extend from mudsill to roof. The upper floor joists rest on a ledger notched into the studs and are nailed to the studs.

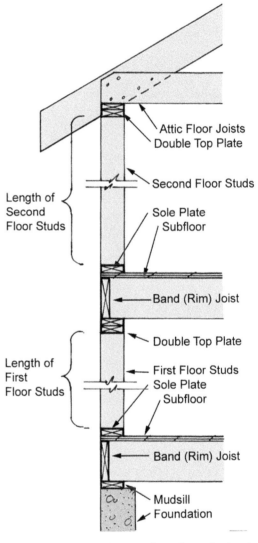

FIGURE 8.5 Platform framing allows the studs of each floor to be constructed sequentially. When the first-floor studs are in place, the upper-floor "platform" is built above them, followed by the upper-floor studs.

and seismic forces. In the earliest stud walls bracing consisted of boards on an angle to the studs. Panels of plywood or OSB have replaced angle bracing in today's homes (see Figure 8.6). Local codes define horizontal bracing requirements as well as other provisions necessary to make the structure resistant to high winds or earthquake danger prevalent in a region.

Each stud of a load-bearing wall shares part of the vertical load imposed from above. 2 × 4s spaced 16″ (406 mm) apart (on center [o.c.]), the standard of the past, have been replaced

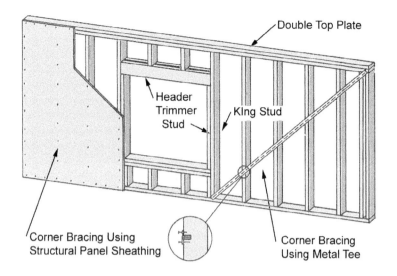

FIGURE 8.6 A typical exterior stud wall contains double studs at the top plate, corners, and openings. Headers above the openings are sized to support the loads from above. Corner bracing, required to resist seismic and lateral forces, is provided by OSB or plywood panels or by metal tee straps.

in cold-climate areas with 2 × 6s, to accommodate the thicker insulation of today's energy codes. When 2 × 6s are used, their spacing is often increased to 24″ (610 mm) for greater economy, but any cost saved on lumber has to be traded off against possibly thicker interior wall cladding. If gypsum drywall is used, ½″- (13 mm) thick panels should be increased to ⅝″ thick (16 mm) to be stiff enough.

Lightweight Steel Wall Framing

In the previous chapter, we saw how light-gauge steel joists can be used as an alternative to wood joists. There are corresponding wall-framing members consisting of C-shape studs and stud runners (see Figure 8.7). The framing goes up quickly, held together with sheet metal screws. But steel-stud wall framing faces the same obstacles in home building as was mentioned for steel-framed floors: unfamiliar technique for carpenters plus special tools and equipment. And there is one other problem with steel-framed exterior walls: The excellent ability of steel to conduct heat makes an easy path for heat to escape to the outside, bypassing the cavity insulation. Any moisture that finds its way into the wall condenses on the cold outer flange of the stud, where it rots the sheathing. Homebuilders solve this problem either by applying rigid foam insulation to the outside faces of the studs or by avoiding steel-stud framing entirely on exterior walls.

Panelized Walls

Walls framed with studs can be erected on the site or in sections at a factory and trucked to the site for assembly. The manufacturer uses the designer's drawings to deconstruct the design into modules that are built in the factory. The advantages over site-built walls include better quality control, savings in time, and less waste. The approach is particularly worth considering for sites too small or difficult to store materials and waste. Costs to panelize are said to be comparable to site building.

Wall Sheathing

Wall sheathing is the membrane material, or "skin", that clads the outer face of the studs, tying them together into a single structural system and providing an anchor for finish materials. Pine boards were the sheathing of choice for homes built prior to the 1940s. They were installed diagonally to brace the studs against horizontal forces. Plywood or OSB panels sheath today's homes.

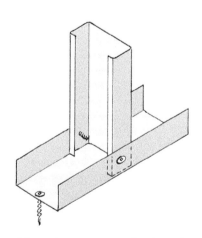

FIGURE 8.7 Framing a wall with steel studs entails setting the studs into the C-shape stud runners and attaching them with sheet metal screws.

Insulating New Framed Walls

The insulation system of a home consists of two parts: thermal insulation and an air/moisture barrier. Thermal insulation can be installed at four possible locations in framed walls:

1. On the outer face of the sheathing
2. At the inside face of the studs between the studs and wall finish
3. In the cavities between the studs
4. Some combination of the above

Because moisture control is so important to high-moisture areas such as kitchens and baths, moisture barriers must be installed in the correct position with respect to the insulation to work. The optimum insulation system for an exterior wall can be determined by following three steps:

1. Determine the desired R-value (see Chapter 4).
2. Determine whether the moisture barrier will go inside or outside the insulation (by whether the region is dominated by the need for heating or cooling).
3. Compare the costs for achieving the desired R-value with various types of insulation available in the area.

The last item is the hardest, since it involves trade-offs with other materials. An R-19 wall, for example, requires insulation with a total R-value of R-18 (the inside and outside air film contributes about R-1). Filling the cavities between 2 × 4 studs with standard R-11 fiberglass insulation yields R-12 (or R-16, with high-density fiberglass). This increases to the desired level with the addition of an inch of rigid polyurethane insulation to the inside (R-7.2 per inch), or by using 2 × 6 studs and R-19 fiberglass; the same results may also be achieved by applying spray foam (see Figures 8.8, 8.9).

The differential cost of wider studs must be compared to the costs of the insulation. But fiberglass used alone requires a separate moisture barrier, usually a sheet of 4- or 6-millimeter poly sheet stapled to the inside of the wall after the insulation is in place.

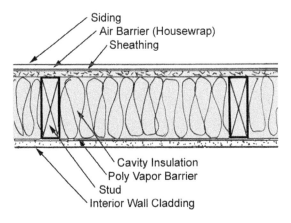

Siding
Air Barrier (Housewrap)
Sheathing

Cavity Insulation
Poly Vapor Barrier
Stud
Interior Wall Cladding

FIGURE 8.8 2 × 4 studs with R-10 insulation between no longer meet the energy codes of many states. The R-value can be increased with 2 × 6 studs with R-19 or R-23 (left), adding a layer of rigid foam insulation to the original wall (right), or applying spray foam, as shown in Figure 8.9.

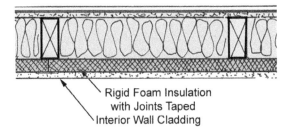

Rigid Foam Insulation
with Joints Taped
Interior Wall Cladding

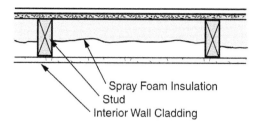

Spray Foam Insulation
Stud
Interior Wall Cladding

FIGURE 8.9 Spray foam provides a good way to both achieve high levels of insulation and seal walls against air and moisture penetration. The cavities can be partially filled (left) or completely filled (right) with the overflow material scraped off after the foam has set.

You can avoid using a separate moisture barrier with a hybrid approach combining foil-faced rigid foam with fiberglass cavity insulation. The foil facing is an excellent moisture barrier, but the system works only if the joints are sealed with a suitable tape. Spray foam, as described in Chapter 4, offers yet another way to achieve a high R-value with minimal thickness.

Insulating Existing Framed Walls

The exterior walls of older houses may have too little or no insulation, which impacts homeowners with high energy costs and discomfort. Any kitchen or bath remodeling project should begin with an assessment of the room's insulation and moisture issues and include measures to upgrade them where needed. People like their baths to be cozy and warm, which requires well-insulated walls. And because baths generate a lot of moisture, the walls should also contain adequate barriers to moisture passage. Before planning an upgrade, investigate the existing walls to see how they are put together. You might get an idea simply by removing a cover plate of a switch or outlet in an outside wall. If not, you may have to drill a test hole.

There are three basic approaches to adding insulation to existing framed walls:

1. Blow loose-fill insulation into the cavities from the outside or inside.
2. Strip off the interior surface and insulate the cavities.
3. Add insulation onto the inside surface.

An adequate moisture barrier must accompany any of these approaches.

Blown Insulation

Cellulose and fiberglass loose-fill insulation are blown into the walls through holes cut in either the outside or the inside finish/sheathing layers. If the insulation is applied from the outside, the insulation contractor removes siding boards at intervals along the outer wall, drills holes in the sheathing between each stud, and inserts a hose to fill the cavity (see Figure 8.10). After the siding is replaced, the original appearance of the exterior of the home is restored with no trace of the work. For inside jobs, holes are cut in interior surfaces and are patched after the cavities are filled. The downside to either method, especially in bathrooms, is the lack of a moisture barrier. If a new interior finish is planned, a layer of poly can be installed beneath the finish to provide a moisture barrier.

Stripping and Insulating

If the interior wall surface is in poor condition or must be removed for other reasons, such as the need to access the cavities to install wiring or for plumbing work, the cavities can be insulated with any of the types of cavity insulation described and a moisture barrier can be installed before a new interior wall finish is applied.

FIGURE 8.10 One way to insulate an existing home is to remove siding at intervals, drill holes in the sheathing, and blow loose fiber insulation into the cavities. The holes are then patched and the siding is replaced.

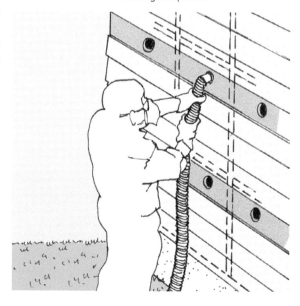

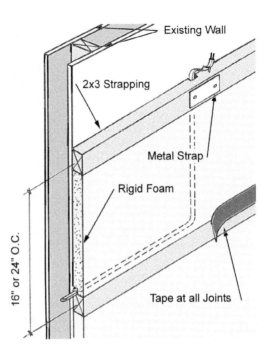

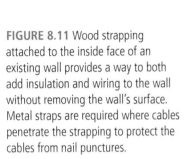
FIGURE 8.11 Wood strapping attached to the inside face of an existing wall provides a way to both add insulation and wiring to the wall without removing the wall's surface. Metal straps are required where cables penetrate the strapping to protect the cables from nail punctures.

Adding Insulation to the Interior

The easiest, most economical method might be to leave the existing wall alone and add an insulated layer onto the inside surface. The simplest way to do this, if the room is large enough to spare the space, is to erect a stud wall inside the exterior wall. The cavities can contain any new piping and wiring as well as the insulation. If space is too small for a new stud wall, rigid foam insulation can be applied to the surface of the existing interior finish, set between strapping applied horizontally to the wall at 24" (610 mm) intervals (see Figure 8.11). The strapping provides a base for attachment of the new wall substrate and finish materials. Moisture control is achieved by either applying a poly sheet over the foam/strapping or by taping all of the joints (but only with foil-faced insulation).

CONCRETE AND MASONRY WALLS

Concrete and masonry materials are massive, high in compressive strength, and immune to decay from organic sources—good properties for a homebuilding material. But masonry materials are also porous, which allows moisture to pass through. Although they retain heat well—a useful property in passive solar homes—they are poor insulators and thus require added thermal insulation in many climates. Finally, while masonry has high compressive strength, it requires steel reinforcement to make up for its lack of tensile strength. That said, the widespread use of masonry materials in homebuilding makes them worthy of discussion here.

Concrete

Although it is not strictly a masonry material, concrete has many of the same characteristics. The material consists of small-size stone (aggregate), sand, and Portland cement, catalyzed into a solid form by the addition of water. In use for years for residential foundation and floor slabs, concrete is now seeing use in above-grade walls, thanks to new forming systems that use foam plastic to form the concrete, as discussed in Chapter 7.

Concrete Block

Often seen in foundations, concrete blocks are also the basic material of above-grade walls in some homes, especially in southern regions. Their susceptibility to cracking makes them less popular in colder regions. Concrete made with small-diameter gravel and sand is used to precast concrete masonry units (CMUs), or concrete blocks.

CMUs come in several modular shapes and sizes, each tailored to a specific use. The most common thickness for walls up to 8' (2,438 mm) high is nominally 8" (actually 7⅝", or 194 mm). Blocks can be set in mortar or dry-set, as described in Chapter 6, and finished with a surface coating or stucco. All CMU walls require steel to reinforce them both horizontally and vertically (see Figure 8.12). Like concrete walls, block walls are poor insulators in themselves. Above-grade walls can be insulated on either face or by using a special type of block that contains foam inserts. Interior surfaces can be left exposed, painted, or furred out to receive another wall finish.

Brick and Stone

Brick, a manufactured material, and stone, a natural one, are both favorite cladding for residential walls. Because they are not considered structural materials capable of supporting any load beyond their own weight, they require a separate structural wall to support the floors and roofs as well as to provide horizontal bracing for the masonry itself. The resulting double-wall assembly is thus called a masonry veneer. The most common masonry veneer walls in houses consist of wood- or steel studs faced with brick or stone (see Figure 8.13). The stud wall fulfills other functions that the masonry cannot, such as providing cavities to house insulation, wiring, and pipes and serving as a substrate for interior finishes.

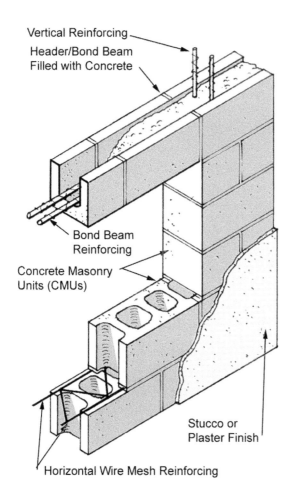

Vertical Reinforcing

Header/Bond Beam Filled with Concrete

Bond Beam Reinforcing

Concrete Masonry Units (CMUs)

Stucco or Plaster Finish

Horizontal Wire Mesh Reinforcing

FIGURE 8.12 A typical CMU wall consists of blocks set in mortar or dry-set and reinforced to meet code requirements. Beams above openings and at the tops of walls utilize U-shape blocks, which contain mortar and steel reinforcing in their cavities.

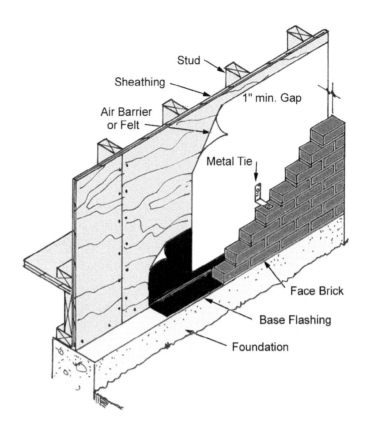

FIGURE 8.13 Brick and stone veneer walls rely on a second wall for structural support. The backup wall may be studs, as shown here, or a structural CMU wall. An air space between the two walls and proper flashing are required to prevent water from penetrating into the inner wall.

EXTERIOR WALL FINISHES

Walls other than brick or stone require an applied finish material that enhances the home and protects the substrate against the elements. The choices vary in material composition, sizes, and shapes. Some of the most common residential cladding materials are discussed next.

Wood Board Siding

Real wood siding is the cladding of choice for many homeowners willing to maintain it. Wood is an organic material that changes over time due to the effects of weather. Rot-resistant species, such as redwood, cedar, and cypress, can be left uncoated. In seacoast and other damp environments, these species weather evenly to a uniform gray. To remain uniform in color in drier regions, the siding requires periodic application of a preservative, stain, or paint. Decay-prone species, such as pine and spruce, always must be coated to protect them against the ravages of the elements.

Clear western red cedar or redwood preprimed on all sides makes the longest-lasting wood siding. The best quality comes from the heartwood of old-growth redwood or cedar trees. The increasing scarcity of these trees has made this source too expensive for many homeowners, who must make do with a lesser grade of redwood or cedar containing knots or with another species, such as pine or spruce.

Wood siding comes in various profiles intended for horizontal or vertical installation. Horizontal siding boards overlap each other and are attached to the wall by nails into the studs (see Figure 8.14). Vertical siding consists of boards that overlap each other or with smaller strips (battens) that overlap the joints. Because vertical joints are more vulnerable to water penetration than horizontal joints, a good backup layer of felt (asphalt-impregnated building paper, tar paper) is first applied to the sheathing. The boards are then nailed to the wall at three points: top plate, midpoint blocking, and bottom plate (see Figure 8.15).

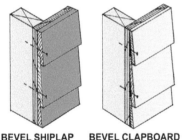

BEVEL SHIPLAP   BEVEL CLAPBOARD

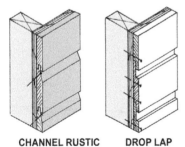

CHANNEL RUSTIC   DROP LAP

FIGURE 8.14 All horizontal wood siding attaches with nails driven into the studs. The optimum location of the nails varies depending on type of siding.

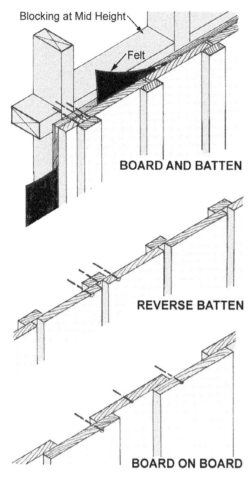

FIGURE 8.15 Vertical siding is applied to a sheathed stud wall, over a waterproofing underlayment, such as asphalt-saturated felt. Boards are nailed to the top and sill plates and blocking is placed at a midpoint.

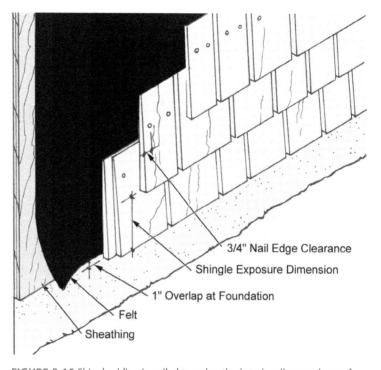

FIGURE 8.16 Shingle siding is nailed to a sheathed stud wall over a layer of asphalt-impregnated felt. Two nails attach each shingle close enough to the top to be concealed by the next course of shingles.

Shingles and Shakes

Wood shingle siding is the hallmark of Cape Cod and some other traditional residential styles. Quality and price is highest for #1 red cedar shingles. Other species and prices are available, all in random widths 16 or 18" (406 or 457 mm) long, tapering from a point to about ½" (13 mm) at the butt end. Shingles install in overlapping layers over a weather barrier of asphalt-saturated building felt. The exposures, or "to weather," vertical dimensions are usually 4½ or 5" (114 or 127 mm). Each shingle is nailed independently, unless panelized shingles are used (see Figure 8.16). Available in 8' (2,438 mm) long strips, panelized shingles cost more but go up much faster, saving on labor.

Wood shakes offer a more rustic appearance. Split, rather than sawn from logs, shakes are thicker and more irregularly shaped. The exposed side is rough; the underside is smooth.

Composition Siding

A number of horizontal siding products made from wood composites offer advantages over real wood, such as longer lengths, consistent quality free from knots, and—with some types— better resistance to weather. Some are made from wood chips or fibers bonded under heat and pressure with chemical resins. Others use wood fibers bonded together with Portland cement. The surface of either type can be smooth or embossed to resemble rough cedar. The boards come in 16' (4,877 mm) lengths of uniform consistency with no knots. Unless it is not pre-primed at the factory, fiber cement siding must be primed and painted on site. Wood composition siding comes preprimed, to receive one or two finish coats after installation.

Plywood Panel Siding

Plywood siding is manufactured in panels of 4' by 8' (1,219 mm by 2,438 mm), ⅜ or ⅝" (10 mm or 16 mm) thick. Grooves cut partway through the surface create the impression of vertical boards spaced at 4 or 8" (102 or 203 mm). Plywood siding makes a good material for horizontal soffits. When installed as siding, the panels are installed over felt or other suitable housewrap material and nailed into the studs. The long sides of each panel are rabbeted to overlap at horizontal joints. If the wall height exceeds the length of a single panel, the horizontal joints between the butt ends of successive panels must be flashed to prevent leaks. Redwood- and cedar-faced plywood siding can be painted, stained, or left unfinished. Fir- or pine-faced panels must be painted or stained.

Vinyl Siding

Siding made from polyvinyl chloride (PVC) has two main advantages of wood siding: It costs less and does not need to be repainted. For these reasons, vinyl siding has steadily edged out wood in new houses as well as a replacement for deteriorated wood siding on existing houses. Vinyl siding is extruded in thin profiles and embossed to look like wood. Viewed up close, it is obviously not wood. The dead giveaway is the joints where the siding meets the trim. Because plastic expands and contracts significantly along its length, each siding length must run behind a vertical trim piece to allow it to move. The necessary gap between the trim and siding always differentiates vinyl siding from real wood siding, which simply butts into the trim. A quality job starts with siding at least .044" (11.17 mm) thick. Lighter colors fare better than dark ones, which may fade in time.

Metal Siding

Aluminum and steel siding are stronger than vinyl and have other advantages. The prefinished coatings hold dark colors better than vinyl does, and metal siding expands much less than plastic. Steel, the most expensive metal siding, is also the strongest. The extra strength might prove worth the money in areas prone to high winds, such as the Gulf South and Midwest.

Stucco and EIFS

Stucco is a traditional cladding that blends well with adjacent materials and can be applied to both framed and masonry walls. Composed of cement, lime, and sand, stucco is troweled onto wire mesh reinforcing over a layer of building felt in three coats. The surface can be left uncoated or painted. To shed water dependably, joints with abutting trim and materials must be properly flashed and caulked.

Cold temperatures cause stucco to shrink and crack—its major flaw. A variety of synthetic exterior coatings grouped under the acronym EIFS (exterior insulation and finish systems) are elastic rather than rigid. They do not crack with temperature changes. EIFS use acrylic polymers as the binding material, alone or combined with Portland cement. Developed as a low-cost alternative to stucco for commercial building façades, EIFs are appearing on an increasing number of homes. EIFS are applied in several layers over rigid foam insulation or directly onto a plywood or cement board substrate (see Figure 8.17). Many textures and colors are available. The colorant is embedded in the material, making it permanent and maintenance free. For all their advantages, EIFSs have leaked in some homes, especially in the South. Manufacturers have responded by publishing installation details that allow any entrapped water to escape to the outside.

Table 8.1 provides a summary of the siding types and other exterior wall finishes.

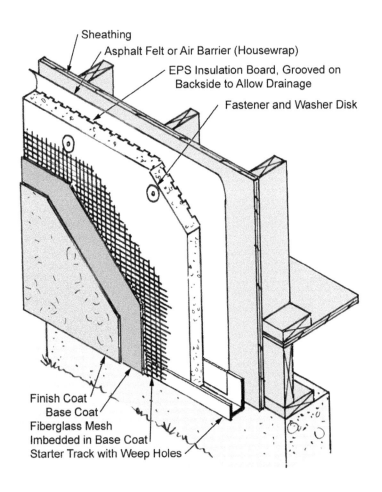

Sheathing
Asphalt Felt or Air Barrier (Housewrap)
EPS Insulation Board, Grooved on Backside to Allow Drainage
Fastener and Washer Disk

Finish Coat
Base Coat
Fiberglass Mesh
Imbedded in Base Coat
Starter Track with Weep Holes

FIGURE 8.17 EIFS employ several layers—felt, rigid foam, fiberglass mesh, and two coats of elastomeric coating—to produce an insulated system that resembles stucco. Proper detailing is required for moisture control.

TABLE 8.1 Exterior wall finish materials

Finish	Cost	Finishes	Pros	Cons
Wood boards	High	Uncoated, paint or stain	Attractive, durable	Periodic refinishing, can weather unevenly
OSB	Low	Preprimed for top coat or prefinished	Uniform lengths, knot free, stiffer than hardboard	Periodic refinishing, limited textures available
Hardboard	Low	Preprimed for top coat or prefinished	Uniform lengths, knot free, wide range of textures and patterns	Periodic refinishing
Plywood panel	Low to medium	Paint or stain; cedar and redwood can remain unfinished	Fast installation	Limited patterns, needs flashing at butt ends
Vinyl	Low	No finish needed	Fast installation, no finish, long warranty	Vulnerable to impact damage, poor appearance at joints
Aluminum	High	Prefinished	Durable, needs no finish	Dents under impact
Steel	High	Prefinished	Durable, needs no finish, resists impact better than aluminum	Can eventually develop rust.
Shingles	High	Leave unfinished or stain	Good appearance, durable, choice of exposure widths	Weathers unevenly if unfinished, slow to install
Stucco	Medium	Uncoated, paint or stain	Durable, long lasting	Prone to cracking and leaks
EIFS	High	Prefinished	Looks like stucco, needs no finish, long lasting, combines finish with insulation	Needs good detailing and meticulous installation to avoid water problems

EXTERIOR TRIM

The right type of trim for the outside is just as important to a quality job as selecting the right siding. Good detailing is important at corners, roof edges, windows, and doors not only for appearance, but also for shedding water. The cladding material and style of the house suggest the appropriate trim material and how it should be installed. Vinyl and metal siding often are trimmed with shapes of the same material. Quality wood siding deserves top-grade wood or composite trim. Brick and stone also need wood trim for eaves, windows, and doors.

Corner Details

The inside and outside corners of wood and shingle siding can meet in several ways. Outside corners can terminate at a vertical trim board, be mitered (or woven, with shingles), or covered with a metal trim piece (see Figure 8.18). Inside corners can meet a vertical inside trim board (all types) or be mitered or woven (shingles and shakes) (see Figure 8.19). Vinyl, aluminum, and steel siding usually terminate in trim shapes of the same material.

Door and Window Trim

The type of windows and doors, wall cladding, and desired appearance all affect the choice of trim for windows and doors. Wood windows typically arrive on the job site with a

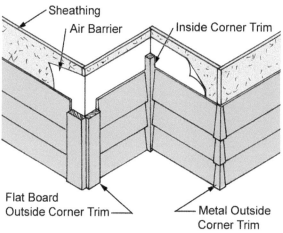

BEVEL SIDING

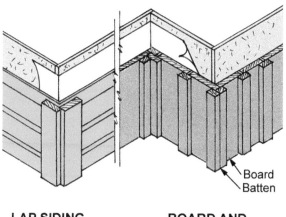

LAP SIDING **BOARD AND BATTEN SIDING**

FIGURE 8.18 Inside and outside corners on wood siding can be trimmed with wood casings or metal corner covers.

preattached brick mold that both trims the outside and nails to the framing to hold the window in place. The sash of wood windows clad on the exterior with PVC or aluminum protrudes past the sheathing, so that the siding can simply abut it without additional trim. The joint between siding and sash is then caulked. However, the thin line of the exposed sash does not evoke the appearance of traditional windows. If this is desired, it can be had by adding a "window frame" trim around the sash (see Figure 8.20). Some of the options are summarized in Table 8.2.

A Better Way to Install Siding and Trim

The installation details shown for each type of finish system described thus far follow traditional methods. However, except for vinyl and metal, all types of siding absorb moisture, even when primed on all sides. The moisture can find its way into the material, causing it to deteriorate and the paint to peel. A newer method for installing finish materials separates the siding and trim from the substrate with an intervening air space, which creates a vertical escape route for any moisture-laden air that penetrates the siding and a drainage plane for water, thus its name, rain screen (see Figure 8.21).

The drainage plane occurs between the housewrap layer and siding and can be achieved with vertical strapping or the application of a manufactured mat, designed to allow the cavity to ventilate and water to drain. Paint on siding installed over a rain screen has proven to last far longer than with traditional installation (see Figure 8.22).

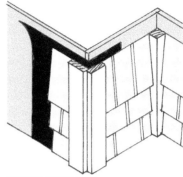

CORNER BOARD TRIM

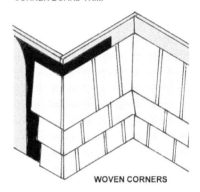

WOVEN CORNERS

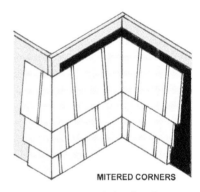

MITERED CORNERS

FIGURE 8.19 Wood shingle siding can turn corners by abutting a casing or by mitering or weaving the shingles themselves.

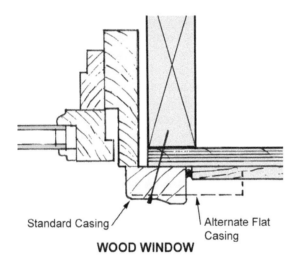

Standard Casing / | Alternate Flat Casing

WOOD WINDOW

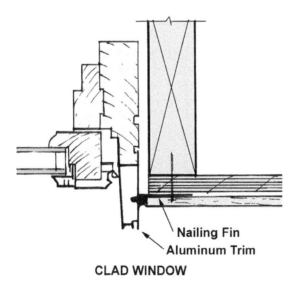

Nailing Fin
Aluminum Trim

CLAD WINDOW

FIGURE 8.20 Wood windows come with an exterior trim piece already attached (above), which is nailed to the wall during installation. Windows clad with vinyl or aluminum (below) typically have a protruding trim attached to the outside of the frame and a nailing fin that is concealed beneath the siding.

TABLE 8.2 Door and Window Trim Options

Building Element	Exterior Wall Finish			Trim Option			
	Wood siding, shingles, shakes	PVC (vinyl) siding	Brick, stone	Integral fin (no additional trim)	Preapplied brick molding	Preapplied flat (1 × 4) trim	Site-applied trim
Article I.							
Doors							
Wood door sash	■				●		●
		■			●		●
			■		●		
PVC-clad wood door sash	■			●			●
		■		●			
			■	●			
Aluminum-clad wood door sash	■			●			●
		■		●			
			■	●			
Windows							
Wood windows	■				●		●
		■			●		●
			■		●		
PVC-clad wood windows	■			●			●
		■		●			
			■	●			
Aluminum-clad wood windows	■			●			●
		■		●			
			■	●			
PVC (all-vinyl) windows	■						●
		■		●			
			■	●			
Fiberglass (protruded) windows	■			●			●
		■		●			
			■	●			

FIGURE 8.21 Installing over a rain screen drainage mat provides a continuous space for drainage and drying and eliminates the threat of trapped moisture between the siding and the substrate.

Courtesy of Benjamin Obdyke Wall and Roof Products Inc.

FIGURE 8.22 A rain screen drainage mat is stapled to the substrate, before siding is installed.

Courtesy of Benjamin Obdyke Wall and Roof Products Inc.

SUMMARY

The exterior walls of a building must reliably serve several functions: as the structural support for other elements, as a barrier to the weather, and as the site of doors and windows. Walls can be built from various structural systems, including logs, timber framing, wood and metal studs, concrete, and masonry.

Framed walls contain cavities that can be filled with insulation. To insulate concrete and masonry walls, other methods must be sought, often a second wall.

Wood- and metal-framed walls offer many choices for exterior finishes, including siding made of wood, wood composite, metal, and shingles, each with assets and liabilities and a proper installation method. A successful exterior finish also requires exterior trim appropriate to the wall construction and consistent with the desired appearance.

CHAPTER REVIEW

1. What is the current method of air-sealing log homes? (See "Log Home" pages 60–61)
2. What materials are used for timber-framed homes? (See "Timber Framing" page 60)
3. How far up do the lower-floor studs extend in platform framing? (See "Stud Wall Framing" page 61)
4. Why have 2 × 6 studs replaced 2 × 4s in many regions? (See "Insulating New Framed Walls" pages 64–65)
5. What materials have replaced board sheathing? (See "Wall Sheathing" page 63)
6. What are two ways to create a moisture barrier? (See "Insulating New Framed Walls" page 64–65)
7. What are some ways to insulate an existing wall? (See "Insulating Existing Framed Walls" page 65)
8. Why are brick walls always constructed as double walls? (See "Brick and Stone" page 67)
9. Describe how one can easily differentiate vinyl siding from wood. (See "Vinyl Siding" page 70)
10. What is gained by providing an air space between the siding and the substrate? (See "A Better Way to Install Siding and Trim" page 73)

Doors and Windows

The openings in the exterior walls of a home constitute yet another of its systems: access from one space to another. Doors provide controlled access from the outside to the inside and from room to room. Windows offer controlled access from the interior to light, view, ventilation, and the warmth of the sun. In this chapter, we discuss how the many choices of these important components differ in their capability to provide the necessary kind of access.

Learning Objective 1: Recognize the criteria that identify each door and window type.

Learning Objective 2: Identify the characteristics of each door and window style.

Learning Objective 3: Specify the appropriate type of door hardware function.

Learning Objective 4: Describe the energy implications of various types of glazing.

DOOR TYPES

Because all doors move in one way or another, it makes sense to classify them first by the way in which they operate. They also vary in style, or appearance, which provides a second means of classification. Except for garage doors, which open vertically on overhead tracks, all other doors in homes either swing from hinges mounted in the side or roll or slide sideways in tracks mounted in the head and sill.

Hinged Doors

Hinged doors can be mounted singly or in multiple units. Single-acting doors provide access into most rooms. Double-acting doors make sense for certain applications.

Single-Acting Doors

Single-acting doors swing only in one direction, either inward or outward. Double-acting doors swing in both directions. You might need a double-acting door for a particular type of interior application, but single-acting doors probably will account for the bulk of your kitchen and bath work. Single-acting doors usually—but not always—open to the inside of the space

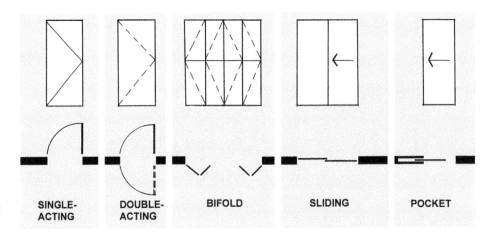

FIGURE 9.1 Doors are classified by type according to the way in which they open and close.

SINGLE-ACTING   DOUBLE-ACTING   BIFOLD   SLIDING   POCKET

accessed. Because doors can open from either side as well as inward or outward, we need two terms to describe their operation (see Figure 9.1). The first term, *hand*, indicates the side where the hinges are located when you are standing outside. The second, *reverse*, is used to designate doors that swing outward. There are four hands: right hand (RH), left hand (LH), right-hand reverse (RHR), and left-hand reverse (LHR). These tags are simpler to remember if you imagine yourself facing the door from the outside (the side in which the key would be inserted; see Figure 9.2).

Double-Acting Doors

Double-acting doors consist of two leaves, each hinged at the jamb, that open in both directions without the need to turn a latch. Often used in restaurants, where waiters have their hands full, double-acting doors see occasional use in some residences, between the kitchen and dining rooms.

Bifold Doors

Doors hinged from each other as well as from a jamb are called bifold doors. A pair of bifold doors actually contains four panels. The outer door of a bifold pair has a pin at the top that rides

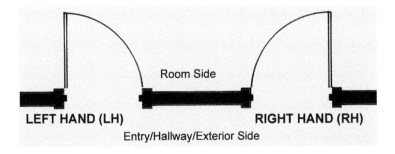

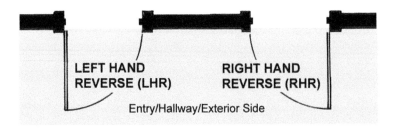

FIGURE 9.2 Single-acting doors are coded, or handed, by the direction in which they open into a room.

in a track, which aligns the doors as they open and close. Bifold doors suit locations where a single-hinged door would be cumbersome and places requiring wide openings, such as wide closets. Two door panels, each 18" (457 mm) wide, create a pair of bifold doors for a 36"-wide (914-mm) opening. Wider openings up to 72" (1,829 mm) are possible with sets of paired panels.

Sliding Doors

The second most common residential entry door type slides in tracks mounted in the head and sill. (Doors other than cabinet doors actually roll on rollers, rather than slide). Sliding (bypass) doors can be installed in sets of two, three, or four panels. Like bifold doors, sliders suit applications where more access width is needed than a hinged door offers or where space is too cramped for a hinged door to operate easily. The most frequent interior application for sliders is on a closet. Exterior sliding doors are usually glazed and called patio doors because they are most always used as a secondary access to a patio or deck. A patio door often makes sense for connecting a kitchen or dining area with a deck or a bath with an enclosed courtyard.

Pocket Doors

Single doors can also slide, but instead of sliding past another door, they disappear into a pocket in the wall. When open, this type of door is completely out of the way within the pocket. Pocket doors are especially useful in kitchen and bath areas where the door remains open much of the time or where a hinged door would cramp the space. The door separating a dining room from a kitchen would be a possible location. Another would be a door to a private bath in a master bedroom suite. Pocket doors are also used sometimes because they provide easier access for people in wheelchairs. On the downside, the gain in unencumbered floor space is offset by the necessity for a pocket in the wall that must be kept clear of wires and pipes. If the wall is load bearing, a header significantly larger than a header for a single-wide door is needed. Items in the wall, such as outlets, vents, or ducts, will have to be relocated.

Pocket doors come in kits containing the track and assembly to be hidden in the wall pocket. Some kits fit into interior walls framed with 2 × 4s.

DOOR STYLES

The term *style* is somewhat vague but generally describes the construction and appearance of the door. Depending on the manufacturer, the door styles described here are shipped as doors only—requiring a separate frame or prehung in frames. Prehung doors generally are preferred in residential work due to their simpler installation.

Flush Doors

The completely flat face of flush doors blends with contemporary houses but looks out of place in more traditional homes. Flush doors come faced with hardboard for a paint finish or in various species of real wood veneers for a natural finish. There are two types of core construction. Hollow core (HC), the most economical, consists of a honeycomb of cardboard sandwiched between the face veneers. The stiles and rails are solid wood. HC doors suit light-duty interior applications. They are not recommended for exterior doors. Sturdier solid-core (SC) doors, with a core made of wood staves, particleboard, or other wood composition material, are used for exterior doors and interior doors subject to abuse or where the client wants quality or better sound control. They are also used between a kitchen and a garage when the code calls for a fire-rated door assembly.

Panel Doors

Traditional-style houses call for wood doors composed of solid wood panels set into stiles and rails glued together with mortise and tenon joinery, although panel (stile-and-rail) doors also blend well with modern-style homes. Interior panel doors are typically 1⅜" (35 mm) thick. Exterior doors are typically 1¾" (44 mm) thick. Economy-class doors intended for paint finish are made of fiberboard. Doors suitable for paint or natural finish are available in pine, fir, and various hardwoods.

One type of exterior composite door panel door is comprised of a skin of steel or fiberglass, molded into shapes that imitate the styles and rails of a wood panel door. A core of solid foam provides thermal insulation.

Exterior panel doors are available with solid or glazed panels in various patterns. Codes require all glazing in doors to be tempered glass for safety. Tempered glass, when broken, breaks into a multitude of small rounded pieces rather than irregular-shape shards that can wound people by cutting or puncturing.

French Doors

Traditional French doors are paired doors that open inward or outward. The term *French door* has gotten somewhat muddled in recent years, with door manufacturers using it to cover a wide variety of glazed doors that include three- and four-door assemblies in in-swing or out-swing configurations. Three-door assemblies typically consist of a central operating door that hinges off one of the stationary side doors. In four-panel configurations, the two middle doors work as double-acting doors, hinged off the outboard door panels.

French doors are made up of a solid frame surrounding an array of glass panes separated from each other by narrow strips called muntins. Where the muntins truly separate individual panes, or lights, the glazing is called true divided light. A more energy-efficient version contains the muntin grid inside an unbroken insulated glass panel with secondary grids married to the inside and outside faces; this style is called simulated divided lights. French doors are made of all wood or wood clad on the outside with aluminum or vinyl.

Patio Doors

As mentioned earlier under "Door Types" patio doors connect interior spaces with the outdoors, opening onto patios, decks, or courtyards. The simplest patio door contains two panels. The movable, or active, panel is indicated in the catalog and on the drawings with the letter "X," the inactive panel with the letter "O." Panel widths are 30" (762 mm), 36" (914 mm), and 48" (1,218 mm), so the smallest single assembly would be 60" (1,524 mm) wide, using a pair of 30" (762-mm) leaves. The widest unit would be 144" (3,658 mm), made up of three 48"-wide (1,219-mm) leaves. Standard heights are 80 and 96" (2,032 and 2,438 mm). Units can be ganged together to create a glazed opening of any width.

Patio doors are available with frames of aluminum, wood, or wood clad with vinyl or aluminum. Heat loss and gain is always a concern with exterior windows and doors, and the frames of glazed doors offer many lineal feet of exposure. Wood or vinyl frames are fairly good insulators, but aluminum is not. In winter, heat travels freely from the interior to the outside through the metal. If patio doors are used in a wet area, such as a bath, moisture can condense on the inside and even turn to ice. Door frames with a nonconductive thermal break gasket sandwiched between the inside and outside portions of the frame minimize this hazard.

Louvered and Mirrored Doors

Closet doors can contain louvers to ventilate the interior or fronted with full-height mirrors. Bifold closet doors with louvers or mirrors are available in various widths. A louvered or mirrored hinged room door probably will have to be special ordered or custom fabricated (see Figure 9.3).

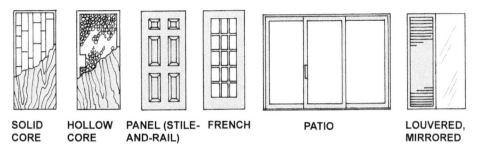

| SOLID CORE | HOLLOW CORE | PANEL (STILE-AND-RAIL) | FRENCH | PATIO | LOUVERED, MIRRORED |

FIGURE 9.3 Some common door styles found in residential construction.

Entrance Systems

The front door means more to the home than a way to get people in and out (see Figure 9.4). As the principal arrival point for visitors, it requires design attributes that express its importance as a focal point of the house. Traditional homes often set their main entrance up a few steps into a porch, which accents the entrance and shelters visitors. Today's homes sometimes have a scaled-down version of a porch, with the front door built into an entrance system consisting of a door flanked by sidelights and topped with a transom window. Entrance systems come in a wide variety of configurations and material choices in prehung frames.

RELOCATING DOORWAYS

Many interior alterations call for relocating the doors by opening a wall for a new door or closing off an old doorway. Creating a new door opening in an interior partition is fairly simple to do unless wiring and/or pipes are in the way. Rerouting wiring is usually feasible and not too costly. Rerouting pipes or ducts may not be possible; if it is, it is sure to be expensive. Before finalizing your design, inspect the job to determine which wires, pipes, or ducts might run through the proposed doorways. You can get a clue about the location of electrical wiring from the location of outlets. Outlets on either side of the proposed opening probably are connected to wiring that runs through the area. You may be able to tell whether piping runs through the area by the location of existing fixtures. Check the floors below, for example, to see if there is a toilet. If so, its waste/vent pipe probably runs upward through the wall above. If, after your sleuthing, you still are not certain, have a portion of the wall finish removed from one side of the wall and peek into the cavity.

Interior bearing walls typically have double top plates. If this is the case, a header beam probably will be required over the new opening to take up the load of the structure above. (See "Modifying Bearing Walls" in Chapter 11.)

Closing off an existing doorway is simply a matter of removing the door and its hinges and casings and filling the void with framing. A sole plate goes down on the floor, followed by trimmer studs nailed to the old jambs and one across the head to provide attachment for the new wall finish.

DOOR HARDWARE

Door hardware includes all of the parts that control movement of the door. It is called hardware because most of the parts are made of metal, although plastic may constitute some interior parts of latch and locks, particularly in the economy lines.

Hinges and pivots afford movement for swinging doors; rollers and tracks for sliding and bifold doors. Push plates, latch sets, and locksets control the movement. Thresholds below doors provide transitions from spaces, while stops, mounted in the floor or wall, can prevent damage from a door swinging into a wall.

FIGURE 9.4 An entrance system combines one or more doors, flanking sidelights, and transom windows into a single frame. Many combinations and styles are possible.

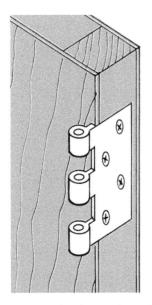

FIGURE 9.5 A door butt is a hinge that fits into a recess routed into the butt edge of a door.

Butts and Hinges

Hinges mount to the face of a door and frame, while butts mount on the edge, or "butt" end of the door, exposing only the pin casing (see Figure 9.5). Prehung doors come with butts already attached. Interior doors up to 36" (914 mm) wide typically require 1½ pairs (3 units) of butts, 3½ by 3½" (89 by 89 mm) in size. Double-acting door hinges have springs that return the door to the closed position. Spring hinges are available for single-acting doors intended to be self-closing.

Locks and Latches

The hardware that controls the movement of the door panel consists of a knob or lever and a mechanism to secure the door in place when it is closed. This assembly is called a lockset, if the door locks and a latch, if the door does not lock. The two most common types of locksets, by their construction, are mortise locks and cylindrical locks (see Figure 9.6). Mortise locks are encased in a rectangular metal box that fits into a mortise carved out of the stile (vertical edge) of the door. They are common in older houses but have been pretty much superseded by cylindrical locks, which fit into a round hole. Cylindrical locksets offer many control options, which have names as well as a standard federal designation number by the American National Standards Institute (ANSI). Some of the more common ones you will most likely need in kitchen and bath installations are listed in Table 9.1.

Lock and latch sets are available with knobs, levers, or handles. Levers are required in any job that must meet Americans with Disabilities Act (ADA) accessibility standards and are a good idea in any door to be operated by an elderly person or a person with limited use of the hands. Levers are, in fact, gradually replacing round knobs for all doors because of they are more easily operated by all users (see Figure 9.7). Handles are used on main entrance doors in tandem with thumb levers that control the latch.

Security deadbolts are used in addition to the primary lock/latch set for extra security at the main entrance. They are accessed by keys only.

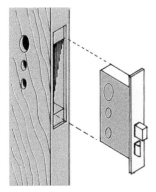

MORTISE LOCK

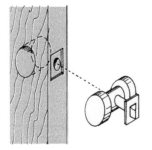

CYLINDRICAL LOCK

FIGURE 9.6 Two types of locksets are commonly used in exterior residential doors: mortise locks (left) and cylindrical locks (right). Interior doors typically contain cylindrical locks or latch sets.

TABLE 9.1 Lock and Latch Functions

ANSI Number	Function Name	Description/Operation	Typical Locations
F75	Passage latch	Knobs both sides always unlocked.	Kitchen, walk-in closet
A20S	Closet latch	Knob on corridor side, thumb turn inside, always unlocked.	Small closet
F76	Privacy lock	Knobs both sides. Push-button on inside for locking. Releases by turning inside knob or opening from outside by inserting flat narrow tool in hole.	Bedroom, bathroom
F81	Entrance lock	Knobs both sides, keyhole on outside knob, turn button on inside knob. Door locked by turning button and unlocked by turning inside knob or key from outside.	Entrance door
B252, E211	Security deadbolt	Double-cylinder dead latch with latch bolt retracted by key from either side.	Entrance door

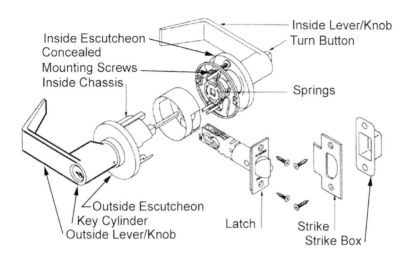

FIGURE 9.7 The parts of a cylindrical lock with a lever-type handle. *Courtesy of Schlage*

WINDOW TYPES

Like doors, windows control access to interior spaces. Well-chosen, quality windows and skylights add both appeal and functionality to kitchens and baths by opening views to the outside and bringing in natural light and ventilation.

Window appearance probably tops the list of criteria for most homeowners and depends on the window's type, material, color, and glazing configuration. The desired appearance also may establish the size and shape of the window, although these are more likely to be determined by the space available and vertical location preferred. Manufacturers' catalogs offer a wide variety of standard and custom window shapes and glazing configurations. Color choices for the inside sash and frame are unlimited for windows intended for natural or paint finish but limited for polyvinyl chloride (PVC) or aluminum windows. Similarly, exterior colors depend on the type of sash and frame. Clad windows come in factory-applied colors, while wood windows can be painted any color. Glass, too, is available in blue, green, or bronze tints as well as clear. However, tinted glass affects energy performance, as we discuss under "Glazing Choices" later in this chapter.

All windows consist of three basic components: glazing, sash, and frame. The glazing is a transparent material that permits vision through the window and allows light to pass through; usually it is glass or plastic. The sash is the component into which the glazing mounts and is either stationary or movable. The sash may be a simple surround consisting of horizontal rails and vertical stiles or subdivided into a number of smaller panes by muntins. Mullions are larger linear components that separate window and/or door units from each other. The frame is the stationary part that affixes into the wall. We classify windows by type, according to how the sash opens and closes (operates).

Fixed Windows

Windows whose sashes do not open at all are called fixed. As it cannot be opened for ventilation, a fixed window would be a poor choice for a kitchen or bath that only has one window, but it may make an economical component of a multi-unit window assembly. Manufacturers typically offer fixed versions of their standard operating units but in more sizes, since size is not limited by the operating mechanism.

Double- and Single-Hung Windows

Vertical windows containing two operable sash units are fundamental to traditional colonial, cape, and cottage-style homes. Both sashes of older, traditional double-hung windows moved up and down, suspended by ropes and counterweights concealed in the jambs. The ropes rode on pulleys in the top of the jamb, balancing the weights of the sashes so they stayed open at the desired position.

Although traditional double-hung windows may have served reliably in an older home, they have some downsides in modern homes. Cleaning the outer panes from the inside is very difficult. The side pockets that contain the ropes and pulleys are a source of heat leaks and ropes and pulleys eventually can break and require replacement. Older double-hung windows are also likely to have only one thickness of glazing (single glazing) and be mounted in frames that leak cold air to the interior, causing discomfort and high fuel bills to homeowners. All of these problems have been solved in today's "tilt-turn" double-hung windows. Instead of ropes and pulleys, sashes glide up and down in weather-tight jambs, held in place by friction and spring counterbalances. A latch at the top of each sash allows it to be tilted inward for easy cleaning from the room side.

Single-hung windows are a recent, more economical product that works in the same manner as the newer double-hung windows, except that the tops sash is fixed in place and only the bottom sash operates. An inoperable upper sash is a drawback only in applications where it is necessary to be able to open both sashes.

Sliding Windows

If you turn a double-hung window on its side, you have a sliding window (also called gliding window), except that the sashes cannot be tilted inward for cleaning. The horizontal shape of sliders blends better with contemporary than traditional homes and is particularly well suited for kitchens and bath walls where an unobstructed lower wall is desired, such as above a tub/shower or above a kitchen sink.

Casement Windows

Casement windows are hinged at the sides to open outward, controlled by a sill-mounted crank. Because the entire sash opens, casements are the best choice for ventilation. They are made even more effective by the projecting sash that funnels passing breezes inside. However, when fully open, they are also vulnerable to rain. Casements work well with modern-style houses but also can suit traditional-style homes if the sash is subdivided into several smaller panes (divided lights).

Some manufacturers configure casement windows into assemblies that project out up to 2' from the wall of the house. Box bay windows have a rectangular footprint, whereas angle bay windows contain side windows on an angle of 30 or 45 degrees. The assemblies come with top and bottom platforms attached, needing only roofing on the top and trim and siding on the base to complete the installation. Bay windows are often the main kitchen window above the sink, where the base and shelves provide platforms for plants.

Awning, Hopper, and Jalousie Windows

If sliders are akin to double-hung windows turned sideways, awning windows resemble casements turned sideways. Because they are hinged on the top and open outward, they shed rain when open (unlike some other window types). Awning windows work well alone or as the vented units of a window group. Because they can take a long horizontal shape, awnings, like sliders, often make good choices above a tub/shower or kitchen sink. When stacked into vertical assemblies, awning windows become hopper, or projected windows. Jalousie windows consist of several panes of glass hinged at the sides. Because the entire assembly opens, this type works well where maximum ventilation is desired, which makes them popular in the South. On the downside, jalousie windows are a poor choice for cold climates. They are poor insulators because they are single glazed and have many cracks between the panes and at the sides.

Skylights, Roof Windows, and Light Tubes

An interior room with no walls to the outside may benefit from sunlight and ventilation with an opening to the roof fitted with a skylight, roof window, or light tube.

Skylights are stationary units with flat or curved domes that can be single- or double-glazed. They mount atop a wood curb attached to the roof deck.

Roof windows are flat and styled to resemble residential windows, hence the name. Increasingly popular in homes, roof windows are available with fixed or operating sashes that tilt outward to open. Frames and sash are usually made of wood and clad with aluminum or vinyl outside. Frames mount on a curb, similar to skylights, or mount directly on the roof deck. Curb-mounted units do not visually blend in with the roof as snugly as deck-mounted ones but are considered by many to be less prone to water penetration, since the skylight is raised above the roof surface. Roof windows come single or double glazed, along with low-e coating (described under "Glazing Choices" later in the chapter). Operating blinds are also available for the underside of the frame to control glare and reduce unwanted solar heat.

Light tubes offer a way to bring daylight into landlocked interior rooms where roof and/or ceiling construction make installing a roof window impractical. They consist of a clear plastic dome on the roof connected to a highly reflective tube that terminates at the ceiling. Because the tube is bendable, it can be adjusted to install in difficult places without reframing the roof and building a light well, an enclosed channel from roof to ceiling, as required for a skylight (see Figure 9.8). The amount of light available from light tubes varies with their diameter and pathway shape. And you cannot see the sky through them, as with skylights and roof windows.

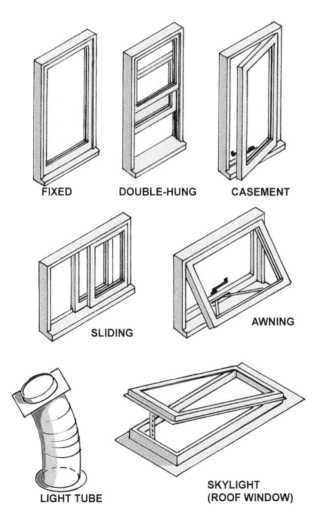

FIXED   DOUBLE-HUNG   CASEMENT

SLIDING   AWNING

LIGHT TUBE   SKYLIGHT (ROOF WINDOW)

FIGURE 9.8 As with doors, windows are classified by the way they open and close. Light tubes offer a means of getting light into a landlocked room where it would not be feasible to install a skylight or roof window.

WINDOW SASH AND FRAME MATERIALS

Traditional window sashes and frames were made of wood, a material that was readily available and could be milled to make intricate profiles (see Figure 9.9). Glass panes were held into the sash with linseed oil putty and the sash, frames, and putty were painted after installation. In time, the paint chipped off, the putty hardened, and the ensuing cracks created pathways for air and water leakage. Today's wood windows incorporate a host of technical improvements to address these problems, including better design, improved sealants, and exterior cladding materials (see Figure 9.10).

Pine is the wood of choice for most windows, but other species, such as mahogany, are available where a natural finish or greater resistance to weather is desired. Wood windows clad on the exterior with PVC vinyl, fiberglass, or aluminum offer the best of both worlds: the appearance of wood inside with a low-maintenance, weather-resistant skin outside.

Residential windows are also available made completely from materials other than wood, including aluminum or all vinyl, in several factory-applied colors (see Figure 9.11). In areas with cold winters, metal windows should contain a nonconductive thermal break material somewhere within the frame to stem heat flow through the metal. Without a thermal break, the cold sash not only leaks heat to the outside but also invites water to condense and run off onto the wall. Window sashes and frames made completely of vinyl are better heat insulators but look heavier than wood due to thicker sash and frame construction necessary for stiffness. Nonetheless, all-vinyl windows have been edging out all other types in recent years for both replacement and new window installations (see Figure 9.12).

GLAZING CHOICES

The type of window glazing affects how much heat it will transmit, which affects both the energy efficiency of the home and the occupants' comfort. A square foot of single-glazed window (R-1) wastes more than 19× as much winter heat than an adjacent square foot of

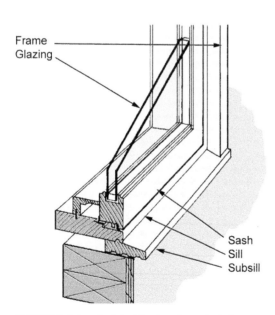

FIGURE 9.9 A typical double-glazed wood window mounted in a wood-framed wall.

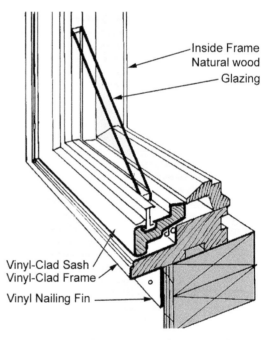

FIGURE 9.10 Clad wood windows have exposed wood frames and sashes on the interior and a weather-resistant cladding of PVC (as shown) or aluminum on the exterior.

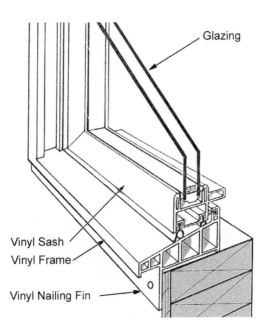

FIGURE 9.11 All-vinyl (PVC) windows, initially used as replacement units in residences, are now popular in new construction as well, thanks to their low cost, easy maintenance, and high energy efficiency.

wall insulated to R-19. Adding a second pane with an encapsulated air space boosts its R value to R-2, a third pane (triple glazing) to around R-3; and a fourth pane (quadruple glazing), to R-4. But adding more than two panes makes the window bulkier, heavier, and costlier. And if the window faces the sun, each successive layer cuts the amount of useful solar heat that penetrates the glazing.

Three advances in recent years have made it possible to get high-performance windows with no more than two glass panes:

1. Low-emissivity (low-e) coatings
2. Encapsulated membranes
3. Inert gas fill

The first improvement came with the development of a microscopically thin metallic oxide coating called low e (for low emissivity), which controls solar heat gain and loss. Low-e coated windows allow various amounts of sunlight and heat to enter while preventing room heat

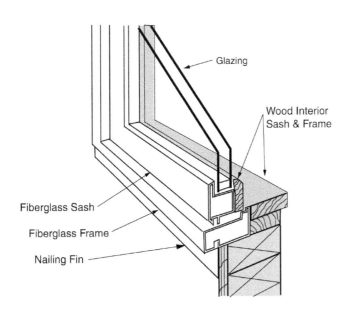

FIGURE 9.12 Windows with fiberglass frames and sashes on the exterior and wood interior are strong, maintenance free, and more dimensionally stable than PVC windows.

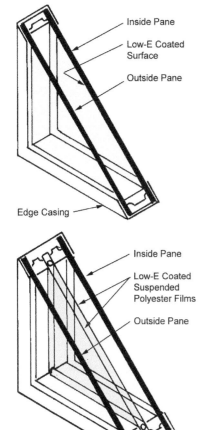

FIGURE 9.13 Some of the advances in high-performance glazing. The double-glazed window at top contains a low-e coating on an interior surface of one of its panes, which boosts its R-value from R-2 to R-3. R-values exceeding 5 are possible with windows containing low-e coated polyester films suspended between two or more panes (bottom) and the air spaces filled with a heavy gas, such as argon.

from escaping back to the outside. The coating typically occurs on the third face of a double-pane window, where the surfaces are numbered 1 to 4, with the surface exposed to the weather numbered 1. A low-e coating boosts a double-pane window's R-value from 2 to 3. The coating also blocks ultraviolet rays, which fade fabrics. Low-e coating also can be selected to block solar heat, a boon to cooling-dominated climates. Window suppliers can help you match the coating to the climate.

The second advance came with substituting thin sheets of coated polyester for glass for the inner panes of triple- and quadruple-glazed windows. The resulting glazing assembly achieves efficiencies up to R-8 without the added weight of two inner panes of glass.

Infusing a heavy gas, such as argon or krypton, into the dead air space between glazing layers yielded the third advance in window energy performance. More viscous than ambient air, these gases flow less within the glazing cavity, which reduces the heat transfer due to convectional movement (see Figure 9.13).

High-performance glazing accounts for only part of the energy efficiency of a window. The other part is its ability to seal out air leaks. State-of-the-art weather stripping usually accompanies any new or replacement window. The weather stripping is usually made of a polymeric EPDM plastic material that stays flexible for several years.

Not all homeowners are eager to pay a premium for the energy savings of high-performance windows that may not be realized for five years or more. But as energy costs continue to climb—as they are expected to—the return on investment (ROI, or payback period) will decrease. And there are other benefits that begin immediately. Because low-e windows block heat radiated from the inside, they reflect back one's body heat, which results in better comfort.

On a remodeling job, any drafty windows should be repaired or replaced as part of the overall project. Drafts can be sealed with new weather stripping. If the windows are single glazed and the house is located in a cold-climate area, the glazing needs improvement. There are three ways to upgrade the glazing. From the most economical to most expensive, they are:

1. Add storm windows to the exterior.
2. Install replacement sashes in the existing frames.
3. Replace the entire window unit.

Storm windows improve the energy efficiency of the basic window in proportion to its condition. The least efficient windows stand to gain the most from having a storm window added to the exterior. Units that are more efficient to begin with will see fewer gains. Storm windows are made to order, according to the size of the net opening inside the exterior window trim. They typically come with two glass panes and insect screens in a double-hung configuration mounted in aluminum tracks and are screwed to the window trim. The main benefit of storm windows is to block cold winds from the main window. Drawbacks include more difficult cleaning of the main windows and the fact that the storm window is what you see, for better or worse.

Replacement sashes yield a more energy-efficient way to improve leaky, single-glazed windows. Many of the same window choices for new windows are available in replacement versions, designed to fit into the existing window frame after the old sash has been removed. The window type is the first decision in choosing a replacement window, followed by the type of glazing and material. Some considerations for material choices are summarized next.

• **Vinyl.** Usually the least expensive, durable, low maintenance. Many color options are available, some with woodlike finishes.
• **Wood.** Goes with traditional houses but requires painting or another finish.
• **Fiberglass.** Stronger while just as durable as vinyl, but likely more expensive.
• **Aluminum-clad wood.** Durable exterior, wood interior, many colors available for aluminum cladding.

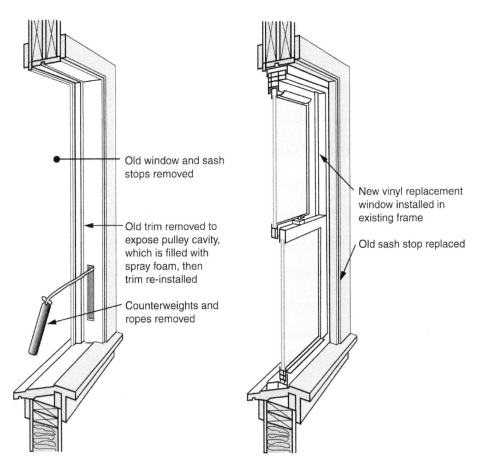

Old window and sash stops removed

Old trim removed to expose pulley cavity, which is filled with spray foam, then trim re-installed

Counterweights and ropes removed

New vinyl replacement window installed in existing frame

Old sash stop replaced

FIGURE 9.14 Replacing an existing double-hung window begins with removal of the old sash, stops, and interior trim to expose the pulley cavity. After removal of the pulleys, counterweights, and ropes, the cavity is filled with spray foam and the interior trim replaced. Exact measurements of the existing frame opening are used to size the replacement window, which is installed in the old frame. Vinyl replacement windows are made to exact sizes. Other types come various standard sizes.

The fabricator begins by accurately measuring the frame opening, then uses these measurements to make a replacement unit that can be installed from the interior, often without disturbing the exterior trim or framing. Replacing double-hung windows that have pulleys and ropes entails an additional step before the new sash goes in: removal of the pulley weights from the side cavities and filling the cavities with foam insulation (see Figure 9.14).

Replacement of the entire window unit, the most expensive improvement, is necessary when the original window frame is in poor condition or the design calls for changing the window size or location. Replacing entails removing all parts of the sash and frame of the existing unit and any enlargement or infill of the existing opening to accommodate the size and shape of the new window.

SUMMARY

Doors and windows are the access system of a residence that controls the movement of persons and elements from outside to inside and from room to room. Doors provide access from space to space by the way in which they operate. Many choices exist in door styles and materials.

Windows provide view to the exterior while controlling the movement of sunlight and solar heat into the interior. A wide variety of window types and materials are available to suit any residential need. Energy efficiency figures high on the list of considerations for window choices in today's homes, and advancements in glazing technology enables designers to specify new or replacement units with much better performance than in the past.

CHAPTER REVIEW

1. What advantage does a double-acting door provide? (See "Single-Acting Doors" page 77)

2. When standing outside a door, which side of the door contains the hinges on a left-hand door? (See "Single-Acting Doors" pages 77–78)

3. What structural consideration must be dealt with in creating an opening for a pocket door? (See "Pocket Doors" page 79)

4. What is a muntin? (See "French Doors" page 80)

5. Why do aluminum doors need a thermal break? (See "Patio Doors" page 80)

6. What issues can come up when relocating doorways? (See "Relocating Doorways" page 81)

7. What does a low-e coating control? (See "Glazing Choices" pages 86–87)

8. What additional step is necessary when replacing a double-hung window beyond other window types? (See "Glazing Choices" page 89)

Roofs

The roof is probably the most important single component of a home. If a kitchen or bath is directly below the roof, its design will affect items such as skylights, vents for exhaust fans, and lighting fixtures. The roof must be designed not only to shelter the occupants from the elements but also include features to maintain comfort inside. The structure must withstand the loads imposed by wind, snow, and seismic forces. This chapter explores how various types of roofs and structural systems meet these challenges.

Learning Objective 1: Use the features of a roof form to match it to the requirements of the application.

Learning Objective 2: Describe the structural systems for framing various types of roofs in connection with the needs of the space below.

Learning Objective 3: Discuss the problems and solutions of controlling the transfer of heat and moisture through roofs.

Learning Objective 4: List the pros and cons of various roofing materials used in residences.

ROOF FORMS

Roof forms follow regional home styles, influenced by the materials and traditions of the region. They may be gable, hip, shed, flat, butterfly, mansard, or gambrel, as shown in Figure 10.1. Interestingly, the fact that flat or nearly flat roofs are found in the dry Southwest as well as wetter Northwest and Northeast suggests that the ability to shed water is determined by factors other than the roof's form.

Gable, shed, mansard, and hip roofs have a long history on houses. Because they all slope, they naturally shed water and do not leak if the roofing material is properly installed and maintained. Even sloped roofs thatched with grass can keep water out. The most vulnerable spots in any sloping roof are the protrusions that interrupt the sloping planes. Each point at which a chimney, dormer, or pipe pokes through the roof is a potential point for water to get in. Careful flashing, sealing, and detailing is required to ensure that these points do not leak. Flat roofs and butterfly roofs do not, by their shape, shed water. In fact, they tend to entrap water. Special provisions needed to prevent leakage include an uninterrupted, continuous roof membrane equipped with roof drains at the interior portions and overflow scuppers at the edges.

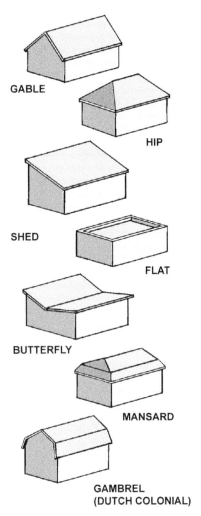

GABLE

HIP

SHED

FLAT

BUTTERFLY

MANSARD

GAMBREL
(DUTCH COLONIAL)

FIGURE 10.1 Some typical residential roof forms.

ROOF FRAMING SYSTEMS

Residential roofs can be framed with rafters, trusses, or panels. Each system has pros and cons, as described in Table 10.1.

TABLE 10.1 Framing systems

Framing System	Characteristics
Rafter framing ("stick framing")	Many individual members (rafters), closely spaced, span between walls or beams. Spans limited to around 20′ for sawn lumber; up to 30′ with manufactured rafters ("I-joists").
Trusses	Made of several slender members assembled into triangular configurations. Usually spaced 24″ apart to clear span up to 60′.
Panel framing	Composite panels span up to 12′ between trusses or timbers (in post-and-beam framing).

Rafter Framed Roofs

Rafters are long, slender members that span between supports, similar to joists in floors, but with one difference. Rafters slope up from the outer walls to a ridge in pitched roofs. Shed roof rafters slope up from an outer wall into the main roof or to the ridge, as shown in Figure 10.2. Shed roofs are also one roof form for dormer windows (Figure 10.3), where they increase headroom and provide an opportunity for windows in an otherwise too-shallow attic.

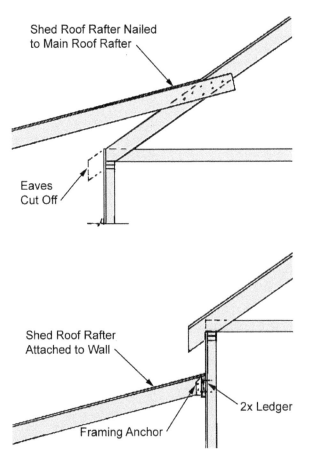

Shed Roof Rafter Nailed to Main Roof Rafter

Eaves Cut Off

Shed Roof Rafter Attached to Wall

2x Ledger

Framing Anchor

FIGURE 10.2 Shed roofs can frame into the main roof of the building (top) or into a wall (bottom).

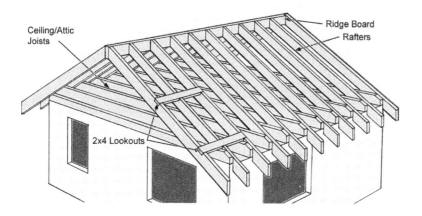

FIGURE 10.3 A typical rafter-framed gable roof. Lookouts (cross pieces set into the end rafters) support the rake (outside rafter) at the gable ends.

Dormers

Dormers are structures built into the roof to provide additional headroom and locations for windows in attics. They can be built with shed roofs or gable roofs (doghouse dormers) and can spring up from the house's outer wall or, with adequate structural support, sit back into the roof (see Figures 10.4 and 10.5).

Supporting Gable Roofs

Roofs that slope downward from a central ridge in a gable roof are the most common form for the main roof of most houses. Framing a gable roof with rafters is a little more complicated than framing over a shed roof, because in addition to supporting the vertical loads imposed on the roof, the system must resist an outward force, or thrust, which can spread the outer walls. Horizontal ties between the rafters provide one way to resist the outward thrust by tying the rafters together. The lower the ties, the more effective they are. The attic floor joists can be effective ties, if they are continuously tied together across their span and secured to the ends of the rafters. Placed higher up, they are called collar ties, but they must

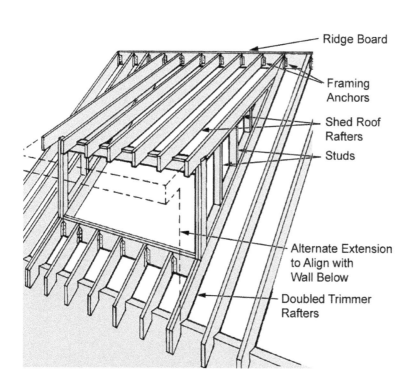

FIGURE 10.4 Shed roof dormers can spring from the ridge of the roof, as shown, or from a point downslope. The front wall can recess behind the wall below or extend out to the outer wall. Note that all framing members around the roof opening are doubled.

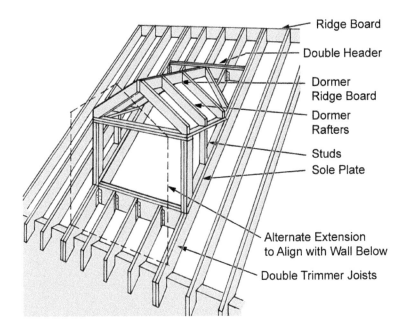

FIGURE 10.5 Framing a gable (doghouse) dormer begins with a double-framed opening in the roof plane. As with shed roof dormers, the front wall can sit back into the roof or align with the outer wall of the house.

be located in the lower third of the roof in order to be of any use in resisting thrust. This presents a dilemma in attics designed for occupancy, since placing the ties low reduces the headroom.

A bearing wall or ridge beam, either below the rafters or in the same plane (face framed) as shown in Figure 10.6, offers another way to counter thrust in gable and hipped roofs. Although a ridge beam takes on the vertical load of the rafter ends that frame into it, it should not be confused with a ridge board, which takes no vertical load, but merely provides a convenient nailer for installing the rafters and ties both slopes of the roof into a single diaphragm for better resisting wind or seismic forces. Gable roofs are also used for doghouse dormers, framed as shown in Figure 10.7.

Sizing Rafters
Rafters are sized according to the loads they carry and their spacing. Rafters are usually spaced 12, 16, or 24" (305, 406, or 610 mm) apart to fit standard sheathing panel sizes and span ratings for ½" (13-mm) and ⅝" (16-mm-) thick sheathing. Rafters must be stiff

FIGURE 10.6 The outward thrust of a pitched roof can be countered by collar ties between the rafters or by the attic floor joists, if care is taken to ensure structural continuity, end to end (left). The attic floor cannot be used for this purpose in attics with unbraced kneewalls (right).

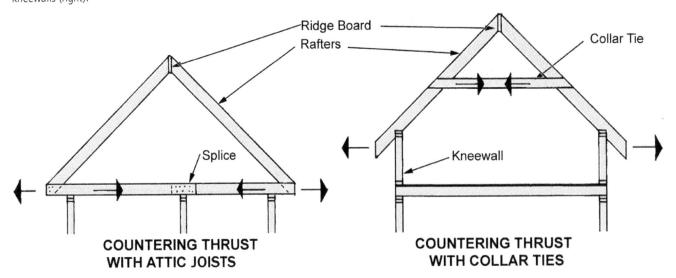

COUNTERING THRUST WITH ATTIC JOISTS

COUNTERING THRUST WITH COLLAR TIES

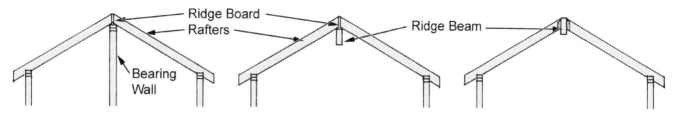

BEARING WALL **RIDGE BEAM BELOW RAFTERS** **RIDGE BEAM IN PLANE OF RAFTERS**

FIGURE 10.7 A bearing wall under the ridge or ridge beam offers an alternative means to counter thrust in pitched roofs.

enough to support their loads without sagging excessively (deflection). Allowable deflection for rafters that do not have ceilings attached to their underside is usually limited to 1/240 of the span (L/240). If the ceiling is attached, the deflection should be limited to 1/360 (L/360)of the span to prevent cracking of the plaster or drywall ceiling. The span for rafters on a sloped roof is the projected horizontal distance between supports rather than their actual length.

As with floor joists, rafters carry two different kinds of loads, live loads and dead loads. Live loads for roofs come from wind and snow and vary from region to region. The local building inspection department is the source for live loads. For dead loads, allow 5 to 8 pounds per square foot (psf) (0.34 kN/m^2 to 0.38 kN/m^2) for light framing with shingle roofing and 8 to 14 psf (0.38kN/m^2 to 0.67 kN/m^2) for tile or slate roofing. Once you have determined the spans, spacing, loading, and allowable deflection, you can select rafters from span tables published by lumber trade associations, following the procedure described for selecting floor joists in Chapter 7. Table 10.2 is an example.

TABLE 10.2 Rafter Selection

Southern Pine, 40-psf live load, 10-psf dead load, deflection limited to L/240									
Size	Spacing	Grade and Spacing (ft-in.)							
	(inches on center)	Dense Select Structural	Select Structural	Non-Dense Select Structural	No. 1	No. 1 Non-Dense	No. 2	No. 2 Non-Dense	No. 3
2×6	12	13–0	12–9	12–6	12–6	12–3	12–3	11–9	10–0
	16	11–10	11–7	11–5	11–5	11–2	11–2	10–8	8–8
	24	10–4	10–2	9–11	9–11	9–9	9–1	8–9	7–1
2×8	12	17–2	16–10	16–6	16–6	16–2	16–2	15–6	12–9
	16	15–7	15–3	15–0	15–0	14–8	14–5	13–10	11–0
	24	13–7	13–4	13–1	13–1	12–6	11–10	11–3	9–0
2×10	12	21–10	21–6	21–1	21–1	20–8	19–11	18–11	15–1
	16	19–10	19–6	19–2	19–2	18–5	17–3	16–5	13–0
	24	17–4	17–0	16–9	15–8	15–1	14–1	13–5	10–8
2×12	12	26–0	26–0	25–7	25–7	25–1	20–2	19–5	15–6
	16	24–2	23–9	23–3	22–10	21–11	20–2	19–5	15–6
	24	21–1	20–9	20–4	18–8	17–11	16–6	15–10	12–8
Source: Southern Pine Marketing Council, *Maximum Spans:* Southern Pine Joists & Rafters.									

Trussed Roofs

When structural components are configured into triangles they can support imposed loads more efficiently than when acting singly, as beams or rafters. Roof trusses constructed with this approach can be custom designed for exposed applications, such as over a cathedral ceiling, or prefabricated for concealed applications. Lightweight, prefabricated trusses are widely used in residential roofs. The most common consist of 2×4s and/or 2×6s connected by sheet metal plates (gussets). Trusses made of light-gauge metal are also increasing in use. Although trusses cost more in material than rafters and beams, they save enormously in labor because they are prefabricated in a factory and arrive on the job ready to place. The labor savings increase with the number of trusses used. (See Figure 10.8.)

Another big advantage of trusses is their ability to span greater distances between supports. Trusses easily span the total width of a typical house, 25 to 40′ (7,620 to 12,192 mm), leaving the space below completely open and flexible for use as living or storage space.

Prefabricated lightweight trusses typically are spaced 24″ (610 mm) apart. That is about the only constant, since trusses can be designed and fabricated in almost any shape that can be subdivided into triangles. This advantage alone makes them useful for framing spaces with unusual ceiling geometry. The simple gable form truss is the most economical shape to roof an interior that has a flat ceiling. Scissors-shape trusses are available for cathedral ceilings. Another truss shape suits a roof where one side has a different slope from the other. Trusses also can be shaped to accommodate thicker insulation or wide openings. Stepped trusses allow framing a hipped roof without additional stick framing (see Figure 10.9). Typically, the designer or builder determines the span, pitch, and loading of the trusses, then transmits these data to the fabricator, who engineers and fabricates them.

Panel Roofs

Post-and-beam framing and roofs framed with widely spaced, heavy trusses are often clad with structural insulated panels (SIPs) as mentioned in regard to walls in post-and-beam houses in Chapter 8. These composite sandwiches of sheathing/foam/sheathing serve as the roof substrate and insulation system and provide a nail-base material on the inside for attaching the ceiling. Most SIP roof panels can be spaced up to 48″ (1,219 mm) apart. In post-and-beam houses where the roofing supports typically are spaced at 8-, 10-, or 12′ intervals (2,438-, 3,048-, or 3,5458-mm), purlins (subframing members) are placed across the roof beams 48″ (1,219 mm) apart.

FIGURE 10.8 Prefabricated, engineered, lightweight roof trusses can be made in many shapes and span openings up to 60′ (18,288 mm). They must be ordered to exact specifications, since they cannot be altered on the job site.

Roofs for Cathedral Ceilings

Varying ceiling heights from one room to the next can add importance to certain rooms and make the house a more interesting grouping of spaces. One way to do this is by raising ceilings in some rooms and lowering them in others. Another is a sloped or cathedral ceiling. Any of the three framing systems described earlier can be used to frame a cathedral ceiling

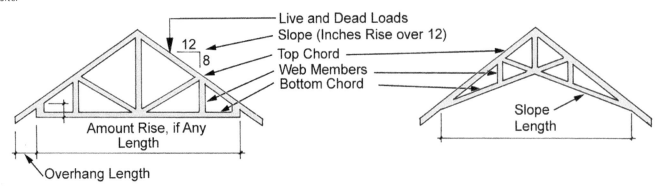

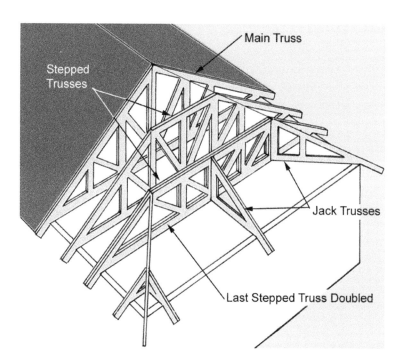

FIGURE **10.9** Hipped roofs can be framed with either rafters or special trusses, each with a different profile, as shown here.

(see Figure 10.10). In rafter systems, the ceiling material is simply attached to the underside of the rafters. Similarly, the interior sheathing of an SIP roof becomes the substrate for the ceiling. In trussed roofs, the trusses must be configured into a shape with a pitched bottom chord (the member of the truss abutting the ceiling). Scissors trusses offer a way to do this.

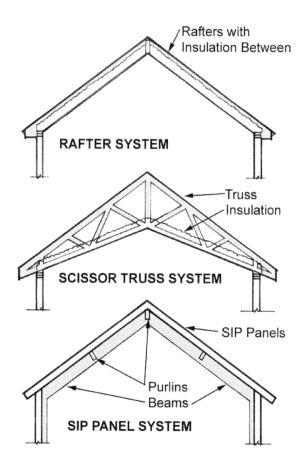

FIGURE **10.10** Three ways to frame a cathedral ceiling.

ROOF SHEATHING MATERIALS

The oriented strandboard (OSB) that makes the top of an SIP sandwich on panel-framed roofs is the sheathing layer that provides a substrate for the roofing material. Rafter- and truss-framed roofs require a separate sheathing layer. Solid boards laid across the main framing served this purpose in houses built before the advent of panel sheathing. Most roofs now are sheathed with solid panels of plywood or OSB, ½ (13 mm) or ⅝" (16 mm) thick, installed with the long panel dimension running across the framing. The span rating for the material is stamped on the surface.

An underlayment material installed between the sheathing and roofing material provides a secondary barrier to moisture penetration. Roofing felt, a material consisting of organic fibers pressed together in a bituminous (petroleum based) matrix, served this purpose for most homes in the past and is still recommended for certain types of roofing, such as tiles and wood shingles and shakes. For other types of roofing, newer polymer-based underlayments are easier to install and are claimed to have better performance. Both types are installed with roofing nails and sheet metal or plastic washers. In areas with severe winters, an additional strip of elastomeric material (ice shield) often is added at the eaves for extra protection against water penetration.

INSULATION AND MOISTURE CONTROL

As with walls, roofs in all climates must be insulated to control heat loss and gain. Also, the thermal insulation must be coordinated with a moisture control strategy. This is especially important for roofs above kitchens and baths, which generate more moisture than other rooms.

The location of the insulation depends on the shape of the roof structure and use of the space inside. For a cathedral ceiling attached to the underside of the roof framing, the insulation can go in the cavities of the framing above the roof sheathing, between the framing and the ceiling, or in some combination.

Houses with attics offer different options. If the attic is sealed off or used only for storage, the insulation can go in the attic floor (see Figure 10.11). For occupied attics, where the space will be heated and/or cooled, the insulation must be placed above and around the sides of the occupied space (see Figure 10.12).

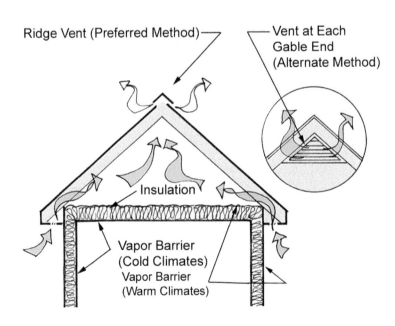

FIGURE 10.11 A "cold" roof system contains the insulation in the attic floor. Vents in the soffit and ridge prevent moisture buildup in the attic. If a ridge vent is not feasible, other means of evacuating the air may be used, such as gable vents (inset).

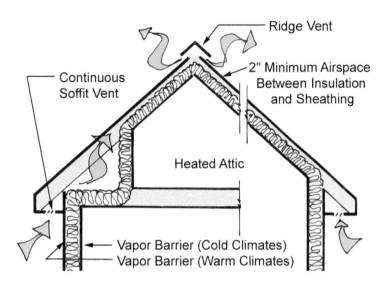

FIGURE 10.12 Occupied attics and cathedral ceiling roofs require insulation around the heated space. Roofs insulated with closed-cell spray foam need no air space between the roof sheathing and insulation. A pathway from eave to ridge is required for other types.

Roofs can be insulated with closed-cell spray foam applied to the inside of the sheathing in the same way as it is applied on walls. For roofs insulated with other materials, an air space between the insulation and roof sheathing is recommended for two reasons. First, it keeps the roof cooler year-round, thus extending the life of the roofing material. Second, ventilation prevents ice dams at the eaves in cold climates. In winter, a roof that stays cold prevents alternate freezing and thawing of ice, which leads to ice dams that cause water to penetrate the roof.

To be effective, the air space must provide a pathway of outside air from the eaves up to and through the ridge. The entire attic space serves as the air space in an open (cold) attic. In a closed (heated) attic, the air space is between the insulation and roof sheathing. It can be achieved by installing foam plastic insulation baffles on the underside of the roof sheathing prior to installing insulation between the rafters.

As stated for walls, humidity is higher indoors in winter than the colder, drier air outside. As the warm, moist air migrates through the building envelope—in this case, the roof/ceiling—it can condense to cause deterioration of the framing members and ceiling finish. The first line of defense against this moisture is a good moisture barrier, usually a layer of 4- or 6-millimeter polyethylene sheet, installed between the insulation and the ceiling finish. If foil-faced foam insulation is used, as it might be in a cathedral ceiling, the joints can be taped to make a good moisture barrier. Closed-cell spray foam insulation provides its own moisture barrier.

ROOFING MATERIALS

The most important function of the "skin" atop the house is shedding water. Other criteria include initial cost, durability, resistance to wind and fire, and local code requirements. Appearance also figures high on the list with most homeowners. The color, texture, and pattern of the roofing must blend with the house for a successful job. Brief descriptions of several common roofing materials are presented next, followed by a table that compares them in summary form (See Table 10.3).

Wood Shingles and Shakes

Cedar and redwood shingles, common home roofing materials prior to the 1940s, now cost so much that they are out of reach of many homeowners.

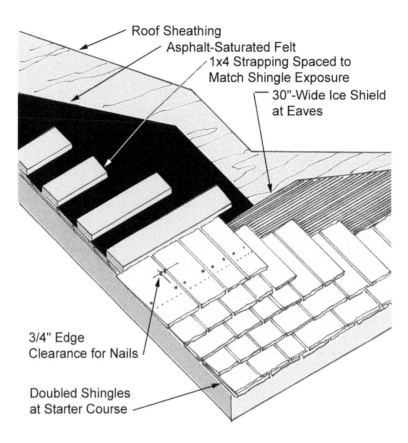

Roof Sheathing
Asphalt-Saturated Felt
1x4 Strapping Spaced to
Match Shingle Exposure
30"-Wide Ice Shield
at Eaves

3/4" Edge
Clearance for Nails

Doubled Shingles
at Starter Course

FIGURE 10.13 Wood shingles typically are installed on strapping the same distance apart as the shingle exposure to prevent entrapped moisture on the undersides of the shingles. Saturated felt below the strapping provides a secondary moisture barrier.

Wood shingles today are available as single units or ganged together in strips. Both install over plywood or OSB sheathing that has been covered with a layer of roofing felt (see Figure 10.13). Shingles are either applied directly over the felt or to 1 × 3 strapping (furring strips) attached horizontally over the felt at the same spacing as the shingle exposure, usually 5½" (140 mm). Recently introduced "shingle breather" materials, available in rolls, are an alternative to strapping. This method allows the undersides of the shingles to breathe, which prolongs their life. The first shingle course is doubled and projects 2" (51 mm) over the drip edge.

Asphalt and Fiberglass Shingles

Asphalt-based shingles reign as the most popular roofing for today's homes because of their low cost; wide range of colors, patterns, and textures; and ease of installation and repair. Traditional asphalt shingles consist of an organic fiber mat saturated with asphalt and topped with mineral granules, which protect the asphalt from degrading under exposure to sunlight. Fiberglass mats were introduced in the early 1970s, to replace the organic fiber mats, reducing the weight and petroleum use, since the latter is used to make asphalt. Today fiberglass shingles are the most common types sold and offer warranties of 20 to 50 years (see Figure 10.14).

Both shingle types come in profiles ranging from flat to textured (architectural), with colored, mineral surface granules in tans, greens, red, grays, and black. The textured varieties achieve a sculptured look by alternating thicker (laminated) layers with single layers of material. As with wood shingles, asphalt and fiberglass shingles are nailed to the sheathing over a layer of roofing felt or polymer underlayment. The starter strip is doubled and, for extra protection in damp locations, set over a strip of bituminous water/ice shield.

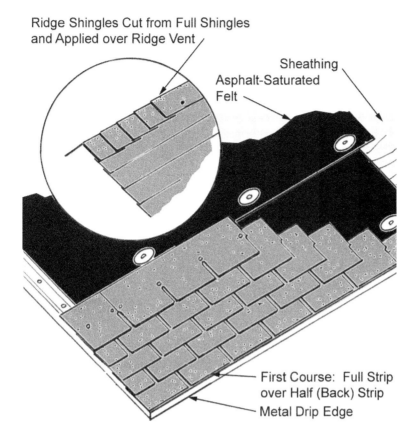

Ridge Shingles Cut from Full Shingles
and Applied over Ridge Vent

Sheathing
Asphalt-Saturated
Felt

First Course: Full Strip
over Half (Back) Strip

Metal Drip Edge

FIGURE 10.14 Asphalt/fiberglass shingles detail.

Metal Roofing

Metal roofing, previously associated with barns and industrial buildings, is now coming into its own as a high-end residential material. The best metal roofing is made of terne, an alloy of metal and copper. Less costly options in steel and aluminum are available in a wide range of baked-enamel colors. Panels 24″ (609 mm) wide in lengths up to 18′ (5,486 mm) make up the bulk of residential metal roofing.

Metal roofing panels are connected to the roof deck by metal clips attached to the edges on the long sides (see Figure 10.15). The edges are raised in various shapes to conceal the fasteners and overlap the adjacent panel for a weather seal. Smaller ribs run down the middle section of the panels to prevent dimpling. Special shapes are required at ridges, changes of directions, and intersections with protrusions, such as dormers and chimneys. These details always stand out and often look awkward, making metal roofing a better candidate for simple roof forms rather than for those with complicated shapes or a lot of protrusions.

Slate

Natural slate is a high-quality roofing material that has been in use for centuries. Installed properly, it can last for many years. Roofing slate is quarried from beds and split into thin sheets. Their natural, irregular shapes have subtle color variations ranging from blacks and grays to blues and greens—some even include reds and browns. Slate is also fireproof.

On the downsides, slate is very expensive, and its brittleness makes it a poor choice in a hurricane-prone area or under a large tree that can drop limbs off from time to time. Standard slates are 12 by 16 and 14 by 20″ (305 by 406 mm and 356 by 508 mm) long and 3⁄16 or ¼″ (5 or 6 mm) thick. Sheets vary somewhat from these target dimensions. Each slate is

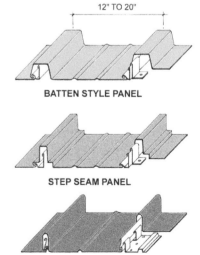

FIGURE 10.15 Metal roofing, once used only in commercial and industrial buildings, is now a popular choice for residences.

laid over a wood deck covered with roofing felt and is secured with two copper nails. Copper wire and roofing cement secure pieces near ridges and hips. A cant strip is installed under the starter course to give it the same pitch as successive courses.

Roofing Tiles

Sun-baked clay tiles topped the roofs of the houses of ancient Crete. Today's fired clay tiles impart the Mediterranean look so common to the stucco homes of California and Florida. Clay tiles come in various profiles and earth-based colors. In addition to clay tiles made by fusing the material together in a kiln, there are other tiles made by other processes, such as concrete tiles made with Portland cement.

All tile roofs are durable, long lasting, and fireproof and are excellent at shedding water. On the downside, tiles impose a hefty dead load requiring a structure capable of carrying the added weight of about 14 psf ($0.67kN/m^2$). Tiles, like slates, are brittle materials that are vulnerable to damage from wind-borne objects and earthquakes. Tiles install over felt-topped roof sheathing, anchored with ring-shank nails or screws over roofs with slopes of at least 3:12. Local codes in high-wind areas may require hurricane clips at ridges and eaves. Metal flashing seals joints at intersections with walls. Mortar is used at ridges and roof bends.

Single-Membrane Roofing

Flat roofs and roofs under upper-story balconies are often roofed with a single membrane made of elastomeric materials, such as EPDM or neoprene. The roof membrane bonds to the roof either by mechanical anchors or adhesive, or it can be loosely laid and held in place by gravel. This type of roofing has all but replaced traditional hot-mopped asphalt traditionally used on low-slope and flat roofs, due to its ease of installation and longer life. A typical residential application might include a roof below an upper-story deck. Membrane roofing is expensive and because it is mostly applied to roofs with very low slopes, it must be installed correctly to avoid leaks. Flashings between abutting walls and other roofs must be installed as well as drip edges at outside perimeters.

TABLE 10.3 Comparing Roofing Materials

	Asphalt Shingles	Wood Shingles	Metal	Tile	Slate	Membrane Roofing
Minimum roof slope (inches rise per foot horizontal)	3:12 2:12[1]	4:12	2½:12	4½:12[2] 2½:12[2]	6:12	(none)
Material cost	Low	Medium	Medium	High	High	High
Installation cost	Low	Medium	Medium	Medium	High	Medium
Life span, years	20–50	10–40	15–40+	20+	30–100	15–30
Weight, psf	2.25–3.85	3–4	0.5–2.7	3.75–11	5–10	2–10[3]
Fire rating[4]	A	B	A	A	A	A

[1]2:12 slope requires installation for "low-slope" applications.
[2]Clay tiles require a minimum slope of 4¼:12; cement tiles can go down to 2½:12.
[3]Higher values are for systems using gravel ballast.
[4]An "A" rating is best. Wood shingles and shakes are treated with a fire retardant and rated "B." Untreated wood shingles and shakes, which are combustible, carry no fire rating.

ROOF EDGES

What happens at the eaves and intersections with projections through the roof is just as important as the choice of roofing material. Because these points interrupt the continuity of the surface, they are the sites most vulnerable to leaks. Keeping water out requires adequate flashing and sealing at each intersection with an adjoining roof surface, wall, chimney, and vent pipe. The roofing itself might suffice for some terminations. For example, asphalt shingles can be bent around the ridges and valleys of a hipped roof with no additional flashing material. But more typically, these junctions require separate flashing material formed into a special shape (see Figure 10.16).

Copper is the best all-purpose flashing for quality roofs of wood shingles, slate, or tiles. Aluminum, galvanized steel, and polyvinyl chloride (PVC) are also used. Nails for metal flashing must resist rust as well as corrosion through contact with a dissimilar flashing metal. Copper nails are used with copper; aluminum nails are used with aluminum. Galvanized or stainless steel nails pair with galvanized steel and vinyl flashing.

SUMMARY

Residential roofs can be constructed in a wide variety of shapes and materials to blend with the style of the home and regional considerations. Regardless of their form and materials, they all must be constructed to bear the loads imposed by winds, snows, and seismic forces while shedding water.

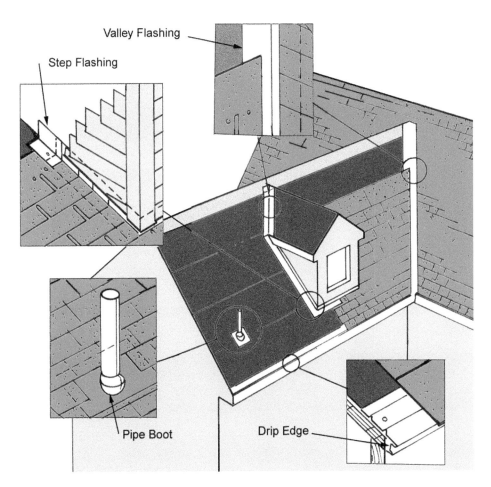

FIGURE 10.16 Roofs must be properly flashed at points where the roofing is interrupted by a projection or abuts another surface. Some critical locations are shown here.

Roofs can be framed with single rafters, trusses, or panels, according to the structure of the building, and be supported by bearing walls and ridge beams. Outward thrust, a problem in gable roofs, can be countered with central supports, ridge beams, or horizontal ties.

Roofs covering cathedral ceilings can be constructed in various ways, with good detailing to address thermal and moisture issues. These roofs can be insulated at the ceiling or roof level, with adequate attention given to ventilation.

Homeowners have a wide variety of roofing materials to choose from. Factors influencing the best choice include the slope of the roof, style of building, initial and lifetime cost, weight, and fire rating.

CHAPTER REVIEW

1. How many slopes does a gambrel roof have? (See "Roof Forms" Figure 10.1, page 92)
2. What two functions do dormers serve? (See "Dormers" page 93)
3. What ways can the ridge of a gable roof be supported? (See "Supporting Gable Roofs" pages 93–94)
4. What function do horizontal ties provide in a roof structure? (See "Supporting Gable Roofs" page 93)
5. What are live loads? (See "Sizing Rafters" page 95)
6. What advantages do trussed roofs offer over stick-framed roofs? (See "Trussed Roofs" page 96)
7. What factors determine the location of the insulation in a roof? (See "Insulation and Moisture Control" pages 98–99)
8. What advantages do fiberglass shingles have over asphalt shingles? (See "Asphalt and Fiberglass Shingles" page 100)
9. Where might membrane roofing be used in a residence? (See "Single-Membrane Roofing" page 102)

Interior Walls and Ceilings

As a kitchen and bath designer, you likely will be more involved with the interior walls and ceilings than with the exterior ones. Because these are the surfaces the client sees, you will naturally want to select the finish materials and colors with care and skill. However, what lies below the finish surface is just as important—even more so in kitchens and baths, where walls have must stand up to high moisture levels, heat, and continual use. This chapter discusses the underlying construction of walls and ceilings and how they can be designed and constructed to serve the demands put on them.

Learning Objective 1: Discuss how an interior wall can be designed to meet the needs imposed on it.

Learning Objective 2: Recognize the areas requiring special framing and the means of achieving it.

Learning Objective 3: Identify the problems and solutions that may be encountered in remodeling walls and ceilings.

PARTITIONS

The interior partitions (walls) of a home are not just ways to divide one space from the next. They perform one or more of these functions:

- Provide acoustic separation between rooms so that sounds from one room are reduced or isolated.
- Provide visual separation between rooms to shut out unwanted light and impart privacy.
- Control access to rooms where security of the contents is desirable.
- Contain water (showers, baths).
- Control airflow between rooms to allow different temperatures and to contain odors
- Provide structural support for floors or roofs above

Meeting these demands requires thoughtful design and competent construction. The next sections describe the various partition systems currently in use.

Stud Walls

The interior walls of most homes in North America are constructed with studs and clad with drywall. These walls go up quickly, are easy to erect in tight spaces, and provide cavities for pipes and wires. When it is time to remodel, these walls are relatively easy to alter or remove.

Wood Stud Partitions

The wood studs that frame most interior walls consist of 2 × 4s 16″ (406 mm) on center, capped with a single 2 × 4 top plate and set on a 2 × 4 bottom plate. If there is enough space on the adjacent floor, the wall sections are nailed together using the floor deck as a working surface, then tilted up into place and fastened to the abutting partitions. Where space prohibits this approach, the base plate is nailed down and the studs are installed one by one (see Figure 11.1).

Wood stud partitions can be tweaked in several ways to suit special needs. If the piping in plumbing walls cannot be contained within a 3½″ (89-mm) cavity, the cavity can be increased to 5½″ (140 mm) by using 2 × 6 studs. Ducts that run in the stud cavity also may require thicker cavities. Interior bearing walls call for a double top plate and properly sized headers to span any openings. Partitions in kitchens and baths require blocking between the studs to support cabinets and fixtures (see Figures 11.2 and 11.3). Blocking is also used to adapt openings in the studs for recessed items, such as medicine cabinets. Finally, if the wall finish is

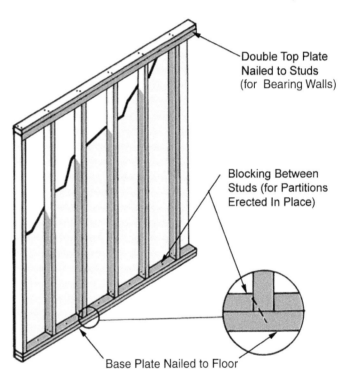

FIGURE 11.1 A typical interior wood stud partition. If the section can be assembled on the floor, then tilted up, the bottom plate is simply nailed to the studs. If not, the bottom plate is first nailed down, followed by the studs, one by one.

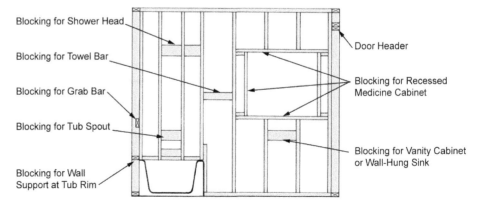

FIGURE 11.2 Stud walls in bathrooms require horizontal blocking to support fixtures, grab bars, and around openings. It is a good idea to build in blocking for grab bars in case they need to be installed later.

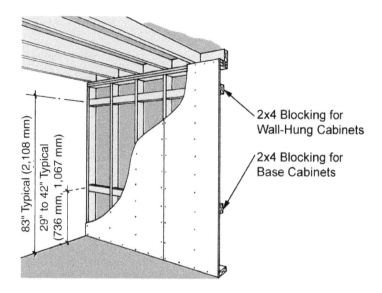

FIGURE 11.3 New stud walls in kitchens should contain horizontal blocking for attaching wall and base cabinets.

anything but drywall, a substrate material may be needed, such as a backerboard under tile, as described in Chapter 12.

Steel Stud Partitions

Steel studs for interior residential partitions are becoming more popular as the quality of wood declines and prices rise. Carpenters who formerly insisted on wood are increasingly willing to learn the sheet metal skills necessary to install steel studs, swayed by the lighter weight, consistency, and dependability of the product. Because steel studs are a manufactured product, they are consistently stable, straight, and uniform, unlike wood. Holes spaced at intervals in the studs provide spaces for pipes or wires.

Steel studs are cold formed from sheet steel in gauges of 25, 20, 18, 16, 14, and 12. (The lower the number, the heavier the gauge.) For typical residential partitions, 25-gauge studs work well.

Studs come in widths of 1⅝, 2½, 3⅝, 4, and 6" (41, 64, 92, 406, and 457 mm), in lengths up to 20' (6,096 mm). Installation typically follows a 1–2–3 sequence. A C-shape track (stud runner) is first screwed to the floor and ceiling (see Figure 11.4). The studs are next fitted into the tracks 16 or 24" (406 or 610 mm) on center and attached with screws. The studs feel flimsy until the final step, attaching the wall finish material, is completed.

Wood 2x stock added to door openings, as shown in Figure 11.5, provides attachment for door frames.

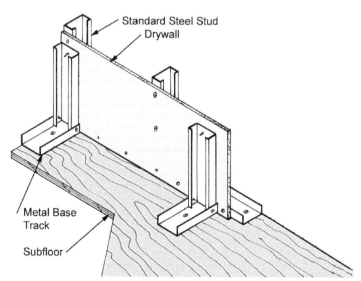

FIGURE 11.4 Steel stud partitions consist of C-shape studs that nest into C-shape tracks screwed to the floor and ceiling.

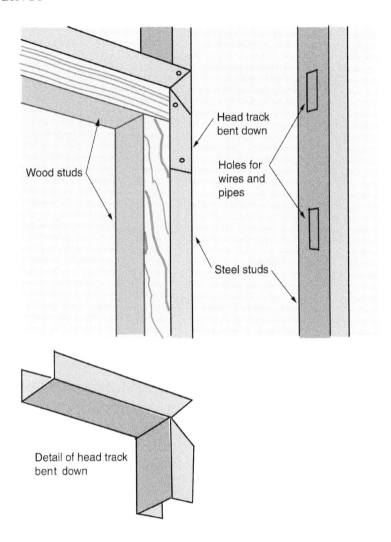

Head track
bent down

Holes for
wires and
pipes

Wood studs

Steel studs

Detail of head track
bent down

FIGURE 11.5 Track sections frame a door opening. The head track is cut longer, the flanges are cut, and a section is bent down to attach to the vertical, as shown below. Wood stud jambs are then added as an attachment for door frames.

Sound-Dampening Partitions

As mentioned, one of the functions of interior partitions is ensuring acoustic privacy. Any parent with teenagers in the household appreciates the need for isolating the transmission of sound within the house. Sound transmission also can be a concern in rooms adjacent to bathrooms, which are exposed to the noise of running water and flushing toilets. Masonry walls have enough mass to make them naturally resistant to sound transmission but are not practical options in homes with stud-framed interior walls.

Sound transmission through walls is measured in STC (sound transmission classification) units. How various STC ratings affect what can be heard on the other side of the wall are listed in Table 11.1.

TABLE 11.1

STC Rating	Sound Transmission
25	Normal speech can easily be understood
30	Loud speech can be understood
35	Loud speech heard but not understood
42	Loud speech audible as a murmur
45	Must strain to hear loud speech
48	Some loud speech barely audible
50	Loud speech not audible
Data obtained from the National Association of Home Builders and other sources.	

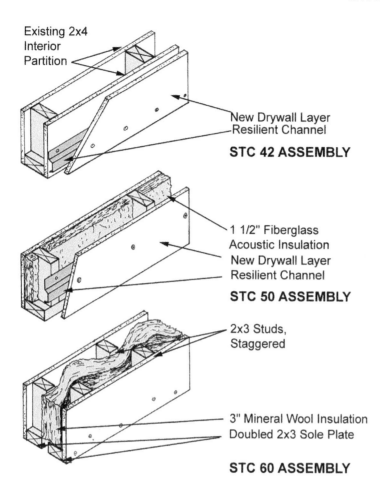

Existing 2x4
Interior
Partition

New Drywall Layer
Resilient Channel
STC 42 ASSEMBLY

1 1/2" Fiberglass
Acoustic Insulation
New Drywall Layer
Resilient Channel
STC 50 ASSEMBLY

2x3 Studs,
Staggered

3" Mineral Wool Insulation
Doubled 2x3 Sole Plate

STC 60 ASSEMBLY

FIGURE 11.6 Three ways to increase the sound-dampening capability of a stud wall.

Standard wood or steel stud partitions clad with drywall do little to shield one room from noise in the next one. However, they can be improved to decrease their sound transmission, as shown in Figure 11.6. Each method cuts sound transmission by adding mass, adding sound-dampening insulation, isolating one wall surface from the others, or a combination of these. Since sound also travels through openings in ducts and door cracks, it is probably not cost effective to try to achieve an STC of greater than 50 without also isolating the ductwork and installing gaskets around the doors. Gasket use is somewhat unusual with interior doors.

SPECIAL FRAMING

It would be unusual for a home requiring the services of a kitchen/bath designer to consist of nothing beyond straight, unbroken interior partitions. Curved walls, surrounds for bath fixtures, and arched openings are some of the ingredients that you should have on your design palette. Although you will not need to know exactly how to frame these items, a general idea of their construction enables you to know what is feasible and what to include in your drawings and specifications.

Enclosing Tubs and Spas

The three-fixture 5- by 7' (1.524- by 22,134-m) bathroom is no longer the norm. Today's baths tend to be larger and likely have more features. Also, there is more choice in fixtures. Some of these fixtures, such as pedestal sinks and claw-foot bathtubs, simply stand free in

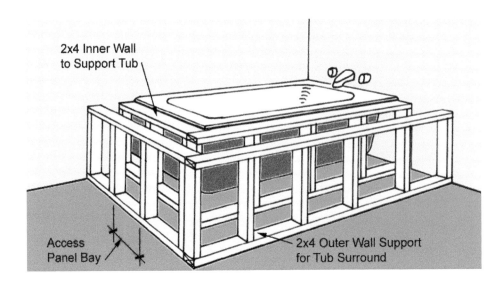

FIGURE 11.7 Whirlpools (spas) typically sit on single or double knee walls with an access to the equipment provided at one end.

an open space. Others, such as toilets, tubs, and whirlpools, are designed to fit into site-built enclosures that may be straight or curved. These enclosures are made of stick framing of the same general type used for interior partitions with added provisions for attached items and finishes. When laying out the design, check the manufacturer's rough-in dimensions of the fixture so you can allow enough clearance for both the fixture and the wall finish above it. Fully recessed bathtubs or whirlpools require support by a single or double cripple wall framed with 2 × 4s. Specify proper blocking to support the bottom of the unit per the manufacturer's data.

Whirlpools are usually larger and hold more water than bathtubs and come with equipment that heats and circulates the water. These differences make the enclosure for a whirlpool more complicated than for a bathtub (see Figure 11.7). In a renovation, first consider how the tub unit can be moved into place. Doorways and stairs in an existing house may not be wide enough for a large unit, which may have to be moved in through a nearby window or opening created in the wall. Next, check out the weight of the unit when full and make sure the floor structure below the installation site is capable of supporting the weight. The supporting platform can consist of a single- or double-width knee (short) wall. Users can step over a single wall but must sit on the platform created by a double wall and swing their legs over into the bathtub. Be sure to specify the location of the access panel for the pump at the plumbing end. Also pin down the location of any blocking required in the surrounding walls for grab bars or other items to be mounted to the walls. Consider specifying insulation around the platform walls both to help control noise and to keep the water warm.

Shower Enclosures

Showers today are just as likely to be separate as combined with the tub. Separate showers are enclosed in several ways, depending on the type of shower. A site-built shower with tiled floor and walls can fit any wall configuration. The enclosing walls are framed with studs similar to other interior partitions with solid blocking installed to support the shower head and any grab bars or other items to be attached to the walls, as shown in Figure 11.8. The floor can be a one-piece preassembled base or tiled, as described in Chapter 12.

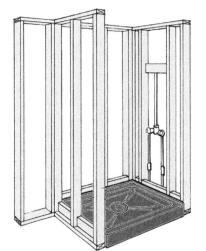

FIGURE 11.8 A site-built shower can surround a tiled floor or prefabricated shower base, as shown.

Fiberglass shower bases come in several sizes and shapes for fully recessed or corner installations. However, the enclosing walls must follow the shape of the base faithfully. The rough opening dimensions of the base determine the position of the studs.

A preassembled shower is shipped as a one-piece unit, with ceiling, walls, and floor formed seamlessly out of acrylic or fiberglass-reinforced polyester (see Figure 11.9). It simply mounts into a stud surround built to the specified rough opening dimensions.

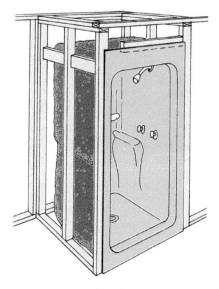

FIGURE 11.9 Studs enclosing a prefabricated shower unit must be coordinated with the requirements of the manufacturer's specifications.

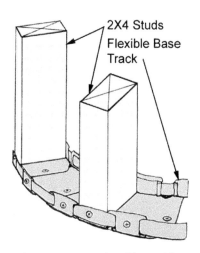

FIGURE 11.10 An adjustable metal floor and ceiling track provides the base for curved walls. The track is simply nailed to the floor and ceiling in the desired curve, then the studs are installed.

Curved Surfaces

Another trend in home design is an increased use of curved walls. Framing a curved wall is similar to framing a rectilinear wall, except that the top and sole plates must take the shape of the curve (see Figure 11.10). Top and base plates can be made of two layers of plywood cut on an arc or metal tracks specifically made for this purpose. Any material that can be bent into a curve can be used for the finish. A common choice is two layers of ¼″ (6 mm) drywall, installed after wetting the top (outward-facing) surface.

Along with curved walls, arched passageways add elegance and interest to many of today's kitchen and bath designs. Three types of arch shapes are common: Roman (half circle), segmental, and elliptical. An arch curves upward from a horizontal spring line that stretches across the opening. Roman arches rise highest above the spring line, making them impractical for wide openings in rooms with standard-height ceilings. Segmented arches are flatter but have sharp corners at the spring points. Elliptical arches can rise as much as desired and meet the spring line at a flatter curve.

All arches are framed below a straight top plate and header, and the header must carry any load above if the wall is a bearing wall (see Figure 11.11). The arch can be framed with sides cut to the shape of the arch and 2 × 4 spacers set between the sides along the bottom of the arch, as shown in Figure 11.12. The sides can be made of 1x pine if the arch height is less than 11″ (279 mm), or ¾″-(19 mm) thick plywood for higher arches. Special PVC and metal corner beads are available to fit around a curve for plaster or drywall wall finish.

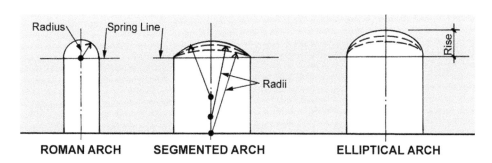

FIGURE 11.11 Roman arches are half circles with the center point along the spring line. The center point for segmented arches lies below the spring line—the lower the point, the flatter the arch. Elliptical arches can be flat or rise as high as desired.

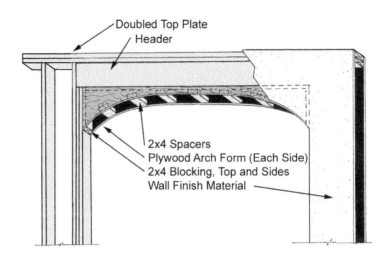

FIGURE 11.12 One way to frame an arch into an opening using plywood sides and 2 × 4 spacers.

Accommodating Recessed Items

Medicine cabinets, toilet paper holders, and other items recessed into the wall require a rough opening with framing on all sides. Most medicine cabinets are available in depths that allow them to fit into a standard 3½″ (89 mm) stud cavity, but they extend into the entire depth of the cavity, with nothing except the wall finish of the adjacent room on the backside. This creates a sound path into the adjacent room that can be a problem. If the medicine cabinet backs up to a bedroom, for example, any sounds in the bath will be heard easily in the bedroom. Possible solutions include substituting a surface-mounted cabinet or relocating the recessed cabinet to another wall, such as one backing into a closet.

CEILING STRUCTURES

The ceiling of a room may simply be a finish material attached to the underside of the floor or roof structure above or be a separate structure built below it. The high ceilings found in many old houses may be an asset in large rooms but make small rooms seem even smaller. A new, lowered ceiling can make the room feel wider and more spacious. It also might provide a needed chase in which to enclose mechanical or electrical systems or lighting.

Codes allow ceiling heights in kitchens and baths to be as low as 7′ (2.134 m). There are two main ways to support a lowered ceiling:

1. Support the ceiling from the walls
2. Hang the ceiling from the structure above

Wall-Supported Ceilings

Framing a lowered ceiling from the walls begins by attaching ledgers to opposite walls on the long sides of the room. Joists are then attached to the ledgers (face-framed) with metal joist hangers, as shown in Figure 11.13. Since the ceiling supports no load other than its own, the joists can be sized accordingly. And if the ceiling finish material is drywall that does not have to carry the weight of insulation, it can be ½″ thick. Table 11.2 provides a guide for sizing ceiling joists.

Suspended Ceilings

Suspending a lowered ceiling from the structure above makes sense when the span is large and/or there is a need to maintain a minimum height of the ceiling joists in order to maintain a space between the structure above and a lowered ceiling for ducts. The ceiling joists are hung from the framing above with short lengths of

FIGURE 11.13 A ceiling supported by the walls is framed by attaching ledgers to the long walls and face framing the joists to the ledgers with framing clips.

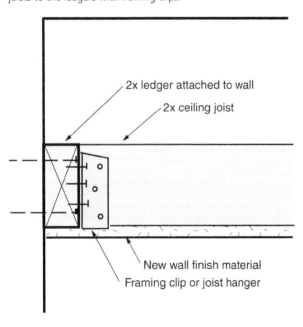

TABLE **11.2** Joists for Lowered Ceilings

Span	Joist Size and Spacing Options	
Up to 8′ (2.438 m)	2 × 4 @ 24″ (610 mm) o.c.	
Up to 10′ (3.048 m)	2 × 4 @ 16″ (406 mm) o.c.	2 × 6 @ 24″ (610 mm) o.c.
10–14′ (3.048–4.267 m)	2 × 6 @ 16″ (406 mm) o.c.	2 × 8 @ 24″ (610 mm) o.c.
14–18′ (4.267–5.486 m)	2 × 8 @ 16″ (406 mm) o.c.	2 × 10 @ 24″ (610 mm) o.c.
Adapted from data published by the Southern Pine Marketing Council. Note: Joists are assumed to carry the weight of the ceiling material only plus a 10-pound live load). o.c.: On center		

2 × 4 or 1 × 6 lumber, as shown in Figure 11.14, spaced to not exceed the maximum spans shown in Table 11.2.

Soffits

A kitchen or bath design may be improved by lowering only some portions of a ceiling. For example, left open, the space between the top of kitchen wall cabinets and the ceiling just collects dust and wastes potentially valuable space. The space can be put to use with taller cabinets that extend fully to the ceiling, creating storage space for infrequently used items, such as punch bowls and party accessories. Alternatively, the space can be closed off with a soffit, or bulkhead, flush with the face of the cabinets or extending outward to contain lighting for the countertops below, as shown in Figure 11.15. In a large bathroom, a dropped soffit over certain fixtures, such as a whirlpool, can help define these areas and make the room more interesting.

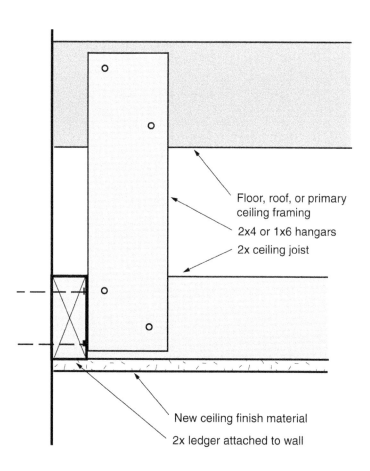

Floor, roof, or primary
ceiling framing

2x4 or 1x6 hangars

2x ceiling joist

New ceiling finish material

2x ledger attached to wall

FIGURE **11.14** Joists for a suspended ceiling are hung from short lengths of 2 × 4 or 1 × 6 lumber attached to the framing above.

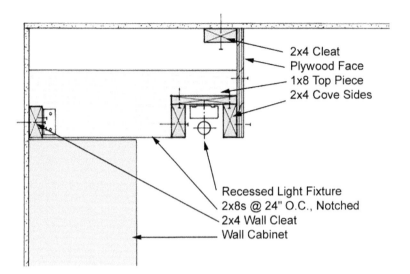

2x4 Cleat
Plywood Face
1x8 Top Piece
2x4 Cove Sides

Recessed Light Fixture
2x8s @ 24" O.C., Notched
2x4 Wall Cleat
Wall Cabinet

FIGURE 11.15 A soffit above a wall cabinet can be flush with the cabinet face or extend outward to create a niche for lighting.

MODIFYING EXISTING WALLS AND CEILINGS

Any redesign to an existing kitchen or bath will likely entail changes to the wall or ceiling surfaces for any of several reasons:

- The wall may need to be removed completely to suit the new design.
- The condition of the existing substrate or finish is too poor to apply a new finish directly.
- A chase is needed to house pipes or wiring.
- The substrate is too uneven or out of plumb for installation of new cabinetry or fixtures.
- Insulation and/or a moisture barrier is needed to upgrade an outside wall.
- A new opening is required in a bearing wall.

You can assess the condition or a wall quickly with a visual inspection, with an eye out for crumbling plaster, dampness, and cracks. Check the straightness of the walls by holding a long straightedge both vertically and horizontally along the length of the wall. When any of the above-mentioned conditions occur on interior partitions, the quickest and easiest solution might be to demolish the partition and replace it with a new one. But don't specify removal of any bearing walls unless you specify an alternative support as well. It may be necessary to gut only one side of a partition, leaving the structure and other side intact.

Modifying Bearing Walls

Partitions that merely separate interior spaces carry no structural loads and can thus be removed or altered without consequence. But bearing wall partitions that support another floor, ceiling, or roof should not be cut into without provisions for an alternate means of transferring the loads down through the structure. The first task, of course, is to be sure that it is a bearing wall. Here are some general clues for spotting interior bearing walls:

- A partition that runs along the long direction of the floor plan near the center is likely a bearing wall.
- If a wall on the first floor sits above and runs parallel to the beam line in the basement, it is likely a bearing wall.
- If there is an attic above the partition in question, inspect the area above the partition to see if joists overlap near the partition. If so, you can assume the partition carries them.

If you can't determine the structural status of a partition, obtain the advice of an architect or structural engineer before proceeding with your design. Some interior walls in earthquake-prone and high-wind regions are reinforced to counter horizontal (shear) forces. Shear walls usually can be spotted by the way they are built. An interior shear wall typically is clad in oriented strandboard (OSB) or plywood or reinforced along the diagonals with metal or wood

TABLE 11.3 Headers for Interior Bearing Walls

Clear Width of Opening in Interior Partition	Header Size	
	Yard Lumber	LVL
3' (.914 m) or less	two 2 × 8s	1 LVL 1¾ × 5½ (44 mm × 140 mm)
4–5' (1.219–1.524 m)	two 2 × 10s	1 LVL 1¾ × 5½ (44 mm × 140 mm)
5–7' (1.219 m–2.134 m)	two 2 × 12s	2 LVL 1¾ × 5½ (44 mm × 140 mm)
7–8' (1.219–2.438 m)	two 2 × 12s	2 LVL 1¾ × 7¼ (44 mm × 197 mm)
8–9' (2.438–2.743 m)	three 2 × 12s	2 LVL 1¾ × 7¼ (44 mm × 197 mm)
The assumed bending stress of the lumber (Fb) is 900 pounds per square inch. The load width assumed is 12' (3.658 m), typical for a bearing wall that runs down the middle of a 24'- (7.315-m-) wide house.		

bracing. When altering shear walls, you have to provide alternate means for transferring the shear stresses and should consult an architect or structural engineer. Interior bearing walls should be temporarily shored on both sides before their structural components are dismantled. Be sure to specify that the shoring start at the ground and extend to the floor or ceiling structure above the walls to be removed.

Any new openings in bearing walls require header beams of the appropriate size. Table 11.3 lists the required header beam sizes for partitions that support a floor or roof above. If the partition supports only an attic floor, the sizes of the table are conservative. If the partition supports more than one floor, the headers are undersize, and you should consult a building design professional for help in sizing. Doubled headers are given in the table except for spans over 8' (2.438 m), which requires three 2 × 12s. Because you can't fit three 2-bys into a 2 × 4 studwall you should consider using a laminated veneer lumber (LVL) header. Provide solid bearing under the ends of each header beam, equivalent to at least one 2 × 4 trimmer stud.

Furring Walls or Ceilings

If an existing surface is too uneven to accept a new finish or if the studs are irregularly spaced, the surface can be made even by attaching furring strips (strapping) across the framing. Furring strips also provide supports for equipment or cabinets, and the space between the furring and old wall can contain pipes, wires, or insulation, providing the proper protection is placed over any wires thus enclosed to prevent puncturing from nails or screws.

The furring material can be standard 1 × 3 wood furring strips, if nothing more than a nail-base substrate is the goal. 1 × 3 furring strips are too thin to even out an uneven wall unless shims are inserted at the hollow portions of the wall. Shimming can be avoided by using stiffer furring made from 2 × 3s or 2 × 4s (see Figure 11.16). Another reason for using 2× furring is that when new wiring must be run through the gap created by the furring, it must be held at least 1¼" (32 mm) back from the face of the framing to meet the electrical code and to prevent the wiring from being punctured by nails. Of course, if the old wall/ceiling finish is stripped off, the wiring can run in the wall cavity.

Sistering Studs

Scabbing new "sister" joists onto the sides of existing ones can level an uneven floor, as discussed in Chapter 7.

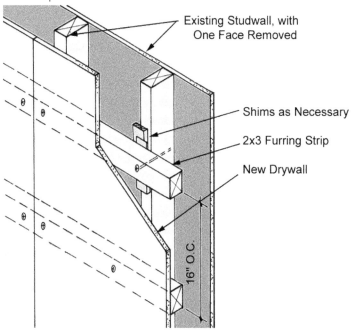

FIGURE 11.16 For a variety of reasons, existing walls often must be furred (strapped) out. The method shown here entails stripping off the old wall finish and attaching furring strips to the framing. Shims between the furring and studs adjust for out-of-plumb or irregular studs.

Existing Studwall, with One Face Removed

Shims as Necessary

2x3 Furring Strip

New Drywall

16" O.C.

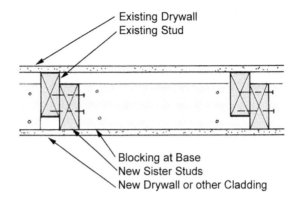

FIGURE 11.17 Adding sister studs onto the existing studs can even out the wall substrate and/or provide needed additional space or piping, insulation, or ducts.

In the same way, sister studs can even out a wall or increase its thickness once the old finish has been stripped off (see Figure 11.17). Before you specify this method, however, make sure the existing studs are spaced close enough together to provide a sound support for the wall finish material. If they are too far apart, you'll probably be better off furring the wall with strips applied horizontally over the old studs, as described above.

SUMMARY

The interior walls of a residence serve many purposes, in addition to separating one room from another. Most homes contain interior walls built with lightweight metal or wood framing, a system that is economical and simple to construct and alter. The cavities between the framing provide spaces for pipes, ducts, and wiring.

Kitchens and baths often require special framing to enclose fixtures. Such framing should be designed to suit the requirements of both the fixtures and the main structure. Designers often can enhance a project with curved surfaces, such as walls or arches. Lowered ceilings can be designed to change the feel of a room or provide a space for ducts or lighting.

There are several ways to alter interior walls, when necessary, in order to make their surfaces true, widen the space behind, or accommodate other needs. Altering bearing walls requires thorough investigation and alternate means of supporting their loads.

CHAPTER REVIEW

1. State three functions provided by partitions. (See "Partitions" page 105)
2. What are two needs that require wider stud cavities? (See "Wood Stud Partitions" page 106)
3. What advantages do steel studs offer over wood studs? (See "Steel Stud Partitions" page 107)
4. Name three ways to improve walls to reduce sound transmission from one room to the next. (See "Sound-Dampening Partitions" page 109)
5. What items must be investigated before specifying a whirlpool in an existing house? (See "Enclosing Tubs and Spas" page 110)
6. How can a top and base plate be made to follow the shape of a curved wall? (See "Curved Surfaces" page 111)
7. What is required of the ceiling in a room with a Roman arch? (See "Curved Surfaces" page 111)
8. What are two ways for supporting a lowered ceiling? (See "Ceiling Structures" page 112)

Interior Surfaces

The surfaces of the floors, walls, ceilings, and cabinets may not be the most important part of your project, but they are what your client sees and will have intimate contact with after the project is completed. If you want satisfied clients, you must understand the various kinds of finishes available and then guide your clients through the decision-making process. Doing this will require an open attitude and ability to communicate the pros and cons of the many options. Also expect to spend some time helping your client sort through a pile of product information, samples, pictures, and cost data. If you do this well, you'll create an appealing interior and leave the project with a happy customer.

Learning Objective 1: Match typical wall and ceiling substrates to their appropriate applications.

Learning Objective 2: Discuss the pros and cons of floor finishes used in kitchens and baths.

Learning Objective 3: Select wall and ceiling finishes to suit their intended use.

Learning Objective 4: Recognize the available types of trim for making transitions between finishes.

BENEATH THE SKIN

The statement "beauty is more than skin deep" is never truer than with the finishes of a room. Too often homeowners paint or paper over an old wall or ceiling to find that the new finish reveals all of the imperfections of the old one. Or, a short time later, the finish chips or flakes off because of the poor condition of the substrate. The proper substrate is crucial, particularly in kitchens and baths, where moisture is always a factor. Thin finishes such as wall coverings require smooth, even substrates to which they can adhere. Paint is likely the least forgiving finish, most demanding of a well-prepared substrate. The next sections describe some of the most common floor, wall, and ceiling substrates, with an eye toward matching them to the desired finish material.

Plaster

The wall and ceiling substrate of most homes built before the 1940s consisted of thin strips of wood lath over which plaster was applied. The process was time consuming and labor intensive but resulted in a sound, perfectly smooth surface capable of accepting paint or wallpaper (the latter was most often the finish of choice). The main ingredient of traditional plaster was quicklime, which is crushed limestone heated to a high temperature. Before the quicklime was mixed with water into a form usable for construction, water was added to it, and the material was left to hydrate (slake) for three weeks on site. The resulting butterlike paste was then mixed with sand and water to create plaster that was troweled on in three separate layers: a scratch coat, a brown coat, and a finish coat. Each layer used a finer grade of sand. Animal hair mixed into the first two coats bound the material together. Rough-sawn wood lath, nailed to the studs with gaps between each lath strip, provided the support for the plaster. Expanded metal lath was used to bend around corners and arches.

Plaster is seldom used in today's homes, except for homeowners who want the best and are willing to pay for it. Today plaster is applied in different ways from former times. Three techniques are in use today:

1. Plaster on metal lath
2. Plaster on gypsum lath
3. Skim-coat plaster on blueboard

Plaster on Metal Lath

Expanded metal lath is a type of mesh that, when stapled to the studs, provides a stable plaster backing that can bend around corners or curves. A skilled applicator can trowel on plaster to create a smooth surface on even the most difficult curves. Metal lath requires three coats of plaster, similar to the process with traditional wood lath, making it the most solid, if most expensive, way to plaster a wall or ceiling.

Plaster on Gypsum Lath

For applications with only straight walls, plaster can be troweled onto panels of gypsum lath, which contains a gypsum core faced with a multilayer paper formulated for good adhesion to troweled-on plaster. Gypsum lath panels are ½" (13 mm) or ⅜" (10 mm) thick, 16" (406 mm) wide, and 48 or 96" (1.210 or 2.438 m) long. They are screwed or nailed across the studs.

Skim-Coat Plaster on Blueboard

A process that has emerged in the last two decades has mostly replaced traditional plastering in residential walls and ceilings. Also known as veneer plastering, skim-coat is a thin layer of plaster applied over a special gypsum panel called blueboard (see Figure 12.1). Done professionally, the process attains a plasterlike quality at far less cost than either of the prior techniques. The process costs more than the more standard drywall (discussed below) but has several advantages. The coating covers the entire surface, leaving no unevenness between the joints of the drywall and center of the panels. It also provides better sound dampening and better fire resistance, requires no sanding, and the surface can be painted within 24 hours of the skim-coat application.

Drywall

Today's most familiar wall substrate is known by several names: drywall, gypsum drywall, gyp-board, and gypsum wallboard. You are more apt to recognize it by the trade name of the most dominant brand, Sheetrock®. The material arose out of the necessity to build a lot of houses quickly at the end of World War II. It became an instant hit, replacing traditional plaster almost overnight, for good reasons. It came in modular panels 4' wide by 8' tall, just tall enough for a ceiling in the postwar housing standard. Panels could be easily cut by scoring one side with a knife, snapping the joint in two, and cutting the backside. Installation required much less skill than plaster. Panels were quickly nailed to the studs, then finished with paper tape applied to the joints with a plaster-based joint compound. The joints were

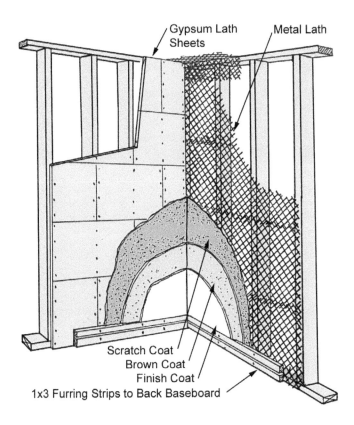

Gypsum Lath Sheets

Metal Lath

Scratch Coat
Brown Coat
Finish Coat
1x3 Furring Strips to Back Baseboard

FIGURE 12.1 Traditional plaster is troweled onto gypsum lath or metal lath in three coats, resulting in a hard, even surface that takes any finish coating.

sanded smooth, yielding a completely flat and even substrate for wall finishes such as paint or wallpaper.

Drywall is a fairly simple sandwich of a gypsum plaster core faced with paper on each side. The core and facing paper can be varied to produce specific products to suit various applications. Four types are in common use in homes:

1. **Standard wallboard**, for walls in dry areas, with a light gray paper that accepts paint and wallpaper.
2. **Water-resisting (WR) wallboard (greenboard)**, containing an impregnated core and water-resistant facing for use as a base for ceramic tile and other nonabsorbent finish materials in areas periodically, but not continually, exposed to water.
3. **Blueboard**, intended for skim-coat plaster finish or tile applied with thinset or elastomeric compounds, but not suitable for inside showers or above tubs.
4. **Fire Code (Type-X)** is used on walls or ceiling surfaces that separate an enclosed garage from living spaces, where the code requires a fire-rated separation.

Drywall panels come in 4' (1.219 m) widths, in lengths of 8, 10, and 12' (2.438, 3.048, and 3.558 m). The ½" (13 mm) thickness is most common in residential walls and ceilings, but ⅝" (16 mm) thick drywall is preferred in quality construction for walls, particularly where an absolutely flat, solid surface is desired. (Note that this is overkill for a skim-coat finish.) Curved walls can be created using two layers of ¼" (6 mm) thick drywall.

A panoply of plastic and metal accessories are available to trim corners and create special surface shapes. The standard metal corner bead that turns a sharp corner has been augmented by polyvinyl chloride (PVC) in 90-degree and rounded (bullnose) shapes for a softer feel (see Figure 12.2).

Standard (gray-faced) drywall can be painted directly; however, the joint compound absorbs paint differently than the uncoated center portions of the drywall, and the difference can be noticeable. One solution is to use blueboard, as mentioned, and apply a skim coat of plaster. Another simpler and more economical method is to spread a thin coating of joint compound over the entire surface, resulting in an even substrate for the paint finish.

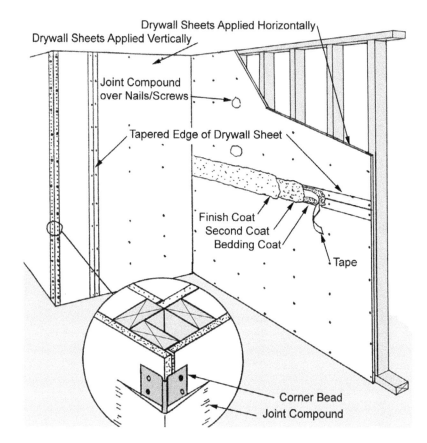

FIGURE 12.2 Drywall panels can install vertically or horizontally. Joints are taped with paper or fiberglass embedded in joint drywall compound. More compound fills screw and nail recesses and other defects. A variety of metal and plastic trim pieces are available for corners and joints.

Backerboards

As mentioned, greenboard drywall is specially formulated to resist water as a tile backer material. However, although it provides an acceptable substrate for tile in basically dry areas, such as kitchen or bathroom walls, it is not suitable for areas continually subjected to water, such as above tubs or inside showers. Cement backerboard, mentioned in Chapter 8 as an underlayment for tile floors, is a long-established material for these wet areas (see Figure 12.3). Another, more recent and lighter-weight option is gypsum backerboard, a material with a gypsum core reinforced with fiberglass mats and faced with a water-resistant paper.

Plywood

Previous chapters cited plywood's uses as a structural wall and roof sheathing. This versatile product also makes an excellent substrate for certain floor and countertop finishes. Plywood can do double duty as both subfloor and substrate for most hardwood flooring and carpeting. If filled and sanded, it also works for sheet floor coverings or vinyl tiles, but it is usually easier and less costly to apply an underlayment of ¼"-thick luan (a type of mahogany) plywood underlayment for these floor coverings.

Plywood can back ceramic tiles on floors or countertops, but tiles applied directly to plywood expand and contract at a different rate from the wood, which can result in cracking. This problem is solved by applying a layer between the tile and plywood that uncouples the two materials Several membrane underlayments are now available to provide this layer, as was discussed under "Membrane Underlayments" in Chapter 7.

Plywood used as an underlayment for tile or stone should be exterior grade, Exposure 1, which appears on the grade stamp as "A-C GROUP 1, EXTERIOR." The "A" surface has been plugged and smoothed and the "Exterior" label indicates that water-resistant glues

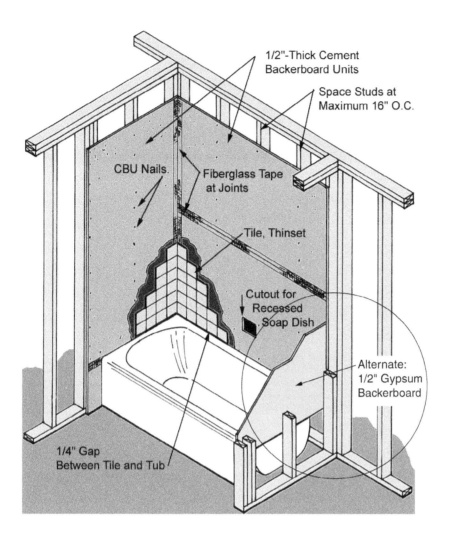

1/2"-Thick Cement
Backerboard Units

Space Studs at
Maximum 16" O.C.

CBU Nails

Fiberglass Tape
at Joints

Tile, Thinset

Cutout for
Recessed
Soap Dish

Alternate:
1/2" Gypsum
Backerboard

1/4" Gap
Between Tile and Tub

FIGURE 12.3 Backerboard is cut by scoring and snapping. Then it is nailed or screwed to the studs and the joints are taped with fiberglass tape. Thinsetting compound bonds tile to the backerboard. Cement backerboard (gray) is shown at left; gypsum backerboard (green) is at lower right.

have been used. Plywood grading can be confusing. In general, plywood is graded according to the appearance of the facing veneer, strength characteristics, and water resistance. The plywood industry uses six letters to code the surface appearance.

N   Smooth-surface "natural finish" veneer is select, all heartwood or all sapwood, free of open defects with a maximum of six repair plugs per 4 × 8 panel, made parallel to the grain and well matched for the grain and color.

A   A smooth, paintable veneer that allows not more than 18 neatly made plugs—boat, sled, or router type—parallel to the grain. It may be painted or used as a natural finish in less demanding applications.

B   Solid-surface veneer permits shims, circular repair plugs, tight knots to 1" across the grain and minor splits.

C   This veneer has tight knots to 1½" (38 mm). It has knotholes to 1" across the grain with some to 1½" (38 mm) if the total width of knots and knotholes is within specified limits. Repairs are synthetic or wood. Discoloration and sanding defects that do not impair strength are permitted. Limited splits and stitching are allowed.

D   Knots and knotholes to 2½" width (63.5 mm) across the grain and ½" (12.7 mm) larger, within specified limits, are allowed. Limited splits are permitted. This face grade is limited to interior (Exposure 1 or 2) panels.

Table 12.1 lists some of the American Plywood Association (APA) grades for the grades of plywood most commonly used in kitchen and bath applications.

TABLE 12.1 Interior Panels

APA Grade	Available Thicknesses, inches (mm)	Grade Designation, Description, and Uses
APA Rated Sheathing Structural 1 Exterior	516 (8 mm) ⅜ (10 mm) ½ (13 mm) ⅝ (16 mm) ¾ (19 mm)	**APA Structural 1 & 2 Rated Sheathing EXT** For engineered applications in construction and industry where resistance to permanent exposure to weather or moisture is required; manufactured as conventional veneered plywood, as a composite, or as a nonveneered panel; unsanded Structural 1 more commonly available.
APA Rated Sturd-I-Floor Exterior	⅝ (16 mm) ¾ (19 mm)	**APA Rated Sturd-I-Floor EXT** For combination subfloor-underlayment under carpet where severe moisture conditions may be present, as in balcony decks; high concentrated and impact load resistance; manufactured as conventional veneered plywood, as a composite, or as a nonveneered panel; available square-edge or tongue-and-groove.
APA A-C Exterior	½ (13 mm)	**APA A-C Ext** For use where appearance of only one side is important: soffits, fences, structural uses.
APA Underlayment C-C Plugged Exterior	⅜ (10 mm) ½ (13 mm) ⅝ (16 mm) ¾ (19 mm)	**APA Underlayment C-C Plugged EXT** For application over structural subfloor; smooth surface for application of carpet and high concentrated and impact load resistance; touch-sanded; for areas to be covered with thin resilient flooring (using panels with sanded face).
APA Rated Sheathing Exposure 1	516 (8 mm) ⅜ (10 mm) ½ (13 mm) ⅝ (16 mm) ¾ (19 mm)	**APA Rated Sheathing Exp 1 or 2** Specially designed for subflooring and wall and roof sheathing but also used for a broad array of other applications; manufactured as conventional veneered plywood, as a composite, or as a nonveneered panel; Exposure 1
APA Rated Sturd-I-Floor Exposure 1	⅝ (16 mm) ¾ (19 mm)	**APA Rated Sturd-I-Floor Exp 1 or 2** Specifically designed as a combination subfloor-underlayment; smooth surface for application of carpet and high concentrated and impact load resistance; manufactured as conventional veneered plywood, as a composite, or as a reconstituted wood panel (waferboard, oriented strandboard, structural particleboard); available square-edge or tongue-and-groove.
APA Underlayment C-C Plugged Exterior	⅜ (10 mm) ½ (13 mm) ⅝ (16 mm) ¾ (19 mm)	**APA Underlayment C-C Plugged EXT** For application over structural subfloor; smooth surface for application of carpet and high concentrated and impact load resistance; touch-sanded; for areas to be covered with thin resilient flooring (using panels with sanded face).
APA Underlayment Group 1 Interior	⅜ (10 mm) ½ (13 mm) ⅝ (16 mm) ¾ (19 mm)	**APA Underlayment INT** For application over structural subfloor; smooth surface for application of carpet and high concentrated and impact load resistance; touch-sanded; for areas to be covered with thin resilient flooring (using panels with sanded face).
APA A-D Group 1 Interior	¼ (6 mm) ⅜ (10 mm) ½ (13 mm) ⅝ (16 mm) ¾ (19 mm)	**APA A-D INT** For use where appearance of only one side is important; paneling, built-ins, shelving, and partitions.
APA B-D Group-2 Interior	¼ (6 mm) ⅜ (10 mm) ½ (13 mm) ⅝ (16 mm) ¾ (19 mm)	**APA B-D INT** Utility panel with one solid side; good for backing, sides of built-ins, shelving, etc.

TABLE 12.2 Suitable Wall or Ceiling Substrate

Substrates	Proposed Wall or Ceiling Finish		
	Paint	Wall Covering	Ceramic Tile
New plaster	Acceptable, if primed	Acceptable	Acceptable in dry areas
Drywall	Acceptable if joints taped and sanded smooth and primed	Acceptable if joints taped and sanded smooth	Greenboard in walls/ceilings only occasionally wet
Old wallpaper, sound condition	Acceptable if sealed with shellac or oil-based primer	Acceptable if old wallpaper is sound and sealed	Not acceptable
Old wallpaper, poor condition	Strip paper and patch wall beneath or apply new substrate	Strip paper and patch wall beneath or apply new substrate	Not acceptable
Old vinyl wall covering, sound condition	Seal first with shellac or oil-based primer	Seal first with shellac or oil-based primer	Not acceptable
Old vinyl wall covering, poor condition	Strip wall covering and patch wall beneath or apply new substrate	Strip wall covering and patch wall beneath or apply new substrate	Not acceptable
Cement or gypsum backerboard	Not acceptable	Not acceptable	Acceptable
Plywood, filled and sanded	N grade acceptable for natural finish. A grade for paint finish.	Acceptable	Acceptable except in showers and around tubs. Membrane underlayment recommended.
Concrete or concrete block	Acceptable if dry and rustic effect desired	Not acceptable unless skim coated or furred out	Acceptable if smoothed and filled or mortar set

Concrete and Concrete Block

Concrete and concrete block work fairly well as a substrate for porous finish materials, such as plaster, ceramic tile, or stone. A skim coat of plaster must be applied first to yield a substrate that is smooth enough to accept a wall covering finish material. Alternately, the wall can be furred out and drywall installed as a substrate for the finish.

Table 12.2 summarizes the basics of substrates and what must be done to each to provide an acceptable base for various wall or ceiling finishes.

FLOOR FINISH MATERIALS

Designers today have a wider variety of floor finishes to select from than ever before. However, the success of the finish depends on a sound floor structure, the proper substrate, provisions for moisture control and attention to the specific installation requirements of the finish. And the finish must suit the function. When bath floors get wet, they get slick and become hazardous, so it doesn't make sense to specify one that is slick to begin with. Described below are some of the most popular kitchen and bath floor finishes and some of the things important for specifying them effectively.

Ceramic Tile, Cement Tile, and Stone

The variety of tiles made from mineral sources abounds, in color, pattern and size. Ceramic tiles are made of various colors of clay, fused into a solid under high temperatures in a kiln. Unglazed tiles are preferred for floors because of their better traction—an especially important feature in baths. Cement tiles are made in much the same way as concrete, by combining portland cement with water and a fine aggregate. Stone tiles of granite, shale, bluestone and other species, are increasing in popularity. Several types of manufactured tiles augment the list. Most all mineral-based tiles install on floors in one of two basic methods:

1. Thinsetting them into a special thinset mortar compound troweled over the substrate
2. Mudsetting them into a mortar bed

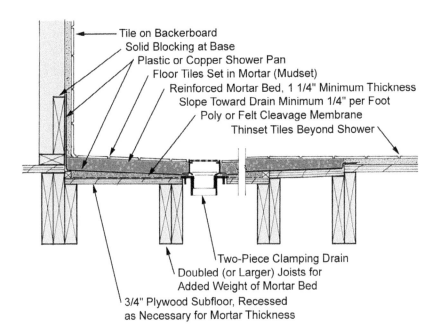

Tile on Backerboard
Solid Blocking at Base
Plastic or Copper Shower Pan
Floor Tiles Set in Mortar (Mudset)
Reinforced Mortar Bed, 1 1/4" Minimum Thickness
Slope Toward Drain Minimum 1/4" per Foot
Poly or Felt Cleavage Membrane
Thinset Tiles Beyond Shower

Two-Piece Clamping Drain
Doubled (or Larger) Joists for
Added Weight of Mortar Bed
3/4" Plywood Subfloor, Recessed
as Necessary for Mortar Thickness

FIGURE 12.4 The mortar bed of a mudset installation can provide the necessary slope for a tile floor in a shower. The tile outside the shower can be thinset over a membrane underlayment.

Thinsetting works well for all but shower floors, which must be sloped for drainage. The best solution for shower floors is to set them in a full mortar bed. The mortar bed slopes a minimum of ¼" per foot toward the drain, which usually requires a mortar bed thickness that varies from 1 to 2" for an average-size shower (see Figure 12.4). Framing below the mortar bed must be recessed by the maximum thickness of the mortar, if the finished floor surface is to align with the adjacent floor. Concrete slabs simply can be recessed by the required maximum mortar thickness. To support the heavy weight of the mortar and tile, the joists in a framed floor should be doubled or engineered for the load. After the subfloor has been installed, a 6-millimeter polyethylene (poly) or felt cleavage membrane is applied over it to allow the wood structure to move without cracking the mortar and tiles. A waterproof shower pan consisting of 40-mm PVC or copper goes on next, upon which the mortar bed is laid.

Resilient Flooring

Resilient flooring gets its name from the fact that it is flexible, unlike brittle mineral-based tiles. It comes in two forms, sheet goods and tiles, adhered to the substrate with troweled-on adhesive or adhesive preapplied to the back of the tiles for a peel-and-stick installation directly to the substrate. Toweled-on adhesive is the preferred application method.

Designers today can choose between several types of resilient flooring, including vinyl (PVC), linoleum, and cork, each with its own pros and cons. Linoleum and cork are considered more environmentally friendly than vinyl but are pricier options. Vinyl has sparked controversy over the release of toxins during production as well as the release of toxins when PVC products are burned. Once installed in a floor, however, the product has little if any effect on indoor air quality.

All resilient flooring requires a compatible substrate that is completely smooth (see Figure 12.5). The plywood or oriented strandboard (OSB) subfloor of a wood-framed floor would suffice if it is filled and sanded, but an underlayment of ¼" luan plywood or particleboard likely would be easier to work with. Resilient flooring also can be applied to existing flooring if it is tightly adhered, free of checks and voids and edge curls. If the existing floor covering is dubious, it should be removed before the new floor covering is applied.

Resilient flooring can be applied over concrete slabs, if they are first troweled smooth and filled, but never over slabs subject to dampness or moisture, which is present in many basements. If the slab isn't consistently dry, a subfloor on wood sleepers should be installed before applying the flooring, as described in the next section.

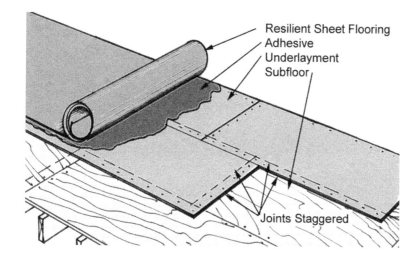

Resilient Sheet Flooring
Adhesive
Underlayment
Subfloor

Joints Staggered

FIGURE 12.5 Resilient flooring installs in troweled-on adhesive over a suitable substrate. Note that the joints of the underlayment panels do not coincide with those of the subfloor.

Wood Flooring

Wood's vulnerability to moisture makes it a less practical option for baths than for kitchens, but that doesn't hamper its appeal to homeowners, so it nevertheless ends up in many baths. Two flooring types are in use today:

1. Glue-down strip/plank and parquet flooring
2. Traditional strip or plank flooring

Glue-down strip and plank and parquet ("mosaic") flooring consists of a hardwood veneer bonded to a thin plywood substrate. The strips or parquets install over underlayment or filled and sanded plywood subflooring by means of troweled-on mastic or can be applied directly to concrete slabs if two conditions are met:

1. The slab is smooth and free of voids.
2. The slab is free of moisture.

Filling voids and grinding the slab smooth satisfies the first condition. The second is more of a challenge. Slabs in today's new homes are poured over a granular base with a moisture barrier, usually 4- or 6-mm poly sheet. If you can determine that your client's home was constructed in this manner, you can be relatively sure that the slab won't wick up moisture from the ground. Short of cutting through part of the slab, likely you won't be able to determine the construction of a slab in an existing home. You might find out by using an electronic moisture meter or employing a simple test. Tape a piece of 1′ (304 mm) square poly to the surface of the slab. Check it after 24 hours. If condensation appears on the undersurface or the slab is damp, there is enough moisture to make installing a wood floor risky.

If the slab is such that a glue-down installation is iffy, the flooring can be applied over a wood subfloor attached to sleepers, as shown in Figure 12.6.

Traditional wood flooring consists of hardwood tongue-and-groove strips or planks that are prefinished or require sanding and finishing, after they have been installed. Both types are typically 25/32″ (19 mm) thick and come in random lengths with tongue and groove edges on all four sides that interlock each piece to the next. Each strip is nailed to the subfloor with nails driven at angles through its tongue. The interlock allows the pieces to shrink slightly with changing moisture content but not to move out of vertical alignment with each other.

Strips and planks can run in any direction over the floor to suit the design objectives, but for a squeak-free installation, the flooring needs a solid substrate and should run across the joists to allow nails to penetrate the joists (Figure 12.7). If the flooring runs in another direction, a solid subfloor with a minimum ¾″ (19 mm) thickness should underlie the flooring, and the nails should penetrate the subfloor by at least ¾″ (19 mm).

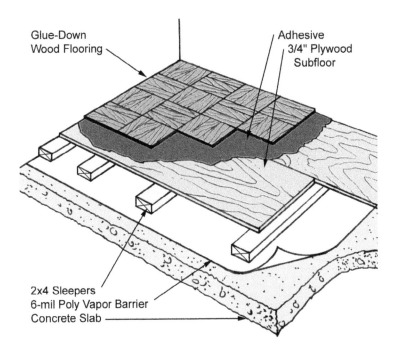

FIGURE 12.6 Glue-down wood flooring is applied to a plywood substrate with adhesive. If the floor is concrete as shown, 2 × 4 sleepers support the subfloor. A poly vapor barrier between the concrete and sleepers keeps moisture out of the wood above.

Oak, maple, birch, and walnut—the most frequently used hardwood flooring in the past—are now joined by several exotic hardwoods, as well as bamboo.

A wood floor should have a plywood or OSB subfloor at least ¾" (19 mm) thick. The nails should penetrate the subfloor by at least ¾" (19 mm).

Wood flooring over concrete slabs require a wood subfloor over sleepers.

Laminate Flooring

Laminate flooring consists of several layers of material bonded together under high pressure, similar to laminate products used for countertops. A clear melamine wear layer protects the next layer, a resin-impregnated paper with a wood grain pattern printed on. A structural

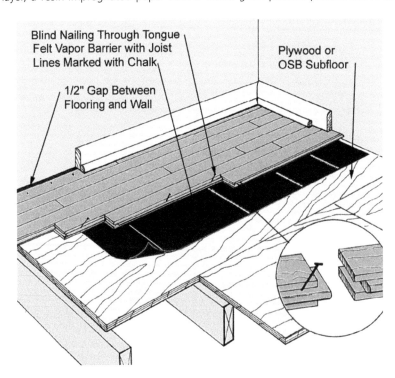

FIGURE 12.7 Wood strip flooring is blind-nailed through the tongue of each strip (inset) through the subfloor. For a squeak-free installation, the nails should penetrate into the floor joists. The position of the joists can be determined from the nailing pattern on the subfloor, then chalked onto the felt moisture barrier. A ½" (19 mm) gap at the walls allows the flooring to expand and contract.

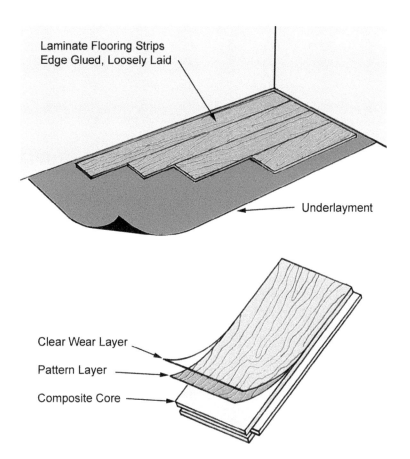

Laminate Flooring Strips
Edge Glued, Loosely Laid

Underlayment

Clear Wear Layer

Pattern Layer

Composite Core

FIGURE 12.8 Laminate flooring strips are glued only on the edges and float on the floor underlayment.

fiberboard core is the next layer, followed by a backing of melamine. Because the wear layer is smooth, laminate flooring can be slippery when wet, which makes it a questionable option for bath floors.

Installing laminate flooring entails applying glue to the tongue-and-groove edges of each piece and pressing it into the abutting piece on an underlayment mat. Because the pieces are attached to each other and not to the subfloor, the finished floor "floats" above the substrate (see Figure 12.8).

There are currently two choices of underlayments, a ¼" (13 mm) thick low-density fiber panel, 24 by 30" (610 by 737 mm), or a closed-cell foam cushion, which is shipped in rolls. Laminate flooring installs over concrete slab floors in much the same way as over wood-framed floors, except that a poly vapor barrier is placed over the slab before the underlayment material.

WALL AND CEILING FINISH MATERIALS

Walls surrounding showers, baths, and sinks are constantly subject to moisture, so a water-resistant finish that can be washed periodically is essential. Even bath walls outside the wettest areas are subject to the constant high levels of humidity and are prone to develop mold and fungus so they too should be washable. In the kitchen, wall surfaces surrounding cooking areas frequently are spattered with grease and food scraps, so they too need to be able to withstand regular washings.

Paint

Paint is a versatile finish. Available in endless colors and various sheens and textures, it can be applied to many substrates quickly and easily. Painted surfaces also can be repainted or serve as a substrate for other wall finishes. Though economical compared to other finishes, a quality paint job requires quality paint, a properly prepared substrate, and competent application.

Paint is a liquid composed of a binder material, pigments, and a solvent. The petroleum-solvents of the past contained lead and volatile organic compounds, or VOCs, which are now recognized as health hazards. Lead has been eliminated, and petroleum-based (oil) paints containing VOCs, though still available, now have equivalent water-based paints that contain no or low levels of VOCs.

Paint suppliers use computers to mix paints to any desired color. The sheen of a paint indicates its glossiness or flatness. There are four standard sheens:

1. **Flat.** The dullest finish hides surface flaws but is hard to clean. Flat paint usually not considered washable so it is not recommended for bath walls or for kitchen walls surrounding food preparation areas. It is never a good choice for woodwork.
2. **Satin (eggshell).** This finish is shinier than flat and somewhat washable—a good choice for most walls and ceilings not requiring frequent cleaning.
3. **Semigloss.** Semigloss paint has a definite gloss but is not shiny. This sheen is washable, so it is a good choice for wet-area walls and ceilings and rooms where surfaces must be cleaned often, such as bathrooms, laundries, and kitchens. It also is a good choice for woodwork in all rooms.
4. **Gloss.** This is shiniest sheen and the most washable finish. Because of its high reflectivity, gloss is most likely to broadcast any flaws or unevenness in the substrate. For that reason, it is used more often on woodwork than on wall surfaces.

Wall Coverings

Although many still call it *wallpaper*, the product sold in rolls today probably contains paper only on the backside if at all. The facing is vinyl, which is much more durable and easy to clean than paper. As mentioned in connection with vinyl used in resilient flooring, issues have been raised in connection with the manufacture and disposal of PVC products, but, once installed, vinyl wall covering has not proven detrimental to the indoor air quality. Numerous colors and patterns are available, many with complementary border strips.

The substrate for a wall covering should be perfectly smooth because any surface irregularities will telescope through the material. Vinyl wall covering is a less-than-ideal surface material for walls surrounding baths and showers because of the potential for water getting behind the seams and causing the wall covering to peel off.

Wood

Like paint, wood is a universal finish material available in many species and forms. It can be another addition to a kitchen and bath design palette if its limitations and installation requirements are understood.

The first thing to recognize is that wood is an organic material that constantly changes in response to its environment. Heat and humidity cause it to swell. Cold and dryness cause it to shrink. Joints consequently open and close, inviting moisture to penetrate and mold and fungus to grow. In a moist environment, the pores in the surface of unfinished wood will also grow microorganisms. Wood used in cabinets is either coated with a moisture-impermeable finish or encapsulated in a veneer, which prevents moisture penetration.

It should come as no surprise, then, that rough, unfinished barn wood probably is the worst choice of a wall finish in a bath. Wood, in fact, should never be used around tubs and showers, but unfinished cedar or redwood is preferred for sauna interiors. Wood on other kitchen and bath walls should be sealed to prevent absorption of moisture. A gloss or semigloss enamel or clear coating makes a good sealer and results in a washable finish.

Wood is available in many species and shapes suited for covering entire walls or trim work. The choices for wall surfaces include veneer paneling, stile-and-rail paneling, board siding,

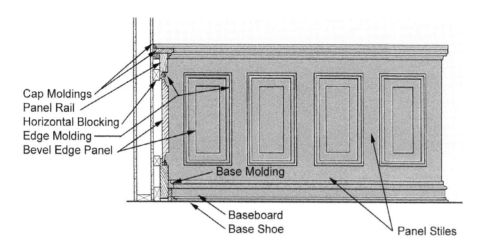

Cap Moldings
Panel Rail
Horizontal Blocking
Edge Molding
Bevel Edge Panel

Base Molding

Baseboard
Base Shoe

Panel Stiles

FIGURE 12.9 A wainscot using traditional stile and rail paneling. Solid panels with beveled edges fit into the frame work.

and plain boards. The environmental impact caused by the depletion of exotic hardwoods from tropical forests is reason to encourage the use of native and sustainable hardwoods, such as maple, birch, walnut, oak, and ash.

Veneer paneling consists of a thin layer of hardwood bonded to a plywood core and installed directly over a substrate or wood furring with edges butted or covered with a trim piece.

Traditional stile-and-rail paneling is an assembly of solid panel boards of a wood such as oak, cherry, or walnut, fitted into a framework of vertical stiles and horizontal rails, as shown in the stile-and-rail wainscot in Figure 12.9. Wood wainscots can be designed with other wood configurations, such as beadboard, as shown in Figure 12.10.

The success of any wood wall surfacing depends as much on the visual characteristics of the wood as how it is put together. Dark colors darken a room. If that's desired, walnut, red oak, mahogany, cherry, and redwood are better choices than lighter woods stained dark. Lighter woods, such as ash, birch, maple, white oak, and pine, with a clear finish tend to make the room lighter. Of course, wood can be painted any color, but the lightness or darkness of the color has the same end effect as naturally finished woods.

Natural Wood Finishes

Appearance figures high as one of the reasons for selecting a particular species of wood for an interior application. A natural finish is the only way to let the wood's unique color, texture and grain show through. Choices remain for specifying the sheen, depth, and color of the finish. A wide range of natural finishes with different levels of opacity, color, and surface durability are available to help obtain the desired end result. To make the correct choice, you must understand the functional requirements of the application, the nature of the wood species, the color and sheen sought by the customer, and, finally, the products available to suit the job.

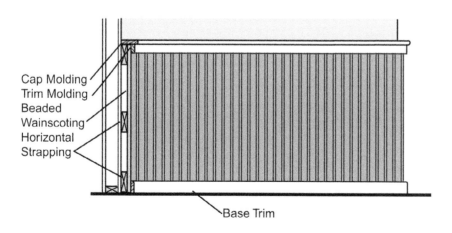

Cap Molding
Trim Molding
Beaded
Wainscoting
Horizontal
Strapping

Base Trim

FIGURE 12.10 A wainscot made up of tongue-and-groove beadboard. If the beadboard is installed vertically, as shown, horizontal strapping is required to attach it to the wall surface.

As with paints, formulations for natural finishes have evolved over the years. Some oil- and lacquer-based coatings now have nontoxic water-based (waterborne) alternatives. However, the newer products don't always yield the same appearance as the formulations they replaced, and they require different application techniques. Clear latex floor finish, for example, is harder to apply and looks milkier than polyurethane, which is oil based.

All natural finishes are either penetrating or film forming, depending on whether they seep down into the matrix of the wood or build a film on the surface. Penetrating finishes bring out all of the nuances of the grain and color of the wood, resulting in a rich "bare wood" appearance. Not all woods have the qualities that show up best with penetrating finishes. Hardwoods tend to take them much better than softwoods. Pine, for example, sucks in a penetrating finish unevenly, resulting in spottiness. Even among hardwoods, species with a lot of character, such as walnut or teak fare, better than those with more subtle grain or nondescript character, such as birch or maple.

Penetrating Finishes

Penetrating finishes include three basic formulations—oil, resin, and varnish—all of which are solvent based. Boiled linseed oil is the most traditional oil finish. It requires several coats and dries slowly, yielding a warm (yellowish), slightly dull patina. Tung oil is a natural oil finish highly resistant to abrasion, moisture, heat, acid, and mildew. Mineral oil is similar and can be used safely on food preparation surfaces, such as butcher blocks. When specifying a penetrating oil finish for butcher blocks used for food preparation, include language that guarantees the product is safe for culinary surfaces. Penetrating resins and stains are polymer-based finishes that bring out the best of hard, open-grain woods, such as oak. Danish oil and antique oil are varieties of these materials. Using penetrating stains on pine and certain other softwoods result in an uneven color, since the wood absorbs the colorant in the stain at different degrees. Porous portions will absorb more, non-porous portions, such as knots, will absorb much less. This can be overcome by priming the wood first with a pre-stain wood conditioner. Rub-on varnish combines penetrating resins with varnish to build up a higher sheen than oils or resins.

Film-Forming Finishes

Surface finishes include solvent-, lacquer-, and water-based products. As stated previously, solvent and lacquer coatings contain VOCs that release hazardous emissions as they dry. Shellac yields a dull sheen but can be rubbed to a higher sheen. White shellac yellows the wood slightly; orange shellac, much more so. Shellac thins with alcohol and dries quickly. It makes a good sealer for other finishes but, when used alone, does not resist heat and moisture or alcohol well. Lacquer also can be rubbed to a high gloss, forming a strong, clear finish, but it is vulnerable to moisture. Because it dries too fast to brush on easily, it is usually sprayed on in several thin coats, making it finish that is better factory applied than site applied. Lacquer thins with lacquer thinner, which is harmful to breathe or touch. Spar varnish and polyurethane varnish are two solvent-based clear finishes that stand up very well to water, heat, and alcohol. That's why spar varnish has long been the finish of choice for ship decks. Both are thinned with mineral spirits (paint thinner) and are brushed on. Polyurethane, available in satin or gloss sheen, is an excellent finish for wood floors.

All water-based finishes are of the film-forming type. They yield stable color and do not yellow when used over light-colored woods—an important plus with today's preference for blond-colored floors. Yet, as mentioned, their appearance is not the same as with solvent-based finishes. You should compare actual samples before specifying one option over the other. Also, raised grain has plagued waterborne finishes since their market debut. While products continue to improve, they still must be applied in strict accordance with the manufacturer's recommendations for success. The best waterborne finishes ship in two containers: the finish and the catalyst. When mixed together the catalyst causes the finish to cure.

Colorants

When the natural color of the wood won't do, or when you want to compensate for the yellowing effect many wood finishes produce, apply a stain before the finish coating, whether the finish is a penetrating or film forming.

There are two basic types of wood stains. Film-forming stains contain finely ground pigments suspended in oil or solvent, much the same as a thin, opaque paint. These stains form a skin coat on the wood, similar to a paint. They work best over light woods with nondescript grain character. Penetrating stains contain organic derivatives dissolved, rather than suspended, in the medium. They penetrate into the grain, allowing it to show through. Both types of stains are available in oil- or water -based solvents.

Laminate

Plastic laminate, or "laminate," can be applied to walls as well as to countertops. One use is a continuous backsplash extending between a kitchen countertop and the wall cabinets. When used this way, the laminate is applied with contact adhesive directly over wallboard.

Tile

Tile ranks as the number one material for wet areas so it's a natural for shower and tub surrounds and sink backsplashes. The many colors, shapes, and sizes of ceramic tile now extend to a host of newer tiles made from natural stone and glass. Because tile, once installed, is relatively permanent, it should serve as the base around which the fixtures and other finishes are based.

Tiles come in various sizes, from 1" (25 mm) to up to about 18" (457 mm) square as well as numerous other shapes. Tiles larger than 4" (102 mm) usually come as single units, whereas smaller tiles are usually attached to mesh backing panels 12" (305 mm) square for easier installation. Any shape and size can be applied to a wall. In dry areas, wall tiles can be applied to any solid, dry substrate. Walls around tubs and showers should go onto only those substrates not affected by water penetration, such as cement or gypsum backerboards described at the beginning of this chapter. Most wall tile today is applied into a troweled-on portland cement–based adhesive (thinset application). After the adhesive sets, cementitious grout is forced into the joints with a rubber trowel. Cleaning off the excess grout from the surface finishes the job.

TRIMMING THE INTERIOR

Unless they abut each other, as a tile wall does where it meets a tile floor, some kind of transitional element is needed between every intersecting surface in a room. This element is usually a linear piece of trim with a profile that suits its application and design intent (see Figure 12.11).

Contemporary homes use trim sparingly and employ simple shapes as baseboards and casings around doors and windows. More elaborate trim work adorns the interiors of older homes. These might include a crown mold cornice around the edges of the ceilings, a horizontal band (picture rail) a few feet down on the walls, and another band (chair rail) about waist height above the floor, to separate the flat wall above from the wainscot below. Matching this kind of elaborate woodwork can be difficult and expensive today and necessitates using less or simpler trim skillfully chosen to blend with the existing trim work without slavishly copying it.

The trim in a room begins at the joint between the floor and the wall. Base trim usually consists of two pieces attached to the wall: a flat baseboard and a smaller toe piece called a base shoe. In quality work, base trim is always mitered at the corner joints. If joints are required for straight sections, the pieces are joined by joints "scarfed" on an angle rather than simply butted together. Casings make the transition between door and window frames and their adjoining walls. They can be as simple as a single flat 1 × 4 or stock casing that runs around three sides

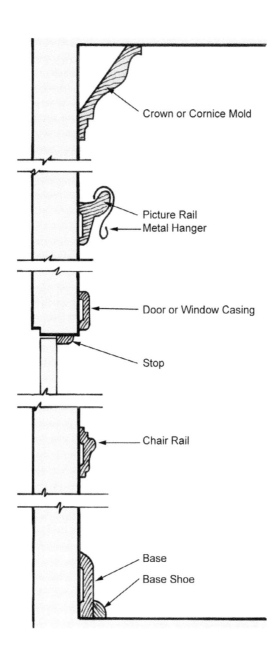

Crown or Cornice Mold

Picture Rail
Metal Hanger

Door or Window Casing

Stop

Chair Rail

Base
Base Shoe

FIGURE 12.11 Moldings serve many purposes, making transitions between finish materials from the floor to the ceiling as well as around windows, doors, and wainscoting.

of the window or door or as complex as an assembly of fluted moldings and rosettes. Windows also may require stools at the base and aprons between the stool and the wall.

Wood Moldings

Some trim is a special shape or color of the same material used on the surface—such as the base and cap pieces used to terminate ceramic tile or the vinyl base that might edge resilient floor coverings—but wood reigns as the most universal trim material. Lumberyards usually stock scores of different trim profiles premilled out of ponderosa pine and can order many of the same shapes in oak, cherry, mahogany, and walnut (see Figure 12.12). Hardwood trim takes a variety of natural finishes, stained or unstained. Softwoods also can be naturally finished, but each has limitations. Pine absorbs penetrating stain unevenly, resulting in a splotchy appearance. All light-colored softwoods tend to yellow over time, a drawback if a lasting light color is desired. The random lengths that make up premilled pine casings are often of slightly different color, which is apparent at the finger joint splices. The color difference easily shows through any light-colored natural finish. This can be overcome by applying a nonpenetrating stain prior to the final transparent finish.

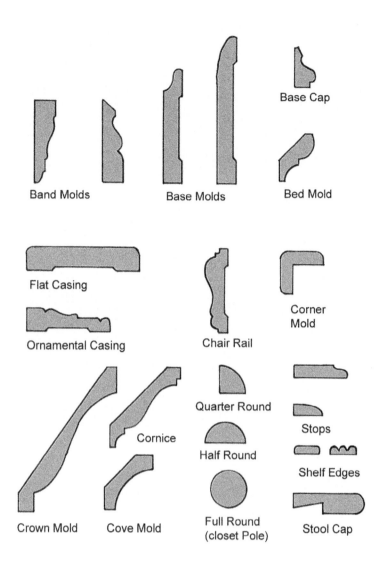

Band Molds

Base Molds

Base Cap

Bed Mold

Flat Casing

Ornamental Casing

Chair Rail

Corner Mold

Cornice

Quarter Round

Half Round

Full Round (closet Pole)

Stops

Shelf Edges

Stool Cap

Crown Mold

Cove Mold

FIGURE 12.12 Wood moldings come in many profiles. Pine is commonly stocked, but other species are available on order.

Manufactured Moldings

Matching the existing ornate wood or plaster trim work in a remodel of a traditional home can be a design challenge. One solution might be joining several stock wood moldings into composite assemblies, although this requires a high level of craftsmanship and can be costly. Another approach is to select from the variety of classical molding shapes now manufactured from such materials as polyurethane or fiberglass-reinforced polyester (see Figure 12.13). Unlike wood, manufactured moldings aren't affected by changes in humidity. Cornices, columns, friezes, niches, and medallions are some of the many shapes available. These moldings typically are preprimed and either nailed or applied with adhesive from a caulking gun. After installation, they can be painted with latex or oil paints.

SUMMARY

Interior surfaces consist of a finish material that is seen and a substrate that isn't. Both work together in a successful installation. Plaster, drywall, backerboard, and plywood substrates behave differently when exposed to moisture. That characteristic, along with their surface different features, determines their suitability as a backing for various wall finishes.

Kitchen and bath floors should be designed to accommodate the needs of these rooms, which may include ease of cleaning, resistance to moisture, and the need to drain. Resilient

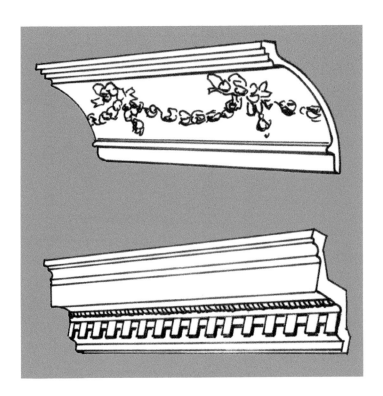

FIGURE 12.13 Moldings with complex surface designs, such as these cornice molds, are made from various plastic and cementitious materials that, unlike wood, don't shrink or crack.

flooring, wood, tile, and laminate can meet these needs, but only if selected and installed properly.

Materials for walls in kitchens and baths share many of the same requirements as for floors and can be finished with a variety of materials, including paint, wood, and wall coverings. Paint choices—are extensive—in types, colors, and sheens—but should be tailored to the needs of the application.

Designers have a wide variety of wood and manufactured trim shapes to select from in order to form successful transitions between finish materials.

CHAPTER REVIEW

1. What qualities are necessary in a substrate for a successful application of wall covering? (See "Beneath the Skin" page 117)
2. Why is a skim-coat plaster application preferable to a standard drywall installation? (See "Skim-Coat Plaster on Blueboard" page 118)
3. Why is a cleavage membrane considered necessary for a tile floor? (See "Ceramic Tile, Cement Tile, and Stone" page 124)
4. What are two ways to adapt a concrete block wall to accept a wall covering (See "Concrete and Concrete Block" page 123)?
5. What feature does a mudset tile floor offer over a thinset one? (See "Ceramic Tile, Cement Tile, and Stone" page 124)
6. What is meant by a floating floor? (See "Laminate Flooring" page 127)
7. How have paints been reformulated to make them less hazardous to health? (See "Paint" page 128)
8. Why is paint with a flat sheen not desirable for wood trim? (See "Paint" page 128)
9. What kind of stain is preferred for pine? (See "Natural Wood Finishes" page 130)

Heating Systems

Most homes in North America, except those on the southern tip of Florida, need some means of heating. It may be as simple as a woodstove or as complicated as a multizone central heating system. With good design, many homes can get much of their heat from the sun. This chapter scans the variety of ways North Americans heat their homes and how these choices might affect kitchen and bath design work.

Learning Objective 1: Discuss the environmental conditions necessary for comfort.

Learning Objective 2: Compare the pros and cons of common fuels used for home heating.

Learning Objective 3: Differentiate between forced-air and hydronic heating systems.

Identify heating systems most appropriate to kitchens and baths.

COMFORT AND HEAT

Heating systems are installed in homes to provide a comfortable environment for the occupants, but how does heat relate to comfort? To begin, the sensation of comfort varies from person to person in the following ways:

- **Age.** Older people need warmer temperatures than younger people.
- **Activity level.** People are more comfortable at lower temperatures when they are active than when they are sedentary.
- **Atmospheric conditions.** The amount of moisture in the air, the movement of air, and solar radiation interact to affect comfort.

These conditions of comfort have been quantified and refined over many years of study by scientists and are displayed in a psychometric chart known as the human comfort zone, shown on Figure 13.1. The chart is based on the comfort felt by people exposed to various temperatures, humidity levels, and air movement. To make a room comfortable, heating and cooling equipment must respond to the variables in the chart and do so dependently, quietly, and efficiently.

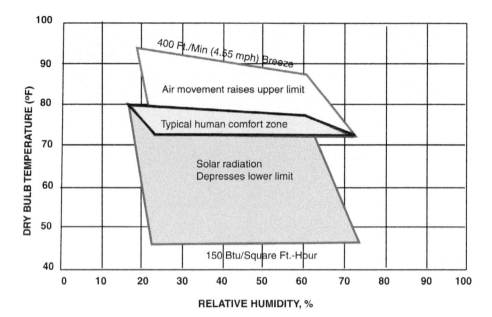

FIGURE 13.1 Most people feel comfortable in the purple-colored zone of the graph. With ventilation, comfort is possible at higher air temperatures (blue zone). Similarly, solar heat extends the comfort zone downward (orange) to about 46° Fahrenheit.

Heat is a form of energy that travels from a hotter to a colder place. It travels in three ways: conduction, convection, and radiation. When you touch the handle of your car door on a January morning, it feels cold, because heat is passing directly from your hand to the handle, by conduction. Now imagine holding a lighted match just above the palm of your hand. The warmth you feel comes from the match transporting its heat by radiation. If you hold your hand above the flame at some distance, you can still feel its warmth, although in this case the heat more likely comes from the air heated by the flame and warms your hand by convection.

Home heating systems employ all three modes of heat transfer, alone or in combination. Because they often rely on more than one mode, it is handier to classify them by the medium they use to distribute the heat. This concept will become clearer as we look at the various ways to heat a house.

Conservation Comes First

All heating systems need some form of energy to create warmth. Regardless of where the energy comes from, the amount needed varies greatly with the climate, the house's solar exposure, and how its envelope (exterior enclosure) is constructed. With the cost of energy growing and the uncertainty of the future fossil fuel supply, homeowners will benefit from anything designers can do to promote energy conservation. Most of the decisions that affect home construction probably will be made by the time you enter the picture as a kitchen and bath designer, but you still can promote conservation by the equipment and appliances you specify. And a basic understanding of energy-conserving design strategies will help make sure your part of the design integrates with the energy conservation goals of the home's construction. An energy-efficient home has:

- Ways to use natural energies to heat, cool, and light the interior.
- An energy-conserving envelope.
- Energy-efficient equipment.

Heat passes in and through the envelope by conduction, radiation, and convection. Earlier chapters described how to create an energy-conserving envelope with adequate insulation, efficient windows, and sealing of cracks and openings and presented some ways to exploit natural energies to heat and cool interiors. These energies exist in some amount in every location and are usually available free or cheap for the taking. For example, breezes can provide much or all of the cooling in most climates. Good window design and location not only capture favorable breezes but also provide an escape route for hot inside air during the cool of the night. The sun can provide much of a home's heating as well as natural lighting. Finally, selecting energy-efficient equipment will save your clients money on whatever fuel they use for heat.

HEATING FUELS

Even solar-heated homes typically rely on another source for backup heat. Sadly, we still depend primarily on fossil fuels for home heat. Natural and bottled gas provides the bulk of home heating in North America, with electricity the next most common source. Wood and other renewable energy sources make up the rest of the energy pie.

Gas

Think of gas as molecules in motion. Gas molecules fill any containing vessel, with equal pressure in all directions. Just as water flows from a higher to a lower level and heat flows from a hotter to a cooler body, gas flows from a place of higher pressure to one of lower pressure.

Gas made its debut in homes in the 1800s as a fuel for lighting. Subsequently it became a common energy source for cooking, space heating, and water heating. These uses continue today, in addition to some newer ones, such as gas-powered refrigerators, heaters, fireplaces, and outdoor barbecues. Because natural gas reserves are apparently ample, this energy source will surely play a big part in residential applications in future years. Its appeal is heightened by the fact that gas is relatively clean burning, producing mainly carbon dioxide in the process, is a convenient fuel to use. A flip of the knob on the kitchen range yields an immediate flame.

Countries using the metric system use calories to measure heat content. In North America we use British thermal units (Btus). One Btu is the amount of heat energy required to raise the temperature of 1 pound of water by 1° Fahrenheit (F). This is roughly equivalent to the heat produced by burning a wooden match. A standard cubic foot of gas, as defined by the American Gas Association, is the quantity of gas contained in cubic foot of volume at a barometric pressure of 30″ (762 mm) of mercury at a temperature of 60° F. Thus, the heating value of any particular gas is the number of Btus it produces per cubic foot.

Gas fuel in buildings is either natural gas or LP gas (liquified petroleum).

Natural gas is mostly methane tapped from wells sunk into gas-bearing sands and piped to a local utility company, which distributes it to homes through its own municipal pipe network. A meter at the point of entry measures the quantity of gas consumed by a home in any given time period.

LP gas may be either butane or propane or a mixture of the two. It may come from natural gas sources or from the distillation process of an oil refinery. In either case, LP gas is liquefied under pressure and shipped in tank trucks. Local gas companies distribute the product to consumers, filling their on-site tanks by hoses attached to the tank truck. Consumers are either billed for each fill or according to a monthly arrangement.

Because both types of gas are constantly under pressure, any leaks in the containers—the tank and distribution piping—pose a fire danger. Two requirements help minimize this danger:

1. All gas piping must be black steel or copper, with joints connected by compression, rather than soldered, fittings.
2. A disagreeable odor added to the gas alerts occupants of any leakage.

Electricity

All matter is made up of atoms. The nucleus, the atom's center, contains positively charged particles called protons and uncharged particles called neutrons. Negatively charged particles called electrons surround the atom. When the balance between protons and electrons is upset by an outside force, an atom may gain or lose an electron. When electrons are lost from an atom, the free movement of these electrons constitutes an electric current.

We get electricity from the conversion of other sources of energy, such as coal, natural gas, oil, nuclear power, and other natural sources. Before electricity generation began over 100 years ago, kerosene lamps lighted houses, iceboxes kept food cooled, and wood- or coal-burning stoves heated rooms. Today electrical power is the primary energy source for equipment and lighting in homes and—along with other fuels—heating.

Electric power is measured in units called watts. Because a single watt is small, when it comes to most household uses, we use units of 1,000 watts, or kilowatts (Kw). The usage over time needs another variable, the hours of usage. Thus, the units of electrical power are measured in kilowatt-hours (kWh). One kWh is equal to the energy of 1,000 watts working for 1 hour. Most electricity is produced from steam turbines, powered by moving water, nuclear energy, or a fuel such as coal, natural gas, or oil. A small but increasing amount is converted directly from the sun by photovoltaic (PV) cells mounted to face into the sun. Wind and biomass (the burning of garbage) also can generate electricity, but at present they account for a very small percentage of the total.

High-voltage electricity from the generating plant travels along cables to a series of transformers. The transformer reduces the voltage down to 220 volts for residential use and then delivers it to the service panel inside the house.

Photovoltaic collectors mounted on the roof can augment the electricity imported from the power grid, as described in Chapter 19.

Oil

Fuel oil is one of the end products of the refining of crude oil. It is heavier than the lightest products of the refining process—gasoline, for example—but lighter than motor oils and tar. As with LP gas, heating oil is delivered to homes by tank trucks.

No. 2 heating oil is the third most dominant energy source for home heating in the United States. It is fuel of choice for 40% of the homes in the Northeast/Mid-Atlantic region of the country as well as much of Canada and is usually the most economical fuel in these regions. It costs somewhere near gas but much less than electricity. If burned in efficient equipment, oil produces minimal exhaust emissions.

Compared to gas, oil has some advantages. First, when leaks occur, heating oil is nonexplosive. Second, liquid heating oil will not burn. It must be vaporized to fire inside a burner. Finally, a large quantity of oil can be stored safely on site. But most oil burners are not as efficient as gas and require periodic cleaning maintenance. A leaking underground oil tank can be very expensive to repair and clean up.

Wood

The warmth and good feeling that comes from sitting near a fireplace or wood-burning stove has ensured a place for wood as a heating fuel since early times. Although only a small portion of today's homes rely on wood for their primary heating fuel, many homeowners desire a wood-burning fireplace or stove as a secondary heat source. Hardwoods such as ash, oak, birch, and maple are preferred over softwoods, because they yield more heat per unit of wood. Firewood is measured in cords. One cord is the quantity of wood that can be stacked in a volume measuring 4' by 4' by 8' (1.219 m by 1.219 m by 2.438 m). Suppliers typically deliver cordwood in sizes that fit most stoves. Wood fuel is also available in the form of pellets compressed from sawdust for burning in pellet stoves.

Using wood as a heating fuel requires much more involvement on the part of the homeowner than other fuels. Even when wood is delivered cut and split, it has to be stored. At least once a day it must be loaded into the appliance, and the ashes must be removed. Unfortunately, burning wood also emits chemical compounds and particulates that pollute the air, some of which pose serious risks to people with respiratory ailments. For that reason, government agencies have taken a variety of measures to minimize the hazard. Some municipalities restrict use of wood heating in times of unacceptable air quality. Others restrict or ban wood-burning appliances in new construction. Some states have air pollutant emission standards and certification programs for wood-burning appliances, modeled on those of the Environmental Protection Agency (EPA). The standards have encouraged manufacturers to equip their appliances with catalytic converters or develop designs that meet the emission requirements. One positive outcome of these efforts is that in becoming more efficient, wood-burning appliances also use less wood to produce the same amount of heat.

Coal

The term *coal* describes a variety of fossilized plant materials with varying heating values, ash melting temperatures, sulfur content, and many other chemical and physical properties. Anthracite, the most common type of coal for home heating, has a heat value of nearly 15,000 Btus per pound. Bituminous coal is a softer, dirtier-burning coal used primarily to generate electricity and fuel some industries.

At one time, meals in almost every home in North America were cooked on a cast iron stove that burned coal, while a coal-burning furnace in the basement heated the home. Both of these vanished when gas, oil, and electricity—all more convenient and cleaner-burning fuels—became widely available. Even though the United States has an ample supply of coal reserves, the extraction and use of coal as an energy source has raised serious safety and environmental concerns. Consensus has been building among climatologists that the rapid rise of carbon dioxide in the atmosphere due to industrialization over the last 150 years has led to an increase in the global average temperature by about 1° Celsius (C). Such a trend threatens profound damage to life on earth, from water and food scarcity, to rising sea levels and greater incidence of disease. According to the International Energy Agency, the burning of coal accounted for 45% of total energy-related carbon dioxide emissions in 2011.

Although coal still is used in heavy industries, coal-burning appliances are rare in homes today.

None of the fuels mentioned so far can heat a house without some means of converting the energy of the fuel into useful heat and getting the heat to where it's needed in the house. The devices for accomplishing these tasks make up a heating system. The various types of heating systems in today's homes are described in the following sections.

FORCED AIR HEATING SYSTEMS

Forced air systems deliver heat by convection. These systems are comprised of two parts: a central heating device—the furnace—and a distribution network—the ducts and accessories. Forced air heating has both pros and cons. On the upside, the ductwork in forced air heating systems can also distribute cold air if coupled with a central air conditioner. On the downside, constantly moving air circulates particulates that can pose a disadvantage to people with respiratory disorders. This can be remedied by the installation of an electrostatic furnace filter. Many types are available, some claiming removal of up to 97% of particles as small as 1 micron.

Furnaces

The heart of a forced air heating system is the furnace. Most furnaces are gas or oil fired, but other fuels include coal, wood, and electricity. The proper choice depends on the cost and availability of each fuel source in a particular region.

In a gas or oil furnace, natural or LP gas is piped to a burner inside the combustion chamber, where it mixes with air. A pilot light or auto-ignition device controlled by a thermostat ignites a flame that heats up a metal box called the heat exchanger, through which room air flows. The flame requires a source of oxygen, or combustion air, which can come from the ambient air, if the furnace is open to it and the walls are not too tightly sealed. The trend, however, is toward more tightly sealed houses to conserve heat, and tight houses should be provided with a separate source of combustion air ducted from the outside directly into the burner and never mixing with the ambient air of the house.

Exhaust gases given off by burners exhaust to the outdoors through a flue through the roof or—with some newer high-efficiency models—through a wall. A separate coil may run through the combustion chamber to heat water for use in the home.

Electric forced air furnaces use resistance heating elements rather than burners to heat the air in the heat exchanger. Because they heat air by moving it over a resistance coil rather than a flame, they need neither a source of combustion air nor venting for flue gases. Even with these advantages, the high cost of electricity in many regions makes electric furnaces the least economical option.

Forced air furnaces come in two versions, according to their position in relation to the duct-work (see Figure 13.2). Upflow furnaces deliver warm air overhead. A typical location for an upflow furnace is the basement, where it supplies one or more floors above. Another possibility is the main floor of a single-floor house whose ducts run through the attic. If this

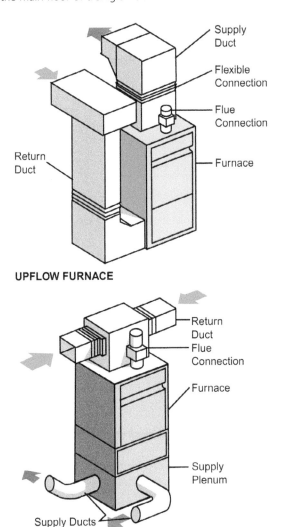

UPFLOW FURNACE

DOWNFLOW (COUNTERFLOW) FURNACE

FIGURE 13.2 The choice of upflow or downflow furnace depends on its location. An upflow furnace is typically in the basement and supplies heated air overhead to the floors above. A downflow furnace is located above the floors it serves.

same house had the ductwork running below the floor, the proper choice of furnace would be a downflow furnace (also known as a counterflow furnace).

The standard measure of their efficiency is the annual fuel utilization efficiency (AFUE), expressed as a percentage. The AFUE compares the amount of fuel converted to space heat to the amount of fuel consumed. Today's furnaces are much more efficient than their predecessors. To qualify for the Energy Star label of the EPA, a furnace must:

- meet or exceed 90% AFUE energy-efficiency ratings.
- have a manufacturer's limited warranty.
- be manufactured by an Energy Star partner.

Duct Systems

The fan in a forced air furnace blows heated air from the heat exchanger into a supply plenum. Smaller-size branch ducts tap into the plenum to supply warm air to the rooms through diffusers (also called registers) (see Figure 13.3). Ducts may be round or rectangular—or both—and made of metal or fiberboard. Typically located below the floor they serve, they may also be run above the ceiling, although delivering warm air downward is less efficient than blowing it upward, since warm air naturally tends to rise. Ducts located in a cold attic or crawl space must be insulated to prevent heat loss. In below-floor systems, diffusers mount either on the floor or on a wall near the floor. Diffusers in ceiling-ducted systems may be mounted either in the ceilings or near the floor, if a duct can be run down from the duct through a wall space (see Figure 13.4).

It is often more difficult to locate diffusers in kitchens and baths than in other rooms for several reasons. First, the rooms—especially baths—are smaller, and equipment or fixtures take up a good deal of the wall space. On the upside, these rooms usually don't need as much supplemental heat as other rooms. The occupants are usually moving around in a kitchen or bath rather than sitting or lying in bed. And cooking, washing, and bathing generate heat, often too much. Still, kitchens and baths should be provided with at least one diffuser. For rooms with no convenient locations on a floor or wall, special diffusers mount in the kick space below a cabinet.

Air supplied to the rooms must somehow find its way back to the source. Room doors should be sized to leave a gap of an inch or so at the bottom to allow the air to circulate. A grille located in a central position, such as a hallway, picks up return air and carries it back to the furnace via a return duct that feeds into a return-air plenum.

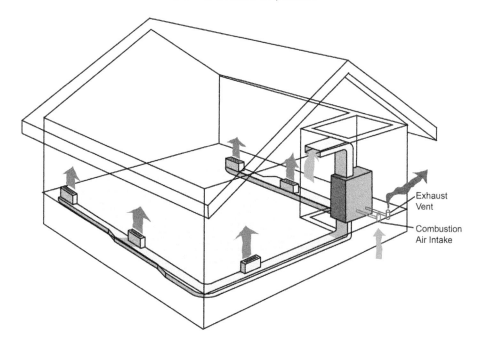

Exhaust
Vent

Combustion
Air Intake

FIGURE 13.3 A forced air heating system supplies warm air through diffusers along the periphery of the house. Cool air returns to the furnace through a return vent typically located in a hallway.

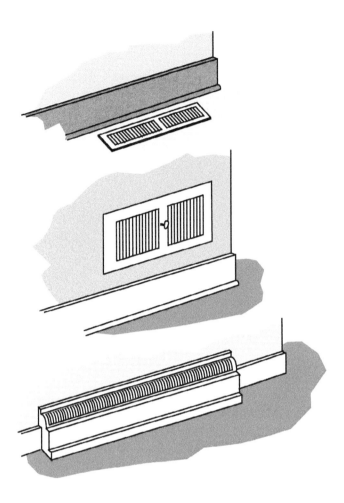

FIGURE 13.4 Diffusers (registers) for air heating and cooling systems come in many shapes and sizes and can be located in any interior surface.

HYDRONIC HEATING SYSTEMS

The word *hydronic* comes from the Greek *hydro*, meaning water, and hydronic systems are sometimes called hot water systems. Where forced air heating systems heat room air directly, hydronic systems heat water that heats the home indirectly via a network of piping running around the periphery of the house (baseboard systems) or tubing arrayed below the floor (radiant floor systems).

Baseboard Systems

Hot water systems have replaced steam heating systems in new construction and can be retrofitted to steam heating systems in older houses, making use of the existing radiators and piping. A boiler heats water in a combustion chamber that circulates through a network of piping to the rooms. Fin tube diffusers—assemblies of aluminum plates attached to the piping—transfer heat to the space. The plates greatly expand the area of heated metal exposed to the air, thereby increasing the heat transfer to the room air. Although some heat is radiated, most of the heat comes from convection, as room air passes up and over the plates. Hydronic baseboard systems have both pros and cons compared to forced air heating.

Pros
- The initial cost of hydronic heating systems is less because the distribution piping and diffusers are more economical than ductwork.
- Because no ductwork is needed, hydronic systems take up less space than ducted systems and are thus easier to fit through the structure—a boon to remodeling and additions.
- Because hydronic systems don't move air around, they are useful to persons with respiratory ailments.

Cons
- A separate ductwork system must be installed if air conditioning is desired.
- Hydronic systems contain no filters to cleanse the air.

Hydronic systems appeal mostly to homeowners in heating- rather than cooling-dominated climates, where the ductwork can do double duty as a conduit for cooled air in the summer.

Gas and oil are both used as fuel for standard boilers in hydronic systems. Oil is more common, for the reasons cited previously. If gas is the fuel, it comes either from an underground pipe connected to a natural gas utility or from an LP tank outside the home. Oil is stored in a tank inside the house near the boiler and gravity-fed into the boiler through a small-diameter pipe. When the thermostat triggers a call for heat, a nozzle in the burner mixes the oil with air and sprays the mixture into the combustion chamber, where it is ignited. The flame wraps around the cast iron sections that contain water, heating it to the target level. A circulator pump (or pumps in multizone systems) then pumps the hot water through the distribution network (see Figure 13.5). As in forced air furnaces, boilers also may contain a secondary loop of piping to heat water for domestic use. Boilers of this type are called combination boilers.

Standard boilers achieve efficiencies of upward of 85%. Condensing boilers (or pulse-type boilers) reach efficiencies of up to 95% by improving the way the fuel is burned. A second heat exchanger recoups some of the heat from the hot exhaust gases to preheat the water in the boiler system. When these boilers are working at peak efficiency, the water vapor produced in the combustion process condenses back into liquid form. This condensate is piped away through noncorrosive piping, since it is acidic. Condensing

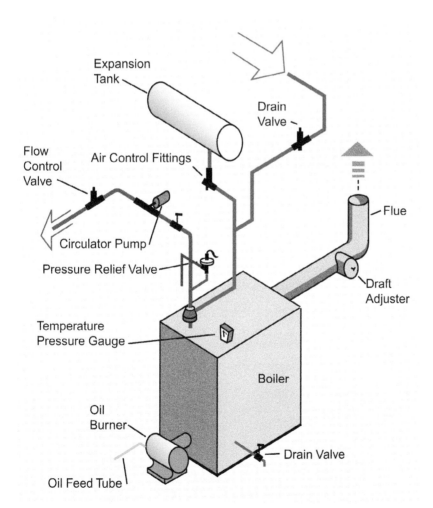

FIGURE 13.5 An oil-fired boiler and its components.

boilers run on either gas or oil. They have one added benefit over standard boilers: They don't need an exhaust flue, or chimney. The relatively low temperatures of the combustion gas produce low-temperature carbon dioxide that can be vented directly to the outside through a 2" (51 mm) diameter polyvinyl chloride (PVC) pipe. A second pipe or concentric pipe around the exhaust pipe brings combustion air into the fire chamber, making the operation of the unit independent of the air supply in the home, which is a great benefit in tightly sealed, energy-efficient houses. Although condensing boilers cost more initially than standard boilers, the difference eventually is recouped in fuel savings. And doing away with a chimney saves on costs while enabling more flexibility in interior planning.

Heated water circulates through copper piping that runs around the perimeter of the house. The simplest circuit is a simple loop with a continuous pipe that connects each fin tube diffuser mounted near the baseboard in each room, as shown in Figure 13.6. The obvious disadvantage of this series perimeter loop layout is that the water temperature drops at each fin tube and gets progressively cooler toward the end of the run. An improved version is the one-pipe system, which allows the main supply/return pipe to bypass each fin tube. A special fitting or valve at each fin tube can control the flow. A two-pipe loop is better still. With a separate supply and return loop, water nearly at boiler temperature is supplied to each fin tube without being cooled by passing through the previous fin tube or accepting cooler return water (see Figure 13.6).

For kitchens that lack sufficient open wall space for diffusers, there are radiators designed to be installed in the toe space below cabinets. A fan comes on when hot water is circulated through the system, to direct warm air into the room.

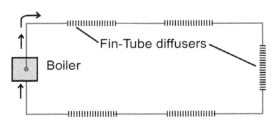

A: SERIES PERIMETER LOOP

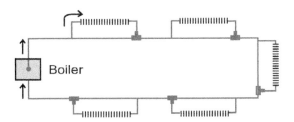

B: 1-PIPE DIRECT RETURN

FIGURE 13.6 A series perimeter loop (A) is the simplest hydronic distribution system but not the best, since diffusers at the end of the loop get the coolest water. This defect is overcome by adding valves, in a one-pipe direct return system (B), and improved more in a two-pipe reverse return system (C), with boiler-temperature water supplied to each diffuser and cooler water returning via a separate line.

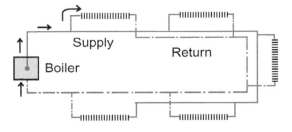

C: 2-PIPE REVERSE RETURN

Radiant Floor Systems

Why not heat people directly instead of heating the air around them, as forced air and hydronic baseboard systems do? This is exactly what radiant heating does. Radiant floor systems also need a piping network to deliver heat, but the piping is expanded over the surface of the floor, making the whole floor the heat diffuser (see Figure 13.7). With a much larger distribution area, the temperature can be lower, so the floor heats the occupants by radiating the heating energy directly to their bodies. They feel warmer, even with the lower air temperature. Advertisements for radiant floor heating drive this point home by showing happy homeowners lounging about on radiant-heated floors in their bare feet.

Radiant heating offers other pluses as well. Lower thermostat settings yield energy savings. The tubing can be coupled with active solar collectors to take advantage of solar energy. Radiant floor heating is quiet, needs no registers in the walls or floor, and doesn't blow dust around, as does forced air. On the downside, it costs more than other systems initially and could be more difficult to work around in future remodels. Also, radiant floors work best with hard, preferably masonry, floor surfaces. This feature makes radiant floors especially attractive heating options for baths and, to a lesser degree, kitchens, for these reasons:

- Cabinetry and fixtures in kitchens and baths, when placed next to walls, occupy spaces where diffusers are typically located.
- Kitchens and baths are more likely to have tiled, or at least uncarpeted, floors.
- The occupants are barefoot much of the time in baths.

Radiant floor heating starts with a gas- or oil-fired boiler to heat the water, as with other hydronic systems. The warm water typically circulates through loops of closely spaced plastic tubing, typically cross-linked polyethylene (PEX). The loops are organized into zones, with the supply to each zone regulated by a distribution manifold near the boiler. The plastic distribution tubing can be embedded in concrete slabs, if insulated below (see Figure 13.8). In wood floors, the tubing can snug up to the underside of the subfloor, between the joists, or be embedded into a 2″ layer of lightweight concrete (or gypsum concrete) topping poured over the subfloor. Of course, the topping costs and adds weight, which must be accommodated by the floor structure.

ELECTRIC HEATING SYSTEMS

Electricity passed through poor conductors generates heat by its resistance, an elegant and simple component of a heating system. Unfortunately, it's also one of the most expensive in many regions, which explains why electric heating takes a backseat to other fuels. (Chapter 14 discusses another form of heating with electricity in connection with heat pumps.) Nonetheless, electric resistance heating may be practical in some situations, such as a bathroom addition with no way to tie into the home's main heating system.

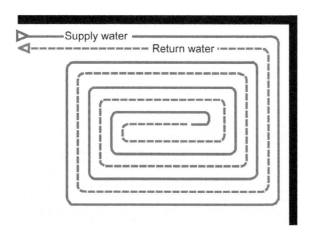

FIGURE 13.7 A simple radiant floor heating system delivers heated water to the floor through one loop and returns cooled water to the boiler through another loop.

TUBING IMBEDDED IN CONCRETE SLAB

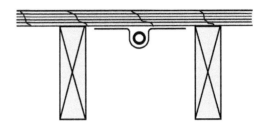

TUBING MOUNTED UNDER SUBFLOOR

FIGURE 13.8 Tubing for radiant floor systems can be embedded in a concrete slab or attached to the underside of a wood floor. Metal plates around the tubing help transfer heat from the tube to the wood.

Electric radiant heating can be installed in floors, as in hydronic systems, as well as in walls and ceilings, which makes it an option to consider for baths that are hard to heat with other alternatives. In electric systems, resistance cable replaces warm-water-carrying plastic tubing of hydronic systems. A water heater containing an electric resistance coil heats the water, as opposed to a boiler.

Electric forced air furnaces provide heat by moving air across resistance heating elements. The hot air is then fan-forced through ducts in the same way as was described for forced air systems. The main advantages are the absence of vents or flues and no need to worry about keeping the LP gas tank or oil tank filled.

Baseboard convectors are likely the simplest way to heat with electricity. Electricity runs through resistance cable inside metal tubing. Fins encase the tubing, as in fin tube hydronic diffusers, to conduct the heat out of the cable, which heats the room by convection (see Figure 13.9).

ACTIVE SOLAR HEATING SYSTEMS

As stated previously, energy-efficient design in a residence reduces its dependence on imported energy sources, resulting in benefits to the environment as well as the homeowner. Chapter 5 described some ways to use solar energy to passively heat the interior. This approach should be considered where a home's site and geometry and layout make it feasible.

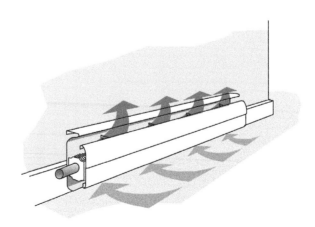

FIGURE 13.9 A fin tube diffuser contains a series of closely spaced metal plates that transfer heat from the supply pipe (or wire, with electric systems) to the room via convection.

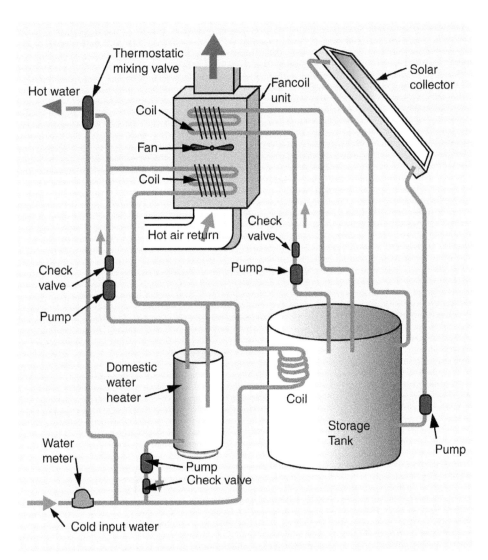

FIGURE 13.10 This active solar space-heating system pumps heated water from the roof-mounted collector into a storage tank in the basement. The water transfers its heat to air in a heat exchanger, which then circulates the air through ducts into the interior. If the water in the tank is not hot enough, water from the domestic water heater is pumped to the heat exchanger to augment it.

The sun's energy also can provide space heat with an active system, which consists of a collector that heats a liquid or air medium and equipment to store and distribute the heat.

Liquid-based systems contain either water that is drained back into a storage tank when outside temperatures are low enough to freeze it or an antifreeze that transfers its heat to water in the storage tank indirectly. Heat from the water reaches the interior either via a distribution system, such as fin tube baseboard diffusers, or via a heat exchanger that heats air that then circulates through ductwork.

Active solar air-based systems employ hollow collectors on the roof, from which the heated air circulates into a storage bin for rocks, usually located in the basement. Fans blow air over the rocks and into ductwork for distribution in the interior (see Figure 13.10).

As with passive solar heating, active solar space heating systems require a south-facing collecting surface. They also require complicated and expensive equipment, which makes them compare unfavorably to passive systems and accounts for the small number of installations.

ALL-IN-ONE HEATING SYSTEMS

All systems described thus far deliver heat to all rooms in the house from a central system comprising a heating device and a distribution system. However, designers often encounter situations not easily served by a central system, such as in an addition or room very far from the heating source. Many products available heat only one room; others can heat a whole house, with proper design.

Stoves

Stoves have evolved over the years and come in a wide variety of shapes, sizes, and materials. They burn wood, coal, pellets, gas, and even corn, all with greater efficiencies and less pollution than their predecessors. Glass-faced models display the flame, which adds esthetic appeal. Except for unvented gas stoves, all require a flue for exhaust gases, and the clearances required between the walls and floors for a stove limit its possible locations in the house. A kitchen or bath is an unlikely location for a stove.

Fireplaces

Fireplaces are wonderful places to sit near on cold nights but are poor heating devices for spaces much beyond the fire, because most of the heat goes up the flue. In fact, open fireplaces rob more heat from the house than they supply. There are, of course, ways to improve this balance. Glass doors enclosing the firebox will keep room air from being sucked up the flue. If such doors are added, there also must be a separate outside air supply to the firebox. Still, uncoupling the fire from the room robs the fireplace of some of its appeal so many people still prefer open fires, at least for occasional use. Fireplaces are rare in kitchens but make luxurious amenities for upscale baths.

Gas fireplaces mimic the effect of burning wood, with fake logs that are constantly engulfed by the flames from the burner below. Although the effect falls short of a real log burning, these units are much less demanding to operate. You simply turn them off and on. They come in vented and unvented models that need no flue. The gas appliance industry has largely addressed earlier concerns about the emissions of unvented gas stoves, specifically carbon monoxide (CO). A national safety standard for vent-free gas appliances, American National Standard Institute (ANSI) Z21.11.2, requires vent-free products to satisfy numerous construction and performance requirements. The safety standard is approved by ANSI and is developed by an independent committee comprised of representatives from various interests, including state and federal regulatory authorities, utilities, manufacturers, and consumers. Vent-free gas products are certified for compliance with this standard to ensure their safety.

Unit Heaters

Gas-fired heating units that mount next to an outside wall make good auxiliary heat sources for hard-to-heat areas, such as a single-room addition (see Figure 13.11). Direct-vent heaters draw combustion air into the fire chamber through a vent in the wall and exhaust the burned gases back out through another, concentric vent. Room air circulates around the fire chamber, never coming into contact with the combustion air. These heaters come in various

FIGURE 13.11 A unit heater provides a way to heat an addition without altering the central heating system. The gas unit shown circulates warmed air around the heating chamber inside. Combustion air enters and exits through the wall without mixing with the room air.

capacities, from 12,000 Btu per hour (BtuH) around 35,000 BtuH. Unvented heaters, which can be located anywhere in the room, also are available.

Heating products are constantly evolving, and there are many variations to the systems mentioned in this chapter. Some heating devices are combined into cooling equipment, as discussed in Chapter 14.

SUMMARY

The goal of home heating systems is to provide comfort for the occupants. Comfort, however, depends on a person's age and level of activity and on conditions of the atmosphere. Ensuring comfort inside a home at a time when dependence on imported energy accounts for an ever-increasing portion of household expenses while exacting greater costs to the environment.

The success of a residential design depends on how it responds to these realities. An energy-efficient home design begins with siting the home to take the best advantage of the energies available from natural sources, including solar energy for heating and breezes for cooling. A well-insulated, tightly constructed envelope can block unwanted heat while keeping the interior warm in cold weather. Choosing energy-efficient equipment will minimize fuel costs to homeowners as well as effects on the environment.

Using energy from the sun benefits the environment as well as homeowners and can be done with passive or active space heating systems. Passive approaches are simpler and more economical. Even homes that are energy efficient and/or derive heat from the sun likely still require some use of imported energy to provide all or part of their space heat. Several fuel sources, including gas, oil, electricity, and wood, are available. The proper choice depends on the amount required, cost in the region, and types of equipment needed to convert the fuel to heat.

Depending on the requirements of the space, it may be heated by a central appliance that delivers heat via a network of ducts or pipes or by an appliance that combines production and distribution in a single unit.

CHAPTER REVIEW

1. Would a person likely be comfortable when the dry bulb temperature is 70° F and relative humidity is 70%? (See Figure 13.1 page 136)
2. What type of heat transfer do you feel by holding a lighted match just above the palm of your hand? (See "Comfort and Heat" page 136)
3. Why would someone choose gas as a heating fuel? (See "Gas" page 137)
4. How is most electricity produced? (See "Electricity" page 138)
5. In terms of how it delivers heated air, what type of furnace would be best suited for a two-story house with a basement? (See "Furnaces" page 140)
6. In a kitchen with no free wall space, where could heated air be delivered from? (See "Baseboard Systems" page 142)
7. What type of heating system has a special appeal for a bath? (See "Radiant Floor Systems" page 145)
8. Why is passive solar heating usually preferred to active solar heating? (See "Active Solar Heating Systems" page 147)
9. Why are most fireplaces inefficient heating sources? (See "Fireplaces" page 148)

Cooling Systems

Comfort is the goal of cooling as well as heating systems. As indicated previously in the graph in Figure 13.1, people feel comfortable when the dry bulb air temperature ranges between around 70° to 80° Fahrenheit (F) (20° to 26° Celsius) when the relative humidity ranges between 20% and 70%. We can feel warm at 45°F (10° C) if we are in the sun. We also still can feel comfortable with temperatures as high as 90° F (32.2° C) if the air is moving. Successful systems for cooling the interior must create the narrow range of comfortable conditions when the ambient conditions are outside of the comfort range shown on the chart.

Learning Objective 1: Recognize the continuum of cooling strategies, from the simplest and least costly to the environment to the most complex and costliest.

Learning Objective 2: List ways a house can be designed to maximize cooling load avoidance.

Learning Objective 3: Identify the potential and limits of passive cooling strategies.

Learning Objective 4: Select cooling systems most appropriate to climate conditions.

COOLING NATURALLY

Cooling with any mechanical means incurs costs. The first cost is that of the equipment and installation. Next comes the expense of fuels and maintenance of the equipment over its expected lifetime. Finally, there are less obvious, harder-to-measure costs to the environment, from extracting the fuels and polluting the air and water in converting the fuels into the energy that powers equipment to make us feel comfortable.

We can do much to minimize our dependence on mechanical cooling by constructing our homes intelligently and drawing on natural energies as much as possible. Not all natural cooling strategies work everywhere or all of the time. Savvy designers understand the climate assets and limitations of their location and how to use them to passively cool homes. Only after exploiting these means do they employ mechanical devices, starting with the simplest and least demanding on outside energy, such as fans. The most complicated and costly devices, such as refrigerated cooling, are the means used when the ambient conditions exceed the capabilities of passive approaches. Load avoidance is the term engineers use to define strategies that minimize the demand, or load, on cooling equipment. Some ways to achieve load avoidance are described next.

Blocking Solar Heat

Windows contribute as much as one third of the total cooling season heat gain in homes in southern regions of the United States. Most of this heat comes directly from solar radiation rather than from hot outside air coming into the house. It stands to reason that the first line of defense against overheating should be some means of blocking this sunshine. Trees do this elegantly; deciduous trees even have the courtesy of dropping their leaves in the winter when we welcome the warmth of the sun. Unfortunately, trees may not be available or in the right location. Roof overhangs, shutters, blinds, and shades can serve just as well, although shades and blinds mounted inside the window are less effective, since the heat of the sun has already penetrated through the window. Roof overhangs should be large enough to block solar heat when it isn't wanted but small enough to admit it in winter. (See the formula for determining overhang projection in Chapter 5 and Figure 5.3.)

Window films and low-emissivity (low-e) coated glass are also effective in keeping out unwanted solar heat. Although window films can be messy and unappealing, low-e coating is invisible. Window manufacturers offer guidelines that tell which low-e coating is the most appropriate for a region's climate conditions.

Natural Ventilation

Air in motion serves two purposes in houses: maintaining indoor air quality and cooling. Ventilation promotes cooling directly or indirectly. When a breeze moves over your skin, it evaporates perspiration and removes latent heat, making you feel cooler. But if the conditions are above the comfort zone (see Figure 13.1), ventilation doesn't work. It can even make you feel hotter. Direct ventilation is an effective means of cooling in the dry bulb temperature range of 80° to 90° F (26° to 32° C), if the relative humidity stays below 80%. Fortunately, these conditions prevail in much of North America for all but the hottest times of summer, usually the month containing the last two weeks of July and first two weeks of August. Another limitation of ventilation is the chance that moving air can contain allergens that some people are susceptible to.

Regions with hot-dry climates, such as in the southwestern desert regions of the United States, typically have large swings in temperature from day to night. Very hot days often are followed by cool or cold nights. Designers can exploit this feature to cool houses through indirect ventilation. Walls and floors made of dense concrete or masonry materials have excellent heat-storing capacities that allow them to absorb and release heat slowly. Simply opening windows at night to allow cool breezes to cool the massive walls and floors naturally cools the interior in much of the year. Closing the windows in the morning allows the cooled materials to absorb heat from the house.

Cross ventilation is another way to take advantage of natural ventilation, by trapping the breezes that blow across the house. Windows on opposite walls of a room are the best way to flood the space with cooling that's free for the taking. But most rooms back up to other parts of the house rather than to an outside wall. Windows on adjacent walls are almost as effective if the windows are far enough apart to ensure a long path for any breeze that enters. A room with windows on only one wall gets little ventilation unless a door on the opposite wall opens to a part of the house that creates a path for the breeze to traverse. Casement and awning windows are better ventilators than double-hung or sliding windows for two reasons. First, they open outward, and the protruding sash directs passing breezes into the room. Second, their entire sash opens, whereas only half of a double-hung or slider opens.

The stack effect provides a third means of natural ventilation, by exploiting the tendency of warm air to rise (see Figure 14.1). Some traditional homes in the southern states had belvederes—roof towers with grilles—atop the center of their roofs. Air from open windows on the first floor rose up a central stairway and escaped through the belvedere, cooling the

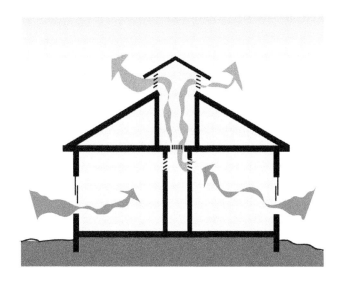

FIGURE 14.1 A house designed to maximize the cooling potential of natural ventilation contains openings situated to promote the flow of air through the entire interior similar to traditional southern houses, such as shown here. Note the openings in the hallway walls and the belvedere on the roof.

house in its wake. This strategy can be had in today's houses with operable skylights in the roof, a particular benefit to kitchens that have limited window area, due to cabinets and appliances taking much of the wall area.

COOLING WITH FANS

Natural ventilation is easy and cheap when it's available. When it isn't, fans can supply natural ventilation, either by separate fans in each room or a central fan capable of ventilating the whole house.

Ceiling fans can both cool a room and distribute the heat more evenly (see Figure 14.2). They make the best sense in larger rooms of the house with ceilings at least 8' (2.43 m) high. Baths usually are not good candidates for ceiling fans because of their smaller size and the need for a means of ventilation to ensure air quality, as we'll see in Chapter 15. Much the same applies to kitchens, even though they may be larger. Ceiling fans need a clearance of at least 10" (254 mm) between the ceiling and fan blades to provide adequate circulation. Guidelines for sizing ceiling fans are shown in Table 14.1.

FIGURE 14.2 Ceiling fans provide a low-tech means of cooling by ventilation.

TABLE 14.1 Sizing Ceiling Fans

Largest Dimension of Room	Minimum Fan Diameter
12' (3.658 m) or less	36" (.914 m)
12–16' (3.658–4.877 m)	48" (1.219 m)
16–17.5' (4.877–5.334 m)	52" (1.321 m)
17.5–18.5' (5.334–5.639 m)	56" (1.422 m)
18.5' + (5.639 m+)	2 fans

A whole-house fan pulls air in through windows opened at least 4" (102 mm) and exhausts it through vents in the attic (see Figure 14.3). It cools the house by moving the air (direct ventilation) and by keeping the heat in the attic from building up. To be effective, whole-house fans should be sized to provide 20 air changes per hour (ACH). The cubic feet per minute (cfm) required for this air change rate is obtained by multiplying the volume of the house by 0.33. The fan typically sits atop a grille in the upper floor ceiling and exhausts the air to the outside via vents in the gable ends of the attic, as shown in Figure 14.3.

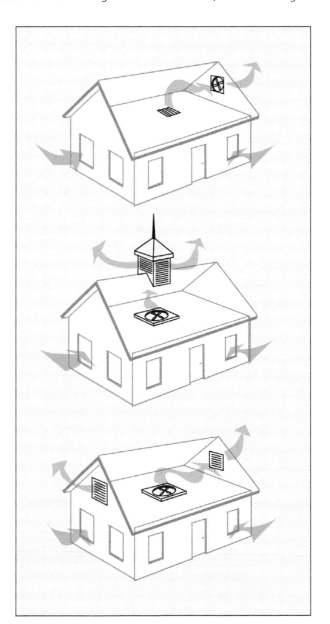

FIGURE 14.3 A whole-house fan can be installed in various ways. Located in the gable end of the attic (top picture), the fan draws inside air from a vent in the attic floor. Mounted in the attic floor, the fan can exhaust air through a belvedere (middle) or gable vents (bottom).

EVAPORATIVE COOLING

The same principle that cools your coffee can cool your house and do it more simply and economically than refrigeration equipment. As the name implies, evaporative cooling works by evaporating water into the airstream. In much the same way as the steam rising off a hot cup of coffee carries its heat away, when you put water in contact with incoming warm air, the water will evaporate into the air. When heat energy in the air changes the water from liquid to vapor, it cools the air in the process. Can this phenomenon be put to use to cool the interiors of houses? It can, but there's a catch: Evaporative cooling works best in dry climates, and even there it is not effective during the hottest times of the year.

The most popular way to use evaporative cooling is with "swamp" coolers, which are widely used in the southwestern part of the United States. How effective they are in lowering the temperature depends largely on how much moisture is already present in the air. Table 14.2 gives an idea of how much cooling to expect for various temperatures and humidity levels.

Evaporative cooling is more complicated and costs more than natural ventilation, but it costs far less than refrigerated cooling (air conditioning). Homes in regions that favor evaporative cooling can enjoy these advantages over refrigerated systems:

- Lower initial cost.
- Lower peak energy usage.
- Lower operating cost.
- Less greenhouse gas production.
- No chlorofluorocarbons (CFCs) or hydrochlorofluorocarbons (HCFCs), hence they do not deplete the ozone in the atmosphere.
- The cooled air is more humid. Refrigerated systems can dehydrate the air too much on a dry day.
- Evaporative cooling constantly floods the house with fresh air.
- The wetted pads through which hot, dry outside air passes en route to the interior also filter the air, which traps dust and other impurities.

Evaporative coolers typically mount on the roof, although through-wall units are also available. There are two types of systems, direct and indirect.

Direct Evaporative Cooling

The direct evaporative cooling system is the most widely used system in the Southwest. A large fan takes in huge amounts of hot outside air and blows it into the house through a pad, or filter, kept constantly moist by recirculated and makeup water (see Figure 14.4). The effect on the occupants is a gently moving stream of cooler air.

TABLE 14.2 Cooling Potential of Evaporative Cooling

Dry Bulb Temperature	Relative Humidity	Number of Degrees Temperature Can Be Lowered
75° F (24° C)	70–80%	3–4° F (1.6–2.2° C)
80° F (27° C)	50–60%	6–9° F (3.3–5° C)
85° F (29° C)	30–55%	10–15° F (5.5–8.3° C)
90° F (32° C)	20–30%	16–20° F (8.9–11° C)
95° F (35° C)	10–20%	21–25° F (11.7–13.9° C)
100° F (38° C)	5–10%	27–29° F (15–16° C)
105° F (41° C)	2–5%	31–33° F (17.2–18.3° C)
110° F (43° C)	2%	35°F (19.4°C)

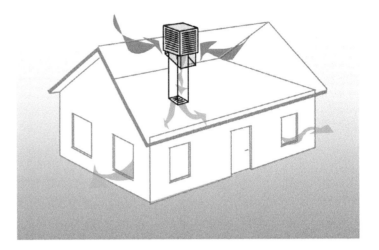

FIGURE 14.4 Direct evaporative coolers pull hot outside air through a wetted pad and deliver cooled, humidified air to the interior. This method works best in the hot-dry climates of the U.S. Southwest.

Indirect Evaporative Cooling

Because direct evaporative cooling adds moisture to the air, it does not suit hot humid regions. Another type, an indirect evaporative system, gets around this hurdle by isolating the moist, cooled air from the room air. It does this by passing the cooled air through an assembly of finned coils, around which the room air circulates (see Figure 14.5).

Both types of coolers mount on the roof, with a small-diameter pipe to supply makeup water and another to drain it to the ground. Through-wall units are also available.

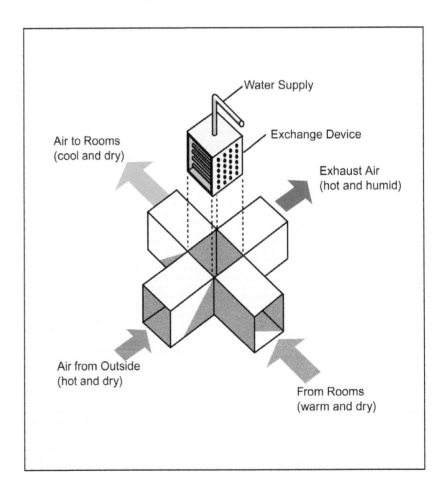

FIGURE 14.5 Indirect evaporative coolers do not mix the air cooled by evaporation with the air supplied to the interior. This feature makes them viable for humid regions.

REFRIGERATED COOLING

Using the simplest, most sustainable, and least polluting cooling strategies benefits everyone. That's why this chapter began by describing passive cooling techniques, such as natural ventilation and solar heat avoidance, followed by approaches that use *some* outside energy, such as fans and evaporative coolers. Mechanical cooling systems have been left to last, because they are the most complicated and energy-consuming cooling systems. Even so, they are the only means of achieving comfort when the outside conditions exceed the capabilities of other approaches. This occurs whenever high temperatures combine with high humidity, a condition that prevails in parts of the year in the southeastern and mid-Atlantic regions of the United States and year-round in southern Florida.

Refrigerated cooling (also called air conditioning or mechanical cooling) gets its name from the same process that cools the air inside a refrigerator. In simplest form, it works like this: A compressor compresses gas at room temperature. As it is compressed, it becomes hot. It flows in a compressed state through a coil located on the backside of the refrigerater, which cools it back to room temperature, but still under pressure. When the gas in then released through a nozzle into a coil inside the refrigerator the pressure diminishes, causing the gas to cool *below* the room temperature. Various types of air-conditioning systems use this process to cool building interiors. Some even combine heating capability.

Room Air Conditioners

Devices that contain the refrigeration and distribution equipment in a single unit are called room air conditioners. The distribution system consists of a fan that delivers cooled air at various speeds to the room. Although it is easy and convenient to mount a room air conditioner in the lower portion of a window opening, this method does not cool a room as efficiently as placing the unit in a special opening high in the wall, since cool air tends to sink to the floor (see Figure 14.6). Besides, a unit in a window blocks the light from that portion of the window and degrades the home's appearance from outside.

Room air conditioners come in various sizes and cooling capacities from 5000 to 29,000 British thermal units per hour (BtuH). Bigger is not better when sizing an air conditioner. An oversize unit cycles on and off less frequently, producing greater swings in temperature and humidity than a smaller unit that cycles on and off more often. In general, a well-insulated room requires from 20 to 40 BtuH per square foot of area to be cooled. Electricity is the usual fuel source and units can work off of 120 volts (V) or 220V power sources. Those wired to 220V power are more efficient but require a separate 220V outlet.

Central Air Conditioning

When cooling the whole house is the goal, a central system is the answer. There are two main configurations, a split system and a ducted system. Both divide the task of cooling the air from the means of delivering it to the rooms.

In a split system, the compressor sits on a concrete pad outside the house and is connected to fan-coil units in the walls or ceilings of various rooms (see Figure 14.7). Small-diameter copper piping provides the umbilical cord between the unit and the fan coils. Fans deliver cooled air from the coils to the rooms. In addition to cooling the whole house, split systems have another advantage over individual room units: They are less noisy. With the compressor unit outside, the only noise occupants hear is the sound of the fan. If the compressor unit is a heat pump, as discussed in the next section, a split system also can deliver heat.

The duct network that delivers warm air in winter can do double duty in the summer in a ducted air conditioning system, but with a trade-off (see Figure 14.8). Because warm air rises, the best place to run ducts for heating is below the floor of the rooms to be heated. Just the opposite is true of cooling, so using below-floor ducts for a ducted air conditioning system

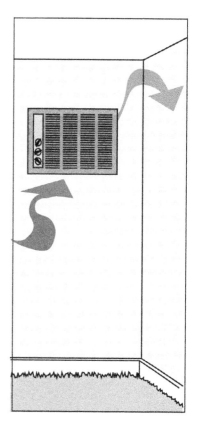

FIGURE 14.6 Because cooler air seeks a lower level, mounting a room air conditioner high in the wall is more effective than placing it in a low window opening.

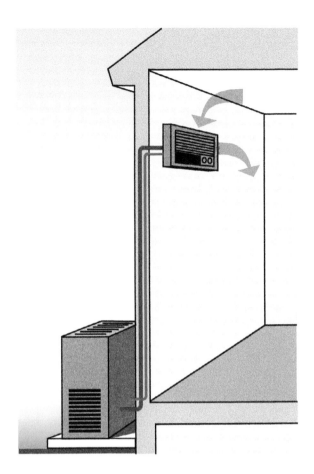

FIGURE 14.7 In a split air conditioning system, the compressor is located outdoors and is connected by piping to fan-coil diffusers in the walls of the rooms.

isn't as efficient as mounting them in the ceiling. This can be done, of course, in regions that need little or no heat in winter. Small kitchens present a special problem, since they probably have little if any free wall space, and floor-mounted diffusers are impractical in kitchens. Whereas heating can be delivered through a toe-space diffuser under a cabinet, cold air squeezed through a narrow aperture this close to the floor will result in little other than cold feet. If you face this situation, try to find a location high on a wall for the diffuser.

Like split systems, ducted systems are quieter than individual room air conditioners. Compared to split systems, ducting is trickier to run and eats up more space than refrigeration piping. However, ducted systems can use the same ducts for forced air heating, if some compromise in efficiency is accepted.

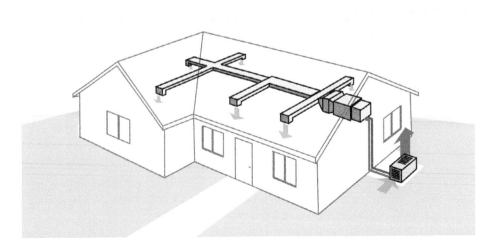

FIGURE 14.8 A ducted air conditioning system with the ducts and diffusers overhead is the best choice for homes in cooling-dominant regions. In heating-dominant regions, the ducts and diffusers are more efficient in the floor.

Rating the Efficiency of Refrigerated Cooling

Refrigerated cooling uses more electrical energy than passive or low-energy means, so homeowners naturally will want the most efficient equipment. Efficiency in a general sense is the output divided by the input, such as miles per gallon in vehicles. We use two measures to rate the efficiency of refrigeration devices.

The energy efficiency rating (EER) measures the efficiency of room air conditioners. It is the ratio of the cooling output in Btus divided by the power consumption in kilowatt-hours (kWh). A room air conditioner with an EER of 9.5 is considered efficient. Each unit bears a label stating its EER.

Central air conditioners and heat pumps operating in the cooling mode are rated by their performance over the cooling season. The seasonal energy efficiency rating (SEER) is obtained by dividing the cooling output in Btu by the energy in kWh required to operate the equipment in the cooling season in an average U.S. climate. A SEER of 10 was established in 1992 as the national appliance efficiency standard for central air conditioners. As of January 2006, all residential air conditioners sold in the United States must have a SEER of at least 13. Energy Star–qualified central air conditioners must have a SEER of at least 14.

Central air conditioners almost always beat out room units in energy efficiency. Features that can help make them operate efficiently include:

- A fan-only switch to allow ventilation only.
- A filter check light that comes on when the filter's predetermined lifetime is exhausted.
- An automatic delay fan switch to turn the fan off a few minutes after the compressor turns off.

SYSTEMS THAT PROVIDE HEATING AND COOLING

If air conditioners are basically refrigerators that pump heat out of the house, why can't we just turn them around in winter to pump heat back inside? We can and do with a device that works much like an air conditioner that can move heat in either direction. Using the same principle as a refrigerated air conditioner, but in reverse, a heat pump extracts heat from a space at low temperature and discharges it to another space at higher temperature. The system consists of two heat exchangers, a compressor and expansion valve, and interconnecting piping filled with a refrigerant. Electricity powers the compressor. By reversing the direction of the refrigerant flow with a valve, the system can be used to either heat or cool.

Heat pumps work well in houses in climates that need both heating and cooling, which includes much of the continental U.S. and southern Canada. They are not likely the most cost-effective choice for climates that seldom or never need refrigerated cooling. Heat pumps come in three configurations, as discussed next.

Single-Room Heat Pumps

Single-room heat pumps are basically room air conditioners equipped to reverse the cycle. They deliver heat efficiently when outside temperatures are above 45° F (7° C). When temperatures drop lower than this, efficiency falls off until the unit produces too little heat to be useful in the heat pump mode. It then shifts the heating task onto a backup resistance heating coil to make up the deficit. This, of course, makes it a costly heating source in regions with cold winters and high electricity costs. You can get an idea of whether a single-room heat pump is cost effective for your region from manufacturers' published data, specifically the heating seasonal performance factor (HSPF). The HSPF equals the total annual heating output in Btus divided by the total electrical output in watt-hours during the heating season.

Split-System Heat Pumps

Split-system heat pumps heat and cool more than one room by separating the compressor from the distribution system similar to a split-system air conditioning system, as described earlier. As with single-room heat pumps, these systems heat efficiently only when outside temperatures are above 45° F (7° C). At colder temperatures, they switch over to heating via an electric resistance element in the fan coil. At these times, the costs increase, particularly in areas with high costs of electricity.

Ducted Systems

Ducted heat pump systems resemble central, or whole-house, air conditioning in their configuration, with the heat pump unit mounted outside and cooled air distributed to the rooms through ducts. They incur the same trade-offs as ducted heating systems, in that overhead ducts work best for cooling while below-floor ducts excel for heating. The best location for ducts depends on the type of structure (a single-level house on a concrete slab has only one possible location, the ceiling) and relative demand for heating versus cooling.

Heat pumps also vary according to the medium they use to extract heat. Three types prevail:

1. Air-to-air heat pumps
2. Ground-coupled heat pumps (GCHP)
3. Groundwater heat pumps (GWHP)

Air-to-air heat pumps use the air as their heat exchange medium and are the simplest and most economical type. Consequently, they are the type most in use. The central unit sits on a pad outside the building, similar to that of a central air-conditioning system.

Another type has gained popularity in recent years. The GCHP uses the warmth or coolness of the ground to heat or cool a house. Because ground temperatures are more stable than air temperatures, GCHPs aren't as sensitive to daily and seasonal swings in temperature as air-to-air systems. GCHPs circulate a heat transfer fluid between the heat pump unit through a buried piping loop that absorbs the earth's natural warmth in winter and transfers heat to the earth in summer (see Figure 14.9).

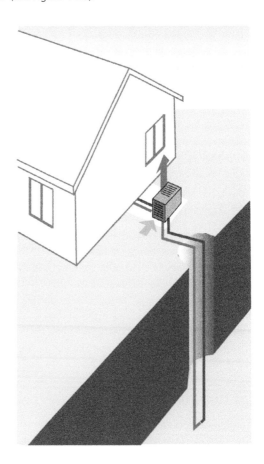

FIGURE 14.9 Because the ground is warmer than the air in winter and cooler in summer, it can be utilized for heating or cooling in GCHPs. Water circulates through piping buried in the ground, extracting heat from the earth in winter and expelling it back into the earth during the cooling season.

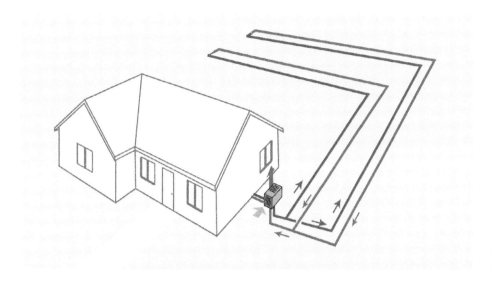

FIGURE 14.10 GWHPs extract heating or cooling from water by piping that extends vertically into a pond or well.

The GWHP, a less common type, draws water from a well or pond, exchanges the heat with a refrigerant, and then discharges the water into a rejection well, disposal pond, or storm sewer (see Figure 14.10). Obviously, this approach is limited to houses close to a water source.

SUMMARY

The need for cooling in houses to make them feel comfortable to the occupants depends on three variables: dry bulb temperature, relative humidity, and solar heat gain. Designers have several means to address these factors, beginning with simple and environmentally responsible measures. Proper landscaping, a well-insulated envelope, and sun-blocking devices on openings can all contribute to reducing the solar heat load. Placement of openings that receive natural ventilation can create comfortable conditions for at least some times of the year.

When conditions exceed the capabilities for comfort through heat-blocking cooling strategies alone, simple mechanical devices such as evaporative coolers and fans often can make up the difference.

Cooling by refrigeration is the costliest method to both the homeowner and the environment, so it should be brought into play only when climate conditions exceed passive and simpler cooling strategies. Refrigerated cooling systems are suited for a single room or a whole house, and some systems distribute cooled air via ducts or fan coils. Heat pumps can provide heating as well as cooling.

CHAPTER REVIEW

1. Would a person likely feel comfortable in a room with a dry bulb temperature of 70° F, relative humidity of 30%, with no moving air? (See "Chapter introduction," page 151)
2. Why are blinds inside the window less effective at blocking solar heat than shutters outside? (See "Blocking Solar Heat" page 152)
3. Would a house in Maine likely benefit more or less in summer than one in Arizona if built with masonry walls and floors? (See "Natural Ventilation" page 152)
4. Which state in the previous question would likely benefit more from evaporative cooling? (See "Evaporative Cooling" page 155)
5. Which two atmospheric conditions combine to limit the capabilities of passive cooling approaches? (See "Refrigerated Cooling" page 157)
6. What two advantages do split air conditioning systems have over ducted systems? (See "Central Air Conditioning" page 157)

Maintaining Healthy Indoor Air

Achieving an energy-efficient home requires minimizing air infiltration through the envelope. There is, unfortunately, a downside to tight houses. Sealing them up to conserve energy also keeps out fresh air that would otherwise cleanse the interior of contaminants. The gases and particles that pollute the rooms of our houses have many sources, some of which are manageable by the occupants: smoking, burning wood in stoves, operating unvented gas appliances, bathing, cooking, and chemicals used for cleaning. Some pollutants are beyond the control of all but the most careful and savvy occupants, including fire retardants in furniture and formaldehyde and organic chemicals used in the manufacture of carpeting and building materials. These substances can gradually release (outgas) to the air in the room.

Some of the culprits that contaminate the air of our houses are not necessarily unhealthy, simply objectionable. Odors produced in the kitchen and bathroom fall into this category. Others, such as secondhand smoke from cigarettes, are definite health hazards, particularly to people with allergies or asthma.

Regardless of the contaminant, occupants will be healthier and happier if it is removed to the outside. Fortunately, we have ways to do this without compromising the goals of energy-efficient design. The culprits that contaminate indoor air are many and varied in their potential for damaging health and well-being. This chapter discusses some of the pollutants and some of the design strategies that can ensure a healthy indoor environment.

Learning Objective 1: Identify the health-impairing gases that can be trapped inside a tightly sealed home.

Learning Objective 2: Discuss the need for some and risks of too much moisture in the interior.

Learning Objective 3: Describe the requirements of effective point source ventilation systems.

Learning Objective 4: Compare whole-house ventilation systems.

SOURCES OF INDOOR AIR POLLUTION

Radon

A radioactive product of the radium that naturally occurs in the earth's crust, radon is a colorless, odorless gas that poses a risk to people in regions with high concentrations of certain types of rock strata. It is believed responsible for 5% to 15% of all lung cancers. Radon gas seeps into houses through minuscule cracks in foundations and basement floors. It also can occur in well water. Preventing radon from getting into a house is easier at the construction stage than after it is built. It begins with carefully sealing up cracks in the floors and walls and waterproofing the foundation on the outside.

A gravel bed below the basement slab can act as a continuous evacuation path to the outside, when it is equipped with a fan that runs continuously at a low velocity to suck air through the gravel and exhaust it to the outside. Homeowners have few means available to mitigate radon in an existing home, short of sealing up visible cracks in the foundation and basement slab and installing a ventilation system in the basement.

Granite, like other stone species, can contain radon. Because it is frequently chosen for countertops, the question arises as to how much risk a granite countertop poses to the occupants. The Environmental Protection Agency (EPA) considers radon originating from the soil beneath a home a far larger public health risk than radon from granite building materials. Also, any radon from a granite countertop in a kitchen or bath is likely to be diluted, since those rooms are usually well ventilated.

Formaldehyde

Formaldehyde is a strong-smelling yet colorless gas embodied that is a component of many common building materials, such as plywood and particleboard, as well as furniture, drapes, and carpets made from synthetic materials. This gas can irritate the nose, throat, and eyes and may case nasal cancer. Today many panel materials contain little or no formaldehyde; care must be taken to specify them at the design stage. Increasing the rate of air changes in the house helps mitigate formaldehyde after the fact.

Combustion Gases

Several noxious gases come from operating kerosene heaters, woodstoves, and unvented gas appliances. Car exhausts in attached garages can also seep into the house through doorways. Deadly in high enough concentrations, carbon monoxide (CO) is a colorless, odorless, tasteless gas produced by burning all fuels. In lesser concentrations, this gas can impair the lungs, eyes, and brain. Nitrogen oxide has no color or odor, while nitrogen dioxide does have an odor at higher levels. Long exposure to either can cause lung damage.

Mitigating pollution from combustion appliances begins at the device. Woodstoves should be properly sized and vented. Appliances should be adjusted correctly. Air into woodstoves and fireplaces should come from the outside rather than from room air. Chimneys need to be kept clean. A car should never be left idling in the garage.

CO detectors that sound an audible alarm are required by the 2012 International Residential Code (IRC) in new construction and in existing dwellings when a permit is required for remodeling. Detectors are to be mounted outside each sleeping area but not within 15' (4575 mm) of a fuel-burning appliance.

Smoke from anything in the house that catches fire contains various noxious gases that can injure or kill the occupants. Smoke alarms detect the presence of smoke and alert the occupants before the smoke or fire can impact their health. The 2012 IRC requires a smoke alarm in the same locations as for CO detectors. The devices in new homes must be hard-wired to the home's electrical system and have battery packs for backup. In existing homes where the remodeling does not require removal of ceiling or wall surfaces, devices equipped with batteries only are allowed. Smoke alarms sound an audible noise when triggered. Devices equipped with strobe lights are available for occupants with hearing impairments.

Particulates

The health hazards smoking poses to smokers are well established. Smoking also releases particles into the air small enough to be inhaled by others. Minor exposure can result in irritation to the eyes and respiratory system. Long-term exposure can cause emphysema, heart disease, bronchitis, and lung cancer.

Other sources of particulates include unvented gas appliances, kerosene heaters, asbestos-bearing construction materials, dust, and pet dander. Solutions include not smoking inside, making sure stove doors don't leak, changing air filters regularly, and providing an outside air source for combustion appliances.

Gases from Household Chemicals

Many organic compounds found in cleaning agents, pesticides, aerosol sprays, paints, and solvents can irritate the eyes, skin, nose, throat, and central nervous system. Some household chemicals are available in "green" versions that do not harm health. Paints containing low levels of volatile organic compounds were mentioned in a previous chapter. Other remedies include following the directions on the label, using chemicals only in well-ventilated areas, and keeping them locked away from children.

You may have noticed that ventilation, in one form or another, is mentioned as a remedy for all of the indoor air pollutants. Having a good grasp of the techniques and devices that provide ventilation will help you achieve clean, healthy indoor air for your clients.

Moisture

Water vapor, while not a noxious gas in itself, can harm both the health of the occupants and the structure itself. For these reasons, moisture levels can't be ignored when we are talking about indoor air quality.

We can't live in a house without producing moisture. For starters, we add moisture to the air every time we perspire or take a breath. We dump large amounts of moisture into the air while showering, bathing, boiling water, and cooking food. In addition, substantial moisture may enter a home apart from anything the occupants do. A house constructed without proper vapor barriers can fall prey to moisture seeping into basements through masonry walls or wicking up through the soil below a crawl space.

We need some moisture in the air to maintain a healthy respiratory system and to keep our skin from becoming too dry. Most people feel comfortable when the air they inhale contains between 40% and 60% relative humidity. Excessive moisture, however, poses a hazard to health by promoting the growth of microorganisms and acting as a solvent for other pollutants.

Mold is one of the microorganisms that thrives in a damp environment. Its threat to health has become more apparent in recent years. A 2007 study funded by the EPA estimated that of the 21.8 million people reported to have asthma in the United States, approximately 4.6 million cases were estimated to be attributable to dampness and mold exposure in the home, resulting in a cost of $3.5 billion—and those are just the health costs exclusive of the cost of remediation. The study also estimated that dampness or mold is present in 47% of homes.

Excessive moisture can damage parts of the house itself. When the indoor temperature is higher than the outdoor temperature, the warm air inside seeks to a path out. As the warm air wends its way through the cracks and crannies of the building envelope, it meets a position in the structure, the dew point, where the dry bulb temperature and wet bulb temperature coincide. Moisture in the air condenses and collects on building materials, where it can rot framing and wall sheathing, peel exterior paint, and create ice dams on the eaves.

The move toward tighter houses requires good design to achieve a moisture-resistant barrier, careful craftsmanship during construction, and means to evacuate moisture. The occupants can do their part by:

- Not intentionally adding moisture by leaving a kettle boiling on a woodstove.
- Not storing green firewood in the heated part of the house.
- Ducting clothes dryers to the outside, not into an attic or basement.
- Using kitchen exhaust fans when cooking.
- Using bath exhaust fans when bathing or showering.

The lion's share of indoor moisture in a home is generated in the kitchen and bath—your area of specialization. As a kitchen and bath designer, you can do your part by properly designing moisture control devices for rooms under your responsibility and communicating the problems and solutions relating to moisture control early to both the client and the building team.

FRESH AIR THROUGH VENTILATION

We saw in Chapter 14 how ventilation, whether natural or fan forced, can help in cooling a house. Ventilation is also needed to ensure good air quality by evacuating contaminated air to the outside and replacing it with cleaner outside air. (Unfortunately, in many large urban, at times in the summer the outside air has high levels of ozone and other contaminants, making it an unhealthy makeup source). In mild weather, obtaining fresh air is as easy as opening a window. Even in cold weather, it presented no challenge in older houses, because enough fresh air leaked in through cracks around windows and doors to maintain a supply of fresh air to the interior. These paths were blocked when houses got sealed up to achieve better energy efficiency. Energy-efficient houses today rely on mechanical means to provide the necessary air changes.

The exact amount of fresh air required for good indoor air quality is stated in air changes per hour (ACH), which is the number of times all of the air in the house is replaced with outside air. The American Society of Heating, Refrigeration, and Air Conditioning Engineers (ASHRAE) recommends a minimum ACH of 0.35 to maintain healthy air inside a house. To put this number into perspective, a well-sealed new home gets in the neighborhood of up to 0.6 ACH and a reasonably tight older home gets around 1.0 ACH. Fairly loose, drafty homes get air changes of 4 ACH or greater.

The Canadian National Building Code (NBC) lists the requirements for ventilation according to the season. Ventilation during the nonheating season can come from natural or mechanical sources. If the room is mechanically cooled, the equipment must provide a minimum of 0.5 ACH. Bathrooms are required to have openable ventilation areas (e.g., the area of an opened window) of at least 0.09 m^2. Other living areas must have a minimum of 0.28 m^2.

The NBC specifies that every dwelling supplied with electrical power must have a mechanical ventilation system for the heating season. Ventilating capacities are specified by volume of air per second in liters/second (L/s) rather than ACH. Ventilating equipment for kitchens and baths must provide at least 5 L/s.

There are many ways to bring in air from the outside through mechanical ventilation. All methods depend on electrically operated fans, acting on their own or coupled with other mechanical equipment. Next we consider some of the main options, from the simplest to most complex.

VENTILATING ROOM BY ROOM

Spot ventilation removes moisture, odors, and pollutants directly at the source. Some of the most common devices that use this approach are discussed next.

Room Exhaust Fans

The simplest, most economical way to move stale air out and fresh air into a room is with an exhaust fan in an outside wall or ceiling, ducted to the outside (see Figure 15.1). Codes state the requirements for mechanical ventilation for baths that don't have direct access to outside air via a window or other opening. The exhaust capacity depends on the size of the room. You can determine the proper capacity by dividing the volume of the room in cubic feet (cf) by 7.5. For example, a bath measuring 8' by 12' with a ceiling height of 8' has a volume of 768 cf. An adequately sized exhaust fan for this room is 768/7.5, or 102 cubic feet per minute (cfm). Capacities of units currently available range between 75 and 600 cfm, so finding one that could handle this room is relatively easy. Fan flow ratings are based on an assumed resistance to air flow. If you are designing an installation with a duct run longer than 5' (1.524 m) or more than one elbow (el), plan on using a fan capacity higher than that which you'll obtain from the formula.

The chief drawback of individual exhaust fans is their noise. Fans produce noise by themselves, and when mounted into a ceiling, they can vibrate the ceiling board to add to the overall noise. Fan noise is measured in units called sones. The quietest kitchen and bath exhaust fans produce around 1 sone, about the same noise as a refrigerator fan. The noisiest ones produce up to 4 sones. The noise plus the inconvenience of having to remember to turn them on and off are probably why exhaust fans don't get used as much as they ought to. To ensure that they get used every time the bathroom is used, the exhaust fan can be wired to the room's light switch.

Kitchen Exhaust Devices

The aroma of bread baking in the oven or a hearty soup steaming on the stove on a cold winter day evokes warm feelings for the kitchen. But cooking also pollutes the air with grease, smoke, undesirable odors, moisture, and even some toxic emissions from gas ranges, making it the major source of air pollution in most homes today. The most effective way to

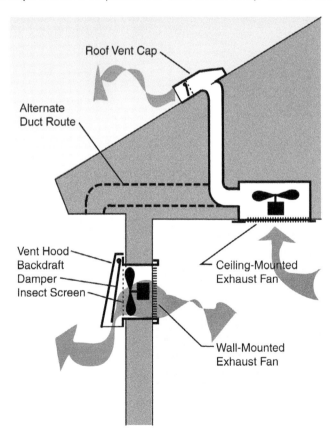

FIGURE 15.1 Room exhaust fans can mount in walls or ceilings. Ducts, when necessary, should be as short and direct as possible.

remove these gases is at the source—the range. Exhaust can be removed from either above or at the cooking surface.

Range hoods, vent hoods, and shrouds capture heated gases as they rise off the cooking surface, suck them through a filter to trap grease, and evacuate them through a duct to the outside. Recirculating, or unvented, models that don't require ducts are also available (see Figure 15.2). They merely pull air through the filter and return it to the room. Because they can't remove combustion gases, they are not as effective as ducted units and should be used only in cases where it is impossible to duct the exhaust to the outside.

Manufacturers offer range hoods incorporating fans and lights in several sizes, capacities, and designs. Off-the-shelf models come in widths of 30", 36", 42", and 48" (762 mm, 914 mm, 1.066 m, and 1.219 m) wide to match the widths of the ranges they serve. Some kitchen designers suggest that the range hood will perform more effectively if its width is wider than the range by one size. As kitchens have become more than a utilitarian place to cook food, so has the equipment. The 30" (762 mm) wide range that served past generations so well no longer satisfies many homeowners today. They look to larger models that incorporate features of commercial ranges. If you are designing a kitchen for this type of range or cooktop, you may be better served by choosing a high-powered commercial-style hood rather than a standard range hood. Custom range hoods made of stainless steel or copper are increasingly common in upscale kitchens.

Regardless of the size and appearance of a range hood, its geometry must be such that it can effectively catch and hold the exhaust gases from the cooking surface while the fan sucks them out (see Figure 15.3). The most effective shape for this is a canopy—think of an inverted bowl. A hood 16" to 21" (406 to 533 mm) deep, front to back, should mount 24" (610 mm) above the range. A 24" (610 mm) deep hood can be 30" (762 mm) above the range.

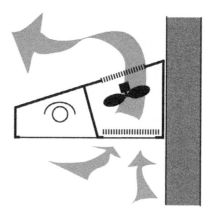

RECIRCULATING RANGE HOOD

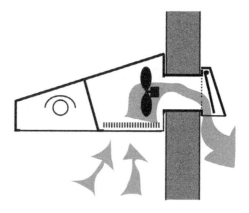

VENTED RANGE HOOD

FIGURE 15.2 A recirculating range hood (left) returns filtered air to the room and should be used only in cases where it is impossible to provide a vented model (right), which exhausts air to the outside.

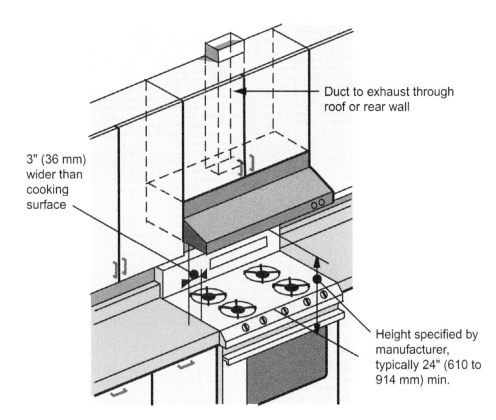

3" (36 mm) wider than cooking surface

Duct to exhaust through roof or rear wall

Height specified by manufacturer, typically 24" (610 to 914 mm) min.

FIGURE 15.3 Typical range hood installation. Note that for best performance, the hood is wider than the range.

When mounted above the range, microwave ovens equipped with an exhaust fan can do double duty as both cooking appliance and venting device for the range (see Figure 15.4). Vented models are preferred for this application over unvented (recirculating) ones for reasons stated earlier. As with vented range hoods, they take in exhaust gases through a filter below the unit and expel them out the top or rear into a duct.

Vented (downdraft) ranges offer an alternative to overhead venting by incorporating an exhaust fan into the range itself (see Figure 15.5). A fan below the cooking surface draws off foul air into a telescoping vent at the rear of the range or a grille in the cooking surface.

FIGURE 15.4 A microwave oven with an exhaust fan in the bottom can serve as both a cooking and a ventilating appliance. A recirculating model is shown here; however, models that vent to the outside are preferred.

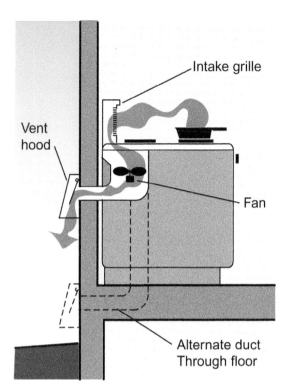

FIGURE 15.5 Vented ranges contain fans that exhaust cooking gases either through the deck or a vertical panel, which is more effective.

COUNTER-LEVEL DOWNDRAFT VENT

FIGURE 15.6 Vented ranges can exhaust through a rear wall or floor. Ducting should be short and direct.

POP-UP DOWNDRAFT VENT

TABLE 15.1 Typical Airflow Rates of Range Exhaust Systems

Range hood	150–600 cfm
Microwave hood	200–400 cfm
Downdraft exhaust fan	300–500 cfm
Island hood	400–600 cfm

Ducting routs through an adjacent outside wall or down through the floor and out through a basement wall (see Figure 15.6). There is no general consensus as to how vented ranges compare to overhead range hoods, except that they don't do as well for cooking with tall pots.

Devices that evacuate stale air from cooking surfaces come in varying capacities, according to the type of device (see Table 15.1). Too much capacity here is better than too little capacity.

The proper capacity or the ventilation device depends on the installation. Some general guidelines are listed next:

- **Hood-against-wall installation:** 50–70 cfm × Area of hood in square feet (150 cfm minimum, 300 cfm liberal)
- **Hood in open space (no back wall):** 100 cfm × Area of hood in square feet (600 cfm minimum)
- **Open grill or barbecue area with or without wall.** 100–150 cfm × area of hood in square feet (600 cfm minimum)

The NKBA recommends that designers always check with cooktop or range manufacturers for cfm recommendations.

The minimum capacity that meets the current ASHRAE standard (62–99) is 100 cfm. Number crunching aside, the safest approach is to give the client flexibility—with variable-speed fans with enough maximum capacity to ensure adequate ventilation even when several pots are boiling at the same time. Most off-the-shelf range hoods contain a fan. When custom-designing a hood, you have the possibility of locating the fan in the duct (in-line fan) for quieter operation.

Range hoods connect to ducting through either the back or the top. The duct can run through the ceiling, above the cabinets, or, if necessary, through cabinets to an exit on an outside wall or the roof. The duct terminates in a wall or roof vent kit that contains a shield to prevent water entry and a flapper that opens to allow exhaust air to escape but flaps shut when wind hits it. On windy days, the noise of the flapper can telescope through the ducting to create an annoying noise in the house.

Preventing Backdrafting

Exhaust fans expel air out of the home without supplying replacement, or makeup, air. In poorly sealed houses, enough air might be drawn back in through cracks around windows and doors to make up the difference. But the lack of makeup air in tight houses can depressurize the house and suck air out of combustion appliances. The result of this backdrafting can be dangerous buildups of CO and other noxious gases. Gas water heater pilot lights and even supposedly airtight woodstoves with outside combustion air can malfunction with only slight negative room air pressures. Here are some ways to avoid the hazard of backdrafting in tight homes:

- Provide a dedicated source of makeup air for the rooms.
- Use only sealed-combustion appliances (appliances that have a ducted supply of combustion air rather than drawing room air into the combustion chamber).
- Use several smaller exhaust fans rather than one large exhaust fan.
- Equip the home with a CO detector.

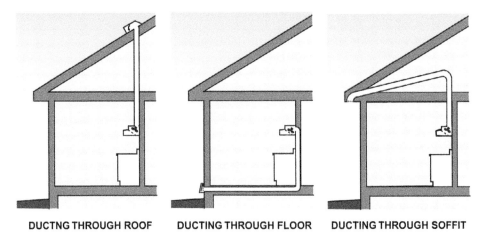

DUCTNG THROUGH ROOF   **DUCTING THROUGH FLOOR**   **DUCTING THROUGH SOFFIT**

FIGURE 15.7 The best route for exhaust ductwork is the shortest path with the fewest turns. The structure may be the deciding factor for the best route. For example, ducting through the floor (center) is possible only if the joists run parallel to the ducts. Otherwise, the duct must run below the joists.

Effective Ductwork

To work well, an exhaust fan must be installed with ductwork capable of evacuating gases to the exterior. The most effective ductwork is smooth inside and has a short path with few, if any, bends, and ends in a wall termination kit or roof jack (see Figure 15.7). Make sure all joints are tight and taped with pressure-sensitive tape that will last after the walls are enclosed. Other good advice includes the following:

• Specify galvanized steel, 28-gauge minimum.
• Never use flexible dryer duct material.
• Provide a backdraft damper at the outlet.
• Specify a small mesh screen at the outlet to keep birds and rodents out.
• Make sure the fan can is accessible for cleaning and servicing.
• Insulate ducts and other parts of the system where they come closer than 6" (152 mm) to wood framing or other combustible materials.
• Insulate ducts that pass through unheated spaces, and insulate all duct runs for a distance of 36" (914 mm) from the point of exit.

Round ducts move air more efficiently than rectangular ones; however, it is not always possible to fit a round duct of the required diameter through the allotted space. Size ducts according to these guidelines:

> **Fan located in ceiling or range hood:** 6" (152 mm) round or 3¼" × 10" (83 × 254 mm) rectangular, for a maximum duct length of 25' (7.620 m).
>
> **Fan located inside the duct (inline fan):** 9" (229 mm) round or 3¼" × 14" (152 × 356 mm) rectangular, for a maximum duct length of 55' (16.764 m).

WHOLE-HOUSE VENTILATION SYSTEMS

Another way to maintain healthy air indoors is with a system that ventilates the whole house. When outdoor temperatures permit, the house can be ventilated simply by opening windows. When the house has to be closed up, ventilation can be done mechanically. All of the fan systems discussed so far are intended to remove contaminated air from the interior. As such, they have two limitations with regard to ensuring a quality interior environment. First, expelling stale air without supplying replacement, or makeup, air depressurizes the interior, with the adverse effects discussed earlier. Second, they can be noisy. A fan in a range hood or bathroom ceiling is close enough to the user to be heard, and the noise of even a relatively quiet range hood can annoy when the fan is operating at maximum speed. Two system approaches address both of these concerns.

Multipoint Fan Systems

Individual exhaust devices typically are installed in kitchens, baths, and laundries—the rooms that generate most of the polluting gases and moisture. Replacing the individual fans in these devices with a central fan at some distance from the point of use solves the noise problem. Systems of this type typically locate an in-line fan in a duct near the point of exit through an outer wall or the roof (see Figure 15.8). Branch ducts below the fan extend to a grille in the ceiling of each room to be served. The fans run continuously at low speed with provision for high exhaust rates on an intermittent basis.

Fresh air for houses with forced air heating/cooling systems enters centrally into the return ducting near the furnace. In houses not heated or cooled by forced air systems, inlet devices installed in outside walls admit the necessary makeup air (see Figure 15.9). These inlets contain regulators to ensure proper airflows at each grille. Inlets are mounted high on a wall to allow the untempered, cold air they bring in to mix with the warm air near the ceiling, so that the air is comfortable by the time it reaches the level of the occupants.

Heat Recovery Systems

Central fan systems properly designed to balance exhausted air with an equal amount of fresh air are excellent means of ensuring clean, healthy indoor air in a home. They fall short in one respect, however. The exhausted air contains heat, along with the polluting gases. Homeowners who invest money to make their homes energy efficient shouldn't have to pay to heat air that is just blown outdoors. Two types of central ventilation systems address this issue by recovering much of the heat contained in the exhaust gases.

A heat recovery ventilator (HRV), also known as an air-to-air heat exchanger, is basically a heat exchanger with two fans inside a metal box. One fan drives stale air out through one channel while another fan sucks fresh outside air in through a second, separate channel. Some of the heat from outgoing air conducts through the metal that keeps the airstreams separate to warm the incoming air. Between 50% and 85% of the heat from outgoing air is thus recovered in the fresh air. HRVs cost more than exhaust-only systems but recoup the initial cost

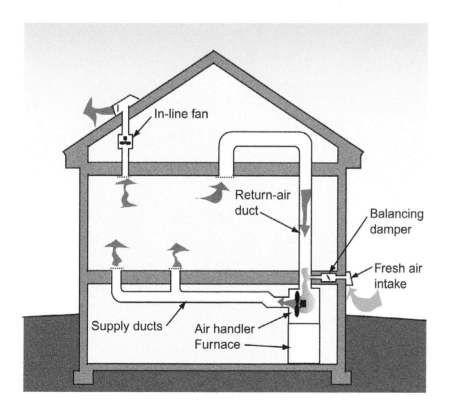

FIGURE 15.8 In a multipoint ventilation system there are no individual kitchen and bath exhaust fans. Instead, grilles in these rooms duct stale air to a central exhaust fan, usually in the attic. Makeup fresh air is introduced through self-balancing air inlets in the walls.

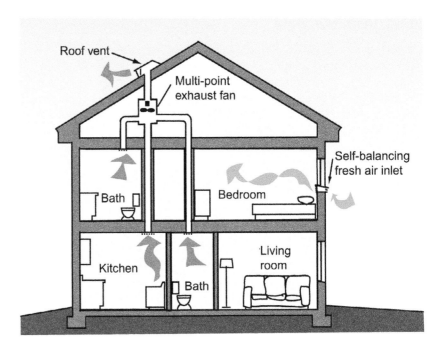

FIGURE 15.9 A whole-house ventilation system can be integrated with a forced-air heating system by combining one or more exhaust fans with a fresh air intake to the furnace fan.

over time through savings on heating fuel. They are more cost effective in cold climate regions, such as the northern-tier states of the United States and Canada, than in more temperate southern regions and are not common in cooling-dominated regions.

A second device, known as an energy recovery ventilator (ERV), recovers energy by the same process as an HRV, except that it is equipped to control humidity as well as temperature. This ability makes it better suited to homes in humid climates, where air conditioning is more

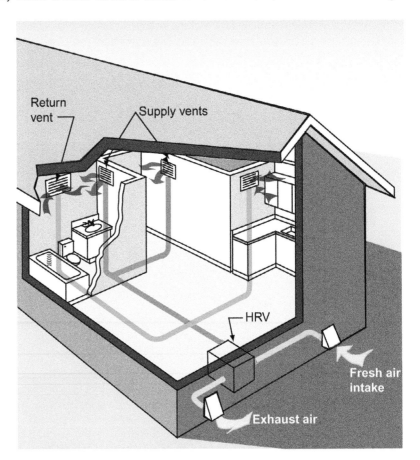

FIGURE 15.10 An HRV or ERV supplies fresh air to the interior and exhausts stale air to the outdoors. Coils inside the unit indirectly capture some of the heat from exhaust air to warm incoming fresh air.

important than heating. The core of the ERV is permeable to moisture, so some of the humidity in the incoming air can cross over to the outgoing air stream, reducing cooling and dehumidification loads. Running an ERV adds moisture to the interior, but the moisture load is less than if an HRV is used instead.

HRVs and ERVs are intended to maintain the air quality of the whole house. As such, they supplement rather than replace point-source exhaust fans above ranges and showers. Both devices mount in either the attic or the basement (see Figure 15.10). Whole-house systems require two distinct duct systems, one for supply air and one for return air. Ducts are smaller in diameter than those of a forced air heating system and may be made of round rigid plastic, round flexible plastic, round sheet metal, or rectangular sheet metal, according to which materials the local building authority accepts. Ducts run between the central unit and pickup points located high on walls of living areas. An HRV or ERV unit typically is controlled by a 24-hour timer or runs continuously. Some units have more than one speed, and most have defrost capability to keep the transfer plates in the unit from frosting up in winter. After the system is installed, the installer should adjust its airflow for proper balance to prevent under- or overventilating.

SUMMARY

Tightening homes in to make them more energy efficient reduces the amount of heat exchange through the building envelope via cracks and leaks but also prevents the free exchange of air between the inside and outside. For this reason, the air inside retains a variety of gases that can imperil occupants' health. Moisture also can build up, encouraging the growth of unhealthy microorganisms and causing the structure to deteriorate.

These problems can be resolved during mild parts of the year simply by allowing fresh air inside by opening windows. A variety of mechanical means address the problem in different ways during other times of the year. Some devices exhaust stale air from sites that generate concentrations of contaminated air, such as above ranges and in bathrooms. When installing these devices in tightly sealed homes, provisions should be made for makeup air in order to preserve healthy indoor air quality. Whole-house ventilation systems include means of admitting fresh air. Heat recovery systems provide fresh air while saving energy of the hot air expelled through the device.

CHAPTER REVIEW

1. What is the negative consequence of a tightly sealed home? (See "Chapter introduction," page 163)
2. What are two effects of excessive moisture inside a building? (See "Moisture" page 165)
3. Which rooms generate the most moisture in a home? (See "Moisture" page 165)
4. How many times must the inside air be replaced with fresh air to maintain a healthy indoor environment? (See "Fresh Air through Ventilation" page 166)
5. When specifying exhaust appliances, what also must be considered? (See "Room Exhaust Fans" page 167)
6. What is backdrafting? (See "Preventing Backdrafting" page 171)
7. What is the main advantage of a heat recovery ventilating system over a system that only expels air to the outside? (See "Heat Recovery Systems" page 173)

Household Water Supply

Clients don't think about the systems that deliver water to the tap unless it smells, leaks, or isn't hot or cold enough. Designers need to understand the systems hidden in walls and floors that deliver water to the tap to make sure the occupants get just the right amount of clean water at just the right temperature.

Household plumbing remained static until plastic piping and other innovations made it both more economical and faster and easier to install. But innovation doesn't automatically mean acceptance, so one of the first things to do when getting established in an area is find out from the local building authority which plumbing codes are in force and any special conditions that apply locally.

> *Learning Objectives 1: Recognize the infrastructure required to get water from the source to the point of use.*
>
> *Learning Objectives 2: Describe the problems and remedies for problems that may be encountered in culinary water.*
>
> *Learning Objectives 3: Compare water heating methods.*

SOURCES OF HOUSEHOLD WATER

Water from the Main

Most homes get their water from a municipal water supply system managed by a public utility that transports it from reservoirs or storage tanks through a network of piping buried below the streets. Water from the street main to the house flows through a meter and shutoff valve that measures consumption in gallons, then into the house (see Figure 16.1). Utility-supplied water enters the house under pressure of 50 to 60 pounds per square inch (psi) (351–421 g/cm^2). For proper function of the fixtures, the pressure should not drop below 30 psi (210 g/cm^2) or exceed 80 psi (g/cm^2). The number of fixtures served and how often they are in use at the same time affect the line pressure, as do the length of the piping runs and number of turns in the system.

Well Water

Rural homes don't have it quite so easy. They must supply their own source of water from a well that taps into an underground aquifer (see Figure 16.2). The level of the aquifer

FIGURE 16.1 The water meter and main shutoff valve usually are located in the front yard near the property line.

goes up or down, depending on how much rain has fallen to recharge it. The level also may drop if other wells near it are withdrawing too much water. In prolonged droughts, the level may go below the level of the pump intake, causing it to pump air and "go dry." Well water quality varies from place to place and from time to time. Whereas utility-supplied water is chlorinated and constantly monitored for quality, well water should be tested regularly for such health hazards as bacteria, nitrates, arsenic, volatile organic compounds (VOCs), and lead.

Pumps come in various designs. Pumps for shallow wells no deeper than 20' (6.096 m) can sit down into the well itself or inside the basement. In deep (drilled) wells, the pump is at the bottom of the well. In either case, the pump should supply a minimum of 5 gallons (19 L) per minute to ensure an adequate flow rate for the fixtures. Water from the pump flows into a holding tank equipped with an air bladder. Water pumped into the tank builds up pressure in the air bladder that forces water to the point of use. Without the bladder, the pump would have to cycle on every time a tap was turned on or the toilet was flushed. The tank can be adjusted to yield the same pressure range as that supplied by a public utility.

FIGURE 16.2 Rural houses often depend on wells for their water. Dug wells are feasible where the water table is consistently within 15' to 30' (4.575 to 9.150 m) of the surface. Drilled wells are necessary when reliable water is deeper down, often hundreds of feet.

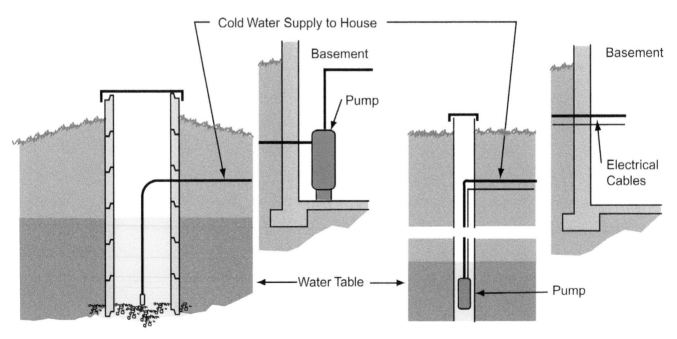

DUG WELL   DRILLED WELL

DISTRIBUTION SYSTEMS

Once inside the house, water must be conveyed through any treatment devices and to the point of use. Until recently, a main pipe carried water from the source or treatment appliance to smaller branch pipes that supplied each fixture. When water was drawn by more than one fixture at the same time, the one downstream suffered a loss of pressure. A newer approach solves this problem and some others by delivering water to each fixture separately. Both systems are described next.

Traditional Distribution Systems

Cold water enters the house through a supply line at least ¾" (19 mm) in diameter or, better, 1" (25 mm) in diameter. Except for water softeners, any devices to treat the water installs on the main supply line near the point of entry. This is because the minerals that make water hard and difficult to use for washing purposes also make it taste good. Water softeners usually are installed on the line that supplies the water heater. The cold-water line remains unsoftened for drinking. After the water heater, the hot and cold water pipes run parallel to the various takeoff points where they are tapped by smaller-diameter branch pipes (usually ½" [13 mm]), to supply appliances and fixtures of the bath, kitchen, and laundry as well as any hose bibs at outside walls.

Hot and cold supply lines usually run horizontally under framed floors, with supply branches, or risers, running up through walls to feed the fixtures (see Figure 16.3). Water supply piping in houses with slab-on-grade construction runs through the attic, where it can be accessed for repairs and alterations. Any piping in an attic should be located near the ceiling surface, tucked under the attic insulation, to protect it from freezing. Hot-water piping should be insulated, regardless of location, to prevent heat loss.

Water supply piping should be laid out in a pattern that minimizes the length of pipe runs and number of fittings the water must course through on its way to the point of use. This

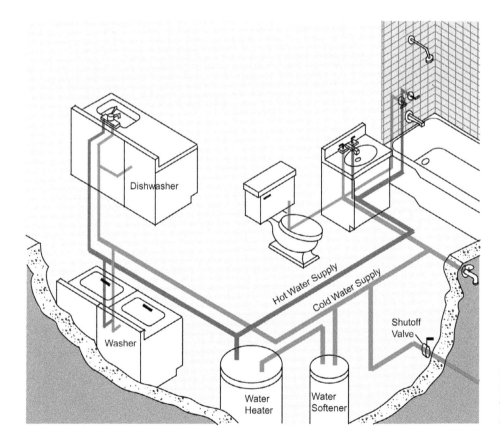

FIGURE 16.3 In a traditional water distribution system, branch pipes tap off the central supply pipe to bring hot and cold water to each fixture.

ensures minimal friction in the line for maximum pressure at the point of use. To achieve this goal, rooms with water-using fixtures should be close to each other. Fixtures in these rooms should back up to common walls. For example, if a laundry can go near a kitchen, try to locate the kitchen sink on the common wall, with the washer backing up to it.

Fixtures inevitably need maintenance, repair, or replacement at some time or another. When that time comes, the water supply to the fixture must be shut off, even for minor repairs, such as replacing a washer in a tap. A shutoff valve installed on the hot and cold supply pipe just before the fixture enables work on the fixture to occur without shutting down the house's entire system.

Manifold Distribution Systems

Traditional galvanized steel or copper distribution piping—parallel hot and cold supply lines with branches to each fixture—requires many fittings for changes in direction and intersections with branch piping. With all fixtures tapping off the main supply pipes, the line pressure can drop when several fixtures are used simultaneously. A newer method for residential water distribution overcomes this drawback. Instead of a central line with tap-off points, the system starts at a distribution manifold, out of which spring a separate home run length of piping to each fixture (see Figure 16.4). Some manifolds also feature fixture shutoff valves allowing users to shut off the water to individual fixtures from one location. Other manifolds—semi–home run or termination ones—are less complicated and may suffice for a few rooms and reduce the number of fittings required in the plumbing system.

Every house has two manifolds. The cold-water manifold connects to the main supply pipe from the meter. The hot-water manifold connects to the water heater. Branch lines tap off the manifolds and run directly to each fixture. Manifolds are 1¼" (32 mm) in diameter (larger than most service lines) to ensure adequate water flow to the fixtures. Because these systems make a direct run to each fixture, they require fewer fittings and thus can use

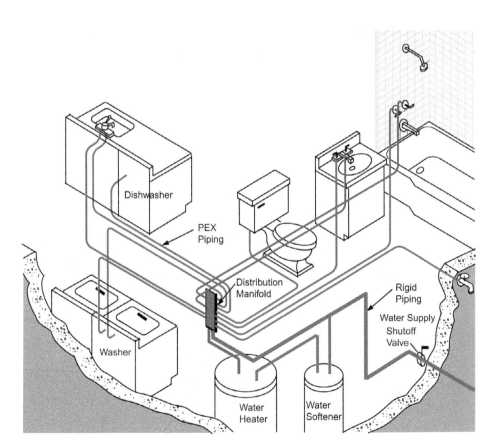

FIGURE 16.4 Manifold water distribution systems make a direct home run of hot- and cold-water lines to each fixture from a central distribution manifold via flexible plastic piping.

smaller-diameter supply piping for the home runs, typically ⅜" (10 mm). A continuous built-in reservoir provides equalized water flow and helps maintain constant pressure to the supply lines. If there is not a shutoff valve for each home run at the manifold, one should be provided at the fixture, as in a traditional system.

Manifold piping systems are made possible by flexible plastic piping made of cross-linked polyethylene (PEX) that can snake around bends without elbows and other fittings. The flexibility of the pipe eliminates the water hammer associated with metal piping systems and has other advantages described later in the chapter.

WATER SUPPLY PIPING

Quality piping withstands temperature extremes, corrosion, and the buildup of minerals (scale) that eventually constrict the flow of water—a tall order (see Figure 16.5). The plumbing code in force in a particular location spells out what's acceptable for a particular application. Next we describe residential water supply pipe materials, from the tried-and-true to the emerging candidates.

Metal Piping

Lead
Common for water supply piping in the 1900s, lead piping was gradually replaced by galvanized steel. Today lead piping turns up only in some lead mains and service piping of old inner-city neighborhoods. The known health hazards of lead have made its use illegal for water supply piping as well as most other construction products.

Galvanized Steel
Galvanized steel piping is steel coated with zinc to resist corrosion. It comes in straight lengths, which are joined by threaded connectors, or fittings. Numerous types of fittings shaped as elbows, tees, wyes, and reducers, are suited to the size of pipe and requirements of the joint. Installing steel pipe is difficult and expensive—the main reason it has been eclipsed by copper and other materials in today's homes. Other flaws include vulnerability to oxidation, or rust, both inside out. Oxidation reduces the interior diameter of the pipe, which restricts the flow of water. Joints weaken, in turn, and may leak. Galvanized steel piping fails sooner at the heavier-used fixtures of the kitchen and bath. The more a fixture is used, the more water and oxygen are present to oxidize, or corrode, the piping. Failure shows up first as round-shape rust growths ("rust warts") on the outside of the pipe. These are failures that have come through the pipe. It is not unusual for the corrosion to seal the failure. If you encounter a home with a steel pipe water system that is failing, you can specify copper for the portions to be remodeled, but the best approach is to replace the whole system, if feasible.

Copper
Copper reigns as the most common water supply piping in houses today and is also used for gas lines. Copper piping comes in rigid, straight lengths and as flexible tubing. Copper or brass fittings are used for both types, but flexible tubing uses fewer fittings, since it bends to change direction. However, care must be taken not to kink the tubing. Two types of fittings are used with copper piping. One type slips over the end of the pipe and bonds to it when solder is applied under a flame. Another type uses compression gaskets plus a threaded nut. This type is used to join pipes of a dissimilar metal or a joint that must be disconnected from time to time, such as the connection to a flexible stainless steel pipe from a sink or toilet.

Copper is a very dependable material but is corroded by acidic water—water with a low pH level. When the walls of the pipe wear thin, the failures appear as tiny, round, green patina

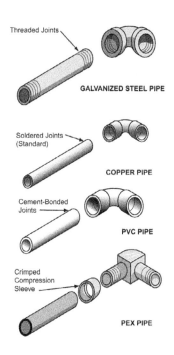

FIGURE 16.5 Four materials make up the bulk of most residential water supply piping. Copper still reigns as the most popular for new construction, while PEX is gaining due to its flexibility and ease of installation.

stains. If these stains are ignored, water may spray through the hole in the center of the round stain. Acidic water can be neutralized by installing a water softener.

There are three types of copper piping for domestic water supply, which vary by the thickness of the pipe walls. The thickest, Type K, identified by a green stripe, is for pipes buried in the ground. Blue-banded Type L (medium thick) and red-banded Type M (the thinnest) are used for indoor water supply (check with your code authority).

Threaded Brass

Brass is a malleable alloy of copper and zinc that has been in use for centuries. Piping made from threaded brass is uncommon but occasionally shows up in homes built before 1940. However, threaded brass is widely used for fittings for copper pipe. Although resistant to rust, brass, like copper, is vulnerable to acidic water.

Plastic Piping

Polybutylene

Plastic piping has made steady inroads into home water supply systems in recent years, because of its greater economy over steel and copper. But not all types of plastic piping are suited to all applications. Polybutylene (PB) piping is a flexible gray or black piping made from polybutylene plastic. Joints fit together with either epoxy or insert fittings and metal crimp rings. Barbed brass or copper insert fittings with crimp ring joints are generally more dependable than the epoxy joints. The joints are vulnerable to chlorine in the water, which causes the plastic to deteriorate. Since its debut in home plumbing systems in the 1970s, subsequent failures of the product have resulted in several individual and class-action lawsuits in the United States. Most municipalities currently do not allow certain types of PB piping for residential potable water.

Polyethylene

Polyethylene (PE) piping is approved only for cold-water systems. Typical uses include service piping from a municipal main or household well. Generally black in color, PE piping is a flexible material easier to install than most other service piping materials. PE pipe sections join together by two stainless steel band clamps. Originally made for radiant floor heating systems in the 1970s, PE pipe began to rupture under exposure to chlorine, causing costly demolition of the concrete slabs that overlaid the piping.

Cross-Linked Polyethylene

An improved version of PE piping was achieved in the 1980s by a process in which the molecules in the plastic were cross linked to form a more durable material. PEX piping typically is joined by crimp fittings, but compression fittings also are used. After 20 years of accelerated testing, PEX has yet to fail under normal conditions. It is the current favorite material for subslab radiant floor heating systems and fast becoming popular for domestic hot and cold water supply. PEX is now accepted for potable water use by codes in most areas. Although the pipe itself costs as much as copper, it installs more quickly for big savings in labor. Its flexibility makes PEX a good candidate for the manifold distribution layouts mentioned earlier. PEX piping offers other advantages over the metal pipe or rigid plastic pipe: It is flexible, resistant to scale and chlorine, doesn't corrode or develop pinholes, is faster to install than metal or rigid plastic, and has fewer connections and fittings.

Polyvinyl Chloride

Polyvinyl chloride (PVC) piping is a white, semirigid plastic joined by fittings bonded with a primer and PVC solvent. PVC is approved for cold water only, which explains why it is popular for irrigation systems outside the house. Another version, called chlorinated polyvinyl chloride (CPVC), is acceptable for both cold and hot water, as long as the temperature stays under 140° Fahrenheit (F) (60° Celsius [C]).

Table 16.1 compares the features of the types of pipe listed.

TABLE 16.1 Comparing Water Supply Pipe Materials

Material	Uses	Connections	Pros	Cons
Lead	(no longer legal)			Toxic
Galvanized steel	Water service, hot and cold water	Threaded galvanized steel fittings	Strong	High cost; corroded by acidic water; hard water causes scale; water hammer
Copper	Water service, hot and cold water	Soldered or compression fittings of copper or brass	Fast, easy to assemble (especially tubing), corrosion resistant	Not very good with very hard or very soft water; joints can be damaged by water hammer
Threaded brass	Hot and cold water	Threaded brass	Corrosion resistant	High cost
Polybutylene (PB)	Hot and cold water	Epoxy, inserts + crimp rings	Few fittings, no freeze damage, no water hammer	Must keep away from heat ducts and flues; joints prone to failure
Cross-linked polyethylene (PEX)	Water service, hot and cold water	Inserts + crimp rings	Same pros as PB, but improved, longer lasting	
Polyvinyl chloride (PVC)	Cold water	PVC fittings joined with solvent cement	Low cost, lightweight	Cold water only; protect from heat sources
Chlorinated polyvinyl chloride (CPVC)	Hot and cold water	PVC fittings joined with solvent cement	Same as PVC plus can use for hot water	Protect from heat
Polyethylene (PE)	Cold water	Stainless steel clamps	Low cost, lightweight, good from well to house	Cold water only

Sizing Pipe for Water Supply

The diameter of the pipe must be appropriate to the type of fixture in order to ensure the desired flow rate at the point of use. The pipe diameter is determined by the line pressure, friction loss, and pipe length. Table 16.2 lists the recommended pipe diameters according to their applications.

WATER SUPPLY PROBLEMS AND SOLUTIONS

It takes more than the right pipe and fittings to make a good water supply system. Several things can cause a water supply system to malfunction or deteriorate.

TABLE 16.2 Sizing Pipe for Water Supply

Application	(Diameter)
House main	1″ (25 mm)
House service	¾″ (19 mm)
Supply riser	¾″ (19 mm)
Tub, spa, whirlpool	½″ (13 mm), ¾″ (19 mm)
Kitchen sink	½″ (13 mm)
Ice maker	¼″ (6 mm)
Dishwasher	⅜″ (10 mm)

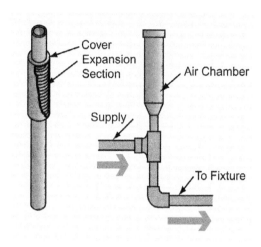

FIGURE 16.6 Two remedies for water hammer. The expansion device (left) allows the pipe itself to expand and contract to absorb the sudden differences in water pressure. The air chamber (right) absorbs the shock with the expansion and contraction of the air.

Water Hammer

Water is not a very elastic material. Although it expands and contracts some when heated or cooled, it doesn't have the same amount of "give" as air. A sudden shutoff of the water supply to an appliance or fixture can abruptly halt the flow of water in the pipes. The resulting jolt, or water hammer, causes an annoying noise. In time, repeated water hammer shocks can loosen joints, resulting in leaks.

Water hammer is easy to prevent. The key is to incorporate something in the piping that can absorb the sudden shock of the water's momentum. There are two ways to do this (see Figure 16.6). One is a loop or coil of the piping itself, which acts like a spring to absorb the shock of the water hammer. The other is a special device that contains an air chamber. Installed in the supply piping to a fixture, the air compresses to cushion shocks to the system.

Dissimilar Pipe Metals

Remodeling work often entails joining existing piping of one material to new piping of another. This is possible, but only with the right kind of fitting. Dissimilar metals can corrode when they are in contact with each other. The small amount of acid in the water sets up an electrolytic action between the two metals that causes electrons from one to flow to the other. A copper-to-steel joint is a likely point of failure. The solution is to keep the two metals apart. A dielectric union separates the two by placing a plastic collar and a rubber washer—both nonmetals—between them.

UNSUITABLE WATER

Even after everything has been done right to get the water to the fixtures and appliances efficiently, the water itself may not be safe to drink or still be unsuitable for other uses, such as cleaning. Numerous contaminants can make it hazardous to health, and its hardness can make it a difficult cleaning medium.

These problems can exist in water from any source. Well water is considered unsafe until it has been tested. Water from a public utility is treated against biological organisms but still can be unsafe to drink. In 1993, for example, 400,000 people in Milwaukee became ill from cryptosporidium ingestion, and 104 died. The system was contaminated by runoff from heavy storms that overwhelmed the filtration plant. Reports of less extreme events of this sort crop up more and more these days. On the whole, North Americans probably have the cleanest drinking water in the world. Nevertheless, problems do occur, and our growing population and encroachment into watershed areas will only make them worse. Households respond by either having their drinking water delivered by a bottled water service or by installing point-of-use (POU) treatment devices to counter contaminants that may be unhealthy or simply objectionable.

Water Pollutants

The Safe Drinking Water Act of 1974 spelled out maximum safe levels for 22 known contaminants. But more than 200 substances have been found in drinking water. The risks these contaminants pose to human health are known and well documented for some contaminants. Some of the main contaminants are discussed next, followed by ways to address them.

Lead

Even at low levels, lead at is a hazard to health, particularly in children. A cumulative poison, lead can damage the nervous system and internal organs and cause anemia. Drinking water is one of the ways we ingest lead. Lead probably gets into most houses today from lead-based solder used in copper water pipes. (Codes now require lead-free solder.) A less likely source might be the pipe from the main in the street to the house or—in very old houses—lead water pipes. Soft (acidic) water dissolves more lead out of these conduits than does hard water.

Arsenic

Arsenic may enter the home from well water that has flowed through arsenic-rich rocks. Industrial effluents also contribute arsenic to water in some places; this inorganic arsenic is mostly found as trivalent arsenite. Organic arsenic species, abundant in seafood, are much less harmful to health and are readily eliminated by the body. Chronic arsenic poisoning from long-term exposure through drinking water causes cancer of the skin, lungs, urinary bladder, and kidney as well as skin changes, such as pigmentation changes and thickening. Increased risks of lung and bladder cancer and of arsenic-associated skin lesions have been observed at drinking water arsenic concentrations of less than 0.05 milligrams per liter (mg/L).

Trihalomethanes

Trihalomethanes (THMs) comprise a group of chemicals that cause cancer in laboratory animals. This group includes chlorine when found in excessive amounts. Chlorine has proven an effective purification agent in public water supplies since 1908. Although the amount added to treat water is probably too low to pose a risk to health, some studies have suggested it might be a contributing factor to bladder cancer. Whether there is any substance to this or not, we do know that chlorine makes water taste bad. The Environmental Protection Agency (EPA) restricts the total maximum concentrations of THM to 0.1 mg/L.

Nitrates

Nitrates are byproducts of fertilizer that can leach into groundwater and contaminate the aquifers that supply both public and private-source drinking water. High nitrate levels in drinking water can pose a special risk for infants. When an infant ingests nitrates, they are converted into another compound called nitrites, which reduces the blood's ability to carry oxygen. The result is a condition known as methemoglobinemia, or blue baby syndrome. Public water is tested and treated for nitrates, but private well water is vulnerable, particularly if the well is located in an agricultural area.

Pesticides

Pesticides are another concern in rural areas and a special danger for private wells. Pesticides that are not taken up by plants, adsorbed by soils, or broken down by sunlight, soil organisms, or chemical reactions ultimately may get into the groundwater. Contamination can result when high concentrations of water-soluble pesticides are used for a specific crop in a vulnerable area. The hazard to human health depends on the kind and amount of pesticide, how long a person has been consuming the water, and the person's overall health. Acute pesticide poisoning symptoms may include headaches, dizziness, stomach and intestinal upset, numbness of the extremities, spasms, convulsions, and heart attacks. While the long-term, chronic effects of pesticides in humans are not completely understood, some pesticides are suspected of causing cancer.

Other contaminants can pose health hazards from minor to severe or simply can make the water taste or smell bad. You probably should recommend that your clients have their water tested before you complete the design, so that you can help them choose the appropriate remedy. There are many sources of information on water quality and testing facilities. The local Cooperative Extension Service is often a good place to begin. The EPA is a repository for a vast wealth of information on a number of issues relating to water quality. The agency's water quality hotline is 800-426-4791 and URL is hotline-sdwa@epa.gov.

Treatment Options

The report from a testing service will spell out the levels of various contaminants in the water and suggest the most effective treatment. POU devices treat water by one or more of five basic techniques, described next. While each has its pros and cons, there is unfortunately no universal fix.

Mechanical Filtration

Mechanical filters remove dirt, sediment, and loose scale from the incoming water by straining it through a sieve made of ceramic material, sand, filter paper, or compressed glass wool. The result is better-looking, better-tasting, and better-smelling water. But because these devices don't treat pathogens, the water won't necessarily be healthier.

Activated Carbon Filtration

Activated carbon filtration uses filters of carbon granules with many exposed pores to trap certain contaminants and remove organic compounds such as chloroform, pesticides, benzene, and trichloroethylene. The filters also remove chlorine and improve the water's taste and color but do not eliminate bacteria. With use, some pores clog and decrease the filter's efficiency. Filter life depends on the design, volume of water processed, and length of time in use. Their effectiveness eventually decreases, requiring replacement of the cartridges.

Reverse Osmosis

Reverse osmosis purifies water by passing it through a semipermeable membrane under normal tap pressure. Up to 95 percent of dissolved contaminants are eliminated. Some membranes even reject many types of bacteria. Reverse osmosis under-sink devices are costly both to install and to operate. They contain three cartridges—one for particulates, one for activated carbon, and the reverse osmosis membrane—each with a different useful life, so replacement is a pain. Less expensive countertop models contain a three-in-one cartridge. These units connect to the faucet via a diverter valve. They run by normal pressure in the water line, so need no outside energy to operate.

Though effective, reverse osmosis filtration is slow and wasteful. Six hours produce a single gallon of water, while four to six gallons of waste water go down the drain. Countertop models yield about 3 quarts (2.8 L) in just over four hours.

Distillation

When water is heated, it produces steam that condenses back to liquid form, purging most of the contaminants in the process. This purification method, known as distillation, is the only one that removes microorganisms and trace amounts of heavy metals with absolute certainty. Even so, certain volatile organic chemicals that have a lower boiling point than water, such as some pesticides, vaporize with the water, recondense, and end up in the processed water anyway. Because distilled water contains no minerals, its taste suffers. It is also very soft and aggressive toward metals in pipes. Distillers are powered by electricity and have a stainless steel, glass, or plastic reservoir with capacities ranging from 1.5 to 15 gallons (5.7 to 56.8 L). Slow and costly to operate, they are also vulnerable to mineral buildup from hard water.

Ultraviolet Water Purification

Ultraviolet (UV) water purification devices utilize a lamp enclosed in a protective transparent sleeve, mounted such that water passing through a flow chamber is exposed to the UV light rays. When harmful microbes are exposed to the UV rays, their nucleic acid absorbs the UV energy, which then scrambles the DNA structure of the organism. Since these devices only kill microorganisms, such as bacteria, viruses, molds, algae, and yeast, and oocysts such as cryptosporidium and giardia, they are often combined with other forms of purification if other contaminants are present in the water.

Table 16.3 lists each impurity described above, along with its treatment options.

Treating Hard Water

Hard water gets its name because it's hard to make it lather with soap. The hardness comes from the mineral salts it contains, mainly calcium and magnesium. These minerals react with

TABLE 16.3 Comparing Water Treatment Options

Contaminant	Maximum Contaminant Level	Mechanical Filtration	Activated Carbon Filters	Reverse Osmosis	Distillation	Ion Exchange (Water Softener)	Ultraviolet Water Purification
Arsenic	0.05 mg/L			•	•		
Asbestos	7 mg			•	•		
Atrazine	0.003 mg/L		•	•			
Benzene	0.005 mg/L		•				
Fluoride	4 mg/L			•	•		
Lead	0.015 mg/L*			•	•	•	
Mercury	0.002 mg/L		•	•	•		
Nitrates	10 mg/L			•	•		
Radium	5 pC/L			•	•	•	
Radon	300 pC/L		•				
Trichloroethylene	0.005 mg/L		•		•		
Total Trihalomethanes	0.1 mg/L		•		•		
Bacteria and viruses			•	•	•		•
Cryptosporidium/giardia				•	•		•
Metallic taste				•	•	•	
Objectionable taste				•	•		
Objectionable odor			•				
Color		•	•	•	•	•	
Sediment	0.5–1.0 NTU**	•					

*EPA action level
**Performance standard

soap to form greasy rings in bathtubs and washbasins. When heated, the minerals turn to hard scale that builds up on pots and pans and the insides of pipes, hot water tanks, and boilers. We measure water hardness in grains per gallon (gpg) or mg/L. Multiply gpg × 17.1 to get mg/L. Moderately hard water contains 3.6 to 7.0 gpg (61 to 120 mg/L). Very hard water contains 7.0 to 10.5 gpg (121 to180 mg/L).

Although detergents cut through hard water, a water softener can wipe out the problem entirely and should be considered for water hardness that exceeds 10.5 gpg (180 mg/L). However, water softened too much—to zero hardness—is corrosive. Water softeners work by a process called ion exchange, where the hard water passes through a bed of softening material charged with sodium ions. The hardening minerals are attracted to the softening material and held there. At the same time, sodium releases into the water (a possible hazard to people who must restrict their intake of sodium, or salt).

In time, the operation depletes the sodium in the bed, and it must be recharged. Salt brine flushed through the bed drives out the hardness and replaces it with sodium. Rinsed with fresh water, the renewed ion exchange material is once again ready for action. Most water softeners use a timer to start the regenerating process automatically. After 600 gallons of water is processed, the softener recharges. The homeowner need only add salt to the brine tank periodically to ensure a constant supply of softened water. Devices come in various capacities, according to the size of the family and projected water usage.

WATER HEATERS

Anyone living in an industrial country today takes hot water for granted, so it's not surprising that a water heater is considered a necessity for any home with a plumbing system. Some water heaters are independent of other equipment; others are integrated with other equipment. There are choices in energy sources as well; although gas and oil fuel most residential water heating in the United States and Canada.

Tank-Type Water Heaters

Conventional water heaters that have their own storage tank are the workhorse for most homes. Basically simple devices, they consist of a thermostatically controlled burner (gas units) or heating element (electric units) that heats the water. An insulated tank stores a ready supply of hot water. Tanks typically are lined with glass to prevent the hot water from corroding the metal. Tank capacities range from 30 to 82 gallons (114 to 311 L). Because the supply has to serve the maximum usage, the right size water heater for a family depends on its peak usage, which usually occurs in the early morning or evening. Table 16.4 presents a way to estimate the required capacity of a water heater, by filling in the column for the number of users per hour. To illustrate, this column has been filled in for a household of two adults and one child for the time in the morning when they are getting ready for the day's activities.

The table indicates that a 50-gallon tank should work for this family. If the family had a couple of teenagers, the water use naturally would go up. In addition to the tank volume, tank-type water heaters also vary in their recovery rate, the amount of water in gallons per hour raised at a given efficiency and Btu input. Manufacturers' specifications state these data for each model. It's better to choose a size a few gallons greater than the estimate to ensure enough hot water at peak times. But an excessively large tank size just wastes money on fuel. The selected model should operate at a maximum pressure of 160 psi (1,103 kPa) and heat water to a maximum 210° F (99° C).

TABLE 16.4 Estimating Water Heater Capacity

Use	Required gallons (liters)	×	Number of users per hour	=	Gallons (liters) used in 1 hour
Shower	20 (76)	×	2	=	40
Bath	20 (76)	×		=	
Shaving	2 (8)	×	1	=	2
Hands/face washing	4 (15)	×	1	=	
Hair shampoo	4 (15)	×	2	=	8
Automatic dishwasher	14 (53)	×		=	
	Total peak hour demand:				50
Adapted from guidelines of the Gas Appliance Manufacturers Association					

In a gas water heater, a burner in a combustion chamber below the tank heats the water (see Figure 16.7). Combustion gases rise up through a flue in the tank and through another flue that exits through the walls or roof.

Electric water heaters contain one or two heating elements called electrodes that project through the wall of the tank into the water (see Figure 16.8). The higher the wattage and voltage of the element, the faster the water will heat. Heated by electricity resistance, the elements produce no exhaust gases, so electric water heaters need no flue. This feature makes them ideal for locating centrally to the rooms that use hot water: bath, laundry, and kitchen. They can safely sit inside a closet, for example—a location not permitted for a gas heater. Kitchens, baths, and laundries are not always close to each other, however, so some designers prefer to locate the main water heater close to the bath and have a second water heater close to or in the kitchen, either in a crawl space or under the kitchen sink. The second unit can be a 20-gallon tank-type water heater or a tankless one, as discussed in the next section.

The same technology that powers refrigeration and air conditioning also works to heat water. Unlike a water heater that uses either gas burners or electric resistance heating coils to heat the water, a heat pump water heater (HPWH) takes heat from the surrounding air and transfers it to the water in the tank (see Figure 16.9). Much less energy is required to "move" the heat than to actually heat the water, unless the surrounding air temperature is very low. Most HPWHs have backup heating elements to heat the water during periods of very low temperatures. Because they consume only half to a third as much electricity as typical electric water heaters, they save dramatically on fuel costs. The savings are offset, however, by much higher initial costs. Another downside is the rate of heating. HPWHs heat water more slowly than electric or gas water heaters, typically about 15 gallons per hour. HPWHs install in two configurations. Both extract heat from room air. One system expels the now-cooled air back into the room—a disadvantage during the heating season. The other type expels the cooled air to the outside.

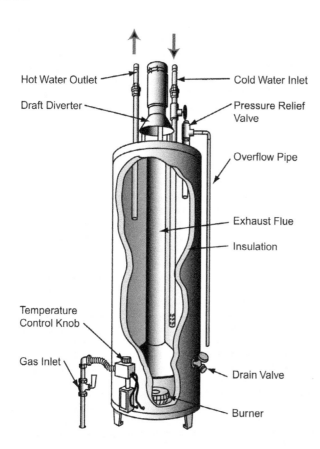

FIGURE 16.7 A gas tank-type water heater requires a gas supply and a flue that expels exhaust to the exterior.

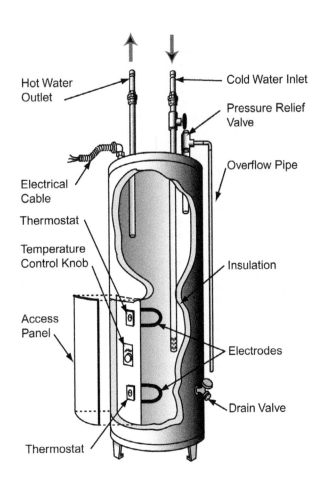

Hot Water Outlet

Cold Water Inlet

Pressure Relief Valve

Electrical Cable

Overflow Pipe

Thermostat

Temperature Control Knob

Insulation

Access Panel

Electrodes

Drain Valve

Thermostat

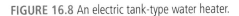

FIGURE 16.8 An electric tank-type water heater.

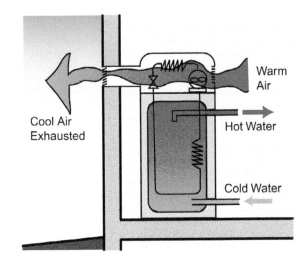

Cool Air Exhausted

Warm Air

Hot Water

Cold Water

FIGURE 16.9 Electrically powered HPWHs supply hot water at one half to one third of the energy used by a standard electric water heater.

Tankless Water Heaters

The cost of heating and storing 50 gallons of water or more in a tank-type water heater can account for much of a home's utility bills, if the water heater is electric and the rates are high. In a typical home, about one fourth of the energy consumed is lost through the tank. This is due to the fact that as hot water leaves the tank, cold water comes into the tank to take its place—gradually diluting and cooling the entire 50 gallon tank. As the hot water goes out and the cold comes in, the tank's heater kicks in to heat the tank. But the rate at which hot water leaves the tank is faster than the heater can heat the cold water coming in and, eventually, we run out of hot water. Once that happens, you'll have to wait because it takes a 50 gallon tank 15 to 20 minutes to heat up enough for the water to feel warm enough depending on the temperature to where it is set. This has been both a waste of energy and an inconvenience for years. In general, the farther a fixture is away from the water heating source, the longer it takes the hot water to get to the fixture. It can take up to 45 seconds while the cold water that was sitting in the line gets wasted down the drain. This can be mitigated by planning the tank in a centrally located place in the home. In warmer climates, a garage can be a good location if it is attached to the home. But tankless water heaters have overcome many of these issues over the last few years.

Tankless water heaters have improved immensely since 2007. Now, in warmer climates, one tankless water heater can accommodate up to four showers at the same time. In colder climates, they can accommodate up to three showers at a time. Even though the cold water in the line still takes a few seconds to clear, there is an endless supply of hot water once it reaches the fixture. When specifying a tankless water heater, carefully consider the flow rate (GPM) required at the fixture or appliance. The tankless unit should be sized based on the demand of the fixtures that are part of the line. Manufactures list the capacity of their units in literature and on their websites.

There are many advantages of the tankless heaters. To begin with, they provide an endless supply of hot water. They are 30% more efficient than a tank, making them a green choice for heating water. This can save up to 40% on a utility bill. The tankless units take up a fraction of the space that the tanks take and they save energy by only heating the water as it goes through the units. In larger homes with two stories, one unit can be delegated to the first story and another unit to the second story. Since they take up less space in the home, it is easier to find a location for a tankless unit, even on the second floor. In addition, there is no danger of a tank full of water failing and spilling 40 to 50 gallons of water through the home. Tankless units can be installed centrally or near the point of use, such as a utility room, garage, basement, attic, or on an outside wall, as well as locations where a tank-type unit may not fit. The biggest drawback is the initial cost, which may be up to three times that of a tank unit.

Tankless units come in gas and electric. The gas units are used for residential as the requirements for an electric model would not make them feasible for residential use on an entire home. The venting for the gas units is different than that of a water heater tank. And depending on the size of the tankless gas unit, the gas line running to the unit may need to be sized to fit. (This is similar in application to the gas ranges that require a larger gas line to put out a higher BTU.)

Sometimes, a client may not want to change the whole house over to tankless but a smaller Point of Use model can make sense in an addition that is at some distance from the tank (see Figure 16.10).These smaller units are available in electric models, and can be put in a cabinet or under the sink. Since they are electric, they don't require venting. Consult the manufacturer's specifications for sizing, makeup air, and piping requirements.

Gas units require a 4", 5", or 6" (102, 127, or 152 mm) in diameter flue, rather than the standard 3" (76-mm) vent of a tank-type heater. They draw large amounts of combustion air, which may rule out some locations. Consult the manufacturer's specifications for sizing, makeup air, and piping requirements.

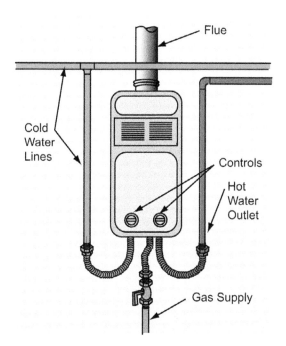

FIGURE 16.10 Tankless water heaters heat water only when it is being used, thus saving the energy lost through storage and distribution piping. They are good choices for fixtures far from the home's central water heater and in some cases as substitutes for a central heater.

Integrated Water Heating

Houses heated by a gas- or oil-fired boiler can do without a separate water heater of any type, if the boiler is equipped with a domestic hot water loop inside the boiler. As with a tankless system, hot water is produced at a constant rate and temperature as it flows through the loop. The downside is that the flow rate is often too slow for more than one fixture operating at any one time. A separate insulated tank added to the system for storage solves the problem, but this hybrid system may not have much edge over a separate, conventional water heater with its own heat source.

Solar Water Heating

Ever-increasing energy prices combined with federal, state, and local tax incentives are making heating water with the sun more popular (see Figure 16.11). In many climates, solar water heating can provide up to 85% of domestic hot water.

There is a wide variety of residential solar water systems, from simple to complex. All systems employ a south-facing collector to heat a fluid and a tank to store the heat. Direct, or closed-loop, systems heat the water used for household purposes directly. Indirect, or open-loop, systems heat an antifreeze fluid, which flows through a heat exchange coil in the storage tank, heating the domestic water indirectly. Beyond that, systems are classified as active or passive, according to the way they operate.

Passive systems circulate the heated water by convection, whereas heated fluid naturally rises and colder fluid falls. The simplest passive system, a batch heater, is comprised of a tank mounted on the roof, that sits above a flat-panel collector. Because the tanks, even

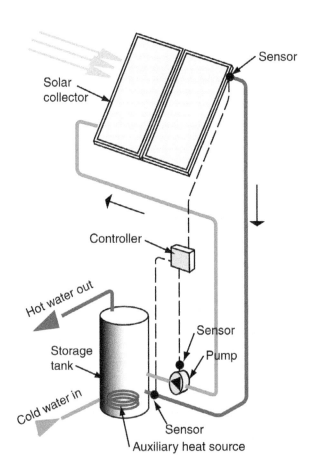

FIGURE 16.11 Simplified operation of an open-loop active solar water heating system. A pump circulates water from collector to tank and, triggered by the sensor, drains the water back into the tank at night to prevent freezing.

insulated, are mounted on the roof, they lose significant heat at night. They also risk freezing. Some devices depend on being manually drained when freezing is expected, an unreliable method. Others employ freeze-tolerant collectors made with flexible polymers, such as silicone rubber, which can expand and contract with changes in temperature. The potential for freezing combined with their somewhat lower efficiency than active systems make passive devices suitable only for milder climates.

Active systems use pumps to circulate the heated fluid directly or indirectly and a sensor to control the circulation. Because the tank is stored inside the heated building, there is less heat loss to the outside at night, so active systems are more efficient than passive systems. Closed-loop systems contain antifreeze as the heat transfer medium. The sensors on direct (closed loop) systems cause the pump to return the water from the collector to the tank ("drainback") at night to prevent freezing. All active systems are more complicated, failure-prone, and expensive than passive systems, but they offer these advantages:

- Better efficiency
- Better control
- Less heat loss from the storage tank
- Storage tank not apparent on the home

Many factors come into play when choosing a solar system over other options. The availability of sunshine on annual basis is likely the most important factor. Another factor to consider is the size of the household to be served. A large family will receive a better payback on the investment in a solar system than a couple, because of greater use of the hot water.

SUMMARY

Providing water for various household uses entails a distribution system that conveys it from the source to the point of use. The piping materials that make up the system offer many choices, each suited to a particular application and with particular installation requirements.

Water from the source often contains contaminants that can affect the health of the occupants or that make the water unpalatable or unsuitable for use. There are many devices available to improve the quality of the water, depending on the contaminant and/or whether the water is hard or soft.

Water for cleansing can be heated by tank or tankless devices, each suited to differing household configurations and fueled by electricity or gas.

CHAPTER REVIEW

1. Why is an air bladder required in a tank supplied by well water? (See "Well Water" page 178)
2. What are the advantages of manifold systems over traditional distribution systems? (See "Manifold Distribution Systems" pages 180–181)
3. What type of copper would you specify for a pipe that runs between the water heater and a sink? (See "Copper" page 182)
4. What causes water hammer? (See "Water Hammer" page 184)
5. What can result from pesticides in the water? (See "Pesticides" page 185)
6. Why would you not choose distillation as a water purification method? (See "Distillation" page 186)
7. Would an active or a passive solar water heater likely be more efficient in North Dakota? (See "Solar Water Heating" pages 192–193)

Drainage Systems

Getting the water to the fixtures and appliances comprises the first half of a home's plumbing system. The other half entails getting it out, along with any accumulated wastes. This is the task of the drain, waste, and vent (DWV) system. This system differs from the water supply system in three significant ways:

1. Waste pipes are not pressurized, so they must slope to enable the contents to flow by gravity alone.
2. Piping must be larger to accommodate solids as well as liquids.
3. The DWV system must have means of preventing sewer gas from flowing back into the house.

In this chapter, we see how each of the components of the DWV system work together to meet these objectives.

Learning Objectives 1: Recognize the functions of each component of a residential DWV system.

Learning Objectives 2: Describe the methods of venting fixtures.

Learning Objectives 3: Compare the pros and cons of various pipe materials.

PARTS OF THE SYSTEM

The network of piping that carries waste out of the house makes up the drainage and waste parts of the DHW system. It begins with small-diameter drain piping at the fixtures that feed into branch pipes of larger size, then into a vertical soil stack—a pipe usually 4" (100 mm) in diameter that carries the waste down to the house drain. The drainpipe, a horizontal pipe the same diameter as the stack, exits the building and connects to the municipal sewer system or septic tank system, if the home is not served by a municipal sewer.

In a septic system, the septic tank buried near the house receives the sewage and holds it while bacteria and other organisms partially digest the waste. In the process, the undigested solids drop to the bottom of the tank as sludge. The sludge accumulates over time, requiring the tank to be pumped out. The liquid effluent runs out the top of the tank to the drain field (leach field). There, a network of piping or shaped conduits receives the liquid effluent and distributes it into the soil, where it breaks down further and purifies.

When adding fixtures to a home with a septic tank, check to make sure the septic tank is big enough for the additional load. A food waste disposer imposes an excessive load on the septic system and many health departments advise against it. The general consensus is that the system should either be oversized by 50 percent or cleaned out twice as often as it would have without the disposer. Water softeners can be detrimental to the system.

Pipes and Fittings

Waste piping mentioned thus far has been referred to as either vertical or horizontal. However, dead-level horizontal pipes can't drain properly. Codes require horizontal branches to slope ¼" (6 mm) per foot. In practical application, this slope varies from ⅙ to ½" (1.6 to 13 mm) per foot.

The diameters of drainage pipes vary according to where they are located in the system. The smallest ones come off the kitchen and bath sinks with diameters usually of 1¼" (32 mm) or, preferably, 1½" (38 mm). Showers, bathtubs, and washing machines typically have drains 1½ or 2" (38 or 51 mm) in diameter, while toilet drains are 3 or 4 (76 or 102 mm). The stack and main sewer pipe are the largest pipes in the system, usually 4" (102 mm) in diameter. Bigger is not always better for drain pipes; pipes that are too big can slow the flow of sewage, so find out from the plumbing inspector in your area which pipe sizes are required for various applications.

Pipes in a DWV system are always straight. Changes in direction are made with a fitting of the right shape. Plumbers name these by the letters they resemble. An el is an L-shape fitting for making a 90° turn. A *wye* has two outlets at a 30° or 45° angle for joining two pipes into one. A *tee* is a similar fitting but with branches at a 90° angle.

Codes require cleanouts at the ends of horizontal piping runs where they change direction more than 45°. All cleanouts must have at least 18" (457 mm) of clearance in front to allow access for cleaning rods, snakes, and other tools.

Traps

The third objective of a DWV system is preventing sewer gas from flowing back into the house. U-shape traps at each fixture do this by retaining a water seal in the bottom of the "U." The seal not only keeps unpleasant gases out of the living spaces but also prevents rodents from entering the house via the sewer pipes. Plumbing codes require every fixture to have a trap. Toilets have a trap built into the structure of the fixture. Traps for other fixtures occur in the drainpipe just below the fixture. The most common type is shaped like the letter "P" lying on its side and is called a P-trap (see Figure 17.1). Codes typically require traps to hold a water seal of between 2 and 4" (51 and 102 mm), be self-cleaning, and not depend on moving parts. Also, no trap outlet can be larger than the fixture drain it serves. Traps must be level with their water seals. Although each fixture must have its own trap, a single trap can serve some side-by-side fixtures, such as a double sink (see Figure 17.2).

Vents

Traps work only if they stay full. If they simply were connected to the piping downstream in a completely sealed environment, the water flowing down would suck out the water in the trap, leaving it filled with air. To prevent the trap from being siphoned in this manner, a vent is added beyond the trap to equalize the pressure. The vent also allows sewer gas to escape to the outdoors (see Figure 17.3). Codes require the drains of each fixture to be vented and specify the minimum size of the vent pipe (see Figure 17.4). The minimum size of any vent can never be smaller than 1¼" (32 mm), or half the diameter of the drain it serves, whichever is larger. Beyond that, the kind of fixture, diameter of the drain being vented, and length of vent pipe all factor in to the required size. Residences typically have 3 or 4" (76 or 102 mm) main soil stack that extends up to vent through the roof.

FIGURE 17.1 A typical P-trap with the maximum permissible length of trap arm.

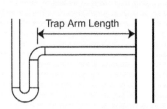

Maximum Length of Trap Arm

Diameter of trap arm	Maximum distance trap to vent
1 1/4"	5'-0" (1 524mm)
1 1/2"	6'-0" (1 829mm)
2"	8'-0" (2 438mm)
3"	12'-0" (3 658mm)
4"	16'-0" (4 877mm)

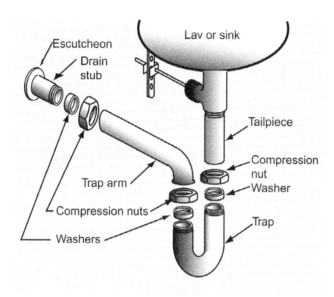

FIGURE 17.2 A typical drain assembly for a sink with a P-trap.

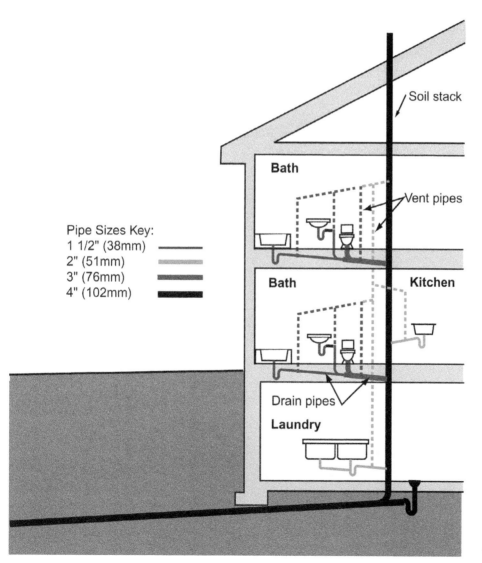

FIGURE 17.3 A typical DWV system for a multistory house.

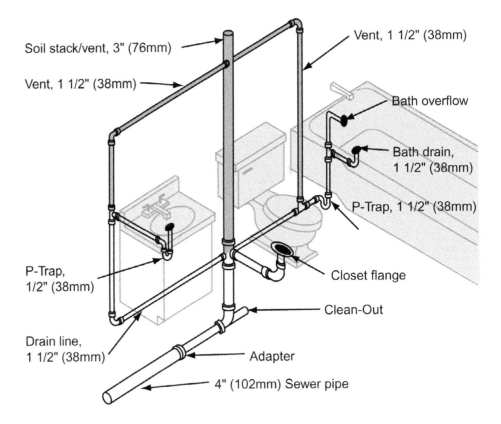

FIGURE 17.4 A typical three-fixture DWV system. The maximum distance between a trap and the vent pipe depends on the diameter of the trap arm piping.

Vent piping normally is installed in walls behind fixtures. This works fine for fixtures that back up to a wall but not for sinks in islands or peninsulas. If fixtures are farther than a code-specified distance from a vent pipe in a wall—typically 8 to 10′ (2438 mm to 2540 mm)—they must contain their own vent. Three ways to vent an island fixture are discussed next. The method chosen should be verified by the local plumbing inspector.

Single-Fixture Wet Vent

In a wet vent, the P-trap from the sink runs horizontally into a larger vertical pipe in the sink base cabinet and discharges into a 3- or 4″ (76- or 102-mm) drain line located in the floor (see Figure 17.5). The drain line must have a cleanout upstream from the entry tee. This system works because oversizing the drain lines beyond the P-trap increases the drain's free-air capacity, allowing the sink to drain without siphoning out the water in the trap.

Bow Vent

Another approach is to connect the P-trap outlet to a vent, as if it backed up to a wall (see Figure 17.6). But instead of the vent continuing up through the countertop, the portion

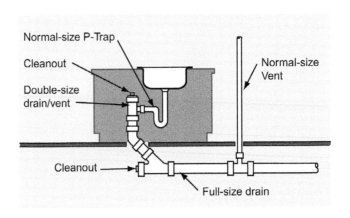

FIGURE 17.5 An island sink can be wet-vented if the trap runs into a vertical pipe at least twice the diameter of the trap before connecting with the main drain and vent piping.

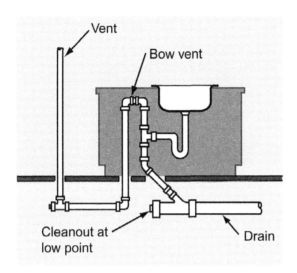

FIGURE 17.6 A bow vent near the sink is another way to vent an island sink, but it consumes a lot of cabinet space.

above the trap loops back down to connect with a remote vent that *is* in a wall. The portion of the vent below the P-trap connects to a drainpipe below the floor. The main drawback of this arrangement is the large amount of space inside the cabinet consumed by the bow vent.

Automatic Vent

The simplest way out of the dilemma may be a simple device that works as a one-way check valve to let makeup air into the system as the sink drains. Automatic vents (bladder vents) typically are glued to the end of the short vertical vent pipe that rises above the P-trap (see Figure 17.7). But if the mechanical valve fails, the room will be suffused with sewer gas.

PIPING MATERIALS

Just as plastics are replacing metals in water supply piping, they have mostly edged out traditional cast iron waste piping in homes because of their greater economy and ease of installation. Plastic is not necessarily a better material, however, as we discuss next.

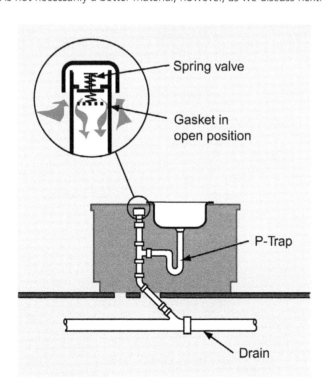

FIGURE 17.7 An automatic one-way check valve that admits make-up air into the system is the simplest and most space-saving solution, if acceptable to the local plumbing inspector.

Cast Iron

Cast iron has been used for indoor waste piping ever since houses had indoor plumbing. In early installations, pipe sections had one straight end and the other end flared into a hub shape. The straight (spigot) end of the previous pipe fitted into the hub of the next pipe. The joint was sealed by first tamping a bituminous-impregnated hemp rope called oakum into it, then pouring molten lead into the joint. Lead and oakum joints are rare today, replaced by joints that rely on compression gaskets to make the seal. Compression gaskets also enable a cast iron pipe to be joined to pipe of other materials—a plus in old houses undergoing alterations (see Figure 17.8).

Cast iron pipe is strong, durable, and heat resistant to the point of being fireproof. Used for the main waste-vent stack in a house, it is much quieter than plastic. This can be important in some installations, such as if the main stack is located in a wall near the living room. The sound of a sudden burst of water plunging down the pipe every time a toilet is flushed upstairs comes through the wall as an annoying noise. On the downside, cast iron pipe is very heavy, expensive, and vulnerable to corrosion from acids or very soft water. In addition, the hubs in hub-and-spigot joints flare out and require extra-wide stud walls or special chases.

Galvanized Steel

With many of the same qualities as cast iron, galvanized steel is accepted by most codes for aboveground DWV piping. Straight sections join together in threaded fittings, as with water supply piping. The very high cost and difficult installation of galvanized steel rule it out for most projects.

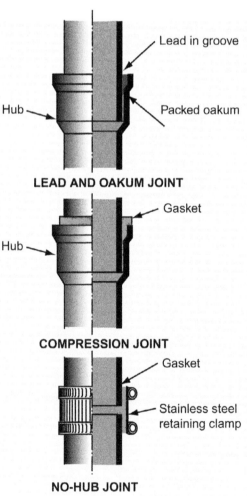

FIGURE 17.8 Cast iron pipe sections initially were joined by molten lead poured into the hub of one section. Oakum packed into the joint kept the lead from running down into the pipe (left). Compressible gaskets (center) can substitute for the lead in a hub-and-spigot joint. Compressible gaskets with steel clamps (right) can join straight pipe sections, eliminating the space-hogging hub.

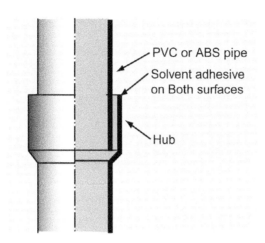

PVC or ABS pipe

Solvent adhesive
on Both surfaces

Hub

FIGURE 17.9 Plastic pipe is joined by coating both surfaces of the joint with the appropriate solvent, then quickly inserting the pipe into the hub.

Plastic

Two types of plastic pipe were introduced in household DWV systems in the 1970s and all but replaced metal piping. Acrylonitrile butadiene styrene (ABS) is a black-colored material first developed for use in oil fields and chemical industries. Polyvinyl chloride (PVC) pipe comes in various colors, according to its code-approved use. White is used for household DWV systems. Both materials are acceptable by the International Residential Code and Uniform Plumbing Code for residential DWV systems.

ABS and PVC piping is lightweight, resistant to chemicals, and good in applications up to 180° F (82° C). Although it is not fireproof like cast iron, it will self-extinguish rather than burn. Two more pluses make them attractive options. First, they don't flare out much at the fittings, such as a hub on a hub-and-spigot joint in cast iron. So a 3" (76 mm) nominal diameter pipe still fits inside a 2 × 4 (51 × 102 mm) stud wall. Second, installation is a snap and can be done by nonplumbers. Pipe sections cut easily with almost any kind of saw.

Joints fit together quickly simply with a solvent (see Figure 17.9). For ABS pipe, both surfaces are coated with the solvent and the sections are fit together. PVC joints must be primed before the solvent is applied. After fitting the sections together, they must be held in place for a short time to allow the solvent to set.

Sections join to steel pipe with a special connection that has threads for the steel pipe and a solvent-weld connection to the plastic end. Compression gaskets usually join plastic pipe to cast iron pipe.

There are downsides to plastic pipe. When it is used for the main stack, it transmits the noise of fluids running inside much more than metal. Expansion and contraction under temperatures above 180° F (82° C) may result in joint failure. And runs longer than 30' (9144 mm) must have expansion loops built in to accommodate expansion/contraction under normal operating temperatures.

See Table 17.1 for the pros and cons of various piping materials.

TABLE 17.1 DWV Piping Materials at a Glance

Material	Connections	Pros	Cons
Cast iron	Lead/oakum, compression clamps	Durable; quiet; resistant to chemicals; heat resistant and fireproof	Expensive; heavy—requiring structural support; difficult and time consuming to install; corroded by acids
Galvanized steel	Threaded fittings	Durable; quiet; resistant to chemicals	Most expensive; difficult and time consuming to install; vulnerable to rust
ABS and PVC plastic	Fittings bonded with ABS or PVC solvent cement	Low cost; lightweight; fast and easy installation	Can be damaged by temperatures above 180° F (82° C); noisy

SUMMARY

A properly designed and installed DWV system ensures that waste materials are evacuated appropriately and reliably from the home while exhausting sewer gases to the exterior. Achieving these goals requires selecting pipes and fittings of the correct size and assembling them in a configuration that allows them to function as intended.

Greater economy, lighter weight, and ease of cutting and installation have caused ABS and PVC plastic piping to largely replace cast iron and galvanized steel in residential DWV plumbing. Plastic pipe is also a good choice for remodeling work, because it can easily be joined to existing piping.

CHAPTER REVIEW

1. What two components are required in a septic system? (See "Parts of the System" page 195)
2. Which pipes in a DWV system are the largest? (See "Parts of the System" page 195)
3. What should be checked before adding a food waste disposer to a home served by a septic system? (See "Parts of the System" page 196)
4. What can happen when a drainage pipe is oversized? (See "Pipes and Fittings" page 196)
5. Why are traps necessary? (See "Traps" page 196)
6. What can happen if a fixture is not vented? (See "Vents" page 197)
7. Why would an installer prefer ABS over PVC pipe? (See "Plastic" page 201)

Kitchen and Bath Equipment

The last two chapters dealt with the parts of the household plumbing system that the occupants don't see and don't think much about, as long as they continue to deliver water and carry away wastes reliably. This chapter discusses the parts of the system they use and interact with: the fixtures and appliances.

The equipment that occupants use includes these items:

- **Plumbing fixtures:** Sinks (lavatories [lavs]), toilets, bathtubs, whirlpools, spas, and bidets
- **Plumbing appliances:** Clothes washers, dishwashers, garbage disposers, water heaters
- **Amenities:** Saunas, steam rooms
- **Accessories:** Controls, valves, drains, and fittings

Kitchen and bath equipment is constantly changing. Many of the changes are genuine improvements in functionality or efficiency, such as low-flow toilets that save water. Some make our lives safer and less complicated. Some make them more complicated. Others, such as full-body showers, are wasteful of water and the energy required to heat it. Manufacturers make many changes simply to sell products or to respond to changing lifestyles.

> *Learning Objectives 1: Explain the functions and hookup requirements of traditional bathroom equipment.*
>
> *Learning Objective 2: Describe recent amenities for baths and their implications for planning.*
>
> *Learning Objective 3: Recognize the support requirements of standard and more recent kitchen equipment.*

FIXTURES FOR THE BATH

The bath is probably the most used room in the house, so it's no wonder that it is the most frequently remodeled room. Many of the changes people make when remodeling a bath relate to changes in family makeup and lifestyles. More women working outside the home has resulted in baths that accommodate two adults during the peak morning rush hour. Design responses to this can include two lavs, an isolated toilet, maybe a separate tub and shower. People today also want the bath to be something more than a utilitarian space for personal hygiene. Spas for relaxation are one response to this need. Saunas are another. But even time-honored utilitarian fixtures, such as toilets, have changed, as we discuss next.

Lavs

Lavs (lavatories), also called sinks, washbasins, and basins, make up one of the fixtures in the standard three-fixture bath. The other two are a tub or shower and the toilet. Every bathroom needs at least one lav, and two-person baths increasingly contain two lavs. Designers today can choose from a bewildering variety of materials, shapes, sizes, and colors. Traditional lavs install either below the countertop (undermount) or overlapping the countertop (self-rimming). The newer bowl models sit on top of the countertop.

Regardless of the type of lav or its installation, the plumbing is separate. Supply piping includes hot and cold water lines—usually ½" (8 mm). The drain line, typically 1½" (38 mm), leads into a P-trap and run horizontal to the main soil stack. If the distance exceeds 8 to 10' (2438 to 3.048 mm)—the maximum distance from a fixture to a vent required by most codes—a separate vent (revent) taps off the drain and leads outdoors or to the main stack (see Figure 17.3 in Chapter 17). Fittings include the faucet set and drain.

Toilets

Strolling through a kitchen and bath showroom or thumbing through a fixture catalog offers convincing proof that toilets—or water closets, as they are more formally called—come in a bewildering variety of colors, shapes, sizes, and styles. Still, the basic function remains the same: getting rid of human waste, which they do with water. Older toilets used a lot of water, 5 to 7 gallons (19 to 27.5 liters [L]) for each flush, which made the toilet the most water-consuming fixture in the house. The U.S. Energy Policy and Conservation Act of 1992 limited the capacity to 1.6 gallons (6 L) for toilets installed after 1994. (At the time of this writing, no such restriction is in force in Canada.) Consumers complained that low-flow toilets were inefficient, sometimes requiring more than one flush to remove solids. And two or more flushes negated the water-conserving intent. Manufacturers have redesigned the trap-ways of low-flow toilets over the past decade, resulting in improved performance. There are three main types of water-flush toilets currently in use: gravity toilets, pressurized tank toilets, and pumped toilets.

Gravity toilets, still the most common type, rely on water from a tank set above the bowl to flush out the contents and refill the trap (see Figure 18.1). Taller, narrower tanks, steeper bowls, and smaller water surface areas in the bowl all contribute to improved flushing with less water.

Pressurized tank toilets use the pressure of water in the cold-water supply line to compress air, which works with a small amount of water—as little as 0.5 gallons (1.9 L)—to flush the bowl. The higher cost of these type of toilet—they are at least three times as much as gravity toilets—limits their widespread acceptance.

Pumped toilets, the most expensive of all, push water through the bowl by a small pump. Pressing a button can set the amount of flush water for 1 or 1.6 gallons (3.8 or 6 L).

Another recent improvement in conserving flush water is the emergence of dual-flush toilets, which have separate controls for flushing liquid and solid wastes.

High-tech toilets developed recently in Japan offer a variety of features, including bidet nozzles (discussed next under "Bidets"), seat warmers, and deodorizers. A control panel at the side lets the user select the feature desired wants.

There are two more types of toilet are not common in urban or suburban homes, but you should be aware of them if you ever design a bath for a vacation house that has no access to a public sewer or septic system. Incinerating toilets use electricity to burn the waste rapidly,

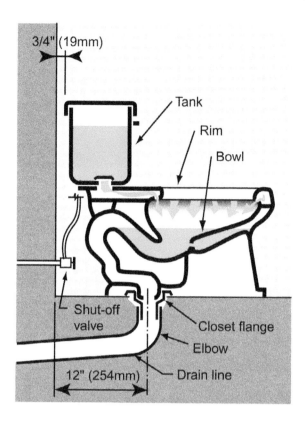

FIGURE 18.1 Gravity toilets rely on water at a higher level to flush out waste in the bowl below. The modern water-saving toilet is the result of several years of evolution, resulting in a fixture that efficiently flushes with 1.6 gallons (3.8 L) or less.

leaving only an odor-free ash that can be dumped with the household trash. Composting toilets work like the compost pile in your backyard to decompose waste. Standard composting toilets sit on the floor like a gravity water toilet and have a composting tank in the basement below. All-in-one units contain a mixer, electric heating element to accelerate composting, and a fan to draw odors up the vent. Residue is removed through a cleanout just below the unit.

In most houses, the house's main waste line runs under the first floor and out through the foundation. A toilet installed in the basement is too low to flush by gravity. This problem is solved with an ejector pump that grinds the solid waste and pumps it up into the house waste line (see Figure 18.2). The typical installation uses a standard gravity toilet mounted on the slab. It drains into an ejector pump that sits inside a tank below the slab. Flushing the toilet raises the level of the waste fluid in the tank, which triggers the pump switch to suck in the waste, grind the solids into a slurry, then pump the mixture up through a 2" (51 mm) diameter pipe into the waste line. A separate vent pipe must run from the tank up through the house and exit to the outdoors. Units that combine a toilet with an ejector pump are also available. In these, both the toilet and the pump sit on a platform above the slab, which eliminates the need to tear into the slab for installation.

Bidets

Bidets are fixtures intended for washing the genitalia and anal regions of the body. They may also be used to clean other body parts, such as feet. In use in Europe since the 1700s, bidets gradually have become in demand in high-end baths in North American homes. A bidet looks something like a toilet with no tank or lid and usually sits beside the toilet. The user sits astride the bidet to cleanse the pelvic area using warm water sprayed from the back of the unit. Both a hot- and a cold-water supply are required as well as a drain.

Bathtubs and Tub/Showers

Many people seldom or never use bathtubs, preferring the speed and convenience of a shower for full-body cleansing. Tub/showers combine both, but although the shower above

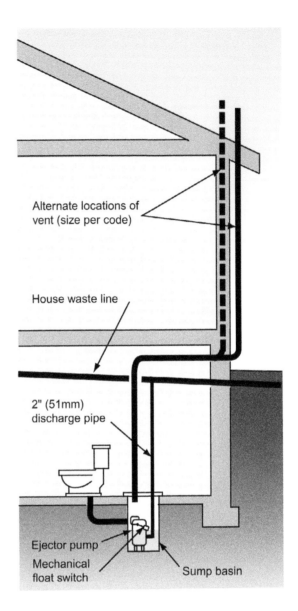

FIGURE 18.2 A sewage ejector pump serves a toilet installed below the waste line of a house. The pump grinds waste into slurry, then pumps it up to the waste line. The device can mount in a pit below the floor, as shown, or be set behind the toilet, if the toilet is installed on a platform above the floor.

a tub saves space, it is not as convenient as a separate shower stall. In any case, babies, small children, and some elderly persons can't use showers so it's probably a good idea for every house to have at least one tub. And a bathtub is still considered a necessary asset when it comes time to resell a house.

Tubs arrive at the site with no fittings. All tubs need a drain/overflow assembly. Hot- and cold-water faucets can be separate or combined into a single-lever control with an integral antiscald device. If a shower is part of the assembly, you also will need to specify the type of shower head (see Figure 18.3).

Not all persons who bathe in tubs can get in and out of standard tubs easily. For these users, there are models with doors on the side that create a water seal when closed (see Figure 18.4). Manufacturers offer a variety of features, such as flip-up seats or jets, which allow the tub to function like a whirlpool.

Shower Stalls

As with lavs and tubs, the plumbing for showers is separate and basically the same as described for tubs, except that there is no spout at the tub level and the controls are at a height reachable while standing (see Figure 18.5). Fittings inside the shower include dual faucets or

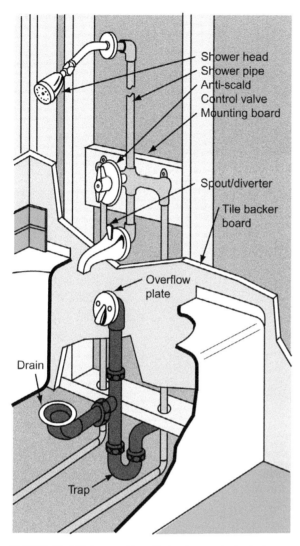

FIGURE 18.3 Fittings and installation for a typical tub/shower unit.

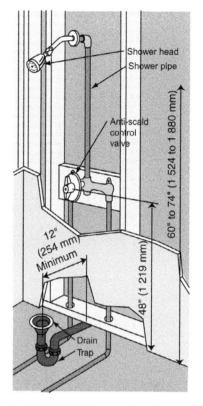

FIGURE 18.4 Fittings and installation for a typical shower.

FIGURE 18.5 Tubs equipped with doors in the side make it easier for persons with special needs to get in and out of the fixture.

a single control, a shower head, and a drain fitting. Showerheads may be mounted in a fixed position or on a flexible hose that allows the head to be hand held to direct the spray as desired, a feature useful for persons who must sit while showering.

For homeowners with a taste for the exotic and budget to pay for it, a whole world of amenities expands the abilities of showers beyond the simple spout mounted on the wall. Manufacturers now offer water delivery systems that spray the whole body by arrays of jets on the wall. Some have pumps that recirculate the water from a reservoir in the base. Others include the steam of a Turkish bath or dry heat of a sauna. Tanning lamps and warm breezes, music, lighting, and aromas are other features available.

Whirlpools and Spas

Whirlpools and spas are increasingly popular, whether installed inside the bath or outside on a deck. Their appeal is their ability to relax people who are stressed out from the pressures of modern life. Whirlpools are basically bathtubs with jets around the bottom to circulate warm water under the pressure of a pump (see Figure 18.6). As they are bathing fixtures, they are drained after each use. Spas evolved from hot tubs and are basically vessels for soaking, not bathing. They are not drained after each use, and users should be clean when they enter spas.

Both fixtures require the same supply and drainage plumbing as described for lavs, tubs, and showers, with two exceptions. First, spas often contain their own water heater, which eliminates the need for a hot-water line. Second, although ½" (8 mm) supply piping will work fine for whirlpools—especially if their main use is for bathing in shallow water—a ¾" (19 mm) pipe will fill the unit more quickly, so it is recommended for spas and for whirlpools intended primarily for soaking.

The pump is what circulates water in a whirlpool or spa. Located under or adjacent to the unit, it must remain accessible via an access panel at the side, front, or rear (see Figure 18.7). After selecting the unit, make sure the electrical service required by the manufacturer's specifications is provided. Pumps are typically 1.5 or 2 horsepower, requiring a dedicated electrical circuit of 15- or 20-amp capacity and a switch protected with a ground fault circuit interrupter (GFCI) device.

Saunas and Steam Rooms

Saunas and steam rooms are two additional fixtures that can add luxury in or adjacent to a bath. Both fixtures are touted for the benefits they offer to health and well-being. Sweating

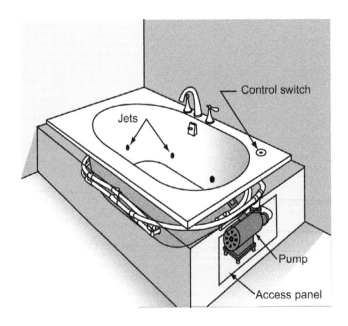

FIGURE 18.6 True whirlpool tubs jet the water into a whirlpool pattern, as shown at left. However, this is just one option. Other units create different patterns of turbulence by varying the arrangement of the nozzles.

opens pores and can temporarily cleanse the outer skin, and may remove toxins from within the body. The heat is relaxing, lowers the pulse and blood pressure by causing blood vessels to dilate, and removes salts from the body. However, scientific evidence doesn't support the widely held belief that using saunas or steam rooms causes weight loss (one reason why many people use these facilities).

Saunas provide dry heat in a wood-paneled room from a wood-fired or electric sauna heater (see Figure 18.8). Rocks on top of the heater absorb and radiate the heat. Water can be poured on the rocks periodically hu-midify the air inside the sauna. The temperature in a sauna typically ranges from 160° to 200° F with a low level of humidity ranging from 5 to 30 percent. Sauna heaters can be fueled by wood, pellets, or electric-ity. Electric models require a 240-volt service. Water for the pail can be delivered from a remote source, or a cold-water line with a faucet can be installed in the sauna.

Unlike saunas, steam rooms provide moist heat from a water-filled generator pumping steam into the enclosed room. The temperature in a steam room typically ranges from 110° to 114° F with a humidity level of 100%. A steam generator supplies steam to a steam room, which can be a shower stall or a prefabricated or site-built compartment equipped with a

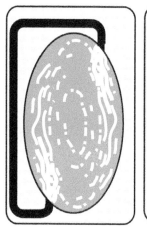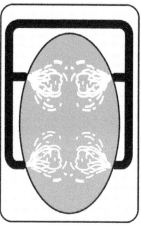

FIGURE 18.7 Whirlpools and spas typically mount on framed platforms. A removable panel must always be provided to access the pump.

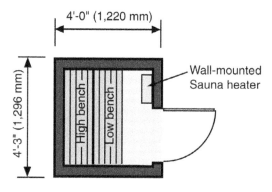

TWO-PERSON SAUNA

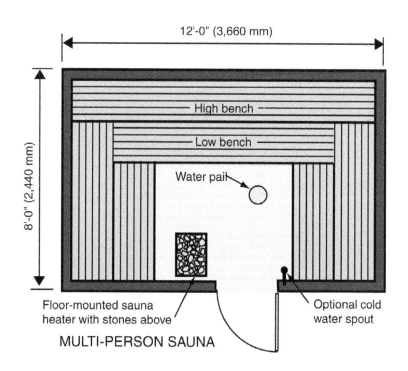

MULTI-PERSON SAUNA

FIGURE 18.8 Saunas can be designed in any size to accommodate any number of users. Small wall-mounted heaters can heat a small sauna, while a larger floor-mounted unit suits a larger one. Water may be carried in or obtained from a cold-water spout installed in the sauna.

floor drain. The generator should be installed in an accessible location and fitted with a cold-water hookup and electrical service of 208V or 240V, depending on the model. All steam rooms require a floor drain.

KITCHEN EQUIPMENT

Once the province of the homemaker—usually a woman—kitchens have become the center of family life and often the focus of home entertaining. Both men and women share the activity of preparing food and drink, with the guests often pitching in. Today's kitchens are places for both preparing full meals and eat-on-the-run snacks. They often also include provisions for recycling and perhaps even a home office space. A wide variety of state-of-the-art fixtures and appliances are available to meet the new needs, but it's up to the designer to incorporate them into a plan that meets the needs and goals of the client.

Sinks

Kitchen sink choices now extend beyond porcelain and stainless steel to include copper, vitreous china, soapstone, and other materials. Styles include apron fronts and many shapes and colors, with chopping blocks, vegetable baskets, and other inserts that can accessorize the sink. Sinks typically mount on or under the countertop.

The current trend is for more than one sink in a kitchen to enable two people to be working at the same time. However, the second unit likely is a special-purpose unit, such as a vegetable washing single sink, rather than a clone of the first, or primary, sink. Sinks not connected to a disposer have a strainer to keep food scraps out of the drainage piping. If there is a disposer below, a stopper fits into the drain, and the stopper is removed to allow food scraps into the disposer.

Except for a disposer that may be installed directly below the sink, the plumbing for sinks is pretty much the same as for lavs, as described earlier, but the fittings may differ. There are many types of faucets available today, some mounted on the countertop, others on the wall. Gooseneck spouts that swivel between sinks are an oft-chosen option to the more common fixed type. A separate spray hose is fairly standard. Various types of water filter devices can connect to the cold-water supply either under the sink or topside.

Disposers connect to the drain under the sink (to the main drain, in the case of a double sink; see Figure 18.9). They are powered from a 120V outlet under the sink. Continuous-feed

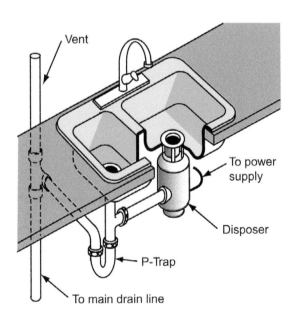

FIGURE 18.9 A kitchen sink installed with a disposer. When installed below a double sink, the disposer is located below the bowl farthest away from the drain line.

disposers are wired to switch under the countertop or a GFCI-protected switch above the countertop. Turning the switch activates the motor in the disposer. Batch-feed disposers operate intermittently, whenever the user turns the strainer device in the sink to the open position. As mentioned in Chapter 17, a food waste disposer imposes an excessive load on a septic system, so it is advisable to verify that the system can handle the additional load before you specify one.

Dishwashers

Once a luxury, dishwashers are now considered basic kitchen equipment. Most dishwashers are built into the base cabinet, under or adjacent to the sink. Plumbing rough-in must be in place before the unit is installed and includes a ⅜″ (10 mm) hot-water line (copper tubing preferred), which enters the dishwasher's space from the side or rear of the base cabinets. The drain rises up the back or side of the dishwasher to connect to the tailpiece of the sink drain by a special dishwasher tee. Some codes require an air gap fitting on the high end of the waste hose loop to prevent siphoning (see Figure 18.10). The air gap assembly mounts on the countertop above the rim of the sink. Some sinks have an extra hole near the faucet assembly for this purpose.

There are also portable models designed to sit outside the cabinetry but that can be installed below the countertop if the homeowner decides to renovate. They need no built-in plumbing. The hot-water supply hose from the unit simply snaps onto the sink faucet, and the drain hose hangs over the sink. Their inconvenience makes these models more suitable for a temporary kitchen, or one in transition, than for a permanent one.

Other Fixtures Requiring Plumbing Connections

As kitchen fixtures and appliances evolve, they add features that may require more than a simple connection to the plumbing system. When specifying appliances, it's a good idea to thoroughly review the manufacturer's technical specifications to obtain the installation requirements so that you can include all necessary plumbing provisions in the plans. Refrigerators equipped to supply filtered cold water or ice cubes need a cold-water supply line, typically a ¼″ (6 mm) copper tube from the back wall, and a drain. Water purification devices installed in the kitchen can mount above or under the countertop. They usually connect to the cold-water supply line with a flexible hose from the device, but consult the manufacturer's data for the plumbing requirements.

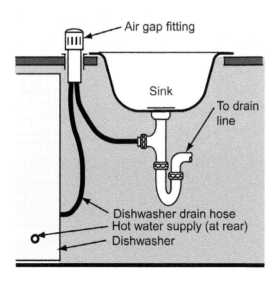

FIGURE 18.10 A dishwasher typically mounts under the countertop next to the sink so that the drain hose from the dishwasher can connect into the trap from the sink. Some codes require an air gap fitting on the high end of the waste hose loop to prevent siphoning.

SUMMARY

Kitchens and baths have evolved beyond their traditional functions. Whereas kitchens once were a place for one person, usually a woman, to prepare food, their uses have expanded to include provisions for eating in, cooking by more than one person, and entertaining. Similarly, the functions of baths have expanded beyond sites for personal hygiene and eliminating bodily waste to include features that promote relaxation and well-being. Accommodating these changes requires an understanding of each fixture and its supporting infrastructure.

CHAPTER REVIEW

1. What major change has occurred in toilet design in recent years? (See "Toilets" page 204)
2. What three ways can lavs can be installed, with respect to the countertop? (See "Lavs" page 204)
3. How can a toilet installed below the house's drain line expel its waste? (See "Toilets" page 205)
4. Why is it a good idea to include at least one tub in a house, even if the occupants prefer to shower? (See "Bathtubs and Tub/Showers" page 206)
5. What is the difference between a sauna and a steam room? (See "Saunas and Steam Rooms" page 209)
6. What can happen if a disposer is connected to a drain line served by a septic system? (See "Sinks" page 211)
7. What may be required to hook up a refrigerator, beyond an electrical connection? (See "Other Fixtures Requiring Plumbing Connections" page 211)

Electrical Systems

Except for rustic cabins in the wilderness, all homes depend on electricity to power the equipment, lighting, and a wide assortment of electronic accessories the occupants have come to regard as essential to their lifestyle—so much that any interruption in the flow of power caused by weather-related events results in great inconvenience. However, climate change has made these occurrences more frequent and less predictable, making the reliable delivery of electricity to the home less certain. And, like other energy sources, the cost of electricity is ever increasing, while its production has raised mounting environmental concerns, particularly where coal and nuclear energy sources are used.

The production of electrical power by sources outside of the home is beyond the scope of this book. However, homeowners are beginning to produce their own electricity, as we see in this chapter, which also covers the flow of electrical power inside the home and issues designers should be familiar with in the process of designating and specifying equipment and appliances that depend on electricity.

Learning Objective 1: Define the terms used to explain electrical current.

Learning Objective 2: Describe the elements that comprise household electrical circuits.

Learning Objective 3: Recognize the challenges posed by incorporating new electrical systems in existing houses.

Learning Objective 4: Discuss the possibilities offered by structured wiring and home automation systems.

Learning Objective 5: Compare the pros and cons of photovoltaic power to power supplied solely by an electrical utility.

ELECTRICITY BASICS

Electrical current is the flow of electrons over conductors. There are two types of current flow. In alternating current (AC), the type of current used in household wiring, the current changes polarity, or alternates, continually from positive to negative and back again at the rate of 60 times a second. Direct current (DC) is steady-state flow, in which the positive and negative wires retain the same polarity. Batteries supply DC current.

We measure the quantity of current flow in units called amperes, or amps, abbreviated as "a" when used to identify the amperage of devices and as "I" in formulas. Electrical current doesn't flow without a force to push the electrons along the line. This force is called voltage and is measured in volts (V). We have electrical power, measured in watts (W), when there is a certain voltage available to force current through a conductor. The power formula tells how much power:

Power = Voltage × Current, or W = VI

Voltage and/or amperage ratings are typically listed for each electrical device in the manufacturer's specifications, so you can determine the power requirements to provide on the circuit. If the amperage isn't given, you can find it by varying the formula and plugging in the known values. For example, if you wanted to find out how many amps a 180-watt exhaust fan consumes on a 120V circuit,

I = W/V = 180/120 = 1.5

The wire that conducts electricity isn't a perfect conductor; there is some degree of resistance, which is given off as heat. The amount of resistance varies with the type of metal used in the wire. Copper wires offer very little resistance, while the tungsten wires inside incandescent light bulbs offers a lot of resistance—so much, in fact, that much of the energy intended for light gets wasted as heat. Resistance is measured in Ohms and stated as "R" in formulas. The resistance in a circuit is determined by Ohm's law, which states the relationship among volts, amps, and resistance (ohms):

R = V/I (or V = IR)

This formula tells us why lights and appliances may draw different amounts of current (amps), even when connected to the same voltage source.

SERVICE ENTRANCE

For homes connected to a power grid, electricity enters the home from the transformer on the nearest power pole. The transformer reduces the voltage to 240V or 220V, depending on the locality, for household use. A supply cable connects the transformer with the home's electric meter via an overhead or underground service cable (see Figure 19.1). This cable continues into the structure to the main service panel, or "distribution central," for the household electrical systems. At the entry point to the panel, the service cable contains three wires, or conductors. Two are "live," or "hot," insulated with red and black plastic. The third is a "neutral," or "grounded," bare copper or aluminum wire (actually a bundle of small wires). The two hot wires carry a potential of 240V between the two conductors. The potential voltage for a device wired to one hot wire and the neutral wire is 120V. Service panels cannot be blocked three feet in front, such as with a window seat or base cabinet.

Inside the Service Panel

The three conductors from the service cable connect to the main breaker, a combination shutoff switch and overload protecting device for the entire home. The main breaker connects to flat bars called buses that run down inside the panel. Circuit breakers for individual household circuits snap onto the buses to tap off 240V or 120V power, according to whether they connect to two hot buses (e.g., water heaters) or a hot plus neutral bus, in the case of household appliances that draw 120V). An electrical circuit is a path of electrons from the power source from a hot wire, through an appliance or device, back to the power source through the neutral, or grounded conductor, as shown in Figure 19.2

Circuit breakers protect branch circuits from electrical overloads or shorts in the circuit. Without this protection, the excess electrical energy would turn to heat and eventually melt the wiring insulation and ignite any combustible material nearby. Older houses had panel boxes equipped with fuses rather than circuit breakers (see Figure 19.3). Because fuses had to be replaced every time they were triggered, or blew, they were eventually superceded by circuit breakers (see Figure 19.4).

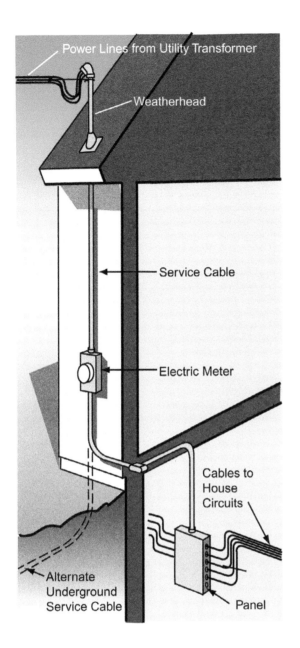

FIGURE 19.1 Electricity enters a home from the transformer on the nearest power pole via overhead or underground cables. After passing through the meter, it flows to the service panel, which distributes power to various circuits.

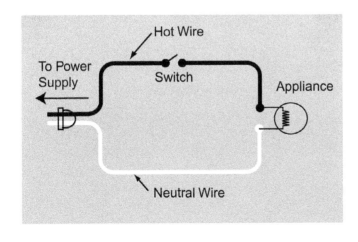

FIGURE 19.2 All electrical circuits require a power source, a positive (hot) wire, a negative (neutral) wire, an appliance that draws current, and a switch to control the flow of electricity through the circuit.

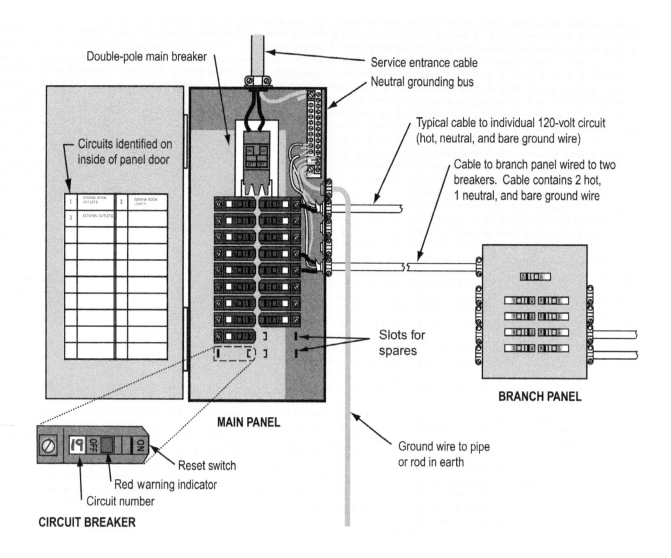

FIGURE 19.3 Fuse boxes provided power distribution and overload protection in older houses. When a circuit was overcharged or shorted, the fuse blew, requiring replacement. Sometimes the occupant, lacking a replacement fuse, placed a penny behind the blown fuse, thus causing a fire danger.

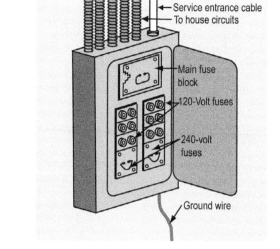

FIGURE 19.4 A typical 100a main service entrance panel. Remodeling or adding to a home may require more circuits than are available as spares, in which case a branch panel can be added, tapping off two breakers in the main panel.

Depending on the size of the house, the panel should have a 100a capacity main breaker (at least), and more likely a 200a one. An electrician is the person to consult on this issue.

Household Circuits

Panels configured to conform to the National Electrical Code (U.S.) and Canadian Electrical Code (Canada) contain four types of circuits: general lighting, small appliance, individual appliance, and ground fault circuit interrupter. There may be one or more of each type, depending on the size of the house and number of appliances.

General Lighting Circuits

General lighting circuits serve lighting and wall receptacles. The code requires 3 watts per square foot of living area, the equivalent of one 15a circuit for each 600 square feet (55.74 m^2) or one 20a circuit per 800 square feet (73.32 m^2). A rule of thumb for the number of receptacles allots 12 outlets for 15a circuits and 16 outlets for 30a circuits. The code also requires a light controlled by a permanent wall switch for each room. Lights in kitchens and baths must be permanently wired rather than the plug-in type.

Small Appliance Circuits

Small appliance circuits distribute power to outlets for plug-in appliances, such as toasters, blenders, and coffee makers. The code requires two 20a circuits in the kitchen and one or more in the pantry and dining or family rooms. These circuits may not be used for lighting.

Individual Appliance Circuits

Individual appliance circuits are dedicated to devices that draw enough current to warrant their own circuits. Table 19.1 lists some of the devices that may occur in kitchens and baths. Always verify the manufacturer's electrical requirements for appliances you specify.

Ground Fault Circuit Interrupters

Kitchens and baths may contain metal pipes or fittings that are grounded. If a person uses an electrical device while in contact with a grounded pipe, electricity could flow through his or her body to the pipe, and the shock could be fatal. A special type of circuit breaker called a ground fault circuit interrupter (GFCI) can sense current flowing through a person because not all of the current is flowing from hot to neutral, as it expects. Some of it is flowing through the person to ground. As soon as the breaker senses that, it trips the circuit and cuts off the electrical power within as little as 1/40 of a second. It works by comparing the amount of current going to and returning from equipment along the circuit conductors. When the amount going differs from the amount returning by approximately 5 milliamperes, the GFCI interrupts the current.

If a GFCI breaker can't be installed in the panel the next best option is a GFCI receptacle, which has a reset button to turn the power back on after any problem that triggers it has been fixed. A third solution is a GFCI receptacle that plugs into an unprotected receptacle. Although this fix is the most economical, it is not the most elegant and risks easy removal by anyone that may not like its appearance.

TABLE 19.1 Electrical Requirements for Kitchen Appliances

Appliance	Voltage	Breaker Capacity, Amps
Garbage disposer	240	20
Electric range or cooktop	120 or 240	50
Dishwasher with water heater Included	120	20
Tankless water heater	240	30
Refrigerator	120	20
Microwave oven	120	20
Exhaust fan	120	20

GFCI protection is required for all receptacles in the bathroom and all receptacles servicing countertop surfaces in the kitchen.

Branch Panels

Service panels in new houses should include several spare, or blank, spaces below the installed circuit breakers to enable the homeowner to add circuits in the future. Remodeling or additions usually require added circuits. What do you do if the panel has no spares? There are two possibilities. If the existing panel is outdated, such as a fuse box type, it's a good idea replace the entire panel with an updated one with adequate capacity for both existing and additional loads. If the panel is adequate but simply lacks spare slots, a branch panel can be added on in piggyback fashion by revising the circuit layout of the main panel.

WIRE AND CONDUITS

Electrical current travels via two types of conductors on its way from panel to appliance: cables and cords. Cables are the hard wiring in houses. They run from the circuit breakers to junction boxes in the walls (or floors). A cord with a plug connects portable appliances to receptacles in the boxes. Hard-wired appliances (those that are not portable) connect to the cable in junction boxes by wires rather than cords.

A cable has two or more wires bundled inside a protective sheathing of plastic or metal. The most common cable for indoor residential wiring is nonmetallic sheathed cable (NM), also called Romex. An NM-type cable for 110V (110 volt) or 120V circuits bundles together a single hot wire encased in black plastic, a white-encased neutral wire, and a bare ground wire. Fourteen-gauge wire used for 15A (15 amp) circuits is indentified as 14/2 with ground and sheathed in white plastic. Twelve-gauge wire for 20A circuits (12/2 with ground) is sheathed in yellow plastic. NM cable for 30a circuits, such as required by a water heater, contains two hot wires, one encased in black, the other in red, plus a neutral wire encased in white and a bare ground wire. Called 10/3 with ground, this cable is sheathed in orange plastic. A special nonmetallic sheathed cable, type UF, is designed for direct burial.

A cord is a flexible conductor of stranded wire containing two or three separate conductors insulated from each other by rubber or plastic.

Another type of cable is contained within a flexible metal sheathing. Armored (BX) cable sometimes is specified for uses needing extra sheathing protection. BX cable is restricted to indoor use in dry locations.

Copper is the material of choice today in residential wiring. Aluminum gained some popularity in the 1960s and 1970s as a more economical alternative for service cable. It fell from grace when its tendency to expand and contract when heated and cooled made it pull away from terminal screws, breaking the connection and causing an arc—a potential fire hazard. Now banned for new construction, in most states, pre-existing aluminum wiring is still legal in homes containing it via a grandfathering clause in the National Electric Code (NEC). Check your local codes for regulations in your area.

Wire Size

We size wire by gauge. The larger the gauge, the smaller the wire diameter (see Figure 19.5). Wire gauges in North America are based on the American Wire Gage (AWG) system, which expresses the size as a whole number. Most household cable uses 12- or 14-gauge wire (14 gauge is the smallest permitted by code, except for low-voltage circuits, such as thermostats and doorbells). Circuits for 120V appliances and lighting typically use 12-gauge wiring. The wire connecting a device with a switch may be 14 gauge. But these are only generalizations. In actuality, the current that the wire must carry determines its size. An undersized wire risks overheating and fire. Twelve-gauge wire is rated to carry a maximum of 20 amps. Fourteen-gauge wire is rated for up to 15 amps.

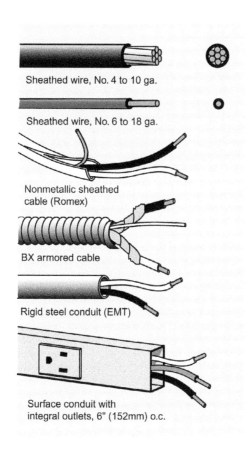

Sheathed wire, No. 4 to 10 ga.

Sheathed wire, No. 6 to 18 ga.

Nonmetallic sheathed
cable (Romex)

BX armored cable

Rigid steel conduit (EMT)

Surface conduit with
integral outlets, 6" (152mm) o.c.

FIGURE 19.5 Many types of cable and conduit are available for residential applications. The gauge and type of cable is noted on the package and/or on the cable itself. NM is used in most indoor circuits. Surface-mounted conduit (bottom) with outlets spaced 6" (152 mm) apart is a good way to ensure enough outlets where they are needed above kitchen countertops.

The size and other traits appear on the outer wrap of cable and wire in abbreviated form. For example, consider the following identifying markings on a Romex cable:

12⁄2 WITH GROUND, TYPE NMC, 600V (UL)

The first number, 12, is the gauge. The second indicates that there are two conductors. "WITH GROUND" tells us that there is a separate ground wire. The type, NMC, means it is nonmetallic cable. Finally, the maximum safe voltage capacity of the cable is given, along with the testing agency, Underwriters Laboratories.

Conduit and Raceways

Whereas cable is an all-in-one wiring conductor, conduit is a kind of sleeve that is installed before the conductors are inserted. In residential wiring, conduit is used mainly outside the house. Service cable from the street to the house is often buried in PVC plastic conduit. Aboveground conduit typically is light-duty electrical metallic tubing (EMT), made of thin-walled galvanized steel. EMT conduit comes in diameters of ½" to 1¼" (13 to 32 mm).

Another type of conduit, a raceway, mounts on the wall surface. Cable can be run through a raceway from one place to another without fishing it through the insides of walls, a boon to remodeling.

Wiring Devices

Various accessories called wiring devices complete the home's electrical system. All wiring systems require a means of connecting wires to each other. Electrical codes require all connections to occur inside a junction box. The most common connector for household wiring is a wire nut, a simple plastic cap that screws over the ends of two or more wires, forming a twisted connection inside while insulating the outside (see Figure 19.6). Wire nuts come in various sizes and colors.

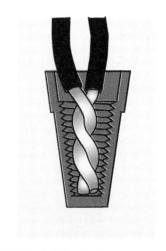

FIGURE 19.6 Plastic wire nuts are a quick and convenient way to join wires. They come in various sizes and colors. Electrical codes prohibit connections outside of accessible junction boxes.

Junction boxes are simple round, octagonal, or rectangular containers that house the terminal points of wires and serve as access points for devices. Junction boxes may not be enclosed in a cabinet. All switches and outlet receptacles must be contained within code-approved junction boxes. Code prohibits splices outside junction boxes. Boxes made of galvanized steel and plastic come in various sizes to fit the number of connections made inside. They can be nailed to the side or face of studs or ceiling joists. Your design drawings should locate all junction boxes that contain switches or outlets. The NKBA recommends that wall outlets be located within 15" and 48" (381 mm and 1219 mm) of the finished floor.

Switches control electricity to appliances by interrupting the flow of current or by adjusting the voltage level (see Figure 19.7). Old houses had switches with two push buttons mounted vertically that the user pushed to turn the appliance on or off. This type was replaced by the familiar single-pole toggle switch that you flip up or down. Other types now in use include rocker switches, controlled by pushing against the top or bottom of the rocker plate, and plate switches, controlled by pushing the entire plate in. Switches other than the single-pole type suit other needs. A three-way switch allows the user to turn a hall lamp on and off from either end of the hall. It is also useful mounted next to a bed, so that the person can turn lights off after getting into bed. Sometimes you may need to control a device from three locations. Simply specify a four-way switch. Wiring for a three- and four-way switch gets complicated, but a competent electrician will know how to install it correctly.

Appliances that run off 240V circuits typically need double-pole switches, which have four, rather than two, terminals, as single-pole switches have.

Dimmer switches with rotary knobs make it possible to control the lighting level, a useful amenity for living, dining, and bedroom lighting. Pushing the knob in turns the device on or off. Turning it adjusts the voltage up or down to control the desired level of lighting.

FIGURE 19.7 Switches come in a wide variety to shut circuits on and off as well as to dim the power to lights. A single-pole switch has two terminals to control a single circuit. A three-way switch has three terminals, one marked "COM," which controls a circuit from two places. Double-pole switches with four terminals control 240V appliances. Four-way switches also have four terminals, for control of a device from three locations.

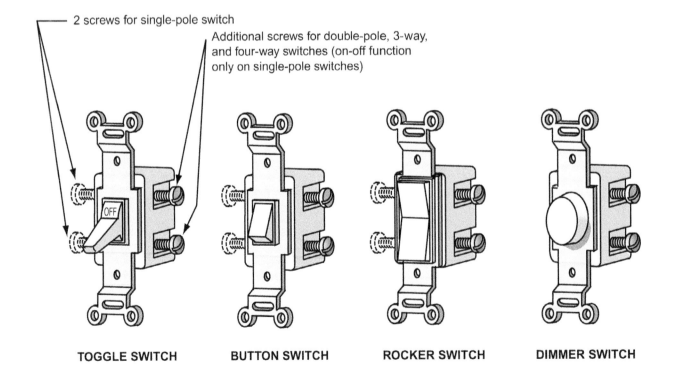

2 screws for single-pole switch

Additional screws for double-pole, 3-way, and four-way switches (on-off function only on single-pole switches)

TOGGLE SWITCH   **BUTTON SWITCH**   **ROCKER SWITCH**   **DIMMER SWITCH**

Receptacles vary by their intended use (see Figure 19.8). The most common type for household circuits running on 120V is a duplex receptacle with two outlets. Each outlet has two side-by-side slots for the hot and neutral prongs of the cord and a semiround slot below for the ground prong. Two-slot ungrounded receptacles found in older houses are no longer acceptable by the code. A special type of receptacle with a slot configuration that prevents a 120V device from being plugged into it is used for 240V appliances. The top portion of duplex receptacles in living rooms and bedrooms often is connected to switches, so the user can plug lamps into them, but all controlled from one switch.

Smart phones, ebook readers, and a variety of portable home electronic devices typically require a power adapter to recharge them via a standard 110V or 120V receptacle. A recently developed wall receptacle eliminates the need for a separate adapter by incorporating one into the receptacle itself (see Figure 19.9). A USB port allows the user to plug an electronic device into the receptacle with a standard USB cable.

The code requirement that receptacles located 6' (1.829 m) or nearer to a moisture source is a problem in baths or kitchens, particularly for receptacles mounted above countertops. The best solution is to protect the entire circuit with a GFCI circuit breaker at the main service panel. If this can't be done, the next best is a GFCI receptacle, which has a reset button to turn the power back on after any problem that triggers it has been fixed. The kitchen and bath industry suggests a single GFCI receptacle in the kitchen or bath, wired to other receptacles downline from it. A third solution is a GFCI receptacle that plugs into an unprotected receptacle (see Figure 19.10). Although this method is the most economical, it is not the most elegant and risks easy removal by anyone who may not like its appearance.

The code requires receptacles to be located such that a 6' (1.829 m) cord can reach them from any point in the room. This works pretty well for baths, as long as there are GFCI-protected receptacles near the lavs, where shaving and hair drying occur. But kitchens never seem to have enough receptacles for the variety of appliances that use them. Aim to provide outlets where they are needed but don't skimp. If you can't provide an outlet every 2' (610 mm) or so in the back wall of the countertop, consider specifying a surface-mounted raceway, such as shown in Figure 19.5, which has integral outlets spaced at intervals of 12" (25.4 mm).

Solving Remodeling Woes

Wiring a new house or addition is a snap compared to wiring a renovation. The electrician has to make your plan work, but the more you know about the pitfalls and solutions, the smoother the installation will be.

The first snag may arise when you discover that the home's service panel is outdated doesn't have any spare slots for additional circuit breakers. If the panel is a fuse box, it should be replaced with a panel containing circuit breakers. If it is up-to-date but lacks sufficient spare slots, a branch panel can be piggybacked onto it for the new circuits.

Getting wires to the outlets and switches can be thorny, particularly with plaster walls. The electrician might be able to fish wires through walls by cutting holes near the floor and ceiling, then using a fish-tape tool to pull the wires through the cavities. Running the wires horizontally may require removing all or part of the wall finish so the wires can be run through holes in the studs, as with new construction. **Any wires run through notches cut into the face of studs must be covered with a metal plate to protect the wires from puncture by nails or screws.** Each project is different, so you should visit the site to size up the situation early on in the design process.

Reuse of existing junction boxes can pose another obstacle. A box may be too shallow for the new switch or outlet or too small for the number of wires that it must accommodate. Replacing the box with a new one entails some demolition, and it may be easier to gut the entire wall finish than try to attempt a cut-and-patch job at the problem box. If the design

2-slot 15-amp, 125V
receptacle, now obsolete

Present 15-amp, 125Vt
receptacle with round
ground slot

20-amp, 125V receptacle
used for large appliances

15-amp, 250Vt receptacle
for window air conditioners

50-amp, 125/250V 3-pole
4-wire grounding receptacle
for ranges

30-amp, 125/250V 3-pole
4-wire grounding receptacle
for clothes dryers

FIGURE 19.8 The number, shape, size, and configuration of the slots in a receptacle determine the type of circuit and amperage it connects to.

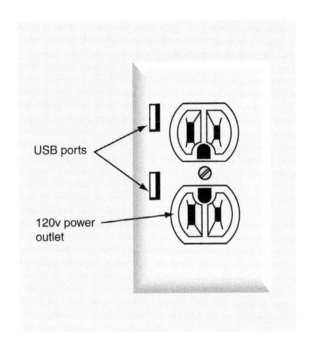

FIGURE 19.9 A recently developed power receptacle contains ports for recharging USB devices, replacing the separate power adapters previously required.

allows the outlet or switch to protrude beyond the face of the wall, a box extension can add the required depth.

The wiring system and devices mentioned so far make up the bulk of electrical systems in North American homes. But they may not be the only option for the future. The revolution in electronic technology during the past two decades has spawned some mind-boggling developments that are bound to change or at least expand the capabilities of household electrical systems, as we see in the following sections.

COMMUNICATIONS WIRING SYSTEMS

Standard home wiring meets the needs of devices and appliances that draw electrical current. But recent developments in electronics have resulted in possibilities previously unimagined for how we use electrical products and services in the home. The applications these possibilities offer are many and continue to expand. Next we discuss some of the most popular at the present time.

Structured Wiring

The low-voltage wire that serves the doorbell and telephone is inadequate for computers and high-definition TV sets and the host of electronic devices yet to emerge. Internet service slows to a crawl on standard telephone cable. Structured wiring handles these needs and offers many more possibilities, such as linking multiple telephone, data, and audio-visual entertainment devices. It enables computers in different rooms to talk to each other as well as to printers and other peripheral devices.

A structured wiring system consists of a network of special cables that make home runs from ports in the walls of various rooms to a central distribution panel located in the basement or a closet (see Figure 19.11). Typically the ports mount near power wiring receptacles and have outlets that fit the jacks of the devices to be plugged into them (see Figure 19.12). A port might, for example, contain a phone jack, a data jack, and a TV jack. Ports can be located according to anticipated use. For example, data and TV outlets might be installed in kitchen walls where these devices might be plugged in.

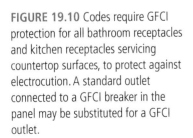

FIGURE 19.10 Codes require GFCI protection for all bathroom receptacles and kitchen receptacles servicing countertop surfaces, to protect against electrocution. A standard outlet connected to a GFCI breaker in the panel may be substituted for a GFCI outlet.

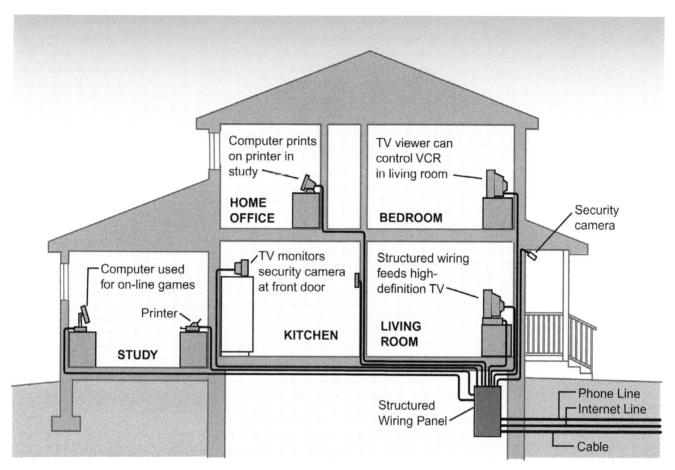

FIGURE 19.11 A Structured wiring system links various electronic devices in a home, enabling them to communicate with each other and to accept automated control. A distribution panel is the site where all cables in the system converge, enabling future changes in the arrangement of devices in the system.

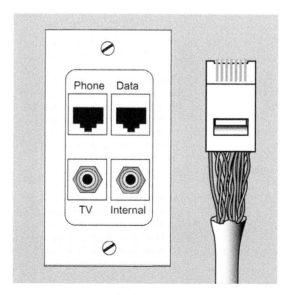

FIGURE 19.12 An outlet for a structured wiring system may contain several jacks for various devices. Jacks can be changed as devices are added or eliminated.

Structured wiring requires two basic types of cable: Category 5e or 6 (Cat 5e, Cat 6) cable, a blend of four insulated wire pairs, twisted to minimize interference, and coaxial cable, type RG 6, a single wire encased within a woven wire sheath. Cat 5e cable comes in several versions. Cat 5e enhanced can handle four phone or data lines, with many times the bandwidth capacity of bell wire. For locations that require both cat 5e and RG 6, such as a living room with a high-definition TV, a single cable that bundles both together is available.

The structured wiring panel is the "brain" of the system that gives structured wiring its flexibility. Terminals in the panel enable a computer in one room to print on a printer in another or a DVD in the living room to send a movie to a bedroom TV. One cable carries the signal to the TV, and one carries instructions from a remote sensor back to the DVD. The homeowner can rearrange the communication between various connected devices by rearranging the connections in the panel.

Structured wiring is sensitive to interference from the home power wiring and should be installed after the primary wiring, with a minimum separation of 6′ (1.52 m) between it and any 120V or 240V lines. Lines should not run parallel to home power lines and should cross these lines perpendicularly, when necessary.

Technology trends may alter the structure of structured wiring systems in the future, as higher-speed wireless networking for both video and data becomes more common. Laptop computers generally have WiFi capability, which is also becoming common for printers and desktop computers. Widespread data cabling may be replaced by distribution to boxes in just a couple of locations that cover a house with strong wireless signals.

Home Automation Systems

Home automation expands the concept of devices communicating with each other, enabling users to control devices within or outside the home. Home automation in one form or another has been around a long time. At the simplest level, it is incorporated in the coffee maker that automatically turns on at a predetermined time in the morning or in a programmable thermostat. At a more complicated level, home automation can turn lights on and off, change thermostat settings, control irrigation, operate home security systems, and provide homeowners with other conveniences. Imagine a home theater that takes care of lights, picture, and sound with one touch or a door that announces when a teenager gets home, a sprinkler system that knows the weather forecast, and a garage door that remembers to close itself if left open for too long. These applications are usually grouped under the "smart home," a label conceived in 1984 by the National Association of Home Builders. The market for home automation applications is growing constantly, spurred on by the increasing number of digital technologies available to consumers today. However, the rate of this growth is slower than initially expected, and some question whether smart homes will truly catch on, or whether consumers even want them. Issues of system complexity and manufacturers' reluctance to adopt compatible standards in consumer electronics are yet to be overcome.

Since home automation systems affect every electrical appliance in the kitchen and bath, designers should be familiar with the approaches currently available.

Home Automation Protocols
Communication between users and home automation devices, as well as between the devices themselves, can be via the home's own electrical wiring system or by radio waves. Currently four protocols are in use:

1. X-10, the oldest protocol, was originally conceived to send signals through the home's existing power wiring. It was later adapted to transmit wirelessly as well. It was found to be vulnerable at times to interference from the radio frequencies emitted by wireless network devices.
2. UPB was designed to counter X-10's weaknesses by utilizing a higher voltage and stronger signal. Its high cost has made UPB prohibitive to buy into and likely has stunted the growth of the technology.

3. Z-wave is a newer protocol using wireless signals, which has made it popular for refitting older homes with home automation. It operates at around 900 megahertz (MHz), a band that competes with some cordless telephones and other consumer electronics devices, while avoiding interference with Wi-Fi, Bluetooth, Zigbee, and other systems that operate on a higher-frequency band. Some of the concerns of Z-wave are its proprietary technology, radio congestion with larger deployments, and low tolerance for failed, moved, or removed devices.

4. Insteon, another newer protocol, utilizes both power line and 915 MHz wireless signals. Each device acts as a transceiver in that it receives a signal and transmits the signal again if it is not the addressed device. Insteon also can communicate via X-10 signals, which has made Insteon popular for homes already equipped with X-10.

Types of Systems

There are three types of home automation controls:

1. Centrally controlled communication systems
2. Distributed-control systems
3. Distributed-control systems

Centrally Controlled Communication Systems

Centrally controlled communication systems route signals between a central computer and appliance controllers or environmental sensors. These systems can control some "dumb" appliances as well as "smart" appliances. If the controller fails, however, the whole system fails. The major distinction in smart home technology is the way electricity is distributed throughout the home. A central control system allots incoming household electricity to a distribution unit (or network box) in each room of the house. The distribution unit does not provide power to the room's outlets indiscriminately, as in a conventional home. The automation outlets contain microprocessor chips that provide power only on request by a smart appliance.

Smart appliances have microprocessor chips that enable them to communicate their identity, power demands, and functional status to the distribution unit when the appliance is plugged in. If the computer system determines that all is well, the distribution unit sends power to that outlet. If the computer system senses potential danger, such as a frayed cord or appliance incompatibility, the distribution unit denies power to the outlet. An outlet is only live when it is utilized by a compatible appliance.

Distributed-Control Systems

Distributed-control systems use wiring already in the home, such as standard power line wiring, telephone wire (four pair), video wire (dual coaxial), radio frequency (RF) signals, and infrared (IR) signals. Microchip controls installed in appliances or outlets enable individual appliances to communicate with each other over the existing electrical wiring without a central controller, although keyboard entry is possible using telephones or personal computers. The system's status can be monitored on the home TV set. Compatible appliances are necessary, but at this time there is no standard in place to make them so. To achieve a common standard, the Electronic Industries Association has developed a standard communications protocol CEBus, short for Consumer Electronics Bus, also known as EIA-600, a set of electrical standards and communication protocols for electronic devices to transmit commands and data that allows appliances and modems from different manufacturers to communicate with each other. Individual semiconductor manufacturers have developed microchips that can be installed in appliances.

Individual Control Devices

Individual control devices are the simplest and most economical home automation system. Devices control single appliances or functions, such as programmable setback thermostats, motion detectors, occupancy sensors, photocell lighting controls, and timers. These systems can also be applied to applications ranging from outdoor lighting to security sensors. The familiar television remote may come to mind, but it's not truly a home automation device, since it requires the user's conscious thought and effort to operate.

ELECTRICITY FROM THE SUN

The space age has spun off many technologies that have benefited society. One of the spin-off technologies that benefits homes came with the development of photovoltaic (PV) systems, which are ways of converting sunlight directly into electrical energy (see Figure 19.13). Conceived in 1950 for space applications, PV systems now provide thousands of houses with some or all of their electricity. The technology is clean, quiet, reliable, and friendly to the environment. What's more, it lessons homeowners' dependency on public electricity, which continues to rise in price. Of course, all of this comes with a price that exceeds the installed cost of a standard wiring system for most houses. However, the added cost can be offset by state and federal tax incentives.

At the present time, PV systems are most cost effective for rural sites remote from a utility power source and for houses located in areas with a lot of sunshine year-round, such as the southwestern United States. Still, constant improvements in the technology over the last 20 years continue to reduce the installed cost of PV systems, making them more attractive options to a greater number of homeowners.

The heart of a photovoltaic system is a silicon cell made of a silicon semiconducting material, the same kind of material from which computer chips are made. When developing the computer chip, engineers found that the electrical output in the computer chip would change when exposed to light. This became known as the photovoltaic effect. When sunlight strikes a PV cell, it knocks an electron loose, creating an electrical current. Tiny wires embedded in the PV cell collect that electricity. Because each PV cell produces just a small amount of electricity, a number of PV cells need to be hooked together into a PV panel, or array, to produce enough electricity for a household. A 100-square-foot (9.3-square-meter) PV system will generate a peak power of about 1 kilowatt, energy enough to meet many power requirements of an average U.S. home.

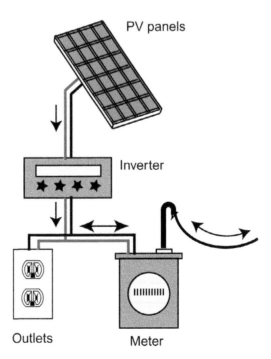

FIGURE 19.13 PV panels typically on a south-facing roof convert solar energy to DC electrical current. An inverter changes it to AC to power household circuits. The inverter interfaces with the utility's power feed in the meter, to enable the homeowner to sell excess power back to the utility.

PV panels can be located on any site that allows them unobstructed access to the south. In homes, they typically mount on a south-facing roof. They feed DC to an inverter that converts the DC power to AC, so it can be used with standard household appliances. Because the sun's energy varies with the time of day and sky conditions, PV systems need some way of storing the electricity for periods when there is insufficient or no sunlight. Arrays of batteries hooked together fill this need for homes remote from an electrical grid and for homeowners who are willing to pay the additional cost to be independent of the grid. But for most homeowners, it is more cost effective to stay connected to the grid and draw on solar power when it is available. These homeowners can sell their surplus power back to the utility company, albeit at a lower rate than they pay for electricity when their homes must draw power from the grid.

Even with tax incentives, equipping a home with PV power exacts an additional cost to the homeowner. To make the decision most cost effective, it behooves homeowners to minimize the demand for household power by choosing appliances and fixtures that run off other energy sources, where possible. Gas-powered water heaters, clothes washers, and ranges should replace their electrical counterparts. Low-voltage and energy-efficient lighting should be chosen, where feasible.

SUMMARY

Energy from electricity is a necessary component of modern home construction. It powers appliances occupants have come to regard as indispensable as well as an ever-expanding variety of devices that have become part of the modern lifestyle. Household electricity, whether provided by an electrical utility or a photovoltaic system, or both, enters the home via a service panel that distributes power to various circuits. Protection from electrical shock is provided for kitchens and baths by ground fault circuit interrupter breakers in the panel or GFCI outlets, and by ordinary circuit breakers in other rooms.

The advent and continuing expansion of electronic devices used for convenience and entertainment has created a need for electrical systems beyond the home's power system to monitor, control, and coordinate these devices.

CHAPTER REVIEW

1. What is the difference between AC and DC? (See "Electricity Basics" page 213)
2. What is the voltage that enters the service panel? (See "Service Entrance" page 214)
3. What is the purpose of circuit breakers? (See "Inside the Service Panel" page 214)
4. What types of circuits do service panels contain? (See "Household Circuits" page 217)
5. What two devices protect persons from electrical shock? (See "Ground Fault Circuit Interrupters" page 217)
6. Does the code allow electrical cable be spliced outside a junction box? (See "Wiring Devices" page 219)
7. What can be done to provide additional circuits when the home's service panel lacks spare slots? (See "Solving Remodeling Woes" page 221)
8. What advantages do structured wiring offer? (See "Structured Wiring" page 222)
9. When would it be advantageous to install a battery pack to back up a PV system? (See "Electricity from the Sun" page 227)

Lighting

Good lighting can spell the difference between a so-so kitchen or bath design and a really successful one. Lighting can be one of the most exciting parts of the design process, and the new products available to the design palette make it even more so. Of course, your role as kitchen and bath designer varies, according to how the project is set up. At most, you may be responsible for determining the type and locations of fixtures for each part of the room, then selecting the fixtures from manufacturers' catalogs or dealers' showrooms. Or—and probably more likely—the homeowner will select the fixtures based on your suggestions. If an architect or electrical engineer has overall responsibility for lighting design, your role may be limited to consulting. But whatever role you play, you should know something about the basics of lighting and the particular needs of kitchens and baths.

Learning Objective 1: Explain three types of lighting needed in an interior space.

Learning Objective 2: Recognize the advantages of natural light.

Learning Objective 3: Compare the pros and cons of various lighting sources.

Learning Objective 4: Identify the types of light fixtures for residential applications.

Learning Objective 5: Apply appropriate light fixtures to specific applications in kitchens and baths.

LIGHTING BASICS

A comprehensive explanation of lighting science is beyond the scope of this book. However, kitchen and bath designers who intend to include lighting in their services should be familiar with the terms that quantify light and the types of lighting best suited to various applications.

We measure lighting intensity by the amount of light generated by a single candle. The total amount of light emitted in all directions from a flame is 1 candela. Luminous flux is the amount of light that strikes a surface at a distance from the candle, measured in lumens (lum) (see Figure 20.1). In the International System (SI) of units, 1 lumen is the amount of light energy that 1 candela yields on a spherical surface of 1 square meter at a distance of 1 meter from the candle. The American System (AS) uses the foot-candle (fc), where 1 fc is the

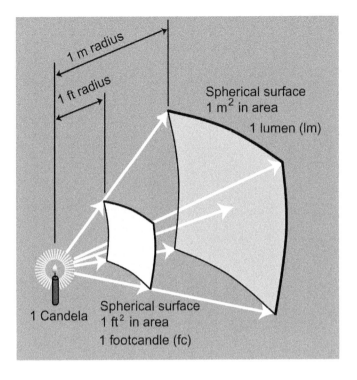

FIGURE 20.1 Luminous flux is the amount of light that strikes a surface, measured in lumens. A candle set 1' away from a curved surface of 1 square foot produces 1 lumen in the American system. In the International System, 1 lumen is the amount of light that falls on a curved surface of 1 square meter at a distance of 1 meter.

amount of light that falls on 1 square foot of spherical surface at a distance of 1' from the candle. The relationship between lumens and foot-candles is:

1 lum = 12.57 fc

You probably have an idea of how much light a 75-watt (W) incandescent bulb delivers. However, as a designer, you should get used to comparing light output in lumens, not watts, because wattage measures only the power consumed, not the light produced. And lamps differ in their light output per watt. A 15W compact fluorescent (CFL) lamp, for example, delivers as many lumens as a 75W incandescent bulb, as do some other types of lamps that have emerged in recent years to replace incandescent lighting.

LIGHTING BY FUNCTION

Good interior lighting provides enough of the right kind of light for whatever activities the occupants are engaged in at the moment. That can mean anything from being able to see the chopping block when cutting up vegetables in the kitchen to creating a relaxing mood with the soft glow of a special lamp above a dining table. Sorted by function, there are three types of lighting: ambient, task, and accent lighting.

Ambient Lighting

All rooms need some general lighting to enable the occupants to get around without bumping into things. During the day, natural sunlight can provide most of the ambient lighting in a house with enough windows in the right locations. Lighting at night can come from direct or indirect sources, or a combination of these. Direct lighting is the light a fixture throws directly into a room or on a task surface. An example is a ceiling fixture that lights up an entire room. Indirect lighting reaches the room after it has bounced off another surface. Lamps mounted in a cove to throw their light up onto the ceiling light up the room below indirectly.

Whatever the source of ambient light, the amount needed is influenced by the colors in the room. Light surfaces reflect light while dark surfaces absorb it. Rooms with a large percentage of dark surfaces will seem darker and more somber with the same amount of ambient lighting as a room with lighter surfaces. Cabinetry accounts for much of the surfaces in kitchens, and although a client may prefer a dark wood, as the designer, you should point out that this choice will make the room feel darker than a lighter wood.

Task Lighting

The general lighting that ambient sources disburse in a room may be adequate for some activities but may fall short for others, such as reading, writing, preparing meals, and other activities that require visual focus on a specific task. Task lighting includes light sources designed to make up this shortfall. The swivel lamp on your desk is a good example. Good kitchen and bath design includes ample task lighting tailored to the activities specific to these areas.

Accent Lighting

Stores would sell far less merchandise if they didn't display it in the most favorable lighting. Commercial lighting designers go to great lengths to make sure the goods are illuminated to catch the eye of shoppers. Homes also can utilize accent lighting to focus attention on special items, such as artwork, china, or collectibles. Lighting fixtures specialized for accent lighting throw a narrow beam that highlights the object of attention without spilling into the room.

DAYLIGHTING

Sunlight can make any kitchen and bath a space pleasant to be in. Skillful use of daylighting can provide the ambient lighting required in a kitchen or bath and often all of the task lighting. The light itself is free, and putting it to use in a new home can likely be done within the budget. And even if it costs a bit more in remodeling projects, the result is often worth it. Some ways to incorporate and optimize daylighting in a room are described next.

Windows

Windows in an outside wall are a good source of daylighting as well as ventilation—an asset in both kitchens and baths. Their type, size, and placement must coordinate with the equipment and fixtures in the room and—in baths—accommodate the need for privacy.

A window on an outer kitchen wall opens the room to a view of the outside, floods the room with ambient lighting, and illuminates the work surfaces. However, the same wall is a natural site for wall cabinets. Fortunately, there are other storage options available, such as separate pantries, tall cabinets, and base cabinets.

Bath windows should be sized and situated to afford privacy. Although any window can be treated with blinds or shades to control view, a narrow window mounted with a sill at least 54" (1,372 mm) above the floor will naturally shield occupants adequately from view from the outside.

Skylights and Roof Windows

Kitchens and baths in one-story homes or on the top floor of multistory homes may be candidates for daylighting via an opening in the roof. A skylight or roof window, centrally located, can illuminate a wide area, providing task lighting on work surfaces as well as ambient lighting for the room.

Borrowed Light

In prior times, kitchens were isolated from the rest of the house. The current design trend for making the kitchen serve for social interaction as well as meal preparation also opens the kitchen to light from adjacent rooms, or borrowed light. The openings between rooms may be full height for circulation or smaller to promote a sense of openness and to bring in daylight borrowed from the next room.

ARTIFICIAL LIGHTING SOURCES

The terms *ambient, task*, and *accent* describe lighting by its intended function. Artificial lighting also varies by the way it is produced, its color, energy consumption, and lamp shape and sizes. And by lamp, we mean the basic item we fit into a fixture, which is the assembly that includes the mounting base, or socket, and features that reflect or disperse the light from the lamp. To select the right type of lighting source for a particular application, you need to understand both. Manufacturers' catalogs, whether in bound copies on your bookshelves or accessed over the Internet, are the best sources of information for fixtures.

Lamps are described by their shape and the way they produce light. In the past few years, the choices have expanded to include types that are more energy efficient and longer lasting than traditional incandescent lamps.

Incandescent

Ever since Thomas Edison invented the first commercially practical incandescent light bulb in the late 1800s, incandescent lamps have been the mainstay of home lighting. They haven't changed much since the early models, either, and still offer a warm, friendly color, a low initial price, and convenience. Their light comes from a tungsten filament that has high resistance to electrical current. Passing an electrical current through the filament converts some of the energy into light, the rest into heat. Because of the high heat, incandescent lamps are the least efficient electric lighting sources available. Their advantage of a low initial cost is eaten away in time, because bulbs burn out after about 750 hours of use. Although incandescent lamps still are available, they are being phased out and likely will disappear in the future. Incandescent lamps come in several shapes, each suited to a special lighting application, as described next (see Figure 20.2).

> **A lamps** are the basic bulbs with standard screw-in bases that come in wattages from 7 to 150. They throw light in all directions from the bulb pretty equally and suit general illumination or task lighting when fitted into a fixture that has a reflector.
>
> **G lamps** are similar to **A** lamps but with bigger and rounder globes, hence the designation "G." The shape, however, is an aesthetic rather than functional feature. These lamps are intended for fixtures that do not hide the bulb, such as strip fixtures around mirrors in baths.
>
> **R lamps** and **PAR lamps** have built-in reflectors to limit the light throw. An R lamp throws out a cone-shape light pattern, whereas a PAR lamp directs its light in a cylindrical pattern, thanks to its parabolic-shape reflector. Both types are used in spotlights and can-type fixtures. Wattages range between 50 and 150.
>
> **B lamps** and **CA-tipped lamps** are small bulbs for decorative uses, such as in chandeliers. B lamps are oval, and CA tipped lamps are flame shape. Both have screw-in bases but are of smaller diameters than A lamps. Wattages range from 25 to 40.
>
> **Miniature (mini) bulbs**, also used for decorative applications, come with wedge bases and bayonet bases.

Fluorescent

Fluorescent lamps yield five times as much light for the same amount of power as incandescent lamps and last much longer (see Figure 20.3). These advantages have made fluorescent lighting the first choice for commercial buildings for years. The first generations of fluorescent lamps had a bluish light color that made people look like ghosts and made meat in counters

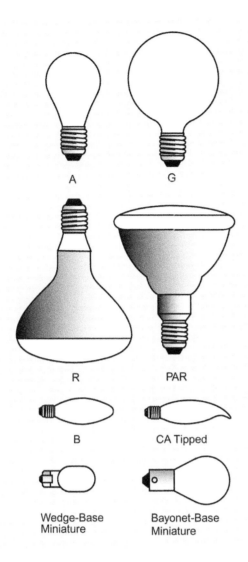

FIGURE 20.2 Although they are being replaced by more efficient lighting, incandescent lamps are still available in several versions. A, G, PAR, and R bulbs screw into standard sockets; B and CA tipped bulbs screw into smaller sockets. Mini bulbs twist into special sockets and require a transformer to step the voltage down to 12 volts.

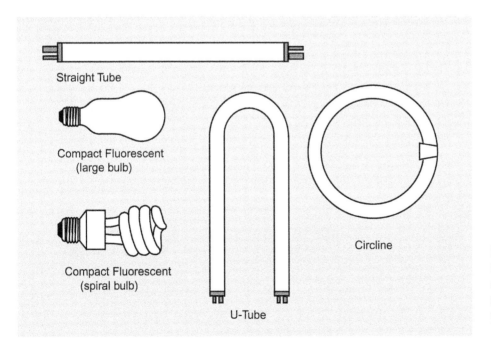

FIGURE 20.3 Fluorescent lamps come in a wide variety of shapes and color renditions. Compact fluorescent bulbs screw into standard 120V sockets and yield outputs from 300 lumens (7W) to 1,600 lumens (23W).

look gray. Due to this problem, even commercial buildings limited the use of fluorescent lighting to general lighting. The color ruled out fluorescent lighting for all but garages and basements of most homes. All that changed in the 1980s when newer coatings for the insides of fluorescent tubes resulted in light that was much warmer colored.

Another change that made fluorescent lighting acceptable in homes came around the same time, when manufacturers found ways to squeeze a long tube into a bulb that screwed into a standard household lighting fixture socket. The result was compact fluorescents that were not only interchangeable with incandescent bulbs but delivered a more flattering light color to skin and most foods. Today's compact fluorescent lamps cost more initially than incandescent lamps but save in the long run due to their lower operating costs and longer lifetimes. For these reasons, they are rapidly replacing incandescent lamps.

Fluorescent lamps do not contain a resistance filament, as incandescent lamps do. Instead, a heated cathode at one end of the tube produces free electrons, which are accelerated by a voltage placed across the electrodes at either end of the tube. As they accelerate, they ionize a gas vapor (mercury) in the tube, causing an arc to flash the length of the tube. The arc excites the vapor in the tube to produce light. All fluorescent lamps need ballasts to heat the cathode and run the tubes at the correct voltages. Straight-tube fluorescents have as separate ballast housed somewhere within the fixture. Compact fluorescents contain the ballast within the base. Standard magnetic-type ballasts produce an annoying flicker as well as perceptible hum, and lamps coupled to them are not dimmable. The newer solid-state electronic ballasts are quieter, with less flicker, and do allow dimming. Another downside of all fluorescents is the small amount of mercury they contain, which poses a risk if the lamps are broken in the home. Municipalities often have regulations for the disposal of burned-out or broken bulbs.

Fluorescent tubes make good candidates for side lighting of bathroom mirrors and under-cabinet lighting for kitchen countertops. But for applications in kitchens and baths, stay away from lamps in the cool-color range. Warmer-colored daylight, deluxe cool white, warm white, or natural lamps complement skin tones and most foods.

Halogen

Tungsten halogen (or simply "halogen") lamps encase the filament of an incandescent lamp inside a capsule containing halogen gas produced by iodine vapor (see Figure 20.4). The gas slows filament wear through a complicated regenerative cycle and improves the lamp's efficiency. Halogen lamps cut energy use by 30 to 50 percent compared to long-life incandescents. Lamp life ranges between 2000 and 3500 hours. The light color is whiter than incandescent lamps, but not bluish enough to make food look bad. Halogen lamps are available in low-voltage (12V) and standard (120V) voltages, in reflector shapes and mini-bulbs. One type of halogen lamp gets its name from the hockey puck, because of its shape. The flat profile of puck lights make them well suited to under-cabinet applications. Other shapes are much the same as incandescent bulbs. Like incandescent bulbs, halogen bulbs burn hot.

FIGURE 20.4 Halogen lamps offer greater efficiency than incandescent lamps and have more precise beams and whiter color, closer to sunlight. The PAR lamp shown is suited to recessed can lights and works on 120V. Other lamps require a transformer to step the voltage down to 12V. MR lamps are suited to track lights, while the bi-pin, mini-can, and puck lamps work well in under-cabinet installations.

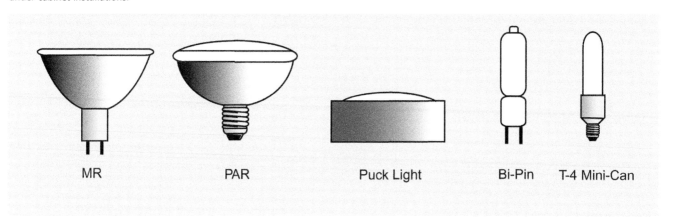

MR   PAR   Puck Light   Bi-Pin   T-4 Mini-Can

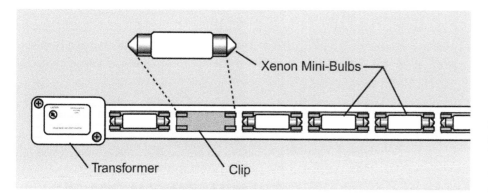

FIGURE 20.5 Small strip fixtures with xenon or halogen mini- bulbs are well suited for under-cabinet installations. The fixture shown uses 5w, 24v xenon mini-bulbs spaced about 2" (51 mm) apart.

Xenon

Xenon bulbs are a more recent invention than halogen and, though more expensive initially, last much longer. Although halogen is dependable, the bulb still uses a filament that eventually burns out; xenon bulbs, however, use only gas and electricity, allowing them to last two or three times as long. Originally developed as brighter lights for auto headlamps and industrial applications, xenon lamps now offer residential designers new lighting opportunities (see Figure 20.5). Xenon lamps contain two electrodes in an extremely small tube filled with inert gases. Electrical current arcing between the electrodes yields a bright light with a color resembling sunlight. The real plus is the lamp life, rated at around 20,000 hours—long enough to last a typical under-cabinet installation for 50 years. Xenon bulbs dissipate their heat more efficiently than halogen, hence they run cooler. Xenon lamps are miniature size with pin bases. Fixtures for under-cabinet or display case applications include strips with lamps mounted at 4" or 6" (102 or 12 mm) apart as well as individual lamps that can mount at any spacing. Transformers are required to convert alternating current to 10V or 12V direct current.

LED

Light-emitting diode (LED) lamps produce light by a solid-state, in which electrons move through a semiconductor material. This technology is the latest lighting innovation to join the energy-efficient options available to designers. LEDs are the costliest initially but save over their lifetime, which is up to 50,000 hours. LEDs contain no mercury so they are a "greener" product than fluorescents. And, with no filament that can be broken, they are more durable than other bulbs. They can be manufactured in very small sizes, which make them good candidates for certain kitchen and bath applications, such as accent and under-cabinet lighting (see Figure 20.6). LEDs are ideal for uses subject to frequent on/off cycling, unlike fluorescent lamps, which fail faster when cycled often. LEDs can be dimmed very easily. Whereas incandescent and fluorescent lamps often require an external reflector to collect light and direct light beams in a usable manner, the solid package of the LED can be designed to focus its light.

Other than their initial expense, LED bulbs have other downsides compared to other types. LED lighting fixtures are integrated systems in which the light sources (LEDs), the fixture housing, and the primary optics are inseparable. The integrated systems contain heat sinks to dissipate the heat. For this reason, they can't be enclosed in separate fixtures. Also, the quality of LED light may not be optimal for some applications. They have a high color temperature and poor color rendering index, however this is continually improving.

FIGURE 20.6 LED technology continues to evolve, producing long-lasting and energy-efficient lighting products, such as shown here. The 6W spotlight contains three diodes in a bulb only 2" (51 mm) high. The strip fixture, intended for under-cabinet lighting, contains clusters of very small diodes.

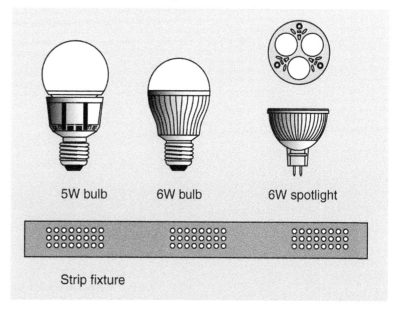

5W bulb   6W bulb   6W spotlight

Strip fixture

LED lamps produce a lighting color of white or warm white with very little heat. LED bulbs range from small to very small and available in A, PAR, MR shapes, which screw into standard 120V sockets. LED mini-bulbs work off transformers and are mounted in clusters in fixtures for under-cabinet installations. This technology is advancing rapidly, and additional products are sure to evolve in the future.

COLOR OF LIGHT

We didn't think much about light color in the old days, when the choices were limited to incandescent or fluorescent lamps. We knew that the warm light of incandescent lamps complemented people's skin tones and enhanced foods, such as meat and most vegetables. The cool light of fluorescent lamps made people look ashen but green salads look more appetizing. But what exactly do we mean by "warm" or "cool" light?

The lighting industry uses two color indices for lighting color: color temperature and color rendition.

Color temperature is an index of how the light source itself looks to us, measured in kelvins (K). Warm-light sources have color temperatures less than 3000K. Light sources between 3000K and 4000K are considered neutral in color. Anything above 4000K is cool (see Figure 20.7).

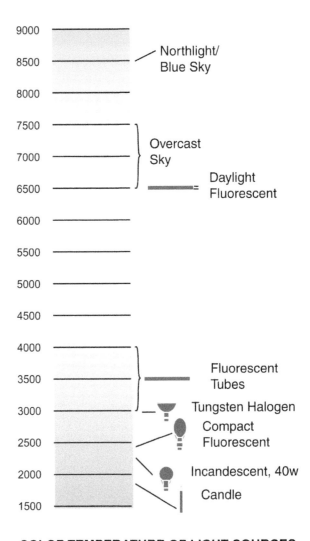

COLOR TEMPERATURE OF LIGHT SOURCES

FIGURE 20.7 Color temperature of light sources.

TABLE 20.1 Comparing Lighting Sources

Type	Output, lumens	Efficacy lum/W	Color Temperature (oK)	Pros	Cons
Incandescent	126–6100	8–20	2550–2800	Low initial cost; good color; convenient; dimmable; many lamp shapes and sizes	Least efficient; bulbs fragile; high ultimate cost; short life; produce heat
Fluorescent (straight tubes)	1350–2900	58–85	3000	Efficient; long life; choice of light color; distribute light evenly; choice of lamp sizes and shapes	Types with magnetic ballasts noisy, flicker, and not dimmable; all contain mercury
Compact Fluorescent	900–1100	40–60	2700	Efficient; long life; choice of light color; choice of lamp sizes and shapes	Higher first cost than incandescent; frequent on/off switching decreases life span; contain mercury
Halogen	2500 (100W)	15-20	2850–3000	Efficient; full-spectrum white color similar to sunlight; small shapes	Higher first cost than incandescent; need transformer; produce heat
Xenon	50 (5W) 120 (10W)	80–90	3000	Full-spectrum white color similar to sunlight; small shapes; more efficient than halogen	Higher first cost than incandescent; need transformer
LED	130–2800	25–30	2600–3500	Efficient; long life; mini-bulbs well suited for under-cabinet fixtures; durable	Highest first cost; poor color rendering index; produce heat

Color rendition is an index of how the light makes objects appear. How accurately a lighting source defines objects is measured by the color rendering index (CRI). The best score is 100, the CRI of sunlight.

Two indices are needed because sources with the same CRI can produce different moods at different color temperatures. When specifying fluorescent lamps for home applications, you'll get the best all-around light color with tubes coated with rare-earth phosphors. Artificial light sources vary widely in their color rendering indices. Incandescent lamps are rated at a CRI of 100—nearly equal to sunlight. Lamps with very low CRI numbers are unacceptable in home lighting. Those ghastly orange street lamps that use high-pressure sodium have a CRI of 22. Table 20.1 compares various lighting sources by their physical characteristics. Here are some rules of thumb for selecting lamps for the right color:

- **Task, accent, and art lighting.** Use halogen or xenon lamps. Small-voltage lamps, such as PAR halogen or MR 16, work better for art, because they throw their heat back away from the object.
- **General lighting.** PAR halogen and compact fluorescents work well, but make sure the compact fluorescents have a color temperature of about 3500K (they range from 2700 to 6500K). If you use fluorescent tubes, choose lamps with a CRI over 80 and a color temperature of between 3000 and 3500K.

BUILT-IN LIGHTING

Getting light to the desired target requires not only a lamp, but also a device that houses the lamp and controls its beam. Lamps can either be built into cabinets or other parts of the home structure or enclosed in manufactured lighting fixtures also called luminaires. Built-in lighting uses a site-built structure to focus or diffuse the light (see Figure 20.8). Some typical applications for built-in lighting are described next.

Under-cabinet lighting. Lamps mounted under wall cabinets near the front edge throw light directly on the countertop where it is most needed for food preparation. Lamps suited for this use include fluorescent tubes, halogen or xenon puck lights, xenon strips, and LED strip fixtures.

FIGURE 20.8 Lighting can be built into the structure or cabinetry to illuminate any selected surface and disperse light directly or indirectly. Direct light, such as shown in the under-cabinet application at left, brightens a countertop. Indirect lighting, shown in the other two examples, creates a softer effect for ambient lighting.

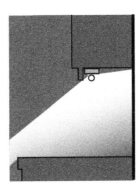

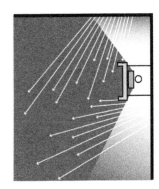

DIRECT, UNDER-CABINET   **INDIRECT, COVE LIGHT**   **INDIRECT, WALL WASHER**

Above-cabinet lighting. The same types of lamps suited for under-cabinet lighting can mount on top of wall cabinets to bathe the ceiling in light for ambient lighting.

Coves and valances. Horizontal baffles running around the room below the ceiling can hide strip lighting, usually fluorescent tubes, for soft, ambient room lighting. A light cove directs light upward onto the ceiling, which reflects it back down in a diffuse pattern. It works best when the ceiling is painted flat white or off-white. A valance is a similar baffle but open at top and bottom to allow the light to wash both the ceiling and the wall below.

LIGHTING FIXTURES

Manufactured lighting fixtures come in an amazing variety that is constantly changing (see Figure 20.9). Previously available only in bound volumes, data relating to these fixtures are increasingly accessible online. The primary types of residential lighting fixtures are described briefly next.

Recessed Ceiling Fixtures

Burying a fixture into the ceiling makes it create the effect of a spot of light coming through a hole in the ceiling. Recessed fixtures offer many designs for getting the light into the room. You can choose between units that hold the lamp in a fixed position or units with the lamp mounted in an "eyeball" that swivels. Some fixtures come with reflectors built in (Alzak type), and take an A-type lamp. Others have corrugated baffles painted white or black. White baffles direct more light downward but are harsher to look at.

Recessed fixtures generally throw a cone-shape beam to illuminate a limited area. A single recessed fixture in the center of a room wouldn't light up the whole room, as would a pendant or surface-mounted one that delivers light in all directions. Thus, recessed fixtures are best installed in multiples, spaced 24" to 42" (610 to 1067 mm) apart. To determine the best spacing for a particular fixture, get the angle of the beam spread from the manufacturer's specs, then position fixtures so that the beams overlap at the intended target. For example, if you are using recessed fixtures to light up a countertop, you want the beams to overlap at a height of 36" (914 mm).

Recessed fixtures give off a lot of heat. The National Electrical Code requires a separation of at least ½" (13 mm) between the fixture and any combustible material and a separation of 3" (381 mm) from any insulation, unless a type IC housing is specified, which may abut any combustible material or insulation.

Surface-Mounted Ceiling Fixtures

Mounting the light source on rather than in the ceiling enables it to throw light in all directions, an asset when designing ambient lighting. Several fixtures arrayed around the edge of a room are likely to be more effective than a single one in the center of the room. Surface fixtures come in single or multiple configurations as drums, cones, squares, and spheres and accept any of the lamp types previously discussed. Manufacturers' specifications state whether they can be dimmed and the maximum wattage permitted to avoid fire hazard.

Suspended Fixtures

Hanging a fixture from the ceiling brings the light source down into the room for more intimacy, particularly in dining areas. There are two types of suspended fixtures, although the distinctions often get blurred. Chandeliers are the descendants of the elaborate assemblies of candles that hung from castle ceilings. Today's versions retain some of the effect with multiple flame-shape or other mini-bulbs that mimic the light of candles. Pendants are a less formal modern adaptation of the idea that hold one or more lamps. Some pendants direct light evenly in all directions. Others focus a beam upward or downward down. Wiring the fixture to a dimmer switch enables diners to adjust the lighting level to suit the mood of the meal.

Track Lights

Lighting fixtures that slide in tracks make it possible to add or reposition the fixtures. They afford even more flexibility because the fixtures swivel and rotate. This versatility enables track lights to wash walls and illuminate countertops or artwork. The tracks mount on the ceiling or hang from legs, if the ceiling is high enough. Individual lamps insert into the track and make contact with two conductors, mounted in parallel inside the track. Lamp housings can be cans with or without baffles and reflectors, much the same as for recessed fixtures. Lamp types used also vary, although many designers favor lamps with built-in reflectors (PAR or MR).

Wall-Mounted Fixtures

After the fixtures, cabinets, and mirrors are located in the design, kitchens and baths tend to have little free wall area for wall lighting fixtures. Still, there may be areas where a wall-mounted fixture makes sense. Sconces are single-bulb fixtures that throw light out, up, down, or a combination of these, based on the design of the diffuser lens, baffle, or reflector housing. They can mount on the wall surface or be recessed.

Another type of wall-mounted fixture is strip lighting, which may be an array of individual lamps mounted into a strip base or a single fluorescent tube with a diffuser lens. Multiple-lamp strips take A, G, or mini-lamps. Tube strips take fluorescent lamps of various lengths, from 16" to 48" (406 to 1219 mm) or arrays of other lamp types. Strip lights are well suited to baths, as we discuss later under "Vanities and Lavs."

LIGHTING KITCHENS

Providing good lighting in the kitchen is probably more difficult than any other space in the house. Food preparation surfaces need adequate task light of the right color and intensity. The rest of the room needs ambient light for general illumination. If a dining area is part of the kitchen, it should be lighted with a source that fosters enjoyment of the meal. All of these goals can be met with proper lighting strategies.

Work Areas

Food preparation is a demanding task that requires good task lighting that puts light on the work surfaces, most of which are on countertops around the periphery of the room. In the quest for economy, many mass-produced houses light the entire kitchen with a single fixture

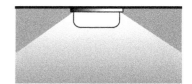

CEILING FIXTURE

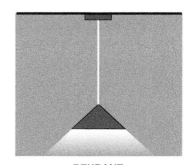

PENDANT

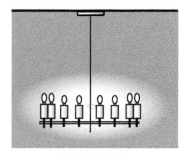

CHANDELIER

SCONCE

STRIP FIXTURE

TRACK LIGHTS

FIGURE 20.9 Lighting fixtures come in an infinite variety to suit any intended application. Track lights allow users to add or subtract fixtures and adjust the direction of the light. Strip fixtures are well suited for installation under kitchen cabinets and along the sides of mirrors.

FIGURE 20.10 A good balance between ambient and task lighting can be had by combining under-cabinet fixtures with fixtures mounted on the ceiling.

in the center of the ceiling, with the worst possible results guaranteed to cast the cook's shadow on any work surface not directly under the fixture. A much better approach is to locate fixtures at the ceiling just in front of the wall cabinets or under the wall cabinets themselves. Ranges can be lighted with lights built into range hoods. Any custom-designed range hood should contain adequate lighting. For downdraft ventilating ranges, mount a recessed or surface-mounted fixture above the range.

The best location for countertop lighting is below the wall cabinets, with the fixtures mounted near the front edge (see Figure 20.10). Lamps mounted here throw their light directly on the work surface, with no objects intervening to cast a shadow. Fluorescent lamps mounted end to end work well if the lamps have a color temperature above 3500K. Another option is a strip fixture that contains several halogen, xenon, or LED lamps clustered or arrayed in a series.

The countertop also can be lighted from the ceiling by locating the fixtures close enough to the wall so that they won't cast the user's shadow on the countertop. Be sure that enough clearance is left to enable wall cabinets doors to open. Fixtures can be recessed or surface mounted on the ceiling or recessed into an overhanging soffit (see Figure 20.11). Can lights and spots work well at the ceiling level. If mounted in tracks, they enable the homeowner to adjust their location and focus (see Figure 20.12).

The Rest of the Kitchen

Successful ambient lighting provides evenly distributed light that doesn't cause glare or discomfort. A single fixture in the center of the ceiling, mentioned earlier, may satisfy the first need but not the second. Anyone sitting in the room can't look up at the ceiling without squinting. If a single fixture is the only choice for ambient lighting, one that bounces light off the ceiling gives a better result. Better still is to use more than a single source, such as strips or individual fixtures mounted on the tops of the wall cabinets.

If a dining area is included as part of the kitchen—on an island or separate table—it should be lighted with a source that provides enough light to see the food and to suit the desired mood, which can change. A breakfast eaten quickly on a dark morning needs a different quality light from a fancy dinner intended to be enjoyed in a relaxed atmosphere. An oft-chosen answer to this is a pendant centered over the dining surface. Another possibility is surface-mounted or recessed cans. If there is a wall surface, a sconce might work. In any case, the fixture should be connected to a dimmer switch, so that the lighting level can be adjusted. Some fluorescent lamps cannot be dimmed. Figure 20.13 shows how combining a pendant at the dining area with above-cabinet lighting provides good ambient lighting for the room. For relaxed dining, the cabinet lights can be turned off, allowing the dining surface to be the focus.

Accent Lighting

As kitchens become a space for living as well as food preparation, they often include areas that display art, china, or collectibles. Wall-mounted art can best be lighted with adjustable

FIGURE 20.11 Another approach mounts task lights in a soffit in front of the wall cabinets.

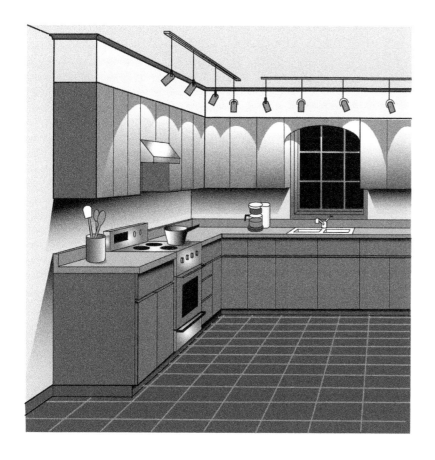

FIGURE 20.12 Task lighting can be supplied by track lighting in front of the cabinets, which enables users to adjust the location and beam of the lighting. The fixtures must be chosen and installed to allow the cabinet doors to open.

FIGURE 20.13 A kitchen that includes a dining area needs a light source above the dining surface, such as the pendant fixture shown here. In this example, the strip lighting under the cabinets can be turned off during dining, while the indirect lights above the cabinets can be dimmed, as desired, for the mood.

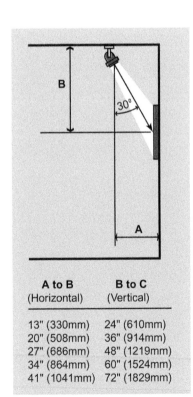

A to B (Horizontal)	B to C (Vertical)
13" (330mm)	24" (610mm)
20" (508mm)	36" (914mm)
27" (686mm)	48" (1219mm)
34" (864mm)	60" (1524mm)
41" (1041mm)	72" (1829mm)

FIGURE 20.14 Guidelines for using track lighting to illuminate objects on a wall, the wall itself, or any vertical surface.
Courtesy of the American Lighting Association

fixtures mounted on the ceiling at a distance out from the wall of 24" to 30" (610 to 735 mm), as shown in Figure 20.14. Another solution is recessed ceiling fixtures, as shown in Figure 20.15. Eyeball-type fixtures that rotate in their housing allow the direction of the light to be adjusted.

Lighting for china and other items displayed behind glass doors can be provided by small, low-voltage strip lighting, such as xenon or LED strip fixtures, mounted at the top of the cabinet just behind the door.

LIGHTING BATHS

The 5' by 7' (1524 by 2134 mm) bath that was the standard in production housing of past decades often made do with a single ceiling fixture for ambient lighting and possibly another fixture above the lav for task lighting. As baths grow in size and amenities, they require a different approach to lighting. For one thing, a larger bath may not be just one room but a room with several subrooms to enclose tubs, showers, or toilets—each needing a source of light. So the goal, once again, is to deliver lighting where it is needed.

Vanities and Lavs

The space between the lav and the wall is one of the most critical but least forgiving areas for bathroom lighting. People have to be able to see the lav or vanity as well as themselves in the mirror above. To do this, the fixture must illuminate the person's face. The simplest solution is a fixture above the mirror. This is also the worst location, since the fixture throws light downward onto the person's face, causing shadows below the eyebrows, nose, and chin—just what you don't want when shaving or putting on makeup. A much better approach is to locate sconces or—better—strip lighting at the sides of the mirror, where they can light the face more evenly (see Figure 20.16). Two fluorescent tubes mounted behind a valence above the mirror can also work by bouncing light off the wall before it hits the

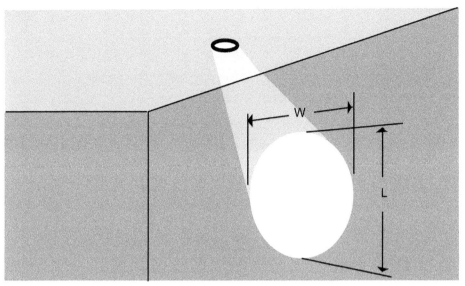

Ceiling Height	Distance from Wall (D)	Lamp Option	Beam Length (L)	Beam Width (W)
8' (1 829 mm)	2' (610 mm)	50W PAR-36 WFL (12V) 50W MR-16 FL (12V) 75W R-30 SP 75W R-30 FL	5' (1 524 mm) 8' (2 438 mm) 4'-6" (1 346 mm) to floor	2'-6" (762 mm) 3' (762 mm) 2" (610 mm) 7' (2 134 mm)
10' (3 048 mm)	3' (914 mm)	75W PAR-38 FL 25W PAR-36 NSP (12V) 50W MR-16 NSP (12V) 50W MR-16 NFL (12V) 75W PAR-38 SP	5'-6" (1 676 mm) 2' (610 mm) 2' (610 mm) 5.-6" (1 676 mm) 3' (762 mm)	2' (610 mm) 1' (254 mm) 1'-6" (457 mm) 3' (762 mm) 1'-6" (457 mm)

FIGURE 20.15 Guidelines for using recessed fixtures for accent lighting. Matching the lamp type correctly with the vertical and horizontal distances shown will ensure light levels of 20 to 60fc at the center of the beam.
Courtesy of the American Lighting Association

person's face (see Figure 20.17). But to work, the wall must be white or near white, and even then this lighting choice might not be as effective as side-mounted fixtures.

Showers, Tubs, and Toilets

A pleasing and economical way to illuminate the small subspaces of a bathroom is directly through their walls. Glass block or obscure (patterned) glass in these walls enables the enclosed space to borrow light from the main space. If this isn't feasible, these spaces usually can be well lighted with a single ceiling fixture, recessed or surface mounted. Many exhaust fans contain a lamp. A separate lighting fixture over a wet area should be a water-resisting type.

Your client may want a heat lamp in the bath. If you include one, locate it in the ceiling above an open area with enough room for the person standing below it to move about. Because heat lamps consume a lot of electricity, they should always be switched separately from other fixtures.

Ambient Lighting

Adequate light levels at the mirror and bathing areas may be all that is needed in a bath. A larger room may require additional ambient light in the form of recessed ceiling fixtures or wall sconces.

FIGURE 20.16 Fixtures mounted at both sides of a mirror are the most effective way to spread light where it is wanted on the user's face. This may provide all of the light required in a small bath. Larger baths may require additional fixtures for task or ambient lighting.

FIGURE 20.17 Task lighting at a vanity can be provided by a fluorescent strip fixture mounted behind a valance.

SUMMARY

Successful lighting design in any interior space requires adequate light of the right color and distribution for three different purposes. Ambient lighting provides illumination for the entire space. Task lighting directs a focused and controlled amount of light on a particular work surface. Accent lighting illuminates certain selected objects.

Kitchens and baths require ambient and task lighting and often accent lighting. A good design begins by taking advantage of daylight through windows, skylights, or openings to other rooms before considering artificial lighting, which can be provided by a wide variety of fixtures and lamps. Lighting fixtures can be selected to control the direction, distribution, and amount of light delivered, while the lamps themselves can be selected for size, shape, light color, and energy use. Incandescent lamps are being phased out. Their replacements are newer types that last longer and use far less energy.

Task lighting on kitchen work surfaces can come from fixtures mounted under wall cabinets, in soffits above the cabinets, or from ceilings. Pendent or ceiling fixtures can provide controlled lighting for dining surfaces. Many possibilities exist for ambient lighting.

Lighting for baths requires task lighting at mirrors, ambient lighting for the entire room, and often special lighting for showers and other enclosed spaces.

CHAPTER REVIEW

1. What is the difference between foot-candles and lumens? (See "Lighting Basics" pages 230–231)
2. In terms of function, what type of light is emitted by a ceiling fixture that illuminates the entire room? (See "Lighting by Function" page 230)
3. What is the lighting consequence of installing walnut cabinets in a kitchen? (See "Ambient Lighting" pages 230–231)
4. What are three advantages windows can provide in a kitchen? (See "Windows" page 231)
5. Why are incandescent lights being phased out? (See "Incandescent" page 232)
6. Which artificial lighting source is said to be "solid-state"? (See "LED" page 235)
7. What is the difference between lighting color temperature and color rendition? (See "Color of Light" pages 236–237)
8. Would a green salad more likely look more appealing with a warm- or cool-color lamp? (See "Color of Light" page 236)

Glossary

A

Accent lighting
Lighting that emphasizes displayed items, such as artwork or china cupboards.

Activated carbon filtration
A means of removing impurities from water by passing it through carbon granules.

Active solar heating
A heating method that collects the sun's heat into a liquid medium or air, then circulates the medium into heat exchangers inside the house for space or water heating.

Alternating current (AC)
The type of current common in home electrical systems that draw their power from a public utility. The current changes polarity, or alternates, continually from positive to negative and back again at the rate of 60 times a second.

Alzak
A type of reflector in recessed lighting fixtures, in silver or gold color.

American Wire Gage (AWG)
A system for classifying wire by size.

Ambient
The environment surrounding us. In the context of buildings, the environmental conditions in the room.

Ambient lighting
General lighting diffused within an entire room.

Ampere, Amp
Unit of electrical current. The current in amps equals the power in watts divided by the voltage in volts.

Annual fuel utilization efficiency (AFUE)
A measure of the efficiency of heating devices, which is the percentage of fuel converted to space heat.

Anthracite
A hard coal used for home heating.

Aquifer
A strata in the ground that contains water.

Armored (BX) cable
Electrical wires encased in a flexible metal sheathing.

Arsenic
A toxic metallic element used in insecticides; also combined with copper to make chromated copper arsenate (CCA) for use in pressure-treated wood.

Artificial lighting
Lighting dependent on an energy source other than sunlight.

Automatic vent
A device used to vent sinks via a check valve that admits air to prevent reverse siphoning of the wastewater.

B

Backdrafting
Sucking air out of combustion appliances caused by depressurizing the home with devices that exhaust air to the outside, without replacing it with fresh air.

Backerboard
Panel materials attached to wall studs in order to provide a substrate for tile.

Ballast
A device that controls the current in a fluorescent lamp.

Batch heater
A type of passive solar device that contains a tank mounted above the collector surface.

Bearing wall
A wall that supports portions of the structure above.

Bidet
A plumbing fixture used for washing the genitalia and anal regions of the body.

Bituminous
A soft coal used primarily to generate electricity and make coke for the steel industry.

Black wire
A "hot" wire in a two- or three-conductor cable.

Board foot
A unit 1" thick by 12" by 12" used to quantify sawn lumber.

Boiler
The central heating device in a hydronic or steam heating system.

Borrowed light
Lighting an interior space via an opening into an abutting space.

Bow vent
A method of venting an island sink via a U-shape vent pipe above the P-trap that leads downward into the floor to connect with a vertical vent in a wall.

British thermal unit (Btu)
A measurement of heat quantity in countries using the British system. One BTU is the amount of heat energy required to raise the temperature of 1 pound of water by 1° Fahrenheit.

BtuH
British thermal units per hour. See "British thermal unit."

Bump-out
A portion of a building cantilevered a short distance toward the outside.

Bus
A flat bar inside an electrical power panel into which branch circuit breakers are plugged.

Butane
A type of natural gas.

Butt
A two-piece hardware device mounted to the edge of a door or window to enable it to swing open or closed.

C

Cable
A bundle of electrical conductors, or wires, containing one or more insulated hot wires, an insulated neutral or white wire, and a bare or ground wire.

Candela
The amount of light generated by one candle.

Carbon monoxide (CO)
A deadly gas that is colorless, odorless, and tasteless.

Chandelier
A lighting fixture hung from the ceiling containing several small lamps.

Chlorinated polyvinyl chloride (CPVC)
An improved version of PVC, suitable for both hot and cold domestic water supply piping.

Chlorine
A chemical of the trihalomethane group that is used to kill microorganisms in drinking water but that is toxic in excessive concentrations.

Chord
In connection with trusses, one of the outermost members of the truss.

Circuit breaker
A protective switch that automatically switches off, or trips, the power to a circuit in the event of an overload or short in the circuit.

Color rendering index (CRI)
A measurement of how accurately a lighting source defines objects. The best score is 100, the CRI of sunlight.

Color rendition
An index of how the light makes objects appear.

Color temperature
An index of how the light source itself looks to us, measured in degrees kelvin (K).

Combustion air
Air required for burning by appliances containing a flame.

Comfort zone
The region of a graph depicting comfort felt by people exposed to various temperatures, humidity levels, and air movement.

Compact fluorescent (CFL)
A type of fluorescent lamp with the fluorescent tube coiled into a compact shape in a size similar to an incandescent bulb.

Concrete
A structural material made by mixing the correct proportions of portland cement, an aggregate material (sand and gravel) and water.

Concrete block (CMU)
Modular structural units made in many shapes and sizes for use in wall construction.

Condensing boiler
An type of boiler that achieves efficiencies of up to 95% by incorporating a second heat exchanger that recoups some of the heat from the hot exhaust gases to preheat the water in the boiler system.

Conduction
The flow of heat energy through a material. Heat flows from the warmer to the cooler side of the material.

Conduit
As used in electricity, a metal or plastic tube containing electrical cables.

Contrast
The difference in brightness between surfaces in the field of view.

Convection
The transmission of heat through a liquid or gas. The cooler feeling you experience in front of a fan in summer is due to convective air movement over your skin.

Cord
The quantity of wood that can be stacked in a volume measuring 4 feet by 4 feet by 8 feet.

Counterflow furnace
See "downflow furnace."

CPVC
See "chlorinated polyvinyl chloride."

Crawl space
An open space below the first floor and ground, usually high enough to crawl through.

Cross-linked polyethylene (PEX)
A flexible plastic piping made from molecules cross-linked to form a durable material and used for domestic hot- and cold-water supply and radiant heating piping.

D

Daylighting
Using light from the sun to light the interior of a building.

Dew point temperature
The temperature at which moisture begins to form on a slick surface indicating 100% saturation. The temperature at which the wet bulb and dry bulb temperatures are the same.

Dielectric union
A pipe fitting that keeps two pipes of dissimilar metals from direct contact with each other to prevent corrosion through electrolytic action.

Diffuser
In heating and cooling systems, a grille, or register, in a floor or wall that delivers conditioned air to the room. In lighting, a transparent or translucent lens that encloses the lamp.

Direct current (DC)
Steady-state current in which the positive and negative wires retain the same polarity. Batteries and photovoltaic collectors supply DC current.

Direct gain
A method of passive solar heating by collecting the sun's heat through windows.

Direct-vent heater
An all-in-one heating device that draws combustion air into the fire chamber through a vent in the wall and exhausts the burned gases back out through another, concentric vent.

Disposer
A device mounted below the drain of a sink to grind food solid wastes into a slurry that can pass through the drain piping.

Distillation
A means of purifying water by boiling it and condensing the steam.

Downflow furnace
A forced air furnace that delivers heated air below the unit.

Dry bulb temperature
The ambient (surrounding) temperature taken with a thermometer.

Drywall
Gypsum-based plaster encased between two layers of facing paper, used for interior wall surfaces as a substrate for paint, wallpaper, or tile finishes.

Duplex receptacle
A common type of receptacle outlets for two plugs.

E

Efficacy
The energy efficiency of a lighting source, or lighting output per watt of power in lumens per watt (LPW).

Elbow (el)
L-shape pipe fittings for making 90° turns.

Electrical metallic tubing (EMT)
A thin-walled galvanized steel conduit used to protect wires from damage.

Electrolytic action
Corrosion that results from two dissimilar metals in contact with each other in the presence of an electrolyte such as water, which contains a small amount of acid.

Energy efficiency rating (EER)
A standard for rating an appliance's energy efficiency. The higher the EER number, the more efficient the appliance.

Energy recovery ventilator (ERV)
A device that exhausts room air to the outside and supplies fresh air while recovering some of the lost heat and humidity

Energy Star
A label by the Environmental Protection Agency that rates the efficiency of energy-consuming appliances.

Envelope
The outermost parts of a building that separate the interior environment from the outside weather, usually the walls and roof.

EPDM
Ethylene propylene diene monomer, a synthetic membrane material used for roofing flat or nearly flat surfaces.

Evaporative cooling
Cooling the air by blowing it through water, which then evaporates, removing heat from the air.

F

Fin tube
A type of diffuser that transfers heat from a pipe to the room via a series of fins attached to the pipe.

Fitting
A supplementary device for a plumbing fixture, such as a faucet, drain, hand-held shower, or valve.

Fixture, lighting
Any light-producing device permanently, or "hard," wired to the home wiring system; (2) The assembly that includes the mounting base, or socket, and any features that reflect or disperse the light from a lamp fitted into the fixture.

Fixture, plumbing
A sink or lavatory (terms used interchangeably in this book), toilet, bathtub, spa, shower, and bidet.

Fluorescent
Lighting produced by arcing an electrical current between electrodes at opposite ends of a gas-filled tube.

Foot-candle (fc)
A measurement in the American System (AS) for the amount of light that falls on a surface. One foot-candle is the amount of light that falls on a surface 1 foot square, placed 1 foot from the source.

Formaldehyde
A colorless gas used in manufacturing melamine and phenolic resins in building materials. Formaldehyde is reputed to be a carcinogen, and exposure is a significant consideration for human health.

Foundation
The below-grade portion of the structure between the footing and the main level.

Furring
Thin strips installed to a wall or ceiling surface to create a substrate for a finish material (also called strapping).

Fuse
A safety device that protects a device or circuit from overload or a short. The mechanism is a low-conductor metal that snaps in two when the fuse blows, making replacement necessary. For this reason, fuses in household circuits have been replaced by circuit breakers.

G

Galvanized
Metal coated with zinc to resist corrosion.

Gauge (gage)
The measurement of thickness of a metal sheet or the diameter of a wire. The larger the gauge, the thinner (metal) or smaller (wire) the size.

Glare
Unwanted brightness that annoys, distracts, or reduces visibility.

Grade beam
A thickening of the outer edge of a concrete floor slab engineered to be used in lieu of a foundation wall.

Ground-coupled heat pumps (GCHPs)
Devices that use the warmth or coolness of the ground to heat or cool a house.

Ground-fault circuit interrupter (GFCI)
A safety circuit breaker required by the National Electrical Code for switches and outlets in areas subject to dampness, such as kitchens and bathrooms.

Ground wire
A wire that carries current into the earth to protect people from becoming electrocuted.

H

Halogen
A variation of incandescent lighting whereby the filament is encased in a capsule containing halogen gas, produced by iodine vapor.

Hard water
Water that contains a high level of dissolved minerals.

Hard-wired
A permanent electrical connection for an appliance or device (as opposed to a cord with a plug).

Heat exchanger
A coil through which heat can be transferred to the heating medium (water or air) without exposing the medium directly to the heat.

Heating element
The cylinder inside a water heater that transfers heat to the water in the tank.

Heating seasonal performance factor (HSPF)
A standard for rating the efficiency of heating equipment, which equals the total annual heating output in British thermal units divided by the total electrical output in watt-hours during the heating season.

Heat pump
A refrigeration device that can reverse the cooling cycle to produce useful heat.

Heat pump water heater (HPWH)
A heat pump adapted to heat water for domestic use.

Heat recovery ventilator (HRV)
A device that exhausts room air to the outside and supplies fresh air while recovering some of the lost heat.

Hinge
A piece of door hardware mounted to the face of a door or window to enable it to swing open or closed.

Home run
In connection with electrical or plumbing systems, a direct route between the supply source and the point of use.

HPWH
See "heat pump water heater."

HVAC
Heating, ventilation, and air-conditioning system.

Hydronic
A type of space heating system that uses heated water as the medium.

I

Incandescent
Lighting produced when an electrical current runs through a poor conductor, such as a tungsten carbide filament in an incandescent bulb.

Inverter
A device that changes DC current to AC.

J

Joist
A horizontal member, usually closely spaced in series with other joists, that transfers the imposed loads to a beam or wall.

Junction box
A metal or plastic box that serves as a terminus for wiring in walls or ceilings.

K

Kilowatt-hours (kWh)
A measurement of power consumption over time. One kWh is the power consumed by a 1,000-watt device operating for 1 hour.

Kilowatts (kW)
One thousand watts.

kPa
Kilo-Pascals. A unit of pressure in the metric system (1 kPa = 6.896 pounds per square inch).

L

Laminate
In interior construction, a material consisting of an exposed layer of a material bearing a design, bonded under high pressure to backing layers, and used for countertops and floor coverings.

Lamp
An interchangeable bulb or tube that constitutes the lighting source in a lighting fixture.

Lath
A layer consisting of wood strips or expanded metal attached to wall studs to support plaster.

LED (light-emitting diode)
A device that emits light via solid-state electronics.

Lens
See "diffuser."

Load avoidance
Minimizing the amount of heating or cooling that must be done by mechanical equipment.

Low-e
Low emissivity. A microscopically thin metallic coating on glass that controls the amount of solar heat that it transfers by radiation.

LP gas
Liquid propane. See "propane."

Lumens (lum)
The amount of light, measured at the lighting source.

Luminaire
See "fixture, lighting."

M

Manifold
In plumbing, a pipe with several take-off points to distribute water to several pipes.

Mansard
A roof form that slopes steeply upward from the eaves toward a horizontal joint, then more gradually upward toward the ridge.

Mold
Various fungi that grow in the form of multicellular filaments. Some diseases of animals and humans can be caused by molds, usually as a result of allergic sensitivity to their spores or caused by toxic compounds produced as molds grow.

Mudsetting
A method of installing tiles, into a thick layer of mortar ("mud").

N

Nitrates
By-products of fertilizer that can leach into groundwater and contaminate the

aquifers that supply both public and private-source drinking water.

Nonmetallic sheathed cable
See "Romex."

O

Oakum
Hemp rope impregnated with a bituminous compound used as a backstop for molten lead in lead and oakum joints for cast iron pipe.

Ohm
The unit of measurement of electrical resistance. The resistance of an electrical device equals the line voltage divided by the device's rated amperage.

Ohm's law
The relationship among volts, amps, and resistance (ohms).

Amps = Volts/Ohms

Oriented strandboard (OSB)
A type of structural panel consisting of thin wood wafers aligned in one direction and bond with adhesives under pressure. OSB is used for roof and wall sheathing and subfloors.

Outgassing
The slow release of chemical gases contained within building materials to the ambient air, such as formaldehyde in particleboard.

Overload
Demand beyond the safe carrying capacity of electrical cables and circuits.

P

Panel
See "service panel."

Parquet
A type of floor covering consisting of small panels of a hardwood veneer.

Particulates
Small particles of soot, dust, or pollen that can irritate the respiratory system.

Passive solar heating
Using the sun's energy to heat a house with minimal dependence on mechanical devices.

PE
See "polyethylene (PE) piping."

Pendant
A lighting fixture hung from the ceiling containing one or more lamps.

PEX
See "cross-linked polyethylene (PEX)."

Photovoltaic (PV)
Electricity directly converted from solar energy. The word devives from "photo" (light) and "voltaic" (electricity).

Plenum
See "return-air plenum."

Plywood
A panel product made by cross-laminating alternate thin layers of wood.

Poly, polyethylene
A type of plastic with many uses in construction, one of which is for vapor barriers in walls, ceilings, roofs, and under slabs.

Polybutylene (PBX)
A flexible gray or black piping used for domestic hot- and cold-water supply.

Polyethylene (PE) piping
A black plastic pipe used for cold-water supply and underground water supply lines.

Polyvinyl chloride (PVC)
A white semirigid plastic material with many uses in the house, including cold-water piping.

Potable
Water sufficiently free from impurities that it can be drunk without posing a hazard to health.

Pounds per square inch (psi)
A unit of pressure in the English system (1 psi = 0.1450 kPa).

Propane
A type of gas delivered to home storage tanks by trucks.

P-trap
See "trap."

PVC
See "polyvinyl chloride (PVC)."

R

Raceway
An enclosure for electrical wires, typically mounted on interior surfaces.

Radiant barrier
A highly reflective material used to block solar heat.

Radiation
The emission of energy from an object. Heat waves from the object radiate to cooler objects. Like radio waves, this form of energy passes through air without heating it; radiation becomes heat only after it strikes and is absorbed by a dense material.

Radon
A colorless, odorless gas released by certain rock strata that can seep through openings in the building envelope and pose a risk to the respiratory systems of occupants.

Rafter
A sloped member of a roof structural system that transfers loads to a beam or wall.

Rail
A horizontal framing member in a built-up wall panel.

Rain screen
A method of installing siding that provides a gap (drainage plane) between the siding and substrate to allow drainage and the backside of the siding to dry out.

Rat slab
A concrete floor slab used to keep rodents from entering basements and crawl spaces.

Reducer
A pipe fitting that joins two pipes of different diameters.

Red wire
A "hot" wire in a three-conductor cable.

Refrigerated cooling
The means by which air conditioners cool air using compressors.

Register
See "diffuser."

Relative humidity
The percentage of moisture in the air compared to the amount of moisture the air could contain.

Return-air plenum
A duct between the supply diffusers in rooms and the furnace of a forced air heating system.

Revent
A separate vent branch connecting the drain line from a fixture or group of fixtures to the outdoors or to the house's main stack/vent.

Reverse osmosis
A means of purifying water by passing it through a semipermeable membrane.

Romex
A type of electrical cable containing a single "hot" wire encased in black plastic, a white-encased neutral wire, and a bare ground wire—all wrapped inside a plastic sheath.

R-value
A measure of resistance to the passage of heat through a material by conductance, in British thermal units per hour (BtuH). Used to rate the heat resisting ability of building insulation, the higher the R-value, the more effective the insulation.

S

Sauna
A compartment that produces hot, dry air for therapeutic uses.

Sconce
A lighting fixture mounted to the wall.

Seasonal energy efficiency rating (SEER)
A standard for rating the annual energy efficiency of appliances that considers the effects of climate. The higher the SEER, the more efficient the appliance.

Septic system
An on-site system for disposing of household sewage, consisting of a tank that partially digests the waste and a drain field that distributes the liquid into the soil.

Service panel
The metal box that is the distribution point for household electricity. It contains the main breaker and branch circuit breakers.

Sewage
Waste containing animal or vegetable matter in suspension or solution.

Soffit
The undersurface of a lowered portion of the ceiling.

Soft water
Water that contains a low level of dissolved minerals.

Solder
An alloy of soft metals that melt to fuse a connection between metal pipe and a fitting. Lead, the traditional base for solder, is no longer acceptable in household water piping and has been replaced by a silver-tin alloy.

Spa
A vessel intended for soaking in heated water.

Stack effect
The tendency for warm air to rise in a space.

STC rating
A system that rates the amount of sound transmitted through walls or floors.

Stile
A vertical framing member in a built-up wall panel.

S-trap
See "trap."

Strapping
See "furring."

Structured wiring
A low-voltage residential wiring system, separate from the power wiring system, used to link telephone, data, and audio-visual equipment.

Sunspace
A method of passive solar heating by collecting the sun's heat into a south-facing room that can be opened or closed to the rest of the house.

Supply plenum
The duct in a forced air heating or air conditioning system that supplies the heated or cooled air to diffusers in the rooms.

T

Task lighting
Lighting focused on an work area.

Tee
A pipe fitting shaped like the letter "T" with three outlets.

Thermal break
An insulating gasket placed between inside and outside portions of a metal window or door frame to stem heat loss and minimize condensation.

Thinsetting
A method of installing tile by troweling a thinset compound over the substrate and pressing the tiles into it.

THM
See "trihalomethanes."

Trap
A section of pipe curved to retain water and make a seal in the line below a fixture. P-traps are shaped like the letter "P," while S-traps (no longer allowed) are shaped like the letter "S."

Trihalomethanes (THMs)
Any of a group of chemicals that are toxic in excessive concentrations. They cause cancer in laboratory animals.

Truss
A structural member consisting of top and bottom chords, each member in pure tension or compression when forces are applied to it.

U

Underlayment
A material installed between a subfloor and floor covering.

UPB
A protocol for home automation systems designed to replace the X-10 protocol.

Upflow furnace
A forced air furnace that delivers heated air above the unit.

USB port
A receptacle into which an electronic USB jack can be plugged.

V

Veneer
A thin layer of wood that creates the finish surface of a panel or, in multiple layers, a plywood panel.

Vent
In plumbing, a pipe or other device that releases sewage gases to the outside. In HVAC, a device through which air enters or exits a duct or piece of equipment.

Volatile organic compounds (VOCs)
Toxic substances contained in paints, solvents, and cleaners derived from petrochemicals.

Voltage, volts
Voltage is the electrical force, or pressure, that pushes the current over the conductors. Volts are the measurement units.

W

Wallboard
See "drywall."

Water hammer
The jolt in a water pipe that occurs when the water is suddenly shut off.

Wattage, watts
The unit of measurement for electrical power. The power in watts equals the voltage times the amperage.

Web
An intermediate structural member inside a truss configuration.

Wet bulb temperature
The lowest temperature level of the air that can be reached by cooling the air by evaporation.

Wet vent
A method of venting a sink by oversizing the drainage pipe below the P-trap to prevent reverse siphoning.

Whirlpool
A bathing fixture equipped with jets around the bottom to circulate warm water under the pressure of a pump.

White wire
The neutral wire in an electrical cable.

Wire nut
A plastic device available in many sizes used to connect electrical conductors by twisting it over the ends of the wires.

Wye
Y-shape pipe fittings with a single inlet and two outlets at a 30° or 45° angle.

X

X-10
The oldest protocol for wiring home automation systems.

Xenon
Lighting produced by current arcing between two electrodes in an extremely small tube filled with inert gases.

Z

Z-Wave
A protocol for home automation systems using wireless signals.

Resources

BUILDING CODE ASSOCIATIONS

Building Officials & Code Administrators International, Inc. (BOCA)
4051 W. Flossmoor Rd.
Country Club Hills, IL 60477
708-799-2300
www.boca.org

International Code Council, Inc. (ICC)
5203 Leesburg Pike, Suite 600
Falls Church, VA 22041-3401
703-931-4533
www.intlcode.org

International Conference of Building Officials (ICBO)
5360 South Workman Mill Road
Whittier, CA 90601
800-284-4406
www.icbo.org

National Research Council of Canada
1200 Montreal Road, Building M-58
Ottawa, Ontario, Canada K1A
613-993-9101
www.nationalcodes.nrc.gc.ca

TRADE ASSOCIATIONS

American National Standards Institute (ANSI)
1430 Broadway
New York, NY 10018
212-642-4980
www.ansi.org

American Society for Testing and Materials (ASTM)
100 Barr Harbor Drive
West Conshohocken, PA 19428-2959
610-832-9585
www.astm.org

Gas Appliance Manufacturers Association (GAMA)
703-525-7060
www.Gamanet.org

National Association of Home Builders (NAHB)
1201 15th Street, NW
Washington, DC 20005
800-368-5242
www.nahb.org

National Association of the Remodeling Industry (NARI)
1901 North Moore Street, Suite 808
Arlington, VA 22209
847-298-9200
www.nari.com

National Electrical Manufacturers Association (NEMA)
780 Lee Street, Suite 200
Des Plaines, IL 60016
800-611-6274
www.nema.org

National Fire Protection Association (NFPA)
Batterymarch Park, P.O. Box 9101
Quincy, MA 02269-9101
617-770-3000
www.nfpa.org

National Kitchen & Bath Association (NKBA)
687 Willow Grove Street
Hackettstown, NJ 07840
800-843-6522
www.nkba.org

Association of Pool and Spa Professionals
2111 Eisenhower Avenue
Alexandria, VA 22314
703-838-0083
www.nspi.org

Sheet Metal and Air Conditioning Contractors' National Association (SMACNA)
4201 Lafayette Center Drive
Chantilly, VA 21151-1209
702-803-2980
www.smacna.org

Underwriters Laboratories, Inc. (UL)
333 Pfingsten Road
Northbrook, IL 60062-2096
847-272-8800
www.ul.com

Index